OXFORD GEOGRAPHICAL AND
ENVIRONMENTAL STUDIES

General Editors: Gordon Clark, Andrew Goudie, and Ceri Peach

OF STATES AND CITIES

Of States and Cities

The Partitioning of Urban Space

Edited by

Peter Marcuse
and
Ronald van Kempen

*Includes an afterword
on September 11*

OXFORD
UNIVERSITY PRESS

OXFORD
UNIVERSITY PRESS

Great Clarendon Street, Oxford OX2 6DP

Oxford University Press is a department of the University of Oxford.
It furthers the University's objective of excellence in research, scholarship,
and education by publishing worldwide in

Oxford New York

Auckland Bangkok Buenos Aires Cape Town Chennai
Dar es Salaam Delhi Hong Kong Istanbul Karachi Kolkata
Kuala Lumpur Madrid Melbourne Mexico City Mumbai Nairobi
São Paulo Shanghai Singapore Taipei Tokyo Toronto

with an associated company in Berlin

Oxford is a registered trade mark of Oxford University Press
in the UK and in certain other countries

Published in the United States
by Oxford University Press Inc., New York

British Library Cataloguing in Publication Data

Data available

Library of Congress Cataloging-in-Publication Data

Of states and cities: the partitioning of urban space / edited by Peter Marcuse and
Ronald van Kempen
p. cm.—(Oxford geographical and environmental studies)
Includes bibliographical references and index.
1. Sociology, Urban. 2. Urban economics. 3. City planning. I. Marcuse, Peter.
II. Kempen, Ronald van. III. Series.
HT155.O37 2001 307.76–dc21 2001035171

ISBN 0–19–829719–X

1 3 5 7 9 10 8 6 4 2

Typeset in Times New Roman MT
by SNP Best-set Typesetter Ltd., Hong Kong
Printed in Great Britain by
Biddles Ltd., Guildford & Kings Lynn

EDITORS' PREFACE

Geography and environmental studies are two closely related and burgeoning fields of academic enquiry. Both have grown rapidly over the past two decades. At once catholic in its approach and yet strongly committed to a comprehensive understanding of the world, geography has focused upon the interaction between global and local phenomena. Environmental studies, on the other hand, have shared with the discipline of geography an engagement with different disciplines, addressing wide-ranging environmental issues in the scientific community and the policy community of great significance. Ranging from the analysis of climate change and physical processes to the cultural dislocations of post-modernism and human geography, these two fields of enquiry have been in the forefront of attempts to comprehend transformations taking place in the world, manifesting themselves in a variety of separate but interrelated spatial processes.

The 'Oxford Geographical and Environmental Studies' series aims to reflect this diversity and engagement. It aims to publish the best and original research studies in the two related fields and in doing so, to demonstrate the significance of geographical and environmental perspectives for understanding the contemporary world. As a consequence, its scope is international and ranges widely in terms of its topics, approaches, and methodologies. Its authors are welcomed from all corners of the globe. We hope the series will assist in redefining the frontiers of knowledge and build bridges within the fields of geography and environmental studies. We hope also that it will cement links with topics and approaches that have originated outside the strict confines of these disciplines. Resulting studies will contribute to frontiers of research and knowledge as well as representing individually the fruits of particular and diverse specialist expertise in the traditions of scholarly publication.

Gordon Clark
Andrew Goudie
Ceri Peach

PREFACE

Two related assumptions about cities are becoming virtual gospel:

(1) that cities are newly divided and polarized; and
(2) that changes in cities today come about because of the competitive market, in the face of an increasingly powerless state.

This book is dedicated to examining these two assumptions.

We believe the first assumption addresses a major development, but requires substantial refinement. Divisions in cities are not new, and 'polarization' is only part of a much more complicated picture and is only contemporary in some aspects. In their present form, division and partitioning are not novel, but rather a further stage in the process of active manipulation of space to protect power and enhance wealth that has been going on for centuries. We prefer the term *'partitioning'* to 'division' or 'polarization' to indicate our belief that the process is an active one, driven by concrete actors advancing concrete interests against concrete opposition, rather than the perhaps unfortunate result of some immutable laws of development.

We believe that the second assumption is only very partially true. While the market is a major determinant of city form and spatial differences within cities, it is not itself an actor, but rather represents the sphere in which actors and major groups of actors operate, actors who also actively influence state policies which are essential to their purposes. Market forces are the drivers (or struggle for the driver's seat) and provide the fuel, but the engine, the steering wheel, and the accelerator are those of the state.

We believe a careful examination of these two assumptions is of much more than purely academic interest. For we believe the partitioning is pernicious: it has extremely negative results for a vast number of people. It increases inequality, threatens democracy, and ultimately undermines the viability of democratic society. And we believe the second assumption is a pernicious one which undercuts attempts to avoid these negative results, disempowers opposition, and conceals the alternatives that are indeed available for the future of our cities. Thus, we believe examining these assumptions is of political as well as academic interest; clarity can make a difference in policy, in action, in people's lives. It is to that aim that this book hopes to make a small contribution.

This book has had a long gestation period. Each of us has grappled with the issues raised here in a number of previous works centring on the way in which cities today are partitioned, divided, quartered, segregated. We assembled the contributors based on their interest in our issues, their extensive and diverse empirical work, and their openness to the kind of interchange we envisaged. In May 1996, we had the opportunity to have a working session in which some of the contributors were able to take part, held in Berlin and at the Bauhaus

Dessau and with its support, which we gratefully acknowledge. We have had significant correspondence with each of the contributors about their pieces (sometimes stretching the limits of editorial roles!), so that this book would not just be an assembly of disparate papers but would cohesively address common questions. We have, however, not tampered with any of the contributions contrary to their author's wishes, and each remains the responsibility of their own author. As will be seen, there are disagreements between various contributions, and we are not ourselves in accord with all the formulations or conclusions of each.

Ronald van Kempen would like to thank the Urban Research Centre Utrecht of the Faculty of Geographical Sciences of Utrecht University (the Netherlands) for the time they gave him for the work on this volume, and the Netherlands Graduate School of Housing and Urban Research (NETHUR) for organizational support. Peter Marcuse would like to thank his colleagues and students in the Planning Program at Columbia University's School of Architecture, Planning, and Preservation for intellectual stimulation throughout. We both thank Ester de Bever for checking all the reference lists, and for making many technical changes to the text.

Our intellectual debts are numerous. Work on city form, on the role of the state in determining that form, on the impact of globalization on cities, on the sociology and economics and geography of partitioning, is vast. We have not been able to absorb or credit all of it in this book, but we want to acknowledge the intellectual efforts of those who have been particularly important and provocative for us, both in agreement and in disagreement, and contributed to our understanding of the issues: Janet Abu-Lughod, Blair Badcock, Bob Beauregard, Jack Burgers, Manuel Castells, Luis Cesar de Queiroz Ribeiro, Sanjoy Chakravorty, Frans Dieleman, Jürgen Friedrichs, Bill Goldsmith, Anne Haila, Chris Hamnett, Doug Henwood, Roger Keil, Christian Kesteloot, Robert Kloosterman, John Logan, John Mollenkopf, Sako Musterd, Klaus Ronneberger, Saskia Sassen, Bill Tabb, Ed Telles, Carlos Vainer, Leo van Grunsven, Jan van Weesep, Thomas Vietorisz, Paul Waley, and William Julius Wilson.

CONTENTS

PART III Conclusions

LIST OF CONTRIBUTORS

Murat Güvenç is an Associate Professor at Middle East Technical University, Department of City and Regional Planning, Ankara, Turkey. He has published studies on the social and industrial geography of Turkey's metropolises. He is currently working on the visualization of micro-data from Turkish censuses, and on the historical geography of Istanbul during the first two decades of the 20th century.

Oğuz Işık is an Associate Professor at Middle East Technical University, Department of City and Regional Planning, Ankara, Turkey. Among his current research interests are illegal housing and urban poverty, and the part played by religion in community building in Turkish cities.

János Ladányi is Professor of Sociology at the Budapest University of Economics. He has published extensively on school segregation, social and economic exclusion, and urban poverty in Hungary.

Peter Lee is Senior Lecturer in Urban and Regional Studies at the Centre for Urban and Regional Studies, University of Birmingham, England. His research interests include the geography of social exclusion and social cohesion, housing and social exclusion, and methodological issues relating to concentrations of deprivation and excluded communities. He has been involved in a number of research projects examining the relationship between crime and social cohesion as well as the geography of 'popular' and 'unpopular' housing areas at local and regional level in the United Kingdom. He has written and researched on the theme of changing and low-demand housing as well as social exclusion.

Peter Marcuse is Professor of Urban Planning at Columbia University in New York City. He has also taught at the University of California at Los Angeles, as well as universities in Johannesburg, Weimar, and São Paulo. He has been president of the Los Angeles City Planning Commission, and a member of a Community Board in New York City. A lawyer as well as planner, he has written widely on comparative housing and planning issues. Recently he edited, together with Ronald van Kempen, *Globalizing Cities: A New Spatial Order?* (Oxford: Blackwell).

Alan Murie is Professor of Urban and Regional Studies and Director of the Centre for Urban and Regional Studies, University of Birmingham. Alan was previously Professor of Planning and Housing at Heriot-Watt University, Edinburgh (1990–4) and has held visiting professorships at the Universities of Utrecht and Amsterdam and City University Hong Kong. He has published over 150 academic papers and was the co-editor of *Housing Policy and Practice*, Macmillan (1999, 5th edition with Peter Malpass) and *Housing, Wealth* *and the Family*, Routledge (1994, with Ray Forrest). His research interests include issues around regional and economic development and housing, social policy, and social change.

Sueli Ramos Schiffer is a Titular Professor of Methodology of Urban and Regional Planning at the School of Architecture and Urban Planning of the University of São Paulo, Brazil. Her research has been developed focusing on the relations between the economic processes, urban transformations, and the socio-economic impacts. In 1999, she edited, together with Professor Csaba Deák, *O processo de urbanização no Brasil* (The Urbanization Process in Brazil), São Paulo: FUPAM/EDUSP.

Eva van Kempen is a Lecturer at the Department of Human Geography, Faculty of Social and Behavioural Sciences, University of Amsterdam, the Netherlands. Her current interests and research are in the field of housing, social policy and social exclusion, and questions concerning the relationship between governance and the construction of socio-spatial inequalities and place as an instrument of social differentiation and identity formation.

Ronald van Kempen is Associate Professor of Urban Geography at the Urban Research Centre of the Faculty of Geographical Sciences, Utrecht University, the Netherlands. He is a member of the editorial board of the *Journal of Housing and the Built Environment* and a vice-chairman of the European Network for Housing Research. His current research focuses on the links between spatial segregation, social exclusion, and the development of cities. Recently, he edited, together with Peter Marcuse, *Globalizing Cities: A New Spatial Order?* (Oxford: Blackwell).

Loïc Wacquant is a Researcher at the Centre de sociologie européenne du Collège de France and Professor at the University of California–Berkeley. He is the author of *An Invitation to Reflexive Sociology* (with Pierre Bourdieu), *Les prisons de la misère, punir os Pobres*, and the forthcoming *In the zone: Life in the dark ghetto at century's end*. As well as urban inequality and imprisonment, his research interests include racial classification and domination and social theory.

Grzegorz Węcławowicz is Professor and Head of the Department of Urban and Population Studies in the Institute of Geography of the Polish Academy of Sciences in Warsaw, Poland. Since 1997, he has been vice-president of the Polish Geographical Association. His current research is on urban issues, particularly the post-socialist transformation concerning social exclusion and segregation at the regional and intra-urban levels in Poland and central Europe. Recently, his book, *Contemporary Poland, Space and Society* (London: UCL Press), was published.

LIST OF FIGURES

LIST OF TABLES

PART I

Introduction and Background

1

States, Cities, and the Partitioning of Urban Space

Peter Marcuse and Ronald van Kempen

Introduction

A spectre is haunting cities around the world: the spectre of globalization. The fear is of convergence on an undesired United States model of urban spatial form and social content, involving increased segregation, shrinkage of public amenities, commercialization of civic life, decline of central cities, and social polarization. In the United States, both the spatial form and its social content reflect deep partitions, indeed chasms, widening between rich and poor, between high-rise citadels of the rich, walled enclaves of the well-to-do and well-educated, sprawling suburbs of a declining middle class, sometimes concentrated in edge cities, mixed and unstable working-class and immigrant quarters, and ghettos of the excluded, often overwhelmingly of racial or ethnic minorities. We may call this model the 'partitioned city'. It is accompanied by the ideological belief that states as well as cities are helpless to do anything but ameliorate, at the margins, some of the more negative aspects of this partitioning. History, geography, culture, local agency, resistance, are all ultimately irrelevant; under the relentless pressure to compete, urban leaders have no choice but to move even faster in the direction all the others are going, each seeking their own bit of competitive advantage over each of the others.

We wish to put the reality of this spectre into perspective. In one sense, it is clearly wrong: however strong the forces of globalization are, and they are indeed strong, their impact on any given city is substantially mediated by that city's history, its physical layout, its location, its built environment, its role in the international economy, its demographic composition. We have, in another volume, examined some of these mediating factors in detail, and concluded that, at least as yet, there has not developed a 'new spatial order' of cities around the world, although we have found strong forces in the direction of convergence (Marcuse and Van Kempen 2000). What we wish to focus on in this volume is a central fear generated by the spectre: that states and cities are powerless to chart their own course, to escape the inevitable, if longer-term and mediated, slide towards convergence. We want to focus on the role of the state, broadly conceived, in dealing with the partitioning of the contemporary city: establishing the partitions, exacerbating the partitions, ameliorating the partitions, avoiding the partitions.

In the contributions to this book, we seek the answers to the following questions:

1. How have cities been partitioned in past periods? What role has the state played in the historical processes of partitioning?
2. Do new forms of partitioning characterize changes in cities today? What role does the state play in the shaping of cities today, in a period in which globalization is generally seen as a dominating force, while at the same time the role of the state seems to be declining, or at least changing? Specifically, do changes in cities today come about because of the competitive market, in the face of an increasingly powerless state?

The Organization of the Book

In Part I of this book, we examine the partitioning of cities historically (i.e., prior to the present stage of globalization), in two contributions by the co-editors devoted specifically to earlier periods. Chapter 2 is a (somewhat presumptuous) broad-scale historical overview, finding that cities have always been subject to partitioning in a variety of ways, some harsh, some moderate, but in ways whose origins and logics fit into clear patterns. Among these patterns is one particularly relevant to our concerns: the role of the state. From ancient times through to the most laissez-faire period of the industrial revolution, the agency of the state, and those who control it, have always been critical factors in the shaping, and particularly the partitioning, of cities, although often in tension with the efforts of those adversely affected by the divisions. The main conclusion is that, historically, the state has been a dominant force in creating and enforcing partitions, but that paralleling state political domination, economic forces have produced their own undercurrent of separation. This chapter also tries to establish a conceptualization of the different partitions of the city, attempting to define in orderly fashion such terms as 'ghetto', 'enclave', 'citadel', etc.

Chapter 3, the second overview chapter, looks historically, not at the actual patterns of partitioning over time, but rather at the various historical attempts to explain patterns. Attention is primarily on the contributions of social sciences, mainly urban sociology and geography, over the last eighty years or so. What is striking about the account is how complex the task of explanation is, and how fragmented the explanations are that the social sciences have developed in the course of the last century. Individual preferences, the role of age, income and family status, various constraints, class distinctions, the role of race, economic, socio-cultural, and demographic variables on different spatial levels, are all adumbrated, in fascinating and provocative theories and theoretical notions. However, the role of the state is not always reflected consistently in the analyses.

We then turn, in Part II, to a number of case studies. Chapter 4, by Peter Lee and Alan Murie, looks at the impact of changes in social housing policies in Great Britain, and finds that the state plays a direct and critical role in shaping the overall residential pattern of two cities (Birmingham and Edinburgh), with present policies leading to increasing segregation. A combination of polarization and professionalization in the economy with a withdrawal of state subsidies from housing leads to a growing residualization of the still large stock of social housing, and thus to an increasing segregation at the bottom end of the economic ladder brought about by the new complexion of state policies.

The following piece by Ronald van Kempen (Chapter 5) examines the emerging patterns and counter-forces in the Netherlands, finding the state the key actor in producing the presence or absence of partitions. He finds some partitioning, but much less than fears of the spectre of globalization and convergence on the United States model would anticipate. Social housing policies, as in Lee and Murie's chapter, play a leading role in avoiding partitioning by income, but are losing their momentum in this direction. Previous welfare state policies have been largely effective in preventing partitioning along either ethnic or income lines, but shifts in state policy may well increase such separation (or are insufficient to prevent it). Of all the presentations in this collection, this chapter best exemplifies both the possibilities and the limitations of a welfare state approach to the spatial form of its cities.

The development of the present form of the black ghetto—the outcast or excluded ghetto—in the United States is then described in a contribution by Peter Marcuse (Chapter 6). He begins with a summary of the first discussions of the ghetto in the United States literature: that by Louis Wirth of the Jewish ghetto over history. He then recounts the changing nature of the black ghetto in the United States after the First World War, traces the shift from a state-reinforced policy of racial discrimination to a market-fostered pattern of overlapping racial and class differentiation. The sharpest lines dividing the ghetto from the rest of the city are created where the lines of race and class overlap. State policies are no longer directly partitioned by race; state policies, however, reinforce ghettoization by increasing economic polarization, and then adapting to and strengthening its spatial consequences. The pattern is quite different from that both of the Jewish ghetto and ethnic immigrant enclaves, where the clustering is voluntary and accompanied by widespread spatial dispersion.

Sueli Schiffer (Chapter 7) discusses divisions in the physical fabric of São Paulo over the span of two centuries. Starting out as a relatively integrated city, the first identifiable separate clusters arose as immigrants from Europe appropriated contiguous areas for their separate settlements at the turn of the century. But real urban segregation, in São Paulo, segregation by class, is an urban phenomenon of the period of heavy industrial development, after 1950. At that point it preserved the radial form that expanded out from the colonial nucleus, and was and is characterized by the settling of lower-income groups in the outskirts. During the 1990s, the elite maintained economic control, guaranteed by the country's fit into global economic patterns. Although this process has introduced new economic measures and has produced changes in the role of the state, it has not brought about structural changes, and has caused Brazilian society to remain unbalanced. Schiffer demonstrates how this is reflected in the urban space of the São Paulo Metropolitan Area today. Simultaneously, with the contemporary expansion of advanced economic activities and the flourishing of expensive leisure activities and shops in upper-class districts, there has been unemployment and a great increase in violence, primarily in the lower-income outlying areas. The sizeable growth of slums and *favelas* has, she argues, occurred side-by-side with an expansion of high-income housing clusters, in the form of gated communities. This contrast makes urban class segregation very visible in today's metropolis.

János Ladányi's Chapter 8 then examines the complex pattern of residential division in Budapest over time. He finds that state socialism produced much less in the direction of egalitarian distribution of population than its theory would have predicted, and he finds the trend towards increasing segregation manifest well before the end of communist domination. He finds a pattern of clustering that is quite different for the higher than for the lower occupationally defined groups: at the upper end, greater homogeneity in larger areas, at the lower, wider distribution and clustering at a smaller scale. Globalization, he argues, accentuates these trends, and produces a suburbanization of the upper classes and a new rural ghettoization of the lower. Regardless of major changes in the nature and role of the state, he shows that discrimination against Gypsies constitutes a residual layer that changes in the state have not influenced. While not examining state policies in detail, the underlying theme seems to be that patterns of location among non-Gypsies today (and to a significant extent in the past also) reflect economic rather than state policies; patterns of location of Gypsies reflect ethnic rather than economic relationships, although aggravated by economic change. He concludes with a reasoned call for a resolute intervention of the post-communist welfare state to deal with the negative developments he describes.

Grzegorz Węcławowicz (Chapter 9) describes the dramatic impact of the major societal change from state socialism to a market economy in Poland, and thus the shift from a state-directed to a market-directed spatial pattern. State socialism represents the furthest extent of state direction of spatial structure in the recent past, analogous only to the directive regimes of a few countries such as Singapore (Van Grunsven 2000), but responding to a diametrically different social, economic, and political base. While the chapter includes the inevitable reference to the extent to which state socialist egalitarianism was imperfectly implemented, the contrast with the increasing differentiation of the post-socialist cities is clear. Because the older more egalitarian structures of the built environment take some time to change, Węcławowicz points out the ways in which differentiation among groups sharing a common space is carried out, in a metaphor also used in various ways by others, in (historical, geographical, and functional) layers (see, e.g., Kesteloot 2000; Marcuse and Van Kempen 2000). His outlook is for a further increase in spatial segregation, consistent with the changed circumstances of the new/old elite, now exercising their influence through the market rather than through state power.

Murat Güvenç and Oğuz Işık break new ground in analysing the social spatial structure of housing in Istanbul, using available data to show a city in which the historical pattern reveals the separation between the rich on the coast and the poor inland, with the state barely visible in producing that pattern (Chapter 10). The direction since then, however, with the end of the cold war and the opening to globalization, suggests a newly developing situation, in which pressure for a new economically externally oriented city will produce changed patterns. Patterns in which the state is called on both to legalize and to commodify the position of the poor where they have informally settled at the same time as the state enables the rich to insulate themselves in contemporary-type enclaves protected from all contact with those poor. However, the authors' essay also describes how the poor have also been able to exert pressure, successfully, for a degree of formalization and legitimization of their status and location.

In Part III of this book, Loïc Wacquant (Chapter 11) analyses the direction in which the future is likely to lead us if the United States model is extended. He describes the newest development in partitioning: the formation of an area of 'advanced marginality', combining race and class in a new economic order, in the United States and France. He does not explicitly take up the state's role in producing the income distribution whose effects he recounts, but others have done this extensively (see, e.g., Levy 1998). The picture he paints of developments in the United States, but not only in the United States, is disquieting in the extreme.

Eva van Kempen's article then spells out the devastating consequences that might in general be expected to ensue where the partitioning of cities has taken a particular form, to the disadvantage of the poor (Chapter 12). She looks at the likely consequences where there is a particular concentration of poverty in what she calls 'poverty pockets'. The United States model, as described by Wacquant, is of course the extreme, but she examines the likely impact of the concentration of poverty when the racial component does not play as prominent a role as in the United States. Spatial form, in particular the segregation of the poor, she theorizes, compounds the difficulties those excluded from the benefits of globalization face, and becomes itself a source of disadvantage and limitation of life chances.

Our concluding chapter then looks to the future (Chapter 13). It is not possible to be 'neutral' in examining the results of present trends in the spatial division of cities, and we examine the possibilities for the creation of alternate ways of developing cities. Of necessity, the discussion is somewhat speculative, since the bulk of present developments point towards increasing rather than decreasing partitioning, convergence rather than resistance or reversal of partitioning. But we believe it important, in view of the prevalence of fears of the spectre and the disabling influence that fear has on those seeking constructive alternatives to its impact, to highlight the real possibilities we see of influencing the outcome, the real tools that are available for that purpose. In short, we believe state action, brought about and undergirded by organized activity at the grassroots, can defeat the realities behind the spectre. The spectre, after all, is ultimately an ideological weapon used by some actors in the globalization process to achieve their particular ends, for which the partitioning of the city is both instrumental and productive. In this sense, our conclusion is also intended to be ideological, or rather, in Mannheim's sense, anti-ideological.

Some Definitions Used in this Volume

For clarity, we provide definitions to help establish consistency in the use of key terms. *Ghettos* and *enclaves* seem critically important to us in the analysis of the partitioning of urban space, because they help clarify the question of what divisions are desirable, which are not, what divisions are consistent with democracy, which are not, what divisions might be considered 'natural' products of individual preferences and which not (see also Marcuse 1997). *Ghettos* are areas of spatial concentration in which their residents live involuntarily, even though in many cases they have adapted to their circumstances and found sources of strength in clustering together. *Enclaves*, by contrast, are largely voluntarily created by their residents, even though in many cases they cluster together for reasons of mutual defence and support in a foreign environment. Ghettos and enclaves thus have elements of the other in them, but it is important analytically to keep the essential elements of each separate. The critical question in each case is the relationship between the residents of the particular area of spatial concentration and those outside it: the residents of the *ghetto* are held in a subordinate position by the outside world, the residents of the *enclave*, although often newcomers and perhaps slightly 'different', are entitled to equality with those outside in all legal, social, economic, and political matters.

It is the concern about ghettos, about the involuntary segregation of minority groups, that is heard almost everywhere around the world today that gives importance to these definitional distinctions. Whether it be of blacks in the United States, Turks in Germany and the Netherlands, Algerians in France,

Muslims in Serbia, Palestinians in Israel, Pakistanis in Birmingham, the worry is that the apparently increasing clustering of individuals of one ethnic or religious or cultural background within a limited area within a city (or a nation) can give rise to a multitude of problems, both to those living within such clusters and to those in the society outside. Yet all clustering is not alike. Clustering may be voluntary, and represent affinity and solidarity, or it may be involuntary, the result of segregation and discrimination. It may be transitional, or it may be permanent, of a group on the way up and out, or a group held down and oppressed. The issues are complex. And what makes the matter even more complicated is that the same clustering, the same concentration of individuals and households, may change its character over time: what had been perceived as transitional may harden into permanence, a separation originally productive of mutual support and cultural enrichment may turn into a ghetto burdensome to all who are forced to live in it. In Chapter 6 more attention is given to the spatial concepts mentioned here.

The *state* we take to be the entire apparatus of government, at all levels, national, regional, local, and including the various institutions of government, for example, the courts and the rules they enforce, the public educational system, all levels of taxing authority, quasi-governmental organizations established by government, and the institutions to which governmental powers are delegated in whole or in part, subject to revocation or control. It is thus a narrower concept than 'regime' in regime theory, but a broader concept than that which equates it only with the particular government in power at any given moment. The reason for choosing an essentially Weberian definition is to highlight the fact that 'the state' is not an organic entity, not an 'actor' as such; even the bureaucracy is often divided within itself, and the bureaucracy is a part only of government, which is a part only of the state. We thus largely follow the discussion in the opening chapter of Evans, Rueschemeyer, and Skocpol (1985). In particular circumstances the state may indeed act, may be autonomous with a separate interest of its own, but in most such cases that interest will be an outgrowth of the interests of the most powerful in the society. A ruling elite may have firm control of the state, as in Hungary between 1949 and 1989, but even here it is not a homogeneous, unitary interest that is involved. Thus, Ralph Milliband (1969) speaks of a 'state system', rather than of 'state', and the formulation permits the clear recognition, very important in the discussions that follow, that 'state' does not speak with one voice, that state policies are often contradictory, and that the purposes of state action are in fact the purposes and interests of different groups, classes, elements, within the society in which the state exists.

We will return to this conception of the state in our conclusion (Chapter 13), in which we want to take up the issue of the extent to which the negative aspects of the partitioning described in this book can be overcome. It will by then be apparent, we believe, that state policy is central to influencing the form and extent of partitioning, but that state policy is not a simple matter of a one-time vote by a legislative body or a simple decision by a president or prime minister, but a much more complex problem involving relations of power and influence in the society as a whole.

References

EVANS, P. B., RUESCHEMEYER, D., and SKOCPOL, T. (1985). *Bringing the State Back In*. Cambridge: Cambridge University Press.

KESTELOOT, C. (2000). 'Brussels: Post-Fordist polarization in a Fordist spatial canvas', in P. Marcuse and R. van Kempen (eds.), *Globalizing Cities: A New Spatial Order?*, 186–210. Oxford: Blackwell.

MARCUSE, P. (1997). 'The ghetto of exclusion and the fortified enclave; new patterns in the United States'. *American Behavioral Scientist*, 41: 311–26.

—— and VAN KEMPEN, R. (2000). 'Conclusion: a changed spatial order', in P. Marcuse and R. van Kempen (eds.), *Globalizing Cities: A New Spatial Order?*, 249–75. Oxford: Blackwell.

LEVY, F. (1998). *The New Dollars and Dreams: American Incomes and Economic Change*. New York: Russell Sage.

MILLIBAND, R. (1969). *The State in Capitalist Society*. New York: Basic Books.

VAN GRUNSVEN, L. (2000). 'Singapore: the changing residential landscape in a winner city', in P. Marcuse and R. van Kempen (eds.), *Globalizing Cities: A New Spatial Order?*, 95–126. Oxford: Blackwell.

2

The Partitioned City in History

Peter Marcuse

Introduction

'Partitioned cities' has recently become a fashionable topic in urban literature. Whether called divided, dual, polarized, quartered, or fragmented, the discussion has often seen the phenomenon as something new historically, something specific to our own age, to the period of globalization, or to post-industrialism, or to post-Fordism. We have elsewhere argued that 'dual' is in any event too narrow a term; that the divisions are far more complex than simply two-part (Marcuse and Van Kempen 2001). This chapter raises a different question about the conception: whether it is historically 'new' or, since that term defies easy definition, what changes have taken place in the division of cities over the long *durée*. It is clearly not conventional history, and does not pretend to the rigour of good historical writing; it is instead intended to raise conceptual questions and perhaps contribute to clarity by putting the way cities are divided today into some historical perspective.

Cities have always been divided. Possibly they always will be—and possibly they should be. A history of divisions in cities would be a fascinating undertaking. It might start with the trenchant comment of Plato:

> For [cities] are each one of them many cities, not a city, as it goes in the game. There are two at the least at enmity with one another, the city of the rich and the city of the poor, and in each of these there are many. If you deal with them as one you will altogether miss the mark. . . .   (Plato *c.* 460 BC/1937: 422)[1]

Or it might go back even further to Hippodamus of Miletus, called by Aristotle the founder of city planning, who argued that cities should naturally be divided into three parts, one for artisans, one for farmers, and one for soldiers, and that the land should further be divided into sacred, public, and private space.

Written records detailing such divisions in these or even earlier settlements are not plentiful. There is however a good deal of information available as to the actual forms of the ancient Chinese cities, the cities of India, and the villages of Africa, and there is certainly ample information about the forms and divisions of Greek, Roman, medieval, and contemporary cities, on all continents. There is certainly enough to make a history of the evolution of divisions worthwhile. It is, however, beyond the scope of what we will attempt here. Rather, we will confine ourselves to exploring three questions such a history might illuminate:

1. Along what lines have cities historically been spatially divided?
2. Do the differing lines of division reflect the characteristics of distinct historical periods and correlate to specific historical societal formations?
3. What role has the state played in each historical period?

This chapter is thus very much exploratory and tentative and, we hope, provocative of further work along the lines discussed above.

What follows is, first, a brief analytic formulation of the way in which we see the lines of division within cities in the past, then a very preliminary historical survey of actual historical divisions, and finally a comment on the role of the state in such divisions.

The Relevant Lines of Division

Cities may be, and have been, divided along a number of lines. Many of these lines, but not all, are social: divisions brought about by the conscious acts of their residents and those who hold power over or among them. We might list the chief possibilities as divisions along lines of nationality, class, income, wealth, occupation, religion, 'race', colour, ethnicity, language, age, household composition, personal cultural preference and lifestyle; other categories can no doubt be defined.

We believe, for purposes of policy-relevant analysis, such divisions fall into three quite separate and distinguishable groups/ideal types:[2] divisions by culture, by functional role, and by position in the hierarchy of power.

Cultural divisions are usually easily visible: by differences in language, in dress, in architectural style, for instance. They may include divisions by ethnicity, by country or nationality or tribe of origin or parentage or descent, by religion or belief, by lifestyle. (We avoid using the term 'race', and see it as conflating cultural division, falsely defined, with differences of status; see below.[3]) While some of these differences may appropriately be called 'cultural' in the strict sense, and others may be the products of manipulation, idiosyncratic choice, or some combination of these, the key element that differentiates cultural divisions from functional or status divisions is that they are based neither on differences in relationship to economic production nor on relationships of power. One ethnic or religious group may in fact also play a specific economic role, and be socially subordinated, to another group. But there are elements of cultural differences that are independent of these economic and social differences; they may reflect them, but are not identical to them. Worship, music, parenting, language, history, holidays, dress, family relations, are not dependent on their economic productivity for their hold on people, nor do they require a relationship of superiority or inferiority to outsiders for their strength (although such feelings may easily be incorporated within them).[4] The lifestyle differences that the real estate market takes into account producing the 'spatial segregation of people by household type, family status, and age, [so that] the different [age] cohorts take up separate quarters' (Kostof 1992: 121), are innocuous, non-hierarchical. Such dimensions of commonality are summarized under the term 'cultural' in the discussion that follows.

Divisions by functional role are the result of economic logic, either physical or organizational: the divisions between farms and factories and residential areas, for instance. They include separate locations for different guilds or the separation of services from manufacturing, or wholesaling from retailing. Residentially, the needs of workers in particular industries to be located in accessible relations to their places of employment may create residential divisions, an extreme example of which would be company-sponsored housing developments. Areas may be set aside for defence, and those involved in defence located there; the externalities of certain industries or occupations may require that those involved in them be near each other, or clustered along transportation routes making them readily accessible to interchange with each other. Such differences are essentially independent of cultural differences, and do not (at least essentially—status differentiates may of course arise out of functional differences) denote relations of superiority or inferiority to other functions, simply differences. Such differences are summarized under the term 'functional' in the discussion that follows.

Zoning is the accepted legal embodiment of such divisions. That zoning should be by function, generally defined as economic use (residential from heavy industrial from light industrial from retail from wholesaling from offices), is not as self-evident as it might seem. 'Performance zoning', for instance, attempts to define permitted uses of land not by their economic nature but by their environmental impact (traffic generated, shadows cast, air circulation impeded, green space occupied, etc.). And, while 'use' may separate manufacturing from retail from residential, it has never been quite clear why residential use for one family should be a different type of use than residential use by two or three families.[5] Be that as it may, separation by function, by use, is accepted today as in general an appropriate division within a city.

Differences in status, reflecting and reinforcing relationships of power, of domination, exploitation, state authority, are exemplified by the imperial enclaves in a colonial town or the black townships of South Africa as extreme examples. But security-guarded luxury residences near central business districts reflect and support relationships of power just as much, as do working-class quarters or 'slums'. Class is a widely relevant current line of differentiation which involves status in the sense used here. Income is often a good surrogate for status, but not identical with it; the same is true of occupation, and even of the cluster of indicators generally known as SES—socio-economic status—which are simply, however, good indicators of an underlying relationship, not the substance of that relationship itself. Power can exist along a multitude of dimensions: military power, political power, economic power, social power, legal power (of which slavery is the extreme case) are examples. They are all summarized under the term 'status' in the discussion that follows. These three divisions both overlap and contradict each other; their intertwining is one of the fascinations of the history of cities. *Cultural* differences may be used to reinforce differences of *status* to the point that the two are at first glance identical; this is notoriously the case with black/white, imperial/indigenous, Jewish/Arab, differences, which frequently reinforce differences of *status* to the point that the two seem at first glance identical. But those divisions often interfere with the effective lines of functional division: groups differentiated by culture and status need to work and be near each other for efficient production. Relations of *status* and *function* often conflict in their impact on space: employers like to have their employees close to their work, but not close to them. Cultural affinities may contradict status differences: within each group, linked by culture, there can be major differences of class as well as of economic function. Interdependence and mutual hostility often go hand in hand. *Function*, *status*, and *culture* were largely merged in imperial enclaves in colonial territories in the past, and may be merging again in today's economies: as Cross and Waldinger point out, 'the ethnic division of labor is, in this sense, the central division of labor in the postindustrial city' (Cross and Waldinger 1992: 173). Since functions are not neutral in the hierarchy of status, the three divisions come together. And so on. The permutations are manifold. We shall see whether, in the long term, a new pattern emerges, whether there is a distinctive pattern to the post-Fordist city with which we are chiefly concerned.

As a final complicating factor: the role of space is not a constant one. Space is socially created; its role shifts with shifting social constellations: cultural, functional, status and power. Of course, geographical considerations influence the location of spatial divisions, and will often correlate to social divisions (e.g., the upper class will live in locations of higher environmental amenity). But even such correlations are fluid and subject to social and economic change: thus waterfront locations may be put to industrial use and occupied by longshore workers in one society, claimed for luxury housing and recreational use in another. Historically viewed, different patterns of division are differentially reflected, fortified, contradicted, by space. The general truth was overstated by Robert Park more than forty years ago: 'social relations are . . . frequently and . . . inevitably correlated with spatial relations' (Park 1952: 177; the contradictory adverbs are in the original). Frequently, yes; inevitably, no, certainly not directly: the slave–master relationship can coexist with slaves living next door to masters, as well as if they live in separate districts of the city. And the direction of influence is reciprocal: social relations determine spatial relations, but these in turn influence, generally but not always reinforcing, social relations. Where the underlying social relations are in flux, or where the allocation and use of space does not closely reflect those relations, there is likely to be conflict, again reflected both in disputes over space and over the underlying relationships themselves. The building of walls (see Marcuse 1997*a*) to create or enforce divisions may be as much a reflection of the instability of underlying relationships as of the hardness of the divisions within them.

While divisions by function and by culture are in general voluntary, divisions by status are not. No group desires low status; it is imposed on them. While those of higher status maintain their separation voluntarily, they need the means to impose it on those of lower status against their wills. Thus, divisions by status require, implicitly or explicitly, the use of force, and in a civilized society such force is (at least in theory) a monopoly of the state. State action may (or may not) also be involved in regulating cultural divisions, and is often involved in shaping functional divisions; but in those cases the state is acting in a purely regulatory role, with the consent and for the benefit of all participants. The source of the state's ability to impose status divisions in space upon its residents may have its source in the simple control of physical force, as was true in many early societies in which monarchs partitioned space for their own benefit, or the state may be itself responding to the desires of the holders of economic or political power, desires likewise reflected in parallel market patterns, and thus benefiting those outside the direct state apparatus. The state's role in establishing the involuntary lines of division that reflect status/power is in both events central in the active process we called 'partitioning' in this book. It is this partitioning along lines of power, implemented by the state, with which we are primarily concerned, for it is that which we consider the most threatening to the prospects for a democratic and just city. And it may be particularly damaging when it is reinforced by divisions of culture and/or function.

The history of spatial divisions reflects these considerations.

Spatial Urban Divisions in History

What follows is, to repeat, only exploratory and hopefully provocative of further thought and research. It is put forward only to suggest three points: that the division of cities is not something new historically; that the nature of divisions has changed significantly over time, in a coherent manner; and that the state has always played a significant role in those divisions.

There are major watersheds within the history of the partitioning of urban space. The first is, of course, the division of city from country. The second is the divide between pre-capitalist and capitalist forms. Within each, there are also major variations; we will be concerned with changes within capitalist forms. There are also major differences between spatial arrangements in capitalist and really existing socialist cities.

We will begin with a brief overview of pre-capitalist forms, taking the separation of city from countryside for granted. At the end, we will give brief consideration to divisions arising in the brief historical period of the existence of socialist cities. But the focus will be on the divisions within the period broadly defined as capitalist, the period in which we still are. The divisions suggested are summarized in Table 2.1.

Pre-capitalist Cities

The earliest explicit reference to internal divisions within cities I have come across is quoted by Spiro Kostof (Kostof 1992: 102) as coming from a Chinese writer, Kuan-tzu:

The scholar-official, the peasant, the craftsman and the merchant . . . should not mix with one another, for it would inevitably lead to conflict and divergence of opinions and thus complicate things unnecessarily . . . Let the scholar-officials reside near school areas, the peasants near fields, the craftsmen in the construction workshops near the officials' palace, and the merchants in the [commercial wards].

We see even here already the ambiguities that beset this area: Kuan-tzu prescribes locations as if he wanted to minimize the 'journey to work', in a manner very similar to Hippodamus, but the purpose seems to be social segregation.

For the city of Amarna, built by Akhenaten in the 14th century BC south of Cairo, a grid was laid out for workers, but the wealthy built where they wished. The residential village at Kahun (perhaps begun as early as 2670 BC to house workers on the pyramids in Egypt) 'was contained by a wall, also intended to prevent people getting out . . .' (Morris 1974: 13). Chinese cities were probably the earliest fully walled cities, with not only conventional exterior walls to protect against invasion but also walled wards 'for the regimentation and control of townsfolk', beginning with the beginning of the Han Dynasty, about 206 BC, and continuing through about AD 1000.

Each ward has four gates. At each gate there are two wardens, four subofficials, and eight guards. These gates were closed in the evening and opened in the morning, at fixed hours and to the beating of drums set up on the main avenues. Entrance was forbidden to non-inhabitants.   (Kostof 1992: 105)

Enforced separation as a means of social control has thus a long history.

Lewis Mumford gives a richer if somewhat more speculative description:

Occupational and caste stratification produced in the ancient city an urban pyramid, which rose to a peak in the absolute ruler: king, priest, warrior, scribe formed the apex of the pyramid; but the king alone, at the highest point, caught the full rays of the sun. Below him the layers widened out into merchants, craftsmen, peasants, sailors, house servants, freed men, slaves, the lowest layer deep in perpetual shadow. These divisions were distinguished and sharpened by the ownership, or lack, of property in various degrees; and they were further expressed in costume, in habit of life, in food, and in

Table 2.1. Spatial urban divisions in history: an overview

Historical type	Society	Status divisions	Cultural divisions	Functional divisions	Role of the state
Early pre-capitalist city	Agricultural, little separation between town and country	State or customary role			Implementing physical power
Developed commercial city	Agricultural, commercial, administrative, towns	State service	Religious position, beliefs	Economic function by guild	Physical domination
Colonial city	Imperial relationships	Imperial v. colonized	Language, religion		Full control, by law and force
Early industrialized capitalist city	Industrial society, separation of home/work place, 'walking city'	Fine-grained by class		Economic function	Slight
Mature, industrialized, Fordist city	Fordist production, national industrial base	Class	Ethnicity	Limited economic function	Market-supporting land use controls, discrimination
Post-Fordist globalizing city	Post-Fordist, globalized economies	Class	Ethnicity		Implementing market: land use controls, exclusion
Socialist city	Really existing socialist societies	State/Party service, ideology of equality		Economic function	Planning and control of economy and land use

dwelling place. Segregated economic functions and segregated social roles in turn created equivalent precincts within the city: not least if not first the marketplace. If the local temple was the magnet for residents of a neighborhood, there would also be a partly visible occupational wall, identifiable by house types, to serve as class envelope. That practice lingers today in the spontaneous grouping of certain occupations, even without the pressure of any municipal zoning ordinance. Thus in Philadelphia, the city where I am now writing these words, the physicians congregate in a small area whose axis is Spruce Street, while the insurance agents fill a whole quarter between Independence Hall and the wholesale provision district. 'Harley Street', 'Madison Avenue', 'State Street', are shorthand expressions not just for occupations, but for a whole way of life that they embody. Rome and Antioch, yes, probably Ninevah and Ur, had their equivalents.   (Mumford 1961: 104–5)

The comparison to Philadelphia (and possibly the reference to Rome; see below) seems overblown, but the elements of a very gross separation are clearly described. The basis for the division was however multiple; in Mumford's account, and many others, military power establishes a space at the top of the pyramid and often at the high point in the landscape. Below that a combination of economic function, religious affiliation, and social status divides cities, largely by custom rather than by state rule.

Some have interpreted the evidence as to Rome somewhat differently from Mumford. 'Rome was essentially an egalitarian city. With the exception of the emperor's palaces built on the Palatine Hill and possible separate working-class districts on the downstream banks of the Tiber and the slopes of the Aventine, high and low, patricians and plebeian, everywhere rubbed shoulders without coming into conflict.' While there were obvious distinctions between the *domus* of the rich and the *insulae* of the plebes, Carcopino states of workers' housing that 'they did not live congregated in dense, compact, exclusive masses; their living quarters were scattered about in almost every corner of the city but nowhere did they form a town within a town' (Jerome Carcopino, quoted in Morris 1974).

Medieval European Cities

Most of medieval Europe was less urbanized than Rome had been, and cities played a less dominant role than in either Greece or Rome. In the transition to feudalism, castles were constructed and rural life organized, with castles not for protection but for domination.[6] Typical paintings show a citadel on a hill, with both church and palace sharing the top of the hierarchy, separated off and protected as buildings, but generally open to public entry and located near to the public marketplace, which in fact was often developed in the immediate shadow of the church. Near it would be a merchants' area, where merchants lived and conducted their business and warehoused their goods, with their workers living on the upper floors. Nearby, or behind, but in the same neighbourhood, would be the workshops and homes of craftsmen, artisans, again with fully fledged guild members, analogous to 'employers' in the present sense, owning the building but their apprentices and journeymen and their families living upstairs in the same building. All of this would be within the walls of the city, used both for military protection and as an economic tool to facilitate the collection of fees and duties. Economic status played a role in location, but mildly; Benevolo says the richer tended to live towards the centre of the city, the poorer more on the outskirts (Benevolo 1980: 310). Peasants lived and worked outside the walls. Spatial arrangements thus reflected both political hierarchies (closely linked to religious) and economic functions, but the lines separating the divisions below the top were open and largely established by custom.

The divisions by economic function, as opposed to those established by the state, also reflected status, and were not uncontested. Kostof quotes Alberti, in the 15th century, who wrote:

There may perhaps be some who would like better to have the habitations of the gentry separate by themselves, quite clear and free from all mixture of the meaner sort of people. Others are for having every district of the city so laid out, that each part might be supplied at hand with every thing that it could have occasion for and for this reason they are not against having the meanest trades in the neighbourhood of the most honourable citizens.   (Alberti 1452/1955: i)

The explanation for the lack of division was perhaps partly economic, partly the inability to organize division. Jacques Heers writes: 'One of the most visible consequences of the disorganization of the city, in these "contrade" of the lesser nobles, was evidently lack of real segregation' (Heers 1990: 262; my translation). Nobles and merchants, wanted to have those who worked for them, those with whom they did business, close to them; although aristocrats may have congregated near the cathedral or on the grand streets, next to, behind, and on the second and third storeys over them, lived much 'lesser' and poorer folk. He speaks of a 'promiscuity' of people of unequal condition, 'tied by tight relationships, by firmly entrenched habits' (Heers 1990: 269). 'They refused (or at least were reluctant) to isolate themselves from their clients, to construct "noble quarters" uniquely of rich houses, no "noble" places surrounded by sumptuous walls, nor "chic" streets reserved for great families, nor even grand palaces protected from their neighbors by gardens surrounded by high walls' (Heers 1990: 269).[7]

The exceptions, of course, were the Jewish ghettos. They were sharply and physically delineated, in such a manner that they could be sealed off at night, without entry or egress to the outside. Thus there was sharp division on ethnic/religious[8] lines. In Spiro Kostof's formulation, Jews were socially segregated, but the segregation 'obviously did not apply to business' (Kostof 1992: 107). Jews were admitted to the city each day and have played an important role its economic life (Richard Sennett 1994, gives a vivid description of this in Venice in the 15th and 16th centuries). Moreover, the existence of the ghetto did not have only negative consequences for its residents; not only did a rich culture flourish in part protected from dilution by the outside world, but in some cases the ghetto was deliberately established and walled in as a matter of purportedly benevolent concern by a lord, in order to protect its Jewish residents from anti-Jewish actions, and ultimately from the pogroms, of their non-Jewish neighbours (for some details and references, see Marcuse 1997*b*: 233, 243).

Colonial Cities

Colonial cities represent one of the clearest examples of the interrelationship between spatial division and political/economic power: between partitioning and domination. Colonial cities have a clear basic typology, although there are variations around the dividing line of the abolition of slavery and the introduction of a capitalist economic system, and according to whether the urban was superimposed on an existing urban pattern or the founding of a new urban system (the formulation is an oversimplification of the picture presented by Anthony King 1985). The basic colonial pattern holds until independence, at which time, if slowly, the non-colonial global pattern is imposed. Non-colonial cities with parallel patterns of slavery and domination exhibit somewhat similar patterns. For example, the southern United States could be visualized as a colony in which the indigenous population had to be imported—enslaved abroad and brought in, rather than enslaved locally.

Colonial divisions are the classic type model of the citadel and the ghetto citadels for the dominant imperial power, ghettos of the native population, a clear separation of the two imposed by the residents of one on the residents of the other. Canton, in 19th-century China, is the prototype, and the word 'enclave' (e.g., British enclave, French enclave) was frequently used to describe what we call here its 'citadels'. Force, the power of the imperial state, established the pattern: partitioning in the fullest sense of the word. Where there was already significant urbanization, citadels were carved out for the dominant group; where cities were first established by the colonial power, ghettos were built for the native population. 'Native towns', built outside of core European settlements, on the one hand, or European canonments established beyond historic 'native towns', on the other, have moulded the new cities of the 'Third World' to this day (Home 1997).

Racial segregation was an accompaniment of citadel formation, but the two are not identical (Ross and Telkamp, cited in King 1985, give 'racial residential segregation' as one of the characteristics of colonial cities, but that is an oversimplification, as King shows). In Delhi, for instance, status was a function both of political/economic position and of race. For individuals, social position was a mix of the two: in the astonishing 'Warrants of Precedence', every position in a hierarchy of 175 roles was listed in order of precedence. Certain indigenous roles ranked relatively high; 'other things being equal, such as rank, seniority or socio-economic status, Europeans had precedence over Indians' (King 1976: 248). Those 'other things' overrode race, as far as social status was concerned. But not as far as residential location was concerned. Delhi had five basic types of location: for gazetted officers, European clerks, indigenous clerks, indigenous elite, and peons. That was all in the Imperial City (see the diagram in King 1976: 245). Thus, there was strict segregation by race between citadel and ghetto. And, of course, conditions were very different between the two: the Imperial City was almost twice the size of the indigenous city, but had 640 residential units, while the indigenous city housed 250,000 inhabitants (King 1976: 248). But the boundary was, although crystal clear on the map and in practice, a matter of social knowledge, not a physical marker; it was simply a street, along which different residential quarters were located (King 1976: 250; the text is not clear as to whether the boundary streets differed visibly from the other thoroughfares). The force of the state lay behind it, but veiled; it was incorporated in, internalized into, custom, so that it was observed without having to be enforced.

The importance of residential partitioning was often in inverse proportion to the extent of established and enforced legal domination: the more understood and effective the hierarchical relationship, the less need for spatial partitioning to enforce:

Kingston [Jamaica] did not demonstrate a high degree of social segregation until after the abolition of slavery. Since status was highly ascriptive, based largely on descent, space was not necessary as a marker of social distance. Only after 1838, as sugar declined as the mainstay of the Jamaican economy, and Kingston lost its status as a free port, did colour, culture and spatial segregation become increasingly important considerations in the urban ecology of Kingston. Even though the town's economy was in decline, there was a steady migration from the equally depressed countryside, so that slums of disadvantaged blacks began to form, until, in 1938, the unemployed rose in major, if unsuccessful, riots. (King 1976: 162)

During slavery, the slums, the 'vile hovels and disgraceful sheds' were 'inhabited by free people of colour who keep petty huckster's shops and by low white people who vend liquors and give rise to many disorderly and indecent scenes'. So no segregation between poor white and poor black. And slaves were scattered throughout. The dynamics are similar to those in southern cities in the United States, as described in Chapter 6 in this volume.

In globalizing cities in the post-colonial era, ghettos tend towards the type of the excluded ghetto (see Chapter 6), in which the residents are excluded from participation in the mainstream economy. That was not the case with the enforced native enclaves in colonial cities. Ghettos in colonial cities were economically integrated with the societies in which they existed:

Every European district needs a native district in order to survive; it will provide indispensable domestic servants, small businesses, and labor . . . [These districts] correspond, in essence, to the business districts and working-class residential neighborhoods of our own modern cities which are, in truth, separated from the bourgeois neighborhoods without a definite line being drawn on a map. (Quoted by Kostof 1992 from Wright 1991, p. 221)

   The Spanish conquest of Latin America reflects the use of spatial segregation to reinforce domination and the intricate interplay of race, ethnicity, status, and power. In Mexico, the divisions were spatial, political, economic, legal: a *república de los españoles* and a *república de los indios* existed side by side, but separate (Cope 1994: 3). A racial hierarchy, the *sistema de castas*, regulated relationships, and created 'status differences among groups that might otherwise have united against their oppressors' (Cope 1994: 4). Yet, Indian labour was essential for the Spanish economy; they may have been excluded from the benefits of their own labours, but those labours were essential to the society in which they lived (Cope 1994: 11). Thus, although the centre of the capital, the *traza*, consisted of thirteen blocks reserved for Spanish occupancy (Cope 1994: 10; see also Bennett 1993: 24), the poor

... were not tucked away into hidden slums: they were visible—indeed, unavoidable—in the most fashionable quarters of the city. Government buildings and elite mansions did not house the rich alone: their lower levels were given over to slaves and servants. Interspersed among the checkerboard of main avenues were narrow alleyways, described as the 'dens of thieves' who terrorized their neighborhoods day and night. (Cope 1994: 9)

Islamic Cities

Islamic cities reveal a variety of patterns with respect to divisions of residential space. There are examples of classic Jewish ghettos in Islamic cities—the oldest separation and spatial confinement of Jews was probably the *mellah* in Muslim Morocco, of 1280—but there are also examples of very mixed forms, in which Jewish activities were separated and demarcated from Muslim activities, but the spatial patterns were intermixed. Tangiers is an example. At one end of the main street was the Islamic Grand Mosque; at the other end was the Street of the Synagogues. Jews tended to live closer to the Street of the Synagogues, but also lived throughout the medina, the central 'old city' of Tangiers. Gibson comments:

With its homes, synagogues, baths, schools, and bread ovens, the Street of the Synagogues was a Jewish mellah in miniature, claiming Jewish space at the crossroads of the political and commercial life of the town. At the same time, this space was protected by, surrounded by, and submerged in the greater synthesis of the city. In spatial terms, the Street of the Synagogues reproduced the dialectic of the social situation of the Jews of Tangiers: simultaneously assertive yet submissive, obvious yet hidden, autonomous yet dependent . . . neither complete assimilation nor strict segregation was the motif in this multi-ethnic community. Boundaries kept the groups separate, but the boundaries were also an important element in social cohesion . . . Jewish schools were located throughout the medina . . . Jews lived throughout the medina; they were not limited to the area of the mellah.   (Gibson)[9]

Other patterns are also reported. In the Mzab valley of Algeria:

... the inhabitants lived in neighborhoods to which their social status assigned them: the religious elite, the tolbas, lived highest up beside the mosque; then the other professions followed, with the merchants and their commerce allotted the lowest level of the town. (Abdulac 1983: 6)

and:

The dividing up of cities into quarters or neighborhoods according to ethnic origins, religious affiliation, or trade also undeniably reflected the segmentation of the society as a whole and its projection onto the city organization. (Abdulac 1983: 11)

In Isfahan, Iran, Shah Abbas in the 16th century developed plans to include existing satellite settlements inhabited by ethnic and religious minorities, such as the Armenians in Julfa, within a still larger city layout. The idea behind Shah Abbas' urban plan was, according to Abdulac (1983: 10), 'that a city should unite and integrate, not divide and exclude'. But he goes on to say that Muslim rulers built new cities primarily for political reasons:

Muslim rulers were more apt to found new cities than they were to plan the redevelopment or the extension of existing ones, probably in part because it was easier to manage social and political problems by removing the ruling minority from a hostile population. (Abdulac 1983: 10)

It seems that, while there were indeed mixed ethnic neighbourhoods in Islamic towns, both religious and ethnic differences and differences of status were often reflected in spatial patterns.

Cities in the Early Stages of Capitalist Industrialization

In the early phase of capitalist industrialization, residential differentiation emerged as a characteristic of the industrial revolution and the growth of manufacturing. Manchester, England in the 1830s was the classic example (Kostof 1992: 118; see also Engels 1845/1958):

... the development of class-specific housing for the 'worthy poor' served to refine the system of spatial segregation established by earlier bourgeois residential development ... [furthering] the ongoing compartmentalization of the various strata of the poor ... (Kostof 1992: 119)

The location of that housing depended on the development of the technology of transportation. At the beginning, economic necessity mandated togetherness, closeness of worker to the factory, overriding the possibility of spatial separation. Separation occurred in various ways: upstairs/downstairs, as in Haussmann's Paris, back of streets and front of streets, as in Engels' Manchester, front building/back building, as in Berlin's *Mietskasernen*. But the mechanisms of separation were significantly different from those of previous periods.

Before the advent of capitalism, spatial divisions were accepted as inevitable, as either the natural accompaniment of power or status and role, or as

God-given. After the advent of capitalism, however, such an acceptance no longer prevailed, but rather the belief grew that markets should be allowed to determine where people lived, letting each decide freely on his or her location. The road to free transactions in land and housing was not smooth; the ending of the rule of primogeniture and other common law restrictions on the free exchange of landed property in England, for instance, took several centuries. But the commodification of land and housing was an essential ingredient of capitalism.

Thus, a sharp line separates divisions under capitalism from all earlier forms of division. Increasingly since the time of Adam Smith—and never before—the spatial form of cities, and in particular the residential location of those in them, were held to be properly (if theoretically) matters of free choice, exercised through the market. No religious precept required the poor to live separately from the rich; no divine right authorized those in power to build palaces or mansions towering over a subject citizenry; no right of conquest authorized some to isolate themselves from a colonized native settlement in an imperial enclave. With the ideology of emerging capitalism, each individual, each household, would acquire such resources as its abilities permitted, and expend those resources in choosing housing according to such preferences as to location and quality as it might have. For the first time in the capitalist city, in other words, the market and the market alone was held to determine spatial patterns. Even the Jewish ghettos became anomalies in this era of market freedom, and the state-imposed walls around cities came down rapidly under the impact, economic as much as physical, of Napoleon's advancing armies and bourgeois ideals and practices.

The social divide that accompanied this economic divide rested on the separation of living place from work place. In a sense, that required a market in residential space. Before, if the apprentice or journeyman lived in space provided by the master, often in the same building as the workshop, the living arrangement was substantively part of the work arrangement; no separate payment for residential accommodation was required. As soon as living space was separated from work place, some other mechanism to provide for it and its allocation was needed, and the market, already functioning in land to some extent before, became a major factor.

Within this general schema of a market-based allocation of space, however, a clear sequence of structural changes (evolution has too teleological a connotation for use here) is visible. The patterns of course overlap; one might speak of the layering of the city (see Marcuse forthcoming), the way in which changes in the built environment must necessarily occur within the parameters made available by what was earlier built and naturally determined. Beyond that, the structural factors that produced change did not, between the period of early capitalism and today, take place as revolutions: they neither altered the underlying social relations of society nor occurred in a brief, identifiable, tumultuous time-span, as revolutions have historically taken place. Thus the overlapping chronology of change is layered over the earlier constructions of the built and the natural environment.

The gradual changes in the role of the state mirrored the gradual development of capitalist society. Initially, the state was a brake on development of the market; in land use in particular, we have already referred to the slow loosening of the bonds that the common law (implemented through the state's legal system) imposed on frozen hereditary spatial patterns. So in its initial stages the growth of the capitalist system was accompanied by a declining role of the state. By the mid 19th century, however, the growing complexity of the economic system and in particular the threats to efficiency, to health, and to social stability caused by the unregulated expansion of both the number and size of cities required action by the state. Thus, the 19th century saw a steadily increasing role for the state in the regulation of the conditions of housing, the layout of streets, the provision of infrastructure—leading to the growth of city planning and the general regulation of land use by government. With it, of course, the nature of divisions within urban space became an object of direct governmental action.

While the development is gradual and very different in different countries, as ideal types a periodization is discernable. The earlier major divide, the separation of town and country, did not mark the inception of the current phase, although what exists today often can be traced backed to earlier urban forms (e.g., in the bulk of western Europe). But while the cities that emerged in the earlier 'pre-capitalist' period were indeed capitalist in some of their relationships, there are major arguments about the precise dating of the transition from pre-capitalist to capitalist systems. While residential land was bought and sold for a profit in certain cases, particularly in England in the past, residential locations were not yet commodified, and it is this factor that we use to determine the major change.

The following periods within and subdividing this market-oriented system of allocation of residential land may then be outlined:

• The period of early industrialization (from about the beginning of the 19th century in England to the end of that century).

• The period of mass production manufacturing (from about the beginning of the 20th century to about the middle of the 1970s), which may in turn be divided into a period of early Fordism, to the end of the First World War, and a period of high Fordism, from then to the 1970s.

• The period of the post-Fordist economy, from the mid 1970s to our day. (We hesitate to use the term 'globalization' in connection with this period, even though the extent of integration with a global economy is one of its characteristics, because globalization, loosely defined, is a feature of capitalism from its outset, and the precise extent of international integration that constitutes 'globalization' as that term is conventionally used still eludes definition; see the introduction and conclusion of Marcuse and Van Kempen (2000).)

Cities in the Fordist Period

The next step in the spatial division of the city, made possible by advances in transportation technology, of which the street car is representative, may be called the commodification of location itself. With it came a renewed role for the state for two reasons, one of efficiency, the other for social and political purposes. For efficiency, slaughterhouses, for instance, could not very productively be located next to residential areas, and zoning by nature of land use was clearly necessary if the economy was to function.

But social and political reasons, having more to do with power than with efficiency or health, also played a role. With the extension of industrial capitalism and the unrest that accompanied it, spatial arrangements became an instrument both for resistance to the domination of capital and a focus of efforts to solidify that domination. Thus, Topalov says

a rational organization of the work force can only be achieved with the disappearance of popular districts of cities where the inhabitants have a strong sense of solidarity, where all sorts of debauchery are deemed to develop and where it is possible for the inhabitants to find seasonal jobs allowing them to survive without the more durable salaries of manufacturing—all reasons for distancing the poor from city centres and placing them closer to factories. (Topalov 1994, cited in Loncle-Moriceau 1995: 463)

At the same time as public attention dealt with scattering the locations of housing for the lower classes, the upper classes were separating themselves as much as they could from groups below them. In England, fencing, walling, and gating had become popular with the development of Regent's Park in 1815. In 1838, a text on suburban design praised those in which 'the houses and inhabitants are all, or chiefly, of the same description and class as the houses we intend to inhabit, and as ourselves' (Loudoon 1838, quoted in Archer 1995: 27). The lineage to today's gated communities is direct (see McKenzie 1994 and Blakely and Snyder 1995). The interrelationship between state and private action also began and continues to be complex, with the precise dividing line sometimes hard to draw. That governmental and quasi-governmental powers were needed to make the divisions secure and effective however, was clear from the beginning.

As systems of production moved from 'low' Fordism to 'high' Fordism, the pattern of residential location, at least in the United States, changed, or rather the incipient pattern accelerated, and suburbs gradually became the dominant residential location for the middle classes, better-paid workers, and many professionals and technical workers. Among suburbs there was also a clear gradation by price and by class, with the highest price and income groups generally being the furthest out from the central city. While there were other spatial changes: the almost complete movement of manufacturing from the central city, the growth of megalopolises, the increased concentration of finance, insurance, real estate and their adjunct services in portions of central cities, we focus here on the evolution of the suburbs as being the sharpest representation of the increasing division of urban space.

To put the development of the suburbs in historical context, we might remember that initially, in the early days of industrialization, it was the poor that lived the furthest out from the city even when their everyday world was directly connected with the centre, forming the bidonvilles and squatter settlements that still characterize many Third World cities (for New York City, see Jackson 1985: 16). Slowly, however, we see a class shift in the use of space on the outskirts of the central city, and with it an increasing role for the state in establishing the parameters of their growth. The chronology and pattern that follows is based on the United States experience which, although not unique, is the extreme example of the tendencies.

• In the period from 1870 to 1920, roughly the period of 'low Fordism', 'street-car suburbs' developed, with the working class moving out as transportation technology improved and they could commute greater distances in to work (see Warner 1962; Edel and Sclar 1984). Thus Queens and Brooklyn developed initially as suburbs of New York City, then primarily Manhattan. In some cases housing in these working class suburbs was self-built; that was the pattern, for instance, in Vienna after the First World War. Parallel development took place outside of Paris, and in Toronto (see Harris 1996, reviewed in *Planning Perspectives*, April 1997).

• From roughly 1920 to roughly 1960, the period of 'high Fordism', the middle class moved more and more out of the central city, massively after the First World War, to the crabgrass frontier of Ken Jackson's account (Jackson 1985). They often leapfrogged over working-class suburbs as the automobile vastly expanded the geographical area that could be a place of residence and yet feed a job in the central city. Where industry moved out, there also continued to be working-class suburbs, but this was formal industry, the primary labor market. The class line between well-paid factory workers and middle class people was blurred, a continuum; exclusion was on race and price, rather than socially on class.

• In the current post-Fordist period, the technoburbs of Robert Fishman, the edge cities of Garreau (maybe also Heinritz and Lichtenberg 1986), again represent a qualitatively new phase of suburban development. For the first time, they represent a move of white-collar and professional work out of the central city (not just manufacturing). And it moves out, not for physical reasons (as factories did, who needed more horizontal space for assembly lines, etc.) but for social reasons, racism a major component. But racism was coupled with class: higher-class white suburbs became by and large open to the few higher-class blacks, and the racist exclusion of lower-income blacks was difficult without the exclusion of lower-income whites. Suburbanites sought a better 'quality of life', often a euphemism for escape from the perceived threat of crime and lower-class behaviour in the central cities, unthinkingly associated with 'race'—the complex, in turn, a function of the growing exclusion and irrelevance of poor and unskilled people to the economy of the edge cities.

In these developments, three forces acted in parallel, strengthening restrictive suburbanization: real estate suppliers and landowners, who stood to gain immediate profit (although with some opposition from those investing in existing central city land and buildings); the advances of technology, which created new opportunities for settlement; and the press for loci of investment in what Harvey calls the 'secondary circuit of capital', excess money seeking an outlet for investment. As the built environment, under this last pressure, is increasingly commodified, the importance of protecting investment is added to the earlier more imagined need to protect actual residential life. The defence of property values plays a greater role in racial exclusion than the protection against the threat of crime.

With these three forces moving together, it is no wonder that government action was directly involved in sustaining the direction of development. The details have been amply documented elsewhere (see Jackson 1985): massive investment in highway construction, exclusionary zoning, mortgage insurance, resistance to metropolitanization of government and sharing of tax bases, increasing disparity in the provision of public services, in particular public education, and in many other actions.

Post-Fordist or Globalizing Cities

The transition from high Fordism to the post-Fordist city produced a number of changes in spatial patterns, many of which are described in detail in our parallel volume (Marcuse and Van Kempen 2000). While most are extensions of earlier patterns, some directly affect the further division of residential space. The market provides no automatic adaptation of residential patterns to the economic, social, and cultural pressures of globalization. The two key changes, for purposes of the discussion here, are changes in employment patterns and changes in the distribution of income and wealth. Both are often lumped together as polarization, although that is in many ways a questionable concept, and it is better to keep the two separate.

In the earlier period of industrialization it was found that 'industrial decentralization has progressed slightly farther than has residential decentralization' (Blumenfeld 1949: 212). In the current period, the concentration of dominant services in central cities and the expansion of both service and manufacturing work in large clusters, sometimes edge cities, outside central cities but within their metropolitan areas, has meant another shift in the location of jobs. Manufacturing has steadily declined in the centre and increased in the periphery. The impact has been very different for different groups, and has accentuated their spatial separation. The increase in service occupations in the centre has meant fewer jobs there for manual workers, and the space they and unskilled workers generally had occupied has been steadily reduced by the process of gentrification. The centre has become increasingly an enclave of the rich. At the same time, the growth of employment at the edge, in new suburban clusters, has increased the attractiveness of such locations for the middle class and skilled workers, whose movement there has meant that the fringes of central cities have witnessed sharper growth than the centre in almost every country.

The new economic relations attendant on globalization have likewise produced changes in the distribution of income and wealth, which accentuate the spatial divisions brought about by changes in the nature and location of employment. In particular, the exclusion of a large minority from participation in the mainstream of the economy has resulted in the growth of concentrations of the very poor, in many countries referred to as 'distressed areas', in the United States because of racial patterns associated with the segregated spaces of the ghetto of the African-American poor (the leading discussion of this phenomenon is in the series of studies by William J. Wilson). The abandonment of whole areas of the central cities is the extreme result of these changes. At the opposite end of the spectrum, the walled enclaves of the well-to-do in the suburbs and the protected citadels of the rich in the central city divide their residents also from the rest of the city. The divisions reflect status—both economic and political power—on the part of their residents.

But whether these divisions actually result from economic change depends a great deal on the actions of the state. The state can ameliorate the extremes of inequality in income, in the first instance, and it can directly control the spatial patterns produced by them, in the second. State action in fact makes the critical difference between European cities and cities in the United States today. Welfare state policies, although declining in extent in almost all countries over the last twenty years, are still substantially more effective in Europe than in the United States. They moderate in Europe (and in most technologically advanced countries of the world) the extreme inequalities of income found in the United States, so that neither the slum conditions of many United States ghettos nor the walled enclaves of the rich are as dominant features of the landscape. State planning and land use controls are likewise much stronger in Europe, as they have been historically, and have by and large been used to lessen rather than accentuate divisions in the city. Details are provided both for the United States and for other cities in other chapters in this volume.

Socialist Cities

Historically, the cities of eastern Europe before state socialism were similar in ecological structure to those of western Europe, but socialist policies achieved very substantial transformations. Ivan Szelényi tentatively characterized the ecological pattern of the socialist city as follows:

The social status of the city declines somewhat, chiefly because of its declining residential numbers. The social status of the transitional zones declines rather faster. There is then high status in the new housing estates, but low status again in the rest of the outer suburbs. Of the two zones of low status, the deteriorating transitional zones are not yet entirely reduced to slums, so that the lowest social status of all is in the outer suburbs, even if physical housing conditions and 'housing satisfaction' are not so bad there. (Szelényi 1983: 147–8)

While Szelényi formulates this as a hypothesis, it is clear that for him the mode of production characteristic of socialism since the early 1950s had profound effects on the ecology of socialist cities. As independent variables he lists: (1) the changed patterns of landownership; (2) the changed distribution of income; and (3) the new role of the state in housing and urban planning. How important the state was may be deduced from his comment:

East European planners do not rely very much on indirect methods of management and motivation, such as regulation and taxation, because they assume they have unlimited powers of direct intervention through their programmes of public investment and housing allocation.   (Szelényi 1983: 149)

The resulting divisions, in contrast to their western parallels, reflect social status secondarily, both because status definitions varied widely from their capitalist counterparts, and because housing policy determined allocations of housing reflecting economic function even more than status, at least in terms of the numbers of those affected. The commitment to equality of incomes was an essential aspect of the ideology of the state socialist system. It meant, on the one hand, that managers, executives, professionals, technicians, were not paid at much higher levels than ordinary workers—and of course business owners, financiers, stockbrokers, speculators, did not legally exist at all. At the other extreme, there was virtually no unemployment, and the level of wages of the unskilled was not that much below that of the skilled. Thus the differentiation based on income and wealth that has existed throughout most of history was significantly rearranged and substantially lessened.

In any event, neither the quality of housing nor its location depended on income or wealth, since most housing was not allocated through the market, but by government regulation. Government policy related housing directly to employment; a key factor in the allocation of housing was the place of employment. Residential space was clearly divided, but by economic function, not by class or position of power. (It should be clear that we speak here of the idealized version of the socialist city; the reality often deviated sharply from the model.) The extreme examples are the new towns built around newly built factories, where indeed the overwhelming concern was with housing for the workers, and all others were of secondary concern and obtained only secondary housing and locations. The discussions of Budapest and of Warsaw today in this volume give a glimpse of the earlier patterns and the later post-socialist developments in these cities (see also Andrusz, Harloe, and Szelényi 1996 and Marcuse 1991, 1992, for former East Germany).

There is thus no question that state action was the decisive force governing spatial patterns in the countries of really existing socialism in eastern Europe and the Soviet Union, and largely also in China.

Conclusions

To sum up what our partial and selective overview of the history of spatial divisions has shown:

• There have always been divisions within cities. It is not the fact that they are divided that is the particular characteristic of the partitioned city today; rather, it is the source and manner of their division. Some divisions are cultural, others arise for reasons of economic functionality, and some reflect and reinforce status, relationships of power. Within these three major lines of partitioning are a variety of minor ones, only tangentially dealt with here.

• Different historic periods have produced different lines of division, not arbitrarily nor as specifically willed agreements about the proper form of a city, but rather as a reflection of the changing fundamental social, economic, political, and ideological characteristics of different historical periods. Broad historical dividing lines (we have suggested six) are reflected in broad changes in the partitioning of cities.

• The state has been decisive in creating, maintaining, or destroying partitions in all periods, but the state has been itself the decisive power in earlier periods, while today its actions largely reflect and reinforce the power of groups external to it and operating through the market. The state has throughout history established both the privileged and dominant position of those in power and variously dictated or left alone but separated those below them. Only in the period of early capitalism did economic forces without state action determine spatial divisions; in later stages, state action was critical in implementing what market forces produced or in moderating their impact.

Notes

1. I owe the reference to the opening of the last chapter of Mollenkopf and Castells (1991: 399). But the translation they use does not contain a critical phrase that is in the Shorey version: 'at the least', and replaces 'many' with 'two'. The translation they use reads: 'Any city, however small, is in fact divided into two, one the city of the poor, the other of the rich, these are at war with one another, and in either there are many smaller divisions, and you would be altogether beside the mark if you treated them all as a single State'. One translation emphasizes the dual character of divisions, the other suggests the possibility of more major partitions.

2. The conceptualization is similar to that others have made, e.g., Archer (2000: 5–6) speaks of three axes of differentiation: 'collective identity, function, and distinction of elite from non-elite'.

3. Glazer and Moynihan (1963) distinguish three 'conflicts' dividing society in the United States: 'interest', 'ethnicity', and 'racism'. It is a confusion of categories; but the distinction between ethnicity and racism is important. Their usage of the term 'race', apparently identifying it with colour, differs from its use here, but their distinction between ethnic differences and separations caused by racism is important. Both relate to a dividing line that looks very similar; but the fact that one self-generates the line, the other imposes it from the outside, needs constantly to be kept in mind.

4. There are indeed situations where cultural differences may be 'created' in order to achieve economic or social results: the revival of religious Judaism among some Russians seeking improvement in their economic conditions, for instance, or a politician discovering ethnic roots to solidify support within a particular community in an election bid. Cultural differences may be used instrumentally; but most cultural differences exist independently of individual purposive choice.

5. The United States Supreme Court struggled with this issue in its landmark decision legitimating zoning under the United States Constitution, *Euclid* v. *Ambler*, and some commentators today consider it to have been mistaken in accepting this particular division. Even a separation between high-rise and low-rise buildings is today often questioned, as in new developments which deliberately mix sizes and configurations for variety and aesthetic appeal.

6. 'Early castles were built on uninhabited, elevated sites, chosen for their defensive positions . . . The purpose of these castles was not to bring security to the country-side, as historians had generally assumed, but to dominate it, to enforce the feudal "ban" on the now servile populations it held, and to defend against neighbouring castles' (Glick 1995: 105).

7. It should be noted that some writers, perhaps using a broader brush, paint a somewhat different picture. Thus, Helen Rosenau speaks of 'the ideal of orderly separation imposed upon the labouring classes in the medieval city, differentiating guild from guild and occupation from occupation' (Rosenau 1983: 38).

8. The overlap of 'ethnicity' and religion is a continuing complexity in the discussion of Jewish relations. For some purposes, clearly, Jewishness was viewed by the outside world as a religion, and Jews could be asked (or compelled) to forswear their faith; but I have seen no indication that acknowledgment of religious affiliation played any role in the determination of where a Jew (defined by ancestry) could live in a medieval community enforcing a ghetto.

9. To my embarrassment, I can not now find the source of this quotation. I apologize to Professor Gibson, and if the proper reference is provided, will be happy to include it hereafter.

References

ABDULAC, S. (1983). 'Large scale development in the history of Muslim urbanism', in *Community and Change: Design Strategies for Large Scale Urban Development*. Cambridge: Aga Khan Progam for Islamic Architecture.

ALBERTI, L. B. (1452/1955). *Ten Books on Architecture: Book IV* (Translation by J. Leoni 1755, edited by J. Rykwert). London.

ANDRUSZ, G., HARLOE, M., and SZELÉNYI, I. (eds.) (1996). *Cities after Socialism: Urban and Regional Change and Conflict in Post-Socialist Societies.* London: Blackwell.

ARCHER, J. (2000). 'Paras, palaces, pathogens: frameworks for the growth of Calcutta', *City and Society* 12(1): 19–54.

BENEVOLO, L. (1980). *The History of the City.* London: Scholar Press.

BENNETT, R. (ed.) (1993). *Settlements in the Americas: Cross-Cultural Perspectives.* Newark: University of Delaware Press.

BLAKELY, E. J., and SNYDER, M. G. (1995). *Fortress America: Gated and Walled Communities in the United States.* Cambridge, MA/Washington, DC: Lincoln Institute of Land Policy/Brookings Institution.

BLUMENFELD, H. (1949). 'On the concentric-circle theory of urban growth', *Land Economics* 25(2): 208–12.

COPE, R. D. (1994). *The Limits of Racial Domination: Plebeian Society in Colonial Mexico City, 1660–1720.* Madison: University of Wisconsin Press.

CROSS, M., and WALDINGER, R. (1992). 'Migrants, minorities, and the ethnic division of labor', in S. S. Fainstein, I. Gordon, and M. Harloe (eds.), *Divided Cities: New York and London in the Contemporary World,* 151–74. Oxford: Blackwell.

EDEL, M., and SCLAR, E. (1984). *Shaky Palaces: Homeownership and Social Mobility in Boston's Suburbanization.* New York: Columbia University Press.

ENGELS, F. (1845/1958). *The Condition of the Working Class in England.* London: Blackwell.

GLAZER, N., and MOYNIHAN, D. P. (1963). *Beyond the Melting Pot. The Negroes, Puerto Ricans, Jews, Italians, and Irish of New York City.* Cambridge, MA: MIT Press.

GLICK, T. (1995). *From Muslim Fortress to Christian Castle: Social and Cultural Change in Medieval Spain.* Manchester, UK: Manchester University Press.

HARRIS, R. (1996). *Unplanned Suburbs: Toronto's American Tragedy, 1900–1950.* Baltimore: The Johns Hopkins University Press.

HEERS, J. (1990). *La ville au Moyen Age en Occident: Paysages, pouvoirs et conflits.* Paris: Fayard.

HEINRITZ, G., and LICHTENBERG, E. (1986). *The Take-off of Suburbia and the Crisis of the Central City.* Stuttgart: Steiner.

HOME, R. (1997). *Of Planting and Planning: The Making of British Colonial Cities.* London: Spon.

JACKSON, K. (1985). *Crabgrass Frontier: The Suburbanization of the United States.* New York: Oxford University Press.

KING, A. D. (1976). *Colonial Urban Development: Culture, Social Power and Environment.* London: Routledge & Kegan Paul.

——(1985). 'Colonial cities: Global pivots of change', in R. J. Ross and G. J. Telkamp (eds.), *Colonial Cities: Essays on Urbanism in a Colonial Context,* 7–32. Leiden: University of Leiden Press.

KOSTOF, S. (1992). *The City Assembled: The Elements of Urban Form Through History.* Boston: Little, Brown.

LONCLE-MORICEAU, P. (1995). 'Review', *International Journal of Urban and Regional Research* 19(3): 463.

LOUDOON, J. C. (1838). *The Suburban Gardener, and Villa Companion.* London: Longman.

MARCUSE, P. (1991). *Missing Marx. A Personal and Political Journal of a Year in East Germany, 1989–1990*. New York: Monthly Review Press.

——(1992). 'Housing in the colors of the G.D.R.', in B. Turner, J. Hegedüs, and I. Tosics (eds.), *The Reform of Housing in Eastern Europe and the Soviet Union*, 74–144. London and New York: Routledge.

——(1997*a*). 'Walls of fear and walls of support', in N. Ellin (ed.), *Architecture of Fear*, 101–14. Princeton: Princeton University Press.

——(1997*b*). 'The enclave, the citadel, and the ghetto: What has changed in the post-fordist U.S. city', *Urban Affairs Review*, 33(2): 233–43.

——(forthcoming). 'The layered city', in P. Madsden and R. Plunz (eds.), *The Urban Lifeworld*. London: Routledge.

——and VAN KEMPEN, R. (eds.) (2000). *Globalizing Cities: A New Spatial Order?* Oxford: Blackwell.

McKENZIE, E. (1994). *Privatopia: Homeowners Associations and the Rise of Residential Private Government*. New Haven: Yale University Press.

MOLLENKOPF, J. H., and CASTELLS, M. (eds.) (1991). *Dual City: Restructuring New York*. New York: Russell Sage.

MORRIS, A. E. J. (1974). *History of Urban Form: Prehistory to the Renaissance*. New York: John Wiley.

MUMFORD, L. (1961). *The City in History: Its Origins, its Transformations, and its Prospects*. New York: Harcourt, Brace.

PARK, R. E. (1952). 'The urban community as a spatial pattern and a moral order', in R. E. Park *et al.* (eds.), *Human Communities*, 165–77. Glencoe, IL: The Free Press.

PLATO (*c.* 460 BC/1937). *Republic* (Translation by P. Shorey). Cambridge, MA: Harvard University Press.

ROSENAU, H. (1983). *The Ideal City*. New York: Methuen.

ROSS, R., and TELKAMP, G. J. (eds.) (1985). *Colonial Cities: Essays on Urbanism in a Colonial Context*. Leiden: Leiden University Press.

SENNETT, R. (1994). *Flesh and Stone: The Body and the City in Western Civilization*. New York: Norton.

SZELÉNYI, I. (1983). *Urban Inequalities under State Socialism*. Oxford: Oxford University Press.

TOPALOV, C. (1994). *La naissance du chômeur, 1880–1910*. Paris: Allbin Michel.

VANCE, J. E. (1971). 'Land assignment in the pre-capitalist, capitalist and post-capitalist city', *Economic Geography*, 47: 101–20.

WARNER, S. B. (1962). *Streetcar Suburbs: The Process of Growth in Boston, 1870–1900*. Cambridge, MA: Harvard University Press.

WRIGHT, G. (1991). *The Politics of Design in French Colonial Urbanism*. Chicago: University of Chicago Press.

3

The Academic Formulations: Explanations for the Partitioned City

Ronald van Kempen

Introduction

As has become clear from the previous chapter, situations and processes of spatial segregation and spatial concentration of population groups, as well as lines of partitioning are as old as the hills. Benevolo (1980; cited in Van Kempen and Özüekren 1998) goes back to Babylon in 2000 BC. Here already distinct quarters could be described. Quarters in the inner city were reserved as residential places for kings and priests, for those who were in power; outer quarters were accessible to everyone. The same structure can be seen in most medieval cities in Europe. Sjoberg (1960) points to the existence of Jewish ghettos (see also Climard 1966) in European pre-industrial cities and in the Middle East, to Muslim quarters in Chinese cities, Christian quarters in Near-Eastern cities, and Hindu quarters in cities in Central Asia. Partitioning and the resulting concentration and segregation patterns often have to do with separation between groups with different resources or different powers. It goes probably without saying that in many cases division lines were erected by those in power. It was however not the national state that had this power, but local elites.

In the late 1800s and the beginning of the 1900s a lot of attention was paid to questions of poverty and social inequality. Sir Edwin Chadwick (1842) described the poor sanitary conditions of the working classes in Great Britain and elaborated on the densely populated and neglected parts of the British cities in that time. Charles Loring Brace (1872) wrote *The Dangerous Classes of New York*, in which he talked about the danger of the homeless unemployed (which turned out to be native Americans instead of immigrants; see Kusmer 1997). Life in the (American) ghetto was described by people like DuBois (1899) and Hapgood (1902). In England the famous work of Charles Booth (*Life and Labour of the People in London*) was written (Booth 1903), as well as

We would like to thank Fred Boal, Gideon Bolt, Jack Burgers, Ben de Pater, Ceri Peach, Erik Snel, and Paul White for their advice for this chapter.

Seebohm Rowntree's *Poverty: A Study of Town Life* (1902). Later, Thomas Burke (1940), Pauline Gregg (1950), and Lewis Mumford (1961) offered lively descriptions of slums in the United States and Great Britain.

In all these publications, explanations of the different roles of different parts of the cities were seldom made. Friedrich Engels (1845/1958) was one of the few who was very aware of the spatial division between rich and poor in the European industrial cities. According to him, the separate territories for the poor were the result of the wish of the rich to keep these poor removed from their sight. Spatial divisions were clearly the result of actions of those in power. As far as we know, the major sociologists of the 19th century who at least had some interest in cities, such as Weber, Durkheim, Simmel, Marx, did not pay attention to questions of spatial segregation, let alone to its explanation.[1]

Only since the beginning of the 20th century have researchers tried to deal more or less systematically with spatial segregation, its features and its explanations. Sometimes this interest was purely academic, but in some cases the reason for this attention was a negative one: residential segregation in terms of income and ethnicity and concentration of the poor and of ethnic or 'racial' groups should or could have ill effects on those living in concentration areas, on those living outside these areas, on the city as a whole or even on society as a whole. This idea is still the motivation for many researchers in this area. The evidence for negative effects is also clear from many more recent studies of American cities (see, e.g., Wilson 1987; Massey and Denton 1993; see also Chapters 11 and 12 in this volume).

For other continents, however, the evidence for negative effects is still not overwhelming. Some have, with more or less difficulty, traced some neighbourhood effects (see, e.g., Musterd and Ostendorf 1998; Andersson 2001), but others still have their doubts and look very critically at the possible influence the neighbourhood and its inhabitants might have on the attitudes and behaviour of individuals (see, e.g., Friedrichs 1997). In Eva van Kempen's Chapter 12 it is clear that negative effects also might exist in European countries. However, still much remains to be proved about the generalizability of the negative effects of separation *per se*.

The aim of this chapter is to give a brief overview on the development of the academic explanations of spatial concentration and spatial segregation. It will be shown that there has always been a clear tendency of looking at the phenomenon of spatial segregation one-sidedly, with attention for only some explanatory factors, while explicitly or implicitly omitting other variables. This also specifically holds for the role of the state. Only recently have more or less integrated explanations become popular.

The search for these more or less integrated explanations has probably also to do with the emergence of new questions and new problems. Some of these have to do with new developments in society, like the transformation of the eastern European political and economic systems, the decline of the welfare states in western European countries, the changing patterns of international migration, and, often debated, but still going strong, the continuing influence of various forms of globalization (see Marcuse and Van Kempen (2000*a*) for a discussion on the role of globalization). How do these changes affect society in general and patterns of segregation and concentration in particular? How does local and national policy react to these effects?

Other questions have to do with a changing academic concern. An example is the question of the relation between social polarization and social inequality on the one hand, and spatial segregation and concentration, on the other. Does increasing social polarization automatically lead to increasing spatial segregation? And if this is not the case: what are the determinants? And what are the effects of spatial segregation on social inequality and social polarization? These questions have only been more or less marginally answered. At the end of this chapter we will address them briefly.

Explanations for Segregation: Traditional Formulations

In explaining patterns and processes of spatial concentration and segregation, the story starts with three 'traditional' spatial analysis approaches: human ecology, social area analysis, and factorial ecology. Good descriptions of these approaches have already been made elsewhere (see, e.g., Bassett and Short 1980; Sarre, Phillips, and Skellington 1989). Here, we will only summarize the basic ideas of these approaches and the main criticisms (drawn heavily from Van Kempen and Özüekren 1998). Where possible, we will explicitly focus on the role of the state here.

The Human Ecology Approach

The enormous influence of the Chicago School, with its human ecology approach, is well known. The structural analysis of neighbourhood change, residential differentiation, and the concomitant processes of spatial segregation and concentration started with the human ecology tradition associated with the Chicago School (see, e.g., McKenzie 1925/1974; Burgess 1925/1974; Park 1925/1974). The city developed through a competition for space to produce concentric zones (Burgess 1925/1974), specific sectors (Hoyt 1939), or multiple nuclei (Harris and Ullman 1945), housing households with different resources and other characteristics. Processes of invasion and succession involved a chain reaction, with each preceding immigrant wave moving outwards and being succeeded by more recent, poorer immigrants (Park, Burgess, and McKenzie 1925/1974). The final pattern of segregation, the 'mosaic of social worlds' (or a residential mosaic; see Timms 1971) was seen as a 'natural' equilibrium. It was a consequence of various processes: invasion, dominance, and succession. Behind it was the idea of immigrant enclaves as transitional stages on the road to eventual acceptance and integration in the larger (American) society (Clark 1996: 110).

In Park's 'The city: Suggestions for the investigation of human behavior in the urban environment', chapter 1 in *The City* (Park, Burgess, and McKenzie 1925/1974), the role of the state is only marginally recognized. Park talks about the role of the city plan, which 'fixes in a general way the location and character of the city's construction, and imposes an orderly arrangement, within the city area, upon the buildings which are erected by private initiative as well as public authority' (Park 1925/1974: 4). A line further on, '. . . and we leave to private enterprise, for the most part, the task of determining the city's limits and the location of its residential and industrial districts. Personal tastes and convenience, vocational and economic interests, infallibly tend to segregate and thus to classify the population of great cities. In this way the city acquires an organization and distribution of population which is neither designed nor controlled' (Park 1925/1974: 5). It is clear that the role of state or government control is only of very minor importance in Park's ideas on the developments of the city.

In his famous chapter 'The growth of the city: An introduction to a research project' (chapter 2 in Park, Burgess, and McKenzie 1925/1974), Burgess' diagram depicted five concentric zones, increasing in socio-economic status and decreasing in density with distance from the central business district. This diagram of urban land use focused on residential uses, ignoring the location of employment, ignoring 'race' or essentially any factor other than income. Human ecologists generally analysed the city as a separate entity and were less concerned with the city as a reflection and manifestation of the wider society (Bassett and Short 1980) and this also applies to Burgess. In 'The growth of the city', the role of the state or government is mentioned nowhere. We have to keep in mind, however, that Burgess' theory and diagram should be seen as a model or an ideal type. In another article Burgess (1928) mentions the role of many factors that in reality influence the form and ecology of the cities. Among situation, site, and natural and artificial barriers, he also mentioned the 'prevailing city plan' as one of the factors (see also Palen 1975).

When comparing the writings of Park and Burgess on the one hand, and Engels on the other, Harvey (1973, p. 133) states that the description Engels made of patterns of segregation in Manchester is '. . . far more consistent with hard economic and social realities than was the essentially cultural approach of Park and Burgess'. Harvey continues: 'It seems a pity that contemporary geographers have looked to Park and Burgess rather than to Engels for their inspiration'.

Of course, Park and Burgess were not the only representatives of the Chicago School. Homer Hoyt's (1939) sectoral approach takes into account the location of industry along river valleys, waterways, and railroad lines; and a significant amount outside the city. In this way he modifies the CBD-centred (Central Business District) position of the 'old' Chicago School. Hoyt has high-rent-paying households as the motor of spatial form: they seek out amenities, expand outward, escape pollution and congestion near the centre. Implicitly he takes into account the role of the state. Already on page three he acknowledges that the organization of (American) cities (probably he refers to the *spatial* and not to the political organization of cities) is not only a result of '. . . the riddle of the internal nature of American cities', but also of, among others, the selection of areas for slum clearance and decisions in regard to zoning or re-zoning of areas within the city. The rest of his book, however, is descriptive (with numerous splendid maps).

Harris and Ullman (1945) present the next major revision of the diagrammatic approach of the early Chicago School. They largely abandon the idea of a unitary city form, and speak of multiple employment centres as forming the nuclei of multiple residential patterns.

The classical formulation of human ecology was criticized for being derived from a biological model, rather than being based on cultural and social processes (Wirth 1944; Firey 1947; Jones 1960). It is argued that the social ecologists paid too little attention to how neighbourhood change actually occurs. Their explanations were insufficiently informed by empirical research referring to choice, preference, and social action (e.g., Hollingshead 1947). Moreover, their neglect of the influence of institutional and political factors, including the national and local state, rendered their account unsatisfactory, even for cities where state intervention through planning and housing provision was limited (Bassett and Short 1989). For countries and cities where the role of the state has strongly influenced patterns of urban growth and residential developments, their approach was even more inadequate. The ideas of the Chicago School were essentially American, and maybe even 'Chicagoan'. They were developed in a specific time period and under a specific system: the free market economy, in which terms such as social security and housing subsidies were not common and the role of the state in general was marginal. The explanatory concepts used by the classical ecologists are not suited to present-day analysis (see Denton and Massey 1991). In particular, they do not apply to cities in western European welfare states.

Despite the critique, the ideas of the human ecologists have stimulated much research. Some of the studies that have come out of the Chicago School are now considered classics in their field. These include of course, *The City*, edited by Park, Burgess, and McKenzie (1925/1974), but also some more sociological/anthropological studies such as Harvey W. Zorbaugh's *The Gold Coast and the Slum* (1929) and Louis Wirth's *The Ghetto* (1928). Also, the approach associated with the Chicago School has resulted in empirical studies that were sensitive to spatial variations and sympathetic to local conditions (Bassett and Short 1980).

Social Area Analysis and Factorial Ecology

The human ecology approach was followed by positivistic-empirical approaches like deductive social area analysis (e.g., Shevky and Williams 1949; Bell 1953; Shevky and Bell 1955) and inductive factorial ecology (e.g., Murdie 1969; Robson 1969; Berry and Kasarda 1977). Factorial ecology uncovered the socio-spatial layout of many cities in the world, though without focusing on causality (De Decker 1985). Census variables were selected and 'run through the statistical mill of principal components analysis or factor analysis' (Bassett and Short 1980). Many analyses revealed sectoral and zonal patterns. Differences between urban neighbourhoods could often (but not always; see Robson 1969) be summarized by three sets of variables: socio-economic status, family status, and ethnicity (Bell 1968).

Critics of social area analysis and factorial ecology said it was descriptive and based on very meagre theoretical notions (Hawley and Duncan 1957; Kesteloot 1980; Bassett and Short 1989; Yeates 1989). Again, the possible role of the state was never mentioned. Other critics pointed out that since most of the research had been done in the United States, the results should not be applied automatically to the European situation (see O'Loughlin 1987). Finally, to the extent that this approach has a theoretical base, it is that the subject is a *Homo economicus*: a fully informed individual with a perfect ability to act in an economically rational way (see Bolt and Van Kempen 1997).

Bringing the Individual into the Explanation: Behavioural Approaches

The General Behavioural Approach

Explanations that explicitly include the preferences, perceptions, and decision-making of the individual in housing and residential mobility were introduced in the behavioural approach. This can be seen as a reaction to the spatial analysis approach. Behavioural models generally focus on the demand side of the housing market. In behavioural approaches, choices of households are directly linked to positions and events in the family life cycle (see, e.g., Clark and Dieleman 1996; Clark, Deurloo, and Dieleman 1997). Household characteristics are major determinants of housing (and locational) preferences (Adams and Gilder 1976; Clark, Deurloo, and Dieleman 1986). Age intersects with the household formation cycle: establishing a durable relationship, starting a family (children are born), contraction of the family (children leave home), and the death of a partner. These are all situations that influence the household's size and its preferred type of dwelling (Rossi 1955; Speare, Goldstein, and Frey 1975; Stapleton 1980).

The behavioural approach has been criticized for its emphasis on demand and the concomitant lack of attention for constraints (see, e.g., Hamnett and Randolph 1988). The role of the state plays, at the most, a minor role. Neither the supply of dwellings nor their accessibility (allocation procedures) get much attention. The shape of the city is, in this approach, a consequence of choices of individuals and not of governmental decisions to build, or to expand an urban area.

The Ethnic-Cultural Approach

The ethnic-cultural approach can be seen as a special form of the behavioural approach. The general argument within the ethnic-cultural approach runs thus: housing conditions and residential patterns differ between groups, and these differences can be attributed to cultural or racial differences between these groups. There is a clear element of 'choice' in this approach. In this vein, Clark (1992) states that whites and Asians have stronger preferences for neighbourhoods populated by their own race than do Hispanics and blacks and that this is one of the main explanations for their different settlement patterns. Robinson (1981) depicts differences in housing situations between Asian and West Indian groups and explains these differences by different cultural orientations.

The ethnic-cultural approach does however allow for the inclusion of constraints in the explanation, but then focuses on constraints arising out of attitudes towards race and culture. The choice for owner-occupied dwellings, for example, can be seen as a cultural preference, but also as a defensive reaction against racist practices of landlords (e.g., Bowes, McCluskey, and Sim 1990). This approach concedes that differences within groups may be just as important as differences between groups. All kinds of subgroups might attach different meanings to many aspects of life, including the kind of housing and neighbourhood in which they would like to live (see, e.g., Ballard 1990).

Introducing the Constraints

A Neo-Weberian Perspective: Housing Classes

Rex and Moore's *Race, Community, and Conflict* (1967) can be seen as the beginning of the neo-Weberian or institutional approach in housing research. Their concept of 'housing classes' has sparked an enormous discussion. It is grounded in the idea that housing, and especially desirable housing, is a scarce resource and that different groups are differentially placed with regard to access to these dwellings. People are distinguished from one another by their strength in the housing market (Rex 1968). Segregation and concentration are thus explained by the 'strength' of individuals or individual households: those with the best position have the best locations.

The main criticism of this approach focused on the implied unitary scale of values of different housing consumers and the unclear basis of the conflict between the classes (see, e.g., Haddon 1970; Dahya 1974; Pahl 1975; Saunders 1979; Sarre, Phillips, and Skellington 1989). But on the other hand, Rex and Moore's study has aroused interest in housing as a scarce commodity. Consequently, many studies have focused on the issue of access to housing and on the resources of individuals.

Different resources of households can be identified (see Van Kempen and Özüekren (1998) for a more elaborate overview). Financial resources refer to income, security of income, and capital assets. Cognitive resources include education, skills, and knowledge of the housing market. Political resources refer to the political power people wield, either formally or informally. And social resources refer to the contacts people have, which may help them to find suitable housing and places to live. Even the present housing situation can be seen as a resource. All these resources are highly influential in explaining the possibilities of households in the housing market and therefore form an important part of the explanation of spatial patterns within cities.

Institutional Approaches

Institutional approaches focus explicitly on the role of the state (or related institutions, or people related to those institutions) as one of the major explanations, or even *the* major explanation of patterns of segregation and spatial concentration. This explicitly holds for all the western European researchers who focus on the role of the welfare state, and especially its decreasing importance, in western Europe. Generally, these researchers focus on the role of the state on the supply of dwellings, in terms of quantity, quality, location, and with respect to allocation or on the role of the state on the income positions of households.

The retreat of the welfare state has an obvious effect on the income position of households of all kinds. When governments pursue a policy of cutting budgets, everyone who depends on the state (pensioners, the unemployed, the handicapped, etc.) will inevitably feel the pinch. Declining incomes may lead to concentration in those parts of the cities where dwellings are still affordable for these households.

Austerity programmes may also lead to lower subsidies for housing. Consequently, fewer affordable dwellings might be built or less maintenance may be done on the existing stock. More generally, transforming housing markets may alter the opportunities for all kinds of groups, including immigrants (see, e.g., Kemper 1998).

In many western European countries, the state has had a strong influence on housing markets. Generally, this role seems to be declining. Especially in countries like the Netherlands and Sweden, the number of social rented dwellings has been very important in the supply of housing. By providing social rented dwellings, the state ensures that low-income households have the opportunity to live in decent housing. In other countries—for example, the United Kingdom—the social rented sector has either been declining very rapidly (Meusen and Van Kempen 1995; Murie and Musterd 1996) or has never been very large (as in Belgium; see Kesteloot, De Decker, and Manço 1997 and Kesteloot and Cortie 1998). In a retreating welfare state, the number of affordable rented dwellings will almost inevitably decline, especially in the newly built stock. This is exactly what has happened in most western European countries since the second half of the 1980s (Özüekren and Van Kempen 1997).

The supply of housing can be a direct effect of political decisions at state level. In Britain, for example, the promotion of home ownership under the Right to Buy led to the heavily subsidised sell-off of council housing. But it also led to strict controls on the production of council houses as well as to higher rents (Phillips and Karn 1992). It is well known from the British housing literature that not everybody profits from the sale of council houses. In particular, the impact on the housing of black households has been highlighted (Mullings 1992).

There are other ways in which the state, in this case the local state, may influence patterns of segregation and concentration. Local government, or housing associations, might decide to allocate dwellings in a certain neighbourhood exclusively to non-immigrants. Housing associations can subtly refuse to register immigrant families by saying that no large dwellings are currently vacant or by asking high registration fees (Van Kempen and Van Weesep 1991).

The crucial role of these and other 'managers' is stressed in the *managerialist approach* of Pahl (1975, 1977) and the work by Lipsky (1980; see also Chapter 12). These authors examine the role of the housing officer in the allocation of resources. Pahl suggests that social gatekeepers (like housing officers) can allocate resources according to their own implicit goals, values, assumptions, and ideologies. This means that stereotypes and racism might influence their decisions (Tomlins 1997).

Discrimination, both direct and indirect, also exists in the private rented sector. Discriminatory practices may be encountered among private landlords as well as among the intermediaries between landlords and prospective buyers or tenants. For instance, landlords might offer a vacancy to a friend or acquaintance rather than rent it to an ethnic household. Also, landlords can place restrictions on prospective tenants, and rental agents may classify the applicants accordingly (see, e.g., Karn 1983). Studies in the United States have shown that real estate agents are primary information brokers and major agents of change (e.g., Galster, Freiberg, and Houk 1987; Turner and Wienk 1993; Teixeira 1995).

Exclusionary policies of local authorities and private landlords may force ethnic minorities into owner-occupation, even, or especially, in an early stage of their housing careers (Phillips and Karn 1992). Some neighbourhoods may thereby become virtually closed to them, forcing them into areas where accessible housing is available (e.g., Ward and Sims 1981; Van Hoorn and Van Ginkel 1986). Discriminatory practices may also exist in the owner-occupied sector. An estate agent may fear that selling a house to immigrants would lead to lower prices in the neighbourhood. Kemeny (1987) reports that some estate agents in the United States deliberately sell to blacks in order to create a chain reaction of sales by whites at knock-down prices. This approach can be very profitable for the estate agent.

In the event of a declining supply, rules may become more influential. Rules, however, are subject to interpretation; for example, they are interpreted by officers who are responsible for the allocation of housing or money. These officers may find themselves torn between all kinds of ideas and pressures that originate from the management board, the housing consumers, colleagues, and of course, from their own preferences (see, e.g., Karn 1983; Tomlins 1997).

The Role of Urban Governance

Related to the widespread retreat of the welfare state in western countries, the central state has devolved many of its duties to other kinds of governments, like provinces, regions, and cities. Within their territory, some cities have shown further decentralization tendencies by giving (some) power to city districts or even neighbourhoods. Other tasks have been privatized. In relation to all these deregulation, decentralization, and privatization processes, some decisions concerning urban developments, neighbourhood policies, and neighbourhood regeneration or reconstruction are in many cases not made by (local) government alone, but by a mix of many different organizations and individuals.[2] According to Elander and Blanc (2001), governments have faced a development towards fragmentation and more differentiated forms of governance: *government* has become *governance*. Privatization, deregulation, and multi-actor policy-making are key ingredients of this trend. In a local setting, local governments no longer play an exclusive role as the leading policy-maker. They are more than ever before merely one of the many actors in the governance arena (Elander and Blanc 2000; Healey *et al.* 1995).

Strongly related to this development, the innovation that seems to have become commonplace all over Europe lately is the creation of 'partnerships'. Partnership has been defined as a coalition of interests drawn from more than one sector in order to prepare and oversee an agreed strategy for the regeneration of a defined area (Bailey, Barker, and MacDonald 1995, cited in Elander and Blanc 2001).

The theme of governance, and the related theme of partnerships, now shows up in many texts about urban developments in general and about neighbourhood regeneration policies specifically (see Bailey, Barker, and MacDonald 1995; Hastings 1996; Walzer and Jacobs 1998; Friedrichs 2001; Jacquier 2001; Kristensen 2001). Although it is probably too early to see the governance approach as a new one that fits in the row of approaches we mentioned before, it is important to mention this focus of analysis. It opens our eyes for the fact that the role of the state is no longer stable, nor defined everywhere in the same manner. Coalitions between parties and stakeholders are formed differently in different cities and the results, in terms of processes and patterns of segregation and concentration, may come out significantly different from each other and from results of, for example, a decade ago.

A few examples may exemplify the possible role of urban governance.

• While housing allocation may have been always the field of local government or housing associations (or both) in a city, partnerships, comprising local governments, housing associations, neighbourhood organizations, private developers, etc. may take over the decision procedure, leading to inclusion of some housing applicants and exclusion of others.

• While urban and neighbourhood regeneration policies have traditionally been the task of local governments, often with a certain kind of support of the local population (at least in many western European cities), presently, also private developers, private firms, and many different kinds of neighbourhood organizations might become involved. This might lead to powerful coalitions, that are successful in generating money (at the local or national, or even European level) or to other coalitions that are not so successful, but do have the same problems in the neighbourhood (see Walliser (2001) who describes this process for the city of Barcelona).

Our expectation is that governance, coalitions, and partnerships will be more influential as explaining variables of processes of concentration and segregation in the near future.

The increasing role of urban governance has some fundamental drawbacks. First and foremost, democratic control of decision-making processes is becoming less (Elander and Blanc 2001; Friedrichs and Vranken 2001). The term 'governance' can therefore easily be seen as a term that conceals the shift of decision-making from the public sphere and the sphere of the state to the private sphere. Whether governance or the privatization of government is the appropriate term here, is a moot question.

Neighbourhood Dynamics

For the above it has become clear that it is difficult, if not impossible, to explain patterns and processes of segregation and concentration by one single theory.

Numerous factors, developments, and variables have to be taken into account, but at the same time every single author or School seems to focus on only a relatively small set of explaining factors. Only a few researchers and theorists have been able and willing to focus on many different variables and developments at different spatial scales at the same time. William Grigsby is one of them. He also explicitly rejected the idea that any single theory could explain residential segregation. Recently, Megbolugbe, Hoek-Smit, and Linnenman (1996) wrote an interesting overview on Grigsby's work. We agree with them that Grigsby's ideas are probably most clearly expressed in *The Dynamics of Neighbourhood Change and Decline* (Grigsby *et al.* 1987).

The basic idea of Grigsby's explanation of neighbourhood succession (the most important indicator of neighbourhood decline) is that a change in any one of a number of social and economic variables (among them are: number of households, household size and composition, income, societal values and attitudes, location and type of business investment, and . . . public sector policies), acting through a system of housing suppliers and intermediaries (owners, developers, brokers, but also public agencies, and neighbourhood groups), causes households to make different maintenance and moving decisions, which then alters the characteristics of residential structures and their neighbourhoods. These changes may then feed back on one or more of the social and economic variables with which the whole process started, or on the intermediate variables, or on the household decisions (Grigsby *et al.* 1987).

From this summary it becomes clear that Grigsby and colleagues do pay attention to a lot of variables and developments. But they also have their limits, which can already be found in their starting points. While the idea that the age of buildings can be stretched almost eternally (by renovation, restructuring, etc.) is not so problematic (although finally there will be some physical limits), their basic premise that neighbourhoods change because of a loss of demand for the dwellings in the area, and the idea that low incomes are the main cause of neighbourhood decline is at least a major point of discussion. Moreover, while there are some hints on the role of public policy and the role of public agencies, their influence is considered to be limited. Of course this is the result of the fact that the theory has developed in the United States. Generalizing Grigsby's ideas to European cities and housing markets can only be done very carefully.

Macro-level Explanations and Political Economy

Work by Anthony Giddens and the late James Coleman has been very influential in using a new focus on societal problems in general and in research on spatial segregation in particular. The basic ideas of both authors are that individual behaviour is influenced by variables on a higher level. Because these variables generally affect many individuals, the compound individual changes affect developments in society. Giddens and Coleman have made clear that developments on a macro-level are thus to be seen as important factors. In our earlier work (Van Kempen and Marcuse 1997; Marcuse and Van Kempen 2000*b*) we have already described the importance of demographic, economic, socio-cultural, and political developments. We have also stressed that many developments (like globalization) do not operate independently, but have to be seen in relation with other variables on different levels. These contingencies differ between countries, metropolitan areas, cities and even smaller areas, such as quarters and neighbourhoods.

Households operate within the societal, demographic, economic, and political context of their countries, regions, and cities. The competition between households and individuals on the housing market (as well as on other markets) may result from changing ideas on the part of an individual or household. Those changes, in turn, may be caused by changes in local structures. But they may even be related to changes on a national or transnational level. In order to explain (spatial) changes on the local level, we have to incorporate structures and developments on other spatial levels (see also Sarre, Phillips, and Skellington 1989; Karn, Kemeny, and Williams 1985; Phillips and Karn 1992; Clark and Dieleman 1996; Van Kempen and Özüekren 1998).

Let us give one simple example on how the context might be introduced in explaining spatial segregation of ethnic groups in a city. At the beginning of the 20th century the location of an ethnic group in the city would simply be explained by the social ecologist by processes of invasion and succession: because stronger groups leave for better places, dwellings become vacant, and the weaker groups are able to move in. The factorial ecologists might find out that there is a clear relation between family status, income, and the ethnic variable, but they would not be able to explain why the patterns exist and how they develop. Behaviouralists and ethnic-culturalists will stress the preferences of the ethnic individuals to move to one place and not the other. Housing class adepts would probably stress the income factor.

Attention for contextual factors gives the explanations more depth. Not only is the income of an individual or household important in explaining segregation and concentration, but also the economic developments that affect the income distribution within a city or country. Preferences are in their turn shaped by general socio-cultural changes which in their turn might also affect demographic developments. The Reagan administration in the United States and the Thatcher government in the United Kingdom have no doubt influenced the ideas of the role of the state in many countries in the world. And this changing attitude towards government has resulted in a declining role of the state in, for example, western Europe, thereby in many cases making surviving for those who are dependent on all kinds of state arrangements (benefits, subsidies, allowances) more difficult.

Much attention has been paid to the role of economic interests in shaping residential patterns by political economists (see, e.g., Harvey 1985; Fitch 1993; Fainstein 1993). That is, there is an interaction between market demand (the expression of preferences, that the ecology school and mainstream economists consider decisive) in shaping patterns, and supply factors, ranging from builders to landowners to speculators to financial institutions, acting with and through political leaders, whose own interests also affect supply and shape demand (e.g., in fostering racism or open housing, through zoning, etc.). The interrelationship between demand and supply factors (neither of which are predominantly economic in conventional self-interest terms) is an open question in any city, region, and country. We should be careful of '. . . any simple, deterministic link between economic change and its consequences for the population . . .' (Harloe and Fainstein 1992: 236). This not only holds for socio-economic positions of individuals, but also for spatial outcomes.

Social Polarization and Segregation

Within many societies there is still increasing talk about a growing social polarization and increasing inequality between groups. Discussions however are still confused. It depends, for example, which variables are used in measuring social exclusion and on which spatial level they are measured. The interesting discussion between Hamnett (1994, 1996) and Burgers (1996) in the journal *Urban Studies* on social polarization in the Netherlands is a perfect example of the difficulties one might encounter when investigating these processes (see also Chapter 12). Hamnett concludes that polarization is not very important in the Netherlands, whereas Burgers shows that this conclusion can only be drawn because Hamnett uses figures of the working labour force, while excluding those people who do not have a job. Burgers argues that polarization should take into account the division between workers and non-workers. Related to this is the role of the state: while the welfare state may be helpful in giving people money in their hands they can, for different reasons, not earn on the labour market, this money is always and everywhere less, and sometimes much less than the money that can be derived from the labour market. So even within highly developed welfare states social polarization does exist.

A specific case in the discussion on polarization and inequality is the talk of dualism and the dual society. Despite the arguments put forward by Marcuse (1989) that clearly makes dualization a very disputable phenomenon (see also Fainstein, Gordon, and Harloe 1992; Mollenkopf and Castells 1991), talks about its existence continue. Two of the most important arguments against the formulation of the dual city is that there are a lot of households with a middle-income or individuals that occupy positions at neither end of the 'dual' spectrum, they are neither rich nor very poor. Possibly, talk about the dual city might better start from the view of a polarization between the real have-nots, on the one hand (the poor, the structurally unemployed, the people with no rights), and the rest of society, on the other.

The other important argument against the use of the dualization idea is that although people might be divided with respect to income, there are a lot of differences among them. This is the case on both sides. With respect to the poor it clearly touches the whole underclass debate. Herbert Gans (1990) already made clear that the underclass concept suffers from at least as many definitional problems as the concepts of dualization and the dual city. One of the main problems is the fact that the underclasses are internally divided. In addition, this also holds for all the poor. Only in some circumstances is it convenient to lump them together, but in many cases it is dangerous to put people together in one category. The young drug addict may have the same low income as the single mother with three children, but their basic problems will differ considerably. The old single, handicapped man might differ very much from the teenage drug dealer threatening him on the street corner. All in all, we might question the use of lumping together people in an income group and then carry out all kinds of analyses.

But also at the top end we should not forget that high-income households might strongly differ in lifestyles, opportunities, and preferences. Some like to live in the centres of major cities, in order to profit as much as possible from the facilities the city offers, in terms of leisure and jobs. Others prefer the suburban scene, with the calm, green environment and safety for the children.

While the discussion on the existence of social polarization is already a difficult one, problems are even greater when the translation from the social to the spatial has to be made. This translation of social polarization into spatial patterns is often made too easy. It is by no means always the case that polarization leads to segregation. This has clearly to do with the spatial structure of the city. In those cities where there is a clear mixture of all kinds of dwellings within neighbourhoods the chance for spatial segregation is much less than in those cities in which cheap dwellings are clustered in one place and more expensive dwellings in another. Also, the availability and accessibility of dwellings is important here. If, with the help of subsidies, people with lower incomes are allowed to live in high-rent dwellings, and if people with higher incomes are allowed to live in low-rent dwellings the chances of spatial segregation are much lower than if there is a strong relation between rent and income. Chapter 5, on the Netherlands, is a case in point here. The low segregation figures can be attributed to exactly these aspects.

Partitioning the City: General Developments

The title of this book suggests that we believe that cities are divided into separate parts. In other words: cities are partitioned and definitely in more than two parts. These parts can be distinguished from each other in terms of

economy, demography, culture, function, and character of the built environment. With this we are not breaking new ground: you do not have to be a social
scientist or a geographer to see that cities have different parts. But with the formulation of the 'partitioned city' we want to put in the foreground the question of agency, of who or what active forces produce the divisions. Cities are
not 'naturally' divided: they are actively partitioned. There are those that do
the partitioning, and those that are subject to it. While the role of the
(national, local . . .) state might have been important on the 'do' side, we have
to be aware of the tendency that the state gradually becomes only one of the
actors, especially when all kinds of coalitions, partnerships, and governance
emerge.

Further, with the partitioned city, we want to suggest that cities have
developed and are developing in a direction that extends prior patterns in a
significantly new way. It is not a dual city, in which there are only two parts, it is
not a polarized city—it is a divided city, but with new connotations, and with
new forces at work influencing the partitioning. The following elements are of
major importance for the development of the partitioned city:

1. The influence of globalization and the way countries and cities cope with
   this. This has been elaborated in Marcuse and Van Kempen (2000*c*).
2. Changes in the form of production and the labour market and the role of
   education.
3. The increasing influence of ethnicity, 'race', and migration.
4. The interrelationship of exclusion with 'race' and class.
5. The hardening of boundaries between/among quarters.
6. The spatial scale of the problem (not only intra-urban, but also differences
   between the city and the remaining metropolitan area).
7. Policy, in different forms can attack the negative effects of the partitioned
   city. For example: the role of housing policy, the role of spatial policy, and
   all kinds of social policies.

We believe the contributions in this volume will help to spell out and clarify
many of these elements. We will return to many of them in our concluding
Chapter 13.

Notes

1. According to Saunders (1985), neither Marx (and Engels) nor Durkheim saw the
   contemporary city as of central theoretical significance, although both of them
   recognized that concentrations of population may facilitate or strengthen the
   developments of certain processes. A radical class consciousness may, for example,
   emerge from the spatial concentration of the industrial proletariat in cities (Engels),
   while Durkheim describes urbanization as an important condition of the development of organic bonds of social solidarity. Simmel talks about the 'metropolitan
   personality' and Weber describes the city mainly in terms of its economy and

history. Clearly, these authors talk about the city as a whole. They do not show any interest in describing divisions within cities (with the exception of Engels, see above), let alone in explaining these patterns.
2. Also, *regime theory* puts emphasis on these relationships, specifically on the interdependence of governmental and non-governmental forces in meeting economic and social goals (see, e.g., Judge, Stoker, and Wolman 1995).

References

ADAMS, J. S., and GILDER, K. S. (1976). 'Household location and intra-urban migration', in D. T. Herbert and R. J. Johnston (eds.), *Social Areas in Cities: Vol. 1. Spatial Processes and Form*, 159–92. London: Wiley.

ANDERSSON, R. (2001). 'Spaces of socialization and social network competition: a study of neighbourhood effects in Stockholm, Sweden', in H. T. Andersen and R. van Kempen (eds.), *Governing European Cities: Social Fragmentation, Social Exclusion and Urban Governance*, 149–88. Aldershot: Ashgate.

BAILEY, N. (with A. BARKER and K. MACDONALD) (1995). *Partnership Agencies in British Urban Policy*. London: UCL Press.

BALLARD, R. (1990). 'Migration and kinship: the differential effect of marriage rules on the processes of Punjabi migration to Britain', in C. Clarke, C. Peach, and S. Vertovec (eds.), *South Asians Overseas: Migration and Ethnicity*, 219–49. Cambridge: Cambridge University Press.

BASSETT, K., and SHORT, J. (1980). *Housing and Residential Structure: Alternative Approaches*. London: Routledge & Kegan Paul.

——(1989). 'Development and diversity in urban geography', in D. Gregory and R. Walford (eds.), *Horizons in Human Geography*, 175–93. London: Macmillan.

BELL, W. (1953). 'The social areas of the San Francisco bay region'. *American Sociological Review*, 18: 39–47.

——(1968). 'The city, the suburb and a theory of social choice', in S. Greer (ed.), *The New Urbanization*, 132–68. New York: St. Martins.

BENEVOLO, L. (1980). *The History of the City*. London: Scholar Press.

BERRY, B. J. L., and KASARDA, J. D. (1977). *Contemporary Urban Ecology*. New York: Macmillan.

BOLT, G. S., and VAN KEMPEN, R. (1997). 'Segregation and Turks' housing conditions in middle-sized Dutch cities'. *New Community*, 23: 363–84.

BOOTH, C. (1903). *Life and Labour of the People in London*. London: Macmillan.

BOWES, A., MCCLUSKEY, J., and SIM, D. (1990). 'Ethnic minorities and council housing in Glasgow'. *New Community*, 16: 523–32.

BRACE, C. L. (1872). *The Dangerous Classes of New York and Twenty Years Work among Them.* New York: Wynkoop & Hallenbeck.

BURGERS, J. (1996). 'No polarization in Dutch cities? Inequality in a corporatist country'. *Urban Studies*, 33: 99–105.

BURGESS, E. W. (1925/1974). 'The growth of the city—an introduction to a research project', in R. E. Park, E. W. Burgess, and R. D. McKenzie (eds.), *The City*, 47–62. Chicago/London: University of Chicago Press.

BURGESS, E. W. (1928). 'Residential segregation in American cities'. *Annals of the American Academy of Political and Social Science*, 140: 105–15.

BURKE, T. (1940). *The Streets of London through the Centuries*. London: Batsford.

CHADWICK, E. (1842/1965). *The Sanitary Conditions of the Labouring Population of Great Britain 1842*. Edinburgh: Constable.

CLARK, W. A. V. (1992). 'Residential preferences and residential choices in a multi-ethnic context'. *Demography*, 29: 351–466.

——(1996). 'Residential patterns: avoidance, assimilation, and succession', in R. Waldinger and M. Bozorgmehr (eds.), *Ethnic Los Angeles*, 109–38. New York: Russell Sage.

——and DIELEMAN, F. M. (1996). *Households and Housing: Choice and Outcomes in the Housing Market*. New Brunswick, NJ: Center for Urban Policy Research.

——DEURLOO, M. C., and DIELEMAN, F. M. (1986). 'Residential mobility in Dutch housing markets'. *Environment and Planning: A*, 18: 763–88.

————(1997). 'Entry to home-ownership in Germany: some comparisons with the United States'. *Urban Studies*, 34: 7–19.

CLIMARD, M. B. (1966). *Slums and Community Development: Experiments in Selfhelp*. New York: The Free Press.

DAHYA, B. (1974). 'The nature of Pakistani ethnicity in industrial cities in Britain', in A. Cohen (ed.), *Urban Ethnicity*, 77–118. London: Tavistock.

DE DECKER, P. (1985). 'Naar een verklaringsmodel voor woonsegregatie', in *Planologische Diskussiebijdragen*, 297–310. Delft: Delftsche Uitgevers Maatschappij.

DENTON, N. A., and MASSEY, D. S. (1991). 'Patterns of neighbourhood transition in a multiethnic world: U.S. metropolitan areas, 1970–1980'. *Demography*, 28: 41–63.

DuBois, W. E. B. (1899). *The Philadelphia Negro*. Philadelphia: University of Pennsylvania Press.

ELANDER, I., and BLANC, M. (2001). 'Partnerships and democracy: a happy couple in urban governance?', in H. T. Andersen and R. van Kempen (eds.), *Governing European Cities: Social Fragmentation, Social Exclusion and Urban Governance*, 93–124. Aldershot: Ashgate.

ENGELS, F. (1845/1958). *The Condition of the Working Class in England*. London: Blackwell.

FAINSTEIN, S. (1993). *The City Builders*. Oxford: Blackwell.

——GORDON, I., and HARLOE, M. (eds.) (1992). *Divided Cities. New York and London in the Contemporary World*. Oxford: Blackwell.

FIREY, W. F. (1947). *Land Use in Central Boston*. Cambridge, MA: Harvard University Press.

FITCH, R. (1993). *The Assassination of New York*. London: Verso Press.

FRIEDRICHS, J. (1997). 'Context effects of poverty neighbourhoods on residents', in H. Vestergaard (ed.), *Housing in Europe*, 141–60. Hørsholm: Danish Building Research Institute.

——(2001). 'Urban revitalization transforms urban governments: the cases of Dortmund and Duisburg, Germany', in H. T. Andersen and R. van Kempen (eds.), *Governing European Cities: Social Fragmentation, Social Exclusion and Urban Governance*, 189–210. Aldershot: Ashgate.

——and VRANKEN, J. (2001). 'European urban governance in fragmented societies', in H. T. Andersen and R. van Kempen (eds.), *Governing European Cities: Social Fragmentation, Social Exclusion and Urban Governance*, 19–39. Aldershot: Ashgate.

GALSTER, G., FREIBERG, F., and HOUK, D. L. (1987). 'Racial differentials in real estate advertising practices: an exploratory case study'. *Journal of Urban Affairs*, 9: 199–215.

GANS, H. J. (1990). 'Deconstructing the underclass; the term's dangers as a planning concept'. *Journal of the American Planning Association*, 56: 217–77.

GREGG, P. (1950). *A Social and Economic History of Britain, 1760–1955*. London: George C. Harrap.

GRIGSBY, W., BARATZ, M., GALSTER, G., and MACLENNAN, D. (1987). *The Dynamics of Neighbourhood Change and Decline*. Oxford: Pergamon.

HADDON, R. (1970). 'A minority in a welfare state society: location of West Indians in the London housing market'. *New Atlantis*, 2: 80–123.

HAMNETT, C. (1994). 'Social polarization in global cities: theory and evidence'. *Urban Studies*, 31: 401–24.

——(1996). 'Social polarization, economic restructuring and welfare state regimes'. *Urban Studies*, 33: 1407–30.

——and RANDOLPH, B. (1988). *Cities, Housing and Profits: Flat Break-Ups and the Decline of Private Renting*. London: Hutchinson.

HAPGOOD, H. (1902). *The Spirit of the Ghetto*. New York: Funk & Wagnalls.

HARLOE, M., and FAINSTEIN, S. S. (1992). 'Conclusion: the divided cities', in S. S. Fainstein, I. Gordon, and M. Harloe (eds.), *Divided Cities. New York and London in the Contemporary World*, 236–68. Oxford: Blackwell.

HARRIS, C. D., and ULLMAN, E. L. (1945). 'The nature of cities'. *Annals of the American Academy of Political and Social Science*, 242: 7–17.

HARVEY, D. (1973). *Social Justice and the City*. London: Edward Arnold.

——(1985). *The Urbanization of Capital*. Baltimore: The Johns Hopkins University Press.

HASTINGS, A. (1996). 'Unravelling the process of "partnership" in urban regeneration policy'. *Urban Studies*, 32: 253–68.

HAWLEY, A., and DUNCAN, O. D. (1957). 'Social area analysis: a critical approach'. *Land Economics*, 33: 337–45.

HEALY, P., CAMERON, S., DAVOUDI, S., GRAHAM, S., and MADANIPOUR, A. (eds.) (1995). *Managing Cities: The New Urban Context*. Chichester, UK: Wiley.

HOLLINGSHEAD, A. B. (1947). 'A re-examination of ecological theory'. *Sociology and Social Research*, 31: 194–204.

HOYT, H. (1939). *The Structure and Growth of Residential Neighbourhoods in American Cities*. Washington, DC: Federal Housing Administration.

JACQUIER, C. (2001). 'Urban fragmentation and revitalization policies in France: a new urban governance in the making', in H. T. Andersen and R. van Kempen (eds.), *Governing European Cities: Social Fragmentation, Social Exclusion and Urban Governance*, 321–46. Aldershot: Ashgate.

JONES, E. (1960). *A Social Geography of Belfast*. Oxford: Oxford University Press.

JUDGE, D., STOKER, G., and H. WOLMAN (eds.) (1995). *Theories of Urban Politics*. London: Sage.

KARN, V. (1983). 'Race and housing in Britain: the role of the major institutions', in N. Glazer and K. Young (eds.), *Ethnic Pluralism and Public Policy: Achieving Equality in the US and Britain*, 162–83. Lexington: Heath.

——KEMENY, J., and WILLIAMS, P. (1985). *Home Ownership in the Inner City: Salvation or Despair?* Aldershot: Gower.

KEMENY, J. (1987). *Immigrant Housing Conditions in Urban Sweden*. Gävle: The National Swedish Institute for Building Research.

KEMPER, F.-J. (1998). 'Restructuring of housing and ethnic segregation: recent developments in Berlin'. *Urban Studies*, 35: 1765–89.

KESTELOOT, C. (1980). *De ruimtelijke structuur van Brussel-Hoofdstad*. Leuven: Acta Geographica Loveniensia.

——and CORTIE, C. (1998). 'Housing Turks and Moroccans in Brussels and Amsterdam: the difference between private and public markets'. *Urban Studies*, 35: 1835–53.

——DE DECKER, P., and MANÇO, A. (1997). 'Turks and their housing conditions in Belgium, with special reference to Brussels, Ghent and Visé', in A. Ş. Özüekren and R. van Kempen (eds.), *Turks in European Cities: Housing and Urban Segregation*, 67–97. Utrecht: European Research Centre on Migration and Ethnic Relations.

KRISTENSEN, H. (2001). 'Urban policies and programmes against social exclusion and fragmentation: Danish experiences', in H. T. Andersen and R. van Kempen (eds.), *Governing European Cities: Social Fragmentation, Social Exclusion and Urban Governance*, 255–71. Aldershot: Ashgate.

KUSMER, K. K. (1997). 'Ghettos real and imagined: A historical comment on Loïc Wacquant's "Three Pernicious Premises in the Study of the American Ghetto"'. *International Journal of Urban and Regional Research*, 21: 706–11.

LIPSKY, M. (1980). *Street-Level Bureaucracy: Dilemmas of the Individual in Public Services*. New York: Russell Sage.

MARCUSE, P. (1989). 'Dual city: a muddy metaphor for a quartered city'. *International Journal of Urban and Regional Research*, 13: 697–708.

——and VAN KEMPEN, R. (2000*a*). 'Conclusion: a changed spatial order', in P. Marcuse and R. van Kempen (eds.), *Globalizing Cities: A New Spatial Order?*, 249–75. Oxford: Blackwell.

————(2000*b*). 'Introduction', in P. Marcuse and R. van Kempen (eds.), *Globalizing Cities: A New Spatial Order?*, 1–21. Oxford: Blackwell.

————(eds.) (2000*c*). *Globalizing Cities: A New Spatial Order?* Oxford: Blackwell.

MASSEY, D. S., and DENTON, N. A. (1993). *American Apartheid*. Cambridge, MA: Harvard University Press.

McKENZIE, R. D. (1925/1974). 'The ecological approach to the study of the human community', in R. E. Park, E. W. Burgess, and R. D. McKenzie (eds.), *The City*, 63–79. Chicago/London: University of Chicago Press.

MEGBOLUGBE, I. F., HOEK-SMIT, M. C., and LINNENMAN, P. D. (1996). 'Understanding neighbourhood dynamics: A review of the contributions of William G. Grigsby'. *Urban Studies*, 33: 1779–95.

MEUSEN, H., and VAN KEMPEN, R. (1995). 'Towards residual housing? A comparison of Britain and the Netherlands'. *Netherlands Journal of Housing and the Built Environment*, 10: 239–58.

MOLLENKOPF, J. H., and CASTELLS, M. (1991). *Dual City: Restructuring New York*. New York: Russell Sage.

MULLINGS, B. (1992). 'Investing in public housing and racial discrimination: implications in the 1990s'. *New Community*, 18: 415–25.

MUMFORD, L. (1961). *The City in History*. New York: Harcourt, Brace.

MURDIE, R. A. (1969) *Factorial Ecology of Metropolitan Toronto 1951–1961*. Chicago: University of Chicago Press.

MURIE, A., and MUSTERD, S. (1996). 'Social segregation, housing tenure and social change in Dutch cities in the late 1980s'. *Urban Studies*, 33: 495–516.

MUSTERD, S., and OSTENDORF, W. (1998). 'Segregation and social participation in a welfare state; the case of Amsterdam', in S. Musterd and W. Ostendorf (eds.), *Urban Segregation and the Welfare State: Inequality and Exclusion in Western Cities*, 191–205. London/New York: Routledge.

O'LOUGHLIN, J. (1987). 'Chicago an der Ruhr or what?', in G. Glebe and J. O'Loughlin (eds.), *Foreign Minorities in Continental European Cities*, 52–69. Stuttgart: Franz Steiner.

ÖZÜEKREN, A. Ş., and VAN KEMPEN, R. (1997). 'Explaining housing conditions and housing market positions', in A. Ş. Özüekren and R. van Kempen (eds.), *Turks in European Cities: Housing and Urban Segregation*, 12–29. Utrecht: European Research Centre on Migration and Ethnic Relations.

PAHL, R. (1975). *Whose City?* Harmondsworth, UK: Penguin.

——(1977). 'Managers, technical experts and the state', in M. Harloe (ed.), *Captive Cities*, 49–60. London: Wiley.

PALEN, J. J. (1975). *The Urban World*. New York: McGraw-Hill.

PARK, R. E. (1925/1974). 'The city: suggestions for the investigation of human behavior in the urban environment', in R. E. Park, E. W. Burgess, and R. D. McKenzie (eds.), *The City*, 1–46. Chicago: Chicago University Press.

——BURGESS, E. W., and MCKENZIE, R. D. (eds.) (1925/1974). *The City*. Chicago: Chicago University Press.

PHILLIPS, D., and KARN, V. (1992). 'Race and housing in a property owning democracy'. *New Community*, 18: 355–69.

REX, J. (1968). 'The sociology of a zone of transition', in R. E. Pahl (ed.), *Readings in Urban Sociology*, 211–31. Oxford: Pergamon.

——and MOORE, R. (1967). *Race, Community, and Conflict*. London: Oxford University Press.

ROBINSON, V. (1981). 'The development of South Asian settlement in Britain and the myth of return', in C. Peach, V. Robinson, and S. Smith (eds.), *Ethnic Segregation in Cities*, 149–69. London: Croom Helm.

ROBSON, B. T. (1969). *Urban Analysis*. Cambridge, UK: Cambridge University Press.

ROSSI, P. H. (1955). *Why Families Move: A Study in the Social Psychology of Urban Residential Mobility*. Glencoe, IL: The Free Press.

SARRE, P., PHILLIPS, D., and SKELLINGTON, R. (1989). *Ethnic Minority Housing: Explanations and Policies*. Aldershot: Avebury.

SAUNDERS, P. (1979). *Urban Politics: A Sociological Interpretation*. London: Hutchinson.

——(1985). 'Space, the city and urban sociology', in D. Gregory and J. Urry (eds.), *Social Relations and Spatial Structures*, 67–89. London: Macmillan.

SEEBOHM ROWNTREE, B. (1902). *Poverty: A Study of Town Life*. London: Macmillan.

SHEVKY, E., and BELL, W. (1955). *Social Area Analysis*. Stanford, CA: Stanford University Press.

——and WILLIAMS, M. (1949). *The Social Areas of Los Angeles*. Los Angeles: University of California Press.

SJOBERG, G. (1960). *The Pre-industrial City*. Glencoe, IL: The Free Press.

SPEARE, A., GOLDSTEIN, S., and FREY, W. H. (1975). *Residential Mobility, Migration and Metropolitan Change*. Cambridge, MA: Ballinger.

STAPLETON, C. M. (1980). 'Reformulation of the family life-cycle concept: implications for residential mobility'. *Environment and Planning: A*, 12: 1103–18.

TEIXEIRA, C. (1995). 'Ethnicity, housing search, and the role of the real estate agent: a study of Portuguese and non-Portuguese real estate agents in Toronto'. *Professional Geographer*, 47: 176–83.

TIMMS, D. W. G. (1971). *The Urban Mosaic: Towards a Theory of Residential Differentiation.* Cambridge: Cambridge University Press.

TOMLINS, R. (1997). 'Officer discretion and minority ethnic housing provision'. *Netherlands Journal of Housing and the Built Environment*, 12: 179–97.

TURNER, M. A., and WIENK, R. (1993). 'The persistence of segregation in urban areas: contributing causes', in G. T. Kingsley and M. A. Turner (eds.), *Housing Markets and Residential Mobility*, 193–216. Washington, DC: Urban Institute.

VAN HOORN, F. J. J. H., and VAN GINKEL, J. A. (1986). 'Racial leapfrogging in a controlled housing market; the case of the Mediterranean minority in Utrecht, the Netherlands'. *Tijdschrift voor Economische en Sociale Geografie*, 77: 187–96.

VAN KEMPEN, R., and MARCUSE, P. (1997). 'A new spatial order in cities?', in *American Behavioral Scientist*, 41: 285–99.

—— and ÖZÜEKREN, A. Ş. (1998). 'Ethnic segregation in cities: new forms and explanations in a dynamic world'. *Urban Studies*, 35: 1631–56.

—— and VAN WEESEP, J. (1991). 'Housing low-income households in Dutch cities', in G. Saglamer and A. Ş. Özüekren (eds.), *Housing for the Urban Poor*, b009–b021. Istanbul: Istanbul Technical University.

WALLISER, A. (2001). 'Decentralization and urban governance in Barcelona', in H. T. Andersen and R. van Kempen (eds.), *Governing European Cities: Social Fragmentation, Social Exclusion and Urban Governance*, 297–320. Aldershot: Ashgate.

WALZER, N. W., and JACOBS, B. D. (eds.) (1998). *Public–private Partnerships for Local Economic Development.* Westport, CT: Praeger.

WARD, R., and SIMS, R. (1981). 'Social status, the market and ethnic segregation', in C. Peach, V. Robinson, and S. Smith (eds.), *Ethnic Segregation in Cities*, 217–34. London: Croom Helm.

WILSON, W. J. (1987). *The Truly Disadvantaged: The Inner City, the Underclass, and Public Policy.* Chicago: University of Chicago Press.

WIRTH, L. (1928). *The Ghetto.* Chicago: University of Chicago Press.

—— (1944). 'Human ecology'. *American Journal of Sociology*, 50: 483–8.

YEATES, M. H. (1989). *The North-American City.* New York: Harper & Row.

ZORBAUGH, H. W. (1929). *The Gold Coast and the Slum.* Chicago: University of Chicago Press.

PART II

Case Studies

4

The Poor City: National and Local Perspectives on Changes in Residential Patterns in the British City

Peter Lee and Alan Murie

Introduction

Residential patterns in cities are changing under the combined influence of economic restructuring and the reshaping of welfare state systems. In the United Kingdom, as elsewhere, major demographic, economic, and labour market changes have contributed to the emergence of new social divisions characterized by a growing inequality in wealth and incomes, social exclusion, long-term unemployment, and growing insecurity of employment. While economic and employment changes are the driving forces for urban change, their consequences for patterns of housing and residence, and patterns of social segregation cannot be taken as given. As has been argued elsewhere, common economic pressures have not and will not produce the same patterns of segregation in different cities (Murie 1994). The reasons for this lie not only in demographic and economic changes taking place but also in political changes that have affected the organization of housing and the welfare state in which the housing system operates. In this context, this chapter focuses upon the 'poor' city in Britain—the location of poor people in British cities, and how it is changing under the combined influence of the state and the market.

The central theme of this chapter, therefore, is that no uniform pattern exists among all cities, each having its own concrete history and circumstances. However, simply reading off the past, as a guide to the future would be a static view of change—the 'concrete history and circumstances' of the past can be modified by the present. We would, therefore, agree that there are general tendencies affecting spatial change, which have applied in the past and which will continue to operate upon all cities. In the post-Beveridge welfare state[1] some cities are better placed than others to mitigate the negative effects of changes in the relationship (implied by post-Fordism) between capital, labour, and the state. The central questions of interest therefore become: 'Which common influences affect social and spatial change?' 'How has spatial partitioning operated to emerge with different patterns in different cities?' 'What has the role of the state been in the development of these patterns?'

Addressing issues of cause and effect in this context is complex. One of the central themes of this book is the changing role of capital and government and how they are reflected in the changing use of space. The way in which capital 'causes' new forms of spatial partitioning can be viewed in at least two ways. First, new spatial partitioning which reflects the cultural symbolism of space and which in turn reflects social partitions and inequality of incomes; and second, new spatial partitions reflecting capital mobility and the erosion of the nation-state.

In both cases, the use of space is simply a reflection of the changing use of capital but causation is never fully attributed. The changing use of space viewed in these two separate ways may have 'similar' causes but the more pertinent question relates to how far causation can be attributed. In this respect post-Fordism cannot be interpreted as a whole without understanding the separate parts. Again, reference to the policy legacies of the past and the role of the central and local state have to be taken into account when explaining new spatial partitions. Structural changes in the mode and regulation of capital will be repeated differently in different cities and countries. In this chapter we review some of the features of post-Fordism contributing to new spatial partitions in British cities with specific reference to the poor city.

Demographic, Economic and Occupational Changes, and Residential Outcomes

Cities are always changing under a variety of pressures. Among these pressures are demographic, environmental, and socio-economic changes. In relation to demographic change there is a growing tendency for households to be formed earlier with a significant increase in the proportion of young adults aged 15–29 living alone. For example, between 1973 and 1993 the proportion of persons living alone aged between 16 and 24 more than doubled from approximately 2 per cent to 4 per cent of all households (HMSO 1995).

At the same time, household changes have also been affected by marital and relationship breakdown. Rates of divorce in Britain have been highest amongst young people aged 18–29. This group has demonstrated the steepest increase since divorce laws were changed in Britain: rising from 3.9 to 33 divorces per 10,000 between 1961 and 1991 (HMSO 1994). With marriage in decline and affected by high divorce rates, single parent households have increased—accounting for just over 1 per cent of all families in 1971 but for more than 7 per cent in 1991 (OPCS 1991). Meanwhile, the dual process of people living longer and changes in household structure are being reflected in the proportions of older people living alone. In 1961 less than 60 per cent of persons above retirement age lived alone compared to almost 80 per cent in 1993 (HMSO 1995). Such changes in household size and structure, the fragmentation of households, and an increase in the population of older people have important consequences for housing demand and the location of households.

The changing economic environment in which they have occurred magnifies the significance of these demographic changes. The driving force for economic change is global. Domestic economic policies are adopted which embrace economic competition in order to stimulate the expansion of low paid employment and compete for inward investment by international companies. The impact of these changes is undisputed and has resulted in a restructuring of work and an erosion in rates of pay and the terms of employment.

Because of a growing need to build a consensus around what a unified Europe offers as its benchmarks of citizenship, the term 'social exclusion' has emerged. As the notion of *exclusion* implies, lack of income and a lack of employment are key indicators: unemployment and poverty exclude individuals from participation in society. However, unemployment is often experienced as a temporary phenomenon. For example, in the spring of 1993 almost a fifth of men in the United Kingdom and more than a quarter of women were unemployed for less than thirteen weeks (HMSO 1994). Unemployment may, therefore, not necessarily lead to social exclusion. The term social exclusion has, consequently, tended to embrace longitudinal factors—the incremental and reinforcing barriers that prevent re-entry to the mainstream. Long-term unemployment is perhaps the most tangible manifestation of this position. Long-term unemployment among men aged 16–24 in the United Kingdom rose both relatively and absolutely over the 10-year period 1984–93. In the spring of 1984, 135,000 men aged 16–30 had been unemployed for between one and two years (19 per cent of the economically active males). By the spring of 1994 this had risen to 22 per cent or 187,000 men aged between 16 and 30 years (CSO 1995). This trend accelerated subsequently and comparison with 20 years earlier when less than a fifth of the unemployed were long-term claimants is illustrative of these trends (Philpott 1994). The evidence on social exclusion suggests that there are incremental or longitudinal effects. During the early part of the 1990s, long-term unemployment in Britain had increased by 84 per cent compared with a rise of 13 per cent in total unemployment (CSO 1995).

Implicit within the notion of social exclusion, however, is a concern for the participation and rights of all members of society—a concept that embraces the poorly employed as well as marginal groups. In such cases the measurement of unemployment or pay and conditions alone would be inappropriate. In addition to increasing unemployment, the restructuring of the British labour market has resulted in insecurity of employment with increasing numbers of people failing to get a firm foothold in the labour market and who experience frequent spells of unemployment. An illustration of the insecurity of unemployment is the number of times the unemployed have been out of work. In June 1991 over a third (33 per cent) of all unemployment claimants in Britain had been unemployed on at least one previous occasion, whilst 13 per cent had been unemployed on two or more occasions (Philpott 1994).

Changes in the occupational structure and the growing difference between remuneration in different occupations have been profound over the past two decades. Both trends in terms of employment and pay have had the effect of undermining job security and increasing divisions of income and wealth. The causes have been structural. For example, the proportion of total employment which is in manufacturing and the primary sector roughly halved between 1971 and 1991—from just over two-fifths to little more than one-fifth (Ford and Wilcox 1994). At the same time there has been a growth in part-time work and self-employment. Over the 10 years 1984–94 there were an extra one and a half million men and women in part-time employment (CSO 1995). The result has been a reduction in the supply of first level entry jobs and unskilled jobs in the 'trade-unionized' manufacturing sector—rates of pay, conditions, and terms of employment had been steady or guaranteed in this sector.

The 'new' British labour market has resulted in a substitution of a service sector for manufacturing 'entry positions' into the labour market. These 'entry level' service sector jobs have experienced relatively modest wage increases over the period 1971–94, whilst highly skilled professions have attracted increasingly higher salaries (HMSO 1994). The new 'entry level' positions include jobs in public services, privatized during the 1980s, as well as clerical or secretarial employment, and work in the burgeoning catering and food industry. Compared to the longer-term security of traditional manufacturing employment low pay and insecurity of employment is now a fact of life for many women and ethnic minorities in these new service jobs. For example, in Britain it is estimated that 5.4 million women are living on or below the poverty threshold of national assistance (Income Support) rates of benefit (Walker 1996). Given these figures, women have a 25 per cent higher risk of being in poverty than men in Britain. Hence, despite growth of employment in these sectors women are still overrepresented amongst the poorest paid—a reflection of their social worth and the low pay in (re)entry level positions.

Periods of unemployment as well as the type of employment affect entitlements to benefits from different sources. In the post-war Beveridge welfare state the role of full employment, as a cornerstone of the welfare state, meant that pension arrangements for the majority were satisfactory. At the same time, pensions were tied to average earnings ensuring that, for the majority, there was no sudden fall in income during retirement. However, in the same post-Beveridge welfare state the growth of inequalities between the unemployed and employed and between sections of the labour market means that a person with several years national insurance contributions (possibly augmented by private or personal pension arrangements), has in prospect a different retirement than the irregularly or casually employed.

The key political element in these changes has been the role of privatization through the processes of removal of state subsidies and the encouragement of individual self-provision. How this connects to spatial partitioning in the British context is crucial. The encouragement of means-tested benefits has had consequences for work incentives and the safeguarding of savings. In a climate of high male unemployment, the benefit regime may especially affect the decisions of some people over their living arrangements. Other changes in policy including those related to energy costs and the development of community care affect the circumstances and numbers of low-income households living in the community and the competition for housing especially in the social rented sector. The interaction of these changes and changes in the structure of welfare benefits has added to the incidence of the 'poverty trap', where the marginal benefits of working do not offset the loss of benefit.

The experience of older workers, young people, or lone parents is very different today than it would have been in a full-employment economy. From the mid 1970s demographic and economic changes as well as the general political shift to the right have precipitated a crisis in the welfare state hastening the end of the 'golden age' (1945–73) of welfare capitalism. Since the mid 1970s a wealth of literature in the United Kingdom on the distributional consequences of these changes has also emerged (see, e.g., Commission on Social Justice 1994; Goodman and Webb 1995; Hills 1995). Early government denials of widening inequality and assertions of the effectiveness of a trickle-down process have been replaced by incontrovertible evidence of widening inequalities. The shares of disposable income of the top fifth and the bottom fifth of households has grown apart between 1979 and 1992 (Hills 1995). There is a wider gap between a growing proportion of households with very low or no earned incomes and other households with relatively high dual incomes. To illustrate this trend, UK government statistics show that the top fifth of households increased their share of total disposable income (after housing costs) from 35 per cent in 1979 to 43 per cent in 1992 (CSO 1995). At the same time the bottom fifth of households have seen their share of the nation's income severely cut from 10 per cent in 1979 to 6 per cent in 1992 (CSO 1995). The mid to late 1990s, however, saw a slow down and eventual reversal of income inequalities. Howarth *et al.* (1998) note that between 1991 and 1996 the number of individuals on relative low income (below average incomes) fell back from 11 million to 10 million (p. 23).

Despite recent changes, the consequence is that income inequality has reached a higher level than at any time since the war (Hills 1995). Average real incomes increased but lower income groups have not shared in this increase.

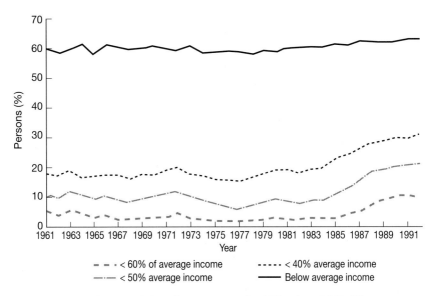

Fig. 4.1. Share of incomes below the average, United Kingdom (1961–92)
Source: Social Trends, HMSO, 1995

The proportion of the population with incomes below the national average had been relatively constant between 1961 and 1992 (CSO 1995). However, the experience of those at the extreme ends of the income distribution—the richest and the poorest people—was one of more dramatic change. Between 1984 and 1992, the proportion of the population earning less than 60 per cent of average income increased from roughly 20 per cent to over 30 per cent, and the share of those earning under 40 per cent of average earnings more than doubled from 5 per cent to 10 per cent (CSO 1995: 95) (Fig. 4.1).

Residential Outcomes

The ending of the circumstances associated with the post-war welfare state along with major economic restructuring has affected all cities in advanced economies. Contributions to debates about urban change have argued that cities are being transformed by changes centred on information technologies and the formation of a global economy (Castells 1992; Sassen 1991). Patterns of change are driven by economic restructuring, de-industrialization, a post-industrial society and globalization and the new global economy shifts control from the macro-economies of the nation-state to the world economy. One of the consequences of globalization is seen to be new patterns of urban poverty and marginality with new spatial patterns of concentration of poverty. Winchester and White (1988), for example, argue that any group characterized by economic marginality (including the unemployed, impoverished elderly, students, single parent families, ethnic minorities, refugees, and handicapped) will be constrained in their residential location. Furthermore, their economic status will then be reflected in their occupation of the poorest sections of the housing stock. However, this account involves a leap in the discussion from reference to globalization of world economies and increasing polarization in occupational and income structures to reference to growing segregation in the housing market. The assumption that rising social inequality is automatically reflected in housing and residential patterns needs to be questioned.

Without resolving the question of the primacy of economic and labour market changes in determining the future of cities there is a need to give attention to institutional and organizational arrangements. The local and national state in particular affect how these changes impact on spatial patterns within cities and on residence. Where the process of economic change involves unemployment, deskilling, temporary and casualized working arrangements, loss of social status, or loss of earning power, the results for households are not automatically a loss of the home, changing residence or homelessness. Whether it will have these consequences depends on the severity and duration of the changes experienced by households but also on how far arrangements for education, training, income maintenance, social security, and housing ameliorate or protect the previously achieved position of the household. Viewed this way Winchester and White's analysis of marginality and segregation could be appropriate for American and Australasian cities whose welfare states and tenure structures differ from European cities. The outcome of economic change may be similar in cities with different tenure structures but this is not always the case and, even where it is, the process is different.

In cities such as Amsterdam, New York, London, Birmingham, Edinburgh, Paris, or Stockholm, economic restructuring does not independently generate new patterns of residential inequality. Even if all of these cities were undergoing the same pattern of economic change, perhaps involving greater social polarization or inequalities in income generated through work, this would not mean that spatial segregation would emerge in the same form and at the same rate. This is because the structure of cities in the 20th century has been strongly influenced by the welfare state. The patterns of spatial segregation which emerge from global economic pressures will be affected by the organization and nature of housing provision and other welfare state arrangements.

Housing and the Welfare State

Highlighting the importance of welfare state interventions in housing and social segregation is not new (Murie, Niner, and Watson 1976). Its basis is demonstrated by differences which developed in research on housing and residential differentiation in the United States and in Europe (especially the Netherlands and Britain). It is useful to reflect on differences in the spatial segregation of cities in the United States compared to Britain, as location of new building and who this is built for is reflected in the national welfare state regime and local political and administrative circumstances. For this reason the United States and Britain can provide alternative models for understanding partitioning.

The post-war US literature on residential differentiation and the processes driving it emphasized the family cycle, socio-economic status, and ethnicity. It presented this in relation to a neighbourhood mosaic with a continuous price structure and price contours relating, in particular, to distance from the city centre. While family cycle, socio-economic status, and (to a lesser extent) ethnicity worked in the British context, the organization of the housing market was very different and in particular the social rented sector was much larger and had a wider role. Housing tenures involved different processes of access and discontinuities which did not fit with the US picture. The emerging literature on access, choice, and constraint in housing in Britain identified housing tenure as a key variable (Murie, Niner, and Watson 1976) and the policies and actions of housing managers and urban gatekeepers as important influences (Pahl 1975). This literature acknowledged that the processes determining what was built where and where people lived were very different in British than in American cities. It is not being argued here that the family cycle or economic changes are of secondary importance in British cities. However, the ways in which pressures, opportunities, and preferences that derive from the family cycle and economic changes translate into residential mobility reflects access to housing and tenure and operates within a segmented and partitioned housing system with significant decommodification. Social rented housing in Britain, prior to the 1970s, did not have a geography which related to the price structure of land or housing; access to social rented housing was not based directly on income and the high quality of housing in the sector encouraged people to continue living in their family home even where incomes rose.

In Britain housing was, therefore, an important element in the post-war welfare state with the development of a large decommodified sector which transformed the physical and social structure of the city. How British cities change under the influence of economic restructuring relates to factors other than technological or economic. British cities in the post-war period up to the mid 1970s developed in an environment of full employment, universal state social security and health provision, and active housing and planning policies. These elements reduced inequalities associated with the life cycle or ill health. They also reduced the impact of unemployment and prevented this experience from creating financial crises, provided access to housing based on need, interfered with market pricing of housing consumption, and broke the links between low income and the worst housing. A crucial consequence of this was the creation of areas of the city with high levels of social mix. Access to social rented housing was not based on direct measures of income and continuing occupation of housing was not based on any test of continuing low income. Early social rented housing was superior to what was available to rent privately. As a result it was attractive to the respectable working class while the unskilled and a growing minority of immigrants remained or were filtered into the poorer quality parts of the private rented sector. Consequently, in Britain where people lived could not be read off simply from household characteristics and data relating to housing quality or distance from the city centre or location. Thus, for example, Robson's conclusion from a study of Sunderland applies more generally:

In addition to making the classical type of ecological analysis largely invalid, the council house areas introduce new elements and new combinations of traits into the structure of this town and, doubtless, of other towns. They are areas in which low class is no longer associated with poor housing (even though the association with high density per room persists) and in which, in terms of age structure and household composition, the population differs radically from areas within the private housing sector regardless of whether such areas are of high or low social class.   (Robson 1969: 154)

Residualization and Polarization

This situation had begun to change by the mid 1960s. The pace of change increased after the mid 1970s because of changes in the economy and the welfare state and, as part of the welfare state, the housing system. The simultaneous effects of demographic change, economic restructuring, and welfare state changes that affected the residential structure of British cities spawned debates about residualization, socio-tenurial polarization, and new social divisions in British cities. The background and its consequences are an important element for understanding the process of restructuring the 'poor city' in Britain.

The rapid decline of the private rented sector in Britain, from the early part of the 20th century onwards, reduced the supply of easy access housing and altered the spatial association between lower income people and poor quality housing in the private rented sector. Meanwhile, the state housing sector became the major accessible tenure for those who could not afford to buy housing and at its peak in the late 1970s, council housing provided for almost one in three households. Long-term patterns of financing made home ownership more attractive and eroded the attractiveness of council housing especially for those with higher incomes. In more recent years the operation of privatization policies and further changes in housing policy and finance have speeded the trend. Changes in housing policy have formed a major part of the restructuring of the welfare state with a central element being the switch from general subsidies to dwellings or tenures and individual means-tested housing benefits operating against a background of higher rents. One of the consequences of this approach was to provide some incentive for those who were in the rented sector, but could have bought, to remain as tenants. In the new policy environment, since 1979, rents in both the private and social rented sectors have increased and subsidies have shifted more rapidly to individual means-tested subsidy. In this environment and especially since the late 1980s, following the passage of the 1988 Housing Act, rent increases have been more dramatic. Average housing association rents increased by 73 per cent over the three year period 1988 to 1991 (Ford and Wilcox 1994; NFHA 1992). By contrast, the most accurate statistics on incomes in Britain show that average incomes increased by just under 35 per cent over the 12 year period 1979 to 1991 (HMSO 1993). A combination of changes in the conditions of tenancy and changes in the funding of housing association developments has been responsible for these sharp increases. Whilst rent rebates or subsidies have offset some of these rising rents, the overall effect has seen those able to afford to buy their home leave the rented sector whereas those qualifying for subsidies and benefits are subject to the poverty 'trap' with little opportunity to leave. Three-quarters of those living in social housing are now in the poorest 40 per cent of the population (SEU 1998).

The changes in the rented sector and the increasing proportion of skilled and other manual workers in home ownership has broken the particular pattern of socio-tenurial polarization identified prior to 1981 (Hamnett 1984). This identified the increasing concentration of professional and managerial groups in owner occupation and of the less skilled in council housing. By the mid 1980s, British social rented housing (council and housing association housing) had narrowed its social base and was increasingly associated with the non-working poor. Alongside this, home ownership had broadened its social base. In 1987 the council sector housed 61 per cent of those in receipt of supplementary benefit (national assistance) and by 1991 almost two-thirds (65 per cent) of the poorest income decile lived in council housing (HMSO 1982, 1992). The concentration of the poorest sections of the community in the sector had increased and in many areas the only households becoming new tenants were those who were classified as homeless (Fig. 4.2).

New tenants, in general, were drawn disproportionately from those outside the labour market (Forrest and Murie 1988; Prescott-Clarke, Allen, and Morrissey 1988; Prescott-Clarke, Clemens, and Park 1994). Furthermore, whilst new tenants will not always have low incomes, the prognosis for the sector continues to be about residualization and a clear welfare housing role. The introduction of rights for council tenants to purchase their homes from 1979 onwards (Right to Buy) and the low rates of investment in new housing in the sector has sealed the future. Nor is the favoured non-municipal arm of the social rented sector experiencing a different pattern. The non-profit, voluntary, housing association sector has grown but still provides only 3 per cent of dwellings. Its tenants and new tenants have a similar profile to council

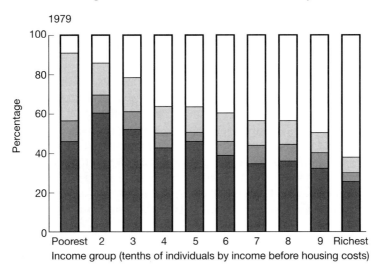

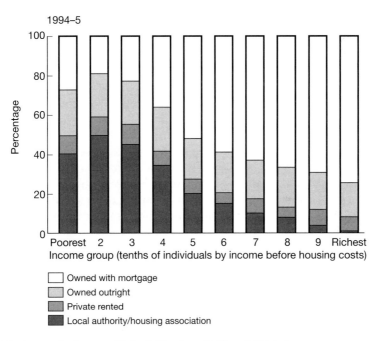

Fig. 4.2. Tenure by income, United Kingdom (1979 and 1994–5)
Source: SEU 1998, p. 24

tenants and concern has been expressed about creating 'ghetto' estates in this sector (Page 1993).

The increasing concentration of low-income households in council housing represents a key element in contemporary patterns of urban division in Britain. The direction of change in the income distribution together with long-term dependency in unemployment have contributed to the process of residualization with the sector having an unambiguous role in housing the 'residual poor'. Council housing's role is more distinct than in the past with less social mix. Data relating to the characteristics of new tenants and the increasing importance of homeless households reinforce the picture of a sector recruiting from a less varied population (Prescott-Clarke, Allen, and Morrissey 1988). However, this pattern is not consistent with a strict view of socio-tenurial polarization because the home ownership sector has not catered more exclusively for higher-income groups and professional and managerial workers. Rather, the owner-occupied sector, with its growth to more than two-thirds of the housing stock, has become a differentiated sector. The result has been the emergence of neighbourhoods that are high-income enclaves within cities, others that represent mass housing estates for younger employed people, others that are highly marginal neighbourhoods of older run down property and areas with high levels of minority ethnic populations and other characteristics. The imagery of polarization is not appropriate to represent what has been happening to housing tenure in Britain. To this extent the spatial structure of tenures has broken down. There is a more complex spatial pattern and it is more difficult to read off from what we know about housing tenure to particular neighbourhoods.

In this discussion it is, therefore, important to recognize that what is happening to the council housing tenure across the country is not always going to be apparent in what is happening to neighbourhoods in cities. Although council housing has become increasingly drawn from a narrow social base (i.e., the economically inactive or lone parents—housing of 'last resort'), this does not mean that areas of housing which were built by local authorities have the same characteristics. Some of these areas are now areas of mixed tenure and the owner-occupiers in the areas may have different social characteristics from council tenants.

This is true not only in relation to those sitting tenants who have bought and continued to live in the area as owner-occupiers but also in relation to those who buy such properties on the open market. They have different characteristics in terms of family structure, income, and age from the council tenants on the estates where they are living. To this extent, again there is a greater differentiation than was apparent in the past. However, it is important to recognize that in some council housing estates there have been very few sales of properties. There has therefore been an increased funnelling of the poorest sections of the community into these areas.

Changing Cities

The evidence presented for Great Britain points to greater social and income inequality and a change in the social role of housing tenures at a national level. At the same time, changes in the welfare state's role as provider of housing have irrevocably changed the relationship between social class and housing tenure. What are the implications of these processes for British cities? Within the city rather than two polar types of area or tenure there are at least three. First, we have council housing neighbourhoods which have become more homogeneous and cater to a much greater extent for those with least bargaining power and in the weakest positions in the labour market. Second, we have a highly differentiated series of segments of the owner-occupied market, some of which are mixed-tenure areas, some of which are wholly owner-occupier areas but all of which have different social characteristics and concentrations. Finally there are neighbourhoods catering exclusively for affluent professional and managerial workers.

But, both the housing market and the extent of social inequality differs between cities. For example, a city such as Liverpool with a long history of declining manufacturing industry and high unemployment (21.1 per cent) has higher city-wide levels of unemployment than London (16.0 per cent Inner London; 8.9 per cent Outer London), Birmingham (14.4 per cent) or Edinburgh (8.6 per cent). All of these cities have very different tenure and built environments. For example, over one-third (33.8 per cent) of Inner London households live in council housing—twice the rate of Outer London (16.5 per cent) and appreciably higher than Edinburgh (19.9 per cent), Birmingham (26.4 per cent), or Liverpool (28.6 per cent) (Table 4.1).

Moreover, where council housing, and especially the least attractive council housing is located differs. There is a range of data which demonstrate the changing composition of council housing neighbourhoods. Studies of the

Table 4.1. Household tenure in UK cities (1991)

	Owner-occupation		Council housing		Housing association		Private rented sector	
	(×1,000)	(%)	(×1,000)	(%)	(×1,000)	(%)	(×1,000)	(%)
Birmingham	225	60.1	99	26.4	21	5.6	25	6.6
Edinburgh	123	66.4	37	19.9	7	4.0	159	8.6
Liverpool	93	51.1	52	28.6	16	8.7	19	10.3
London	1,579	57.2	645	23.3	155	5.6	338	12.2
Inner	423	38.6	370	33.8	102	9.3	179	16.3
Outer	1,156	69.4	274	16.5	53	3.2	159	9.5
Great Britain	14,500	66.3	4,690	21.5	690	3.1	1,970	9.0

Source: OPCS (1991).

processes of housing allocation also show that there has been a systematic tendency to steer households with least bargaining power towards certain parts of the housing stock (see Henderson and Karn 1987; English 1979; and the reviews in Wilmott and Murie 1988; Malpass and Murie 1994).

The early studies relating race to access to housing indicated that minority ethnic groups were disadvantaged in the allocation policies adopted by local authorities (Rex and Moore 1967). Minority ethnic groups in Britain were therefore initially under-represented within the council housing sector. More recent data indicate that there is a very high level of home ownership among Asian households (OPCS 1991). Indeed, with the exception of household heads in professional and managerial employment, the level of home ownership is higher among Asian than white households. Whereas, in 1984, only 40 per cent of white heads of households in semi-skilled manual employment were owner-occupiers this was the case for 70 per cent of Asians (Brown 1984). It is important to note that the parts of the owner-occupied market that are used by minority ethnic groups are often distinctive low-value properties which are older, smaller, and have inferior amenity provision. These are often located in poor localities and reflect a history of undermaintenance of properties previously in the private rented sector (Henderson and Karn 1987).

Over the last decade 'black' (black African or black Caribbean) headed households have gained access to the council sector to a much greater extent. They make up a higher proportion of new tenants but new tenants are more likely to be allocated flats rather than houses and the flats are more frequently on the upper floors. Indeed, the evidence for the council sector is that black council tenants tend to be in less desirable parts of the stock and in older smaller properties. A number of studies have outlined the processes through which black households become concentrated in particular parts of the city often in less desirable properties (Henderson and Karn 1987). The importance of these studies is in demonstrating that it is the way that policies are administered and carried out rather than the formal housing policies themselves that leads to a concentration of minority ethnic groups in particular parts of the council housing system. Despite the relaxation of residential qualifications, which had previously been the greatest hindrance to households from minority ethnic groups, it remained difficult for these households to gain access to social housing and to the best social housing.

The situation is complicated by the operation of transfer policies and the expression of areas of choice as well as by administrative practices designed to cope with the pressures placed upon allocation staff. Owner-occupiers, unmarried cohabiting couples, and joint families tend to be given less priority in the allocation processes and in their study of Birmingham, Henderson and Karn (1987: 273) concluded that: 'It was the attitude of whites towards living in the inner city and older parts of the middle ring which was by far the most powerful element in producing the growing segregation of West Indians and Asians in those areas'.

The strong preference of whites for the suburbs produced a tendency for inner city vacancies to be offered to West Indians or Asians because white applicants tended to reject such properties. This effectively meant that when Asians and West Indians moved into council houses they have mainly moved out of the middle ring and towards the inner city estates.

The interaction between these factors means that national patterns of change are not automatically reproduced locally. Not only is there a contrast in the pattern of economic restructuring between cities, reflected in a wide range of unemployment rates, but the legacy of differentiation and the pattern of housing market restructuring differs. In relation to the latter element the rate of privatization has differed considerably between cities.

Spatial Partitioning: Changes *within* the British City

Changes in the *occupational* structure is another approach in understanding what has been happening to particular cities. Hamnett (1994) has examined Sassen's (1991) thesis of polarization in global cities and suggested that rather than polarization, what has occurred is professionalization. How far this process of professionalization has gone is relevant to British cities and has implications for spatial segregation in the context of an increasingly differenti- ated housing market in which the decommodified sector remains substantial although it has declined. The remainder of this chapter, therefore, looks more closely at changes in the socio-economic profile and patterns of residential segregation in two British cities: Edinburgh and Birmingham. These two cities provide contrasting evidence of how the restructuring of the welfare state and with it the commodification and privatization of the housing market have con- tributed to the shaping of the city in Britain.

Edinburgh is a city with an economy traditionally based on legal, govern- mental, educational, and financial services. The role played by finance and the service sector in Edinburgh's economy makes it noticeably different when com- pared to the role of manufacturing in Birmingham. Indeed, as Hague notes, the social structure of Edinburgh has historically been disproportionately middle class: 'Edinburgh is a rather peculiar city . . . a majestic capital but without the full functions of the capital of a nation state. It has always been a city of consumption and administration rather than a city of production like Glasgow or Birmingham . . . This economic structure begot a social structure that was disproportionately middle class, the most bourgeois town in Britain' (Hague 1993: 7).

Between 1981 and 1991, for example, the proportion of the population in Edinburgh in professional or managerial positions increased from 23 per cent of the workforce to almost 30 per cent (Table 4.2). The key employment sectors over this period were banking and finance (an increase of 56 per cent working

Table 4.2. Socio-economic group of households in Edinburgh and Birmingham (1981 and 1991) (%)

	Edinburgh		Birmingham	
	1981	1991	1981	1991
Employers and managers	14.5	18.9	9.4	12.2
Professional workers	8.4	11.5	3.4	4.9
Intermediate non-manual workers	12.5	16.8	10.1	12.9
Junior non-manual workers	16.7	15.7	20.9	21.1
Manual workers	25.2	19.3	21.7	22.5
Personal service and semi-skilled manual workers	13.9	11.5	23.3	19.3
Unskilled manual workers	6.6	4.7	6.9	5.3

Source: OPCS (1981, 1991).

in this sector over the period), insurance (>114 per cent), and business services (>91 per cent). All of these sectors saw dramatic increases both in relative and absolute numbers employed. In Birmingham, a city with a long history of manufacturing employment, the proportion of the workforce in professional or managerial positions increased more conservatively from almost 13 per cent to just over 17 per cent of the working population.

The relative shares of different socio-economic groups have changed in a way compatible with professionalization rather than polarization. For example, over the period 1981–91 Edinburgh saw the numbers of manual workers decline dramatically whilst junior non-manual workers also declined. Other groups showed a numerical increase. At the same time the proportion of unskilled workers declined with food and drink (<44 per cent) and printing and publishing (<48 per cent) being particularly affected by the restructuring taking place both locally and globally. However, whilst manual employment declined by almost 6 per cent in Edinburgh (leaving a situation whereby it formed less than 20 per cent of the workforce in 1991), Birmingham saw a marginal (0.8 per cent) increase over the period 1981–91—indicating the enduring legacy of manufacturing employment in the city. In Edinburgh, manufacturing industry had declined with the percentage of residents aged 16 and over in the sector falling from 16.9 per cent in 1981 to 11.3 per cent in 1991. Employment in the service sector had increased over the same period from 47.4 per cent to 57.1 per cent. This, together with the relative increases in the proportion of workers in professional or managerial occupations in both cities, might support the thesis of professionalization.

However, this view of professionalization involves a neglect of those individuals that are outside the labour market. The economically *inactive* population are not included in UK unemployment figures as they are not available for employment and are therefore treated separately. Moreover, because they are not working they cannot be included in analysis of occupations because they have no occupational classification. However, a significant proportion of the

Table 4.3. Percentage of the UK working-age population not in employment (1991)

	Unemployed[a]	Not working[b]
Birmingham	14.4	33.7
Edinburgh	8.6	25.2
Liverpool	21.1	42.4
London	11.6	28.2
Inner	15.9	32.0
Outer	9.0	25.8
Great Britain	9.3	28.3

Note: The working-age population is based on those aged between the school leaving age of >16 and the retirement age for women and men in the United Kingdom (aged 59/64).

[a] Unemployed is the economically *active* population not in employment.
[b] Not working includes unemployed and economically *inactive* men and women of working age (i.e., those not seeking work such as the sick, disabled, those caring for relatives and the early retired).

Source: OPCS (1991).

economically inactive form part of the labour market during economic boom periods. Therefore, trends affecting rates of economic inactivity have important implications for the observed occupational structure, and analysis of changes in occupational and labour market stratification should not overlook economic inactivity. Economic inactivity is especially significant in regions with a high dependency upon one employer where subsequent closure and large-scale redundancies can result in 'discouragement' of the labour force and a shrinking of the economically *active* population. An example of this process is provided by the closure of some UK coal mines during the 1980s, which did not lead to an increase in unemployment but an increase in economic *inactivity*. This was a direct result of the process whereby older male workers were *discouraged* from applying for a reduced pool of jobs, and hence entered long-term dependency on state sickness benefits or took early retirement (Beatty and Fothergill 1994).

The difference between unemployment rates reveals the level of 'hidden' unemployment in British cities. Table 4.3 illustrates the difference between unemployment and the non-working rate (i.e., the working age population either unemployed, sick, or inactive for other reasons) for four British cities. In Edinburgh, although the unemployment rate was less than 9 per cent, more than a quarter of the working-age population were not working. The total economic inactivity rate for Edinburgh was around 40 per cent, however, this includes men and women over retirement age.

In Liverpool, the inactivity rate is far greater and the underlying unemployment rate of 21 per cent is more than doubled in a city where more than 4 out of 10 working-age adults are not working. The figure is slightly higher if we include students or those temporarily employed on government training schemes.

Evidence suggests that rates of economic inactivity conform to a continuing upward trend: Edinburgh saw its economically inactive population (including pensioners) rise by 16 per cent to 142,228 (41 per cent of the adult population) between 1981 and 1991; in Birmingham the increase was less marked but totalled some 284,369 adults or 38.3 per cent of the total adult population. When the economically inactive are included, therefore, the evidence is of a marked growth in the 'work-poor', both in absolute and relative terms, contradicting a professionalization thesis. In cities with such high inactivity rates it is illustrative of how the process of 'discouragement' leading to the relabelling of the unemployed as economically inactive or sick requires a more thorough analysis of the stratification of the labour market. Hence, whilst unemployment in Edinburgh increased only modestly from 7.7 per cent to 8.6 per cent and actually declined slightly in Birmingham between 1981 and 1991, the economically *inactive* population in both cities, increased.

Social Change at the Neighbourhood Level

How have these changes in occupational and activity rates affected the residential patterns within Edinburgh and Birmingham? Analysis of residential segregation in Birmingham and Edinburgh illustrates how policy legacies together with recent changes in the welfare state and widening inequalities produce different patterns of residential segregation. To overcome some of the problems of aggregated spatial data within the city we have used small area statistics from the 1991 United Kingdom Census of Population in comparing Edinburgh and Birmingham.[2] Figures 4.3 and 4.4 present 'local area' maps for the two cities showing the estimated percentage of 'poor' households within local areas (neighbourhoods)[3] and show that the location of the poor in these two cities is strikingly dissimilar.

In Birmingham, the inner city forms the core of poverty with some outlying pockets in the suburbs. In Edinburgh, a radial arm of poverty extends westwards out of the city (Fig. 4.3), whilst concentrated pockets surround the outer periphery. There are similar proportions of multiple deprivation in the two cities. For example, 35 per cent and 32 per cent of 'poor' households, respectively, in Edinburgh and Birmingham live in a fifth of the local areas. Comparison of tenure in Britain for 1991 shows that whilst owner-occupation was higher in England (67.6 per cent) than in Scotland (52.1 per cent) (OPCS 1991), Edinburgh (66.4 per cent) was closer to the English average than Birmingham (60.1 per cent) (see Table 4.1). A greater number of households in Birmingham (32.0 per cent) lived in social housing when compared to Edinburgh (23.9 per cent). Social housing in Edinburgh plays more of a role in housing the poor

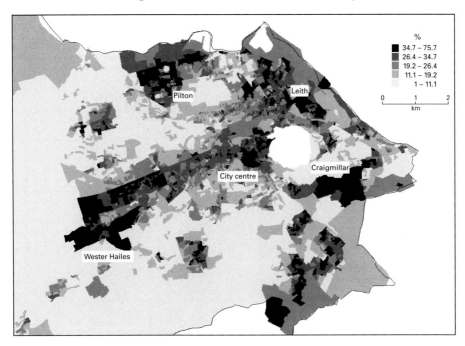

Fig. 4.3. Poverty in Edinburgh: estimated percentage of poor households at the neighbourhood level (1991)

Source: Census Data, Crown © JISC purchase, OPCS 1991

than in Birmingham. Almost 62 per cent of households living in the poorest quintile (20%) of local areas in Edinburgh (when ranked according to the estimated percentage of poor households) lived in social housing. This compares with slightly more than 42 per cent in Birmingham. In Edinburgh, the main concentrations of council housing are in the peripheral estates of Pilton, Leith, Craigmillar, and Wester Hailes (Fig. 4.5). These areas have continuing problems of poverty and had the highest recorded unemployment rates in Edinburgh during 1995—24 per cent compared with 11 per cent for the district (EDC 1996).

In Birmingham, the areas with the highest proportion of social housing also feature as the poorest areas. However, a significant proportion of poor areas are also associated with other tenures. Comparison between the proportion of poor households in local areas in Birmingham (Fig. 4.4) with the proportion of households in council housing (Fig. 4.6) demonstrates how poverty is predominantly an inner city phenomenon in Birmingham. The highest densities being around the very central inner urban core of Aston (to the North), Nechells (to the North East), and Ladywood (to the south of the City centre). Smaller, but significantly dense clusters of council housing are found in Kingstanding in the northern suburb and Bartley Green and King's Norton in the southern belt of

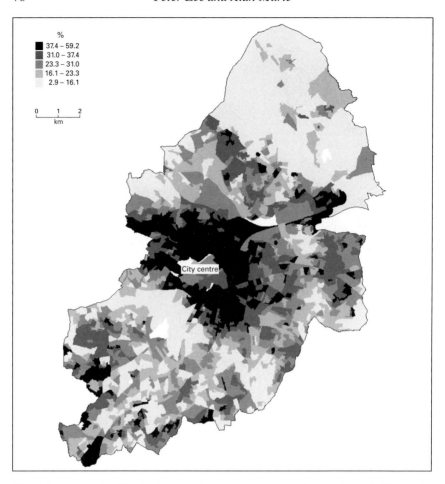

Fig. 4.4. Poverty in Birmingham: estimated percentage of poor households at the neighbourhood level (1991)
Source: Census Data, Crown © JISC purchase, OPCS 1991

Birmingham. In the suburban wards of Kingstanding, Bartley Green, and King's Norton the tenure structure was split almost equally between owner-occupation and social housing. Concentrations of council housing are illustrated in Fig. 4.6 for these areas. In the inner urban wards of Aston, Nechells, and Ladywood only Aston (64 per cent) had a clear majority of households in social housing.

The coincidence of social housing with concentrations of poverty in Birmingham is, therefore, less clear-cut than in Edinburgh. The reasons for this are related to the greater role of the different tenures in the two cities but also to the significance of ethnic minorities in Birmingham and their different distribution between tenures. In Edinburgh, less than 3 per cent of the population iden-

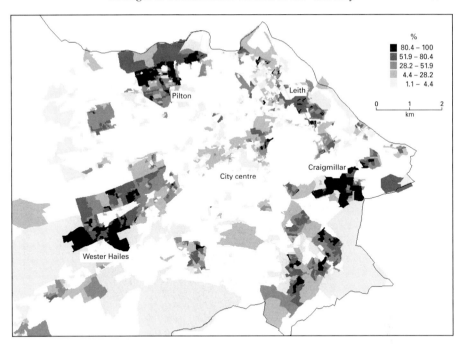

Fig. 4.5. Council housing in Edinburgh (1991)

Source: Census Data, Crown © JISC purchase, OPCS 1991

tified themselves as belonging to a non-white ethnic group. In Birmingham, non-white ethnic groups comprised more than one-fifth of the city's population in 1991—considerably greater than the average for Britain as a whole, which was 5.5 per cent of the population or 2.9 million British residents (Table 4.4). In addition, the suburban council housing locations had proportions of non-white ethnic groups significantly below the city average. These were 6.7 per cent (Kingstanding), 5.2 per cent (Bartley Green), and 4.8 per cent (King's Norton). By comparison, in 1991 more than half (55 per cent) of Aston's population was non-white whilst for other areas of the city, such as Nechells and Ladywood, the figures were 49 per cent and 42 per cent, respectively. The geography of Birmingham's ethnic population is illustrated by Fig. 4.7 showing the densities of black and Asian ethnic groups around the inner city.

Figure 4.7 does not disaggregate for different ethnic groups, however, it is interesting to note that black, black Caribbean and black African ethnic groups have tended to live to the west of the city centre in Handsworth and Soho where there is also a large population of residents with origins in the Asian sub-continent. Meanwhile, the east and south east of the city centre (Small Heath, Sparkbrook, and Sparkhill) has been predominantly populated by residents with origins in Pakistan and Bangladesh. In terms of density,

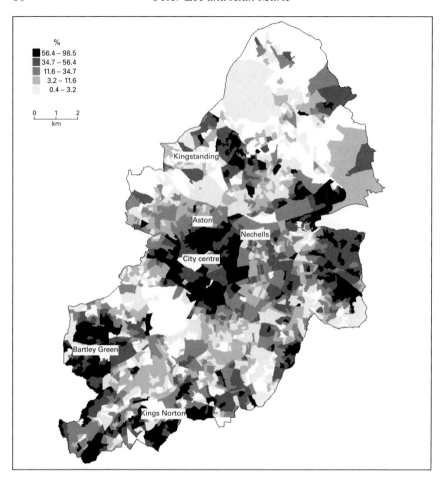

Fig. 4.6. Council housing in Birmingham (1991)
Source: Census Data, Crown © JISC purchase, OPCS 1991

Table 4.4. Residents by ethnic group in the United Kingdom (absolute numbers and percentages) (1991)

	White	Black[a]	Asian sub-continent[b]	Other[c]
Birmingham (abs.)	754,274	56,376	129,899	20,492
(%)	(78.5)	(5.9)	(13.5)	(2.1)
Edinburgh (abs.)	409,044	1,176	4,129	4,570
(%)	(97.6)	(0.3)	(1.0)	(1.1)
Great Britain (abs.)	51,086,144	871,120	1,470,245	628,184
(%)	(94.5)	(1.6)	(2.7)	(1.2)

[a] Black includes black Caribbean, black African, black other.
[b] Asian: Indian, Pakistani, Bangladeshi.
[c] Other: includes Chinese.

Source: OPCS (1991).

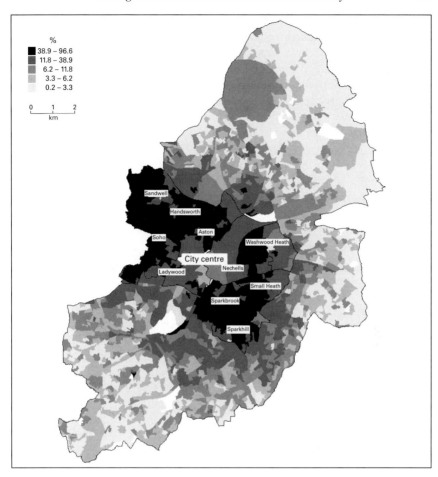

Fig. 4.7. Percentage of residents in Birmingham from a non-white ethnic background (1991)

Source: Census Data, Crown © JISC purchase, OPCS 1991

90 per cent of the population in some neighbourhoods in the east and south east of the city are residents with origins in India, Pakistan, or Bangladesh.

In areas with high proportions of ethnic minority populations in Birmingham only Sparkbrook had significantly high percentages of households in council housing (40 per cent). Despite the modest or relatively low proportions of social housing tenants in these areas of the city comparison with the concentration of poor households (see Fig. 4.4) is striking. In Small Heath, three-quarters of households privately rented or owned their homes, whilst in Sparkhill more than a fifth of households were privately renting their homes and a further three-fifths were owner-occupiers in 1991. Typical properties in these areas are small 'terraced' (adjoining row house dwellings) houses converted into flats or shared dwellings (bedsits). The areas are characterized by small living spaces and low-cost owner-occupation or private rented accommodation controlled by a few local landlords. More than 70 per cent of dwellings in Sparkhill, for example, were terraced or converted flats compared to an average of 42 per cent for Birmingham as a whole. Whilst the processes of residualization in the council sector in Great Britain have resulted in the sale of the superior houses (rather than flats) in the better locations, council housing continues to provide housing of a high standard.

Hence, in Aston and Ladywood, areas with higher than average concentrations of council housing, less than 35 per cent of households lacked central heating in their homes. By comparison, in areas with high rates of owner occupation or private renting, such as in Sparkhill and Small Heath, between 50 per cent and 60 per cent of households lacked central heating in 1991. These areas also continue to be characterized by overcrowded conditions and absence of amenities (i.e., lacking or sharing a bath or lavatory).

Conclusions

Although there is recognition that there has been an increase in inequality of incomes between households and individuals within the United Kingdom, there has been much debate about how such changes are reflected at the city or local neighbourhood level. Common economic pressures in the global economy will not produce the same patterns of segregation in different cities. This is true both within and between national economies. Tracing back original debates about global effects and welfare states shows the need to recognize the importance of the welfare state regime and its legacy in determining the geography of poverty in British cities. In this respect it is important to note the differences between cities within national economies and not just internationally. In this chapter we have illustrated this by referring to Edinburgh and Birmingham.

The economies of these two British cities could not be more opposite in their history and enduring emphasis. In both cities there has been an increasing tendency for the workforce to be in the categories of manager, employer, or professional. However, Hamnett's representation of this pattern as professionalization is partial and rests on omitting reference to the economically *inactive* population. In Great Britain this has been an expanding group, which has experienced declining resources. They form part of the low-income pole in what can be seen as polarization rather than professionalization.

Moving beyond this debate, it is unclear that the pattern of changes is best represented either as polarization or as professionalization. The picture emerging from data on incomes in Britain suggests an increasingly polarized society with the numbers with middle incomes in decline. However, the income distribution presented earlier (Fig. 4.1) can also be characterized as one of differentiation with the *direction* of change leading to a situation of polarization. Such a direction of change would fit with the pattern of demographic, economic, and welfare changes which has led to a growth in inequalities of income and wealth and in the growing phenomenon of 'work-rich' (one or more earners) and 'work-poor' (no earner) households. However, in the general context of economic, welfare, and social change this pattern of income distribution could also be seen as a reflection of new patterns of household formation. Simple dichotomies between the 'work-rich' and 'work-poor' are inadequate as there also needs to be a recognition of the increasing number of households in low-paid and/or insecure employment. It may be argued, therefore, that what is emerging are a greater number of groups with very different interests and stakes in society. These relate to:

(1) the elderly and long-term sick who are permanently dependent on welfare and outside the labour market;
(2) the long-term unemployed and those who are unable to enter the labour market because of care responsibilities but who in terms of age would normally be seen as part of the labour market;
(3) those who are on the fringes of employment, moving in and out of work in the flexible labour market in part-time work and self-employment; and finally,
(4) those in secure career occupations with considerable entitlements to work-related fringe benefits.

Reference to this increased differentiation in the labour market is a more appropriate contrast to the full employment situation that has existed through most of the post-war era and is a clearer picture than that presented by polarization.

It has also been argued in this chapter that if we look at the way in which the housing market has changed it is also more appropriate to refer to residualization and differentiation rather than polarization. Whereas the role of council housing and the other rented sectors has become more narrow and focused on those with least choice in the housing market, the role of owner-occupation has become more differentiated. While council housing could be seen as one end of the housing market with other parts of the rented sector also associated with this end, it is less easy to identify home ownership as representing an alternative pole. The home ownership sector is too varied to be categorized easily in this way. Again therefore it is more appropriate to see a pattern in which differentiation within the owner-occupied market operates alongside an increased identity of rented housing with the lowest-income groups.

If we adopt this picture both of economic and labour market change and of changes in the housing market and look at the patterns which emerge between Edinburgh and Birmingham there are striking differences. Although both cities have been subject to the same economic pressures, the resulting patterns of residential differentiation are very different. Some of this relates to the legacy of what was built and especially the location of council housing and differentiation within the home ownership sector.

But more important is the evidence of the different roles of the owner-occupied and council housing sectors especially relating to minority ethnic groups. The Edinburgh picture is much closer to the stereotype view. Council housing is the predominant tenure for the poorest sections of the community and the geography of poverty relates very strongly to the geography of council housing. This pattern has become more clear with the impact of the right to buy. The residual council housing sector is the part of the sector that had increasingly catered for the poorest and consequently the relationship between the geography of poverty and the geography of council housing has become stronger.

The owner-occupied sector in Edinburgh is relatively highly priced, reflecting demand from professional groups. In this respect the cultural symbolism of space (living in the prestigious inner city of Edinburgh) coincides with the changing mode and regulation of capital (the growth of Edinburgh as a financial capital). People on the margins of the labour market or outside the labour market have little recourse to tenures other than council housing and their concentration in peripheral estates is striking. In Birmingham, the association between poverty and council housing is less dramatic. A considerable proportion in council housing neighbourhoods do not fall into the category identified as poor. There is considerable differentiation within the council sector according to its role in housing minority ethnic groups. Whilst peripheral concentrations of poverty are predominantly white, the inner urban core of poverty is more mixed in terms of ethnicity. The explanations for this relate to the history of access to council housing and home ownership and a similar pattern is likely to be apparent in other British cities with substantial ethnic minority populations. The Birmingham situation is not only different in relation to the role of council housing and differentiation within the council housing sector. It is also different because a more significant proportion of those in poverty are living in tenures other than council housing. Again, this relates to a concentration in parts of the inner city and in smaller 'Victorian' houses built before 1919. These were often the most accessible parts of the housing market to these groups when they first arrived in the city and which have become the preferred locations for these groups subsequently.

What emerges from the processes of economic restructuring, labour market change, housing market change, and changing state policies, are very different geographies of poverty and segregation. This cautions against assuming that common and global economic processes will produce common residential outcomes or that they are the sole determinants of spatial change in cities. However, the new spatial partitioning of British cities reflects general tendencies affecting spatial change which chime with other contributions in this volume.

Notes

1. The Beveridge welfare state refers to the combination of public welfare policies (education, health, and housing) in post-1945 Britain, the broad political consensus that existed to support those policies and the role of full employment in maintaining the welfare of the majority of citizens. Hereafter, we refer to the post-Fordist state.
2. In Edinburgh, Output Areas were used whilst in Birmingham, Enumeration Districts were the basis for analysis. These were the only comparable spatial boundaries for Scottish and English local authorities allowing us to reflect the 'neighbourhood'. However, the average population within Birmingham Enumeration Districts was roughly four times that of Edinburgh. Small populations within Output Areas (typically averaging 100 residents) will particularly affect the range of percentage values in Edinburgh.
3. The estimated percentage of poor households was based on regression results from a survey of poverty carried out in Britain in 1990 (Gordon and Pantazis 1995). An index of poverty containing the variables: *households with no car, lone parent households, single pensioner households, households containing a person with limiting long-term illness,* and the *unemployed* weighted to reflect the degree of risk of poverty in each category. The result is a representative estimation of the proportion of poor households in small areas.

References

BEATTY, C., and FOTHERGILL, S. (1994). 'Registered and hidden unemployment in areas of chronic industrial decline: the case of the UK coalfields'. Paper presented at the Regional Studies Association Conference: *Tackling Unemployment and Social Exclusion,* Sheffield, UK, 15 November.

BROWN, C. (1984). *Black and White Britain,* 3rd PSI survey. Aldershot: Gower.

CASTELLS, M. (1992). *European Cities, the Informational Society and the Global Economy.* Amsterdam: Centrum voor Grootstedelijk Onderzoek.

Commission on Social Justice (1994). *Social Justice: Strategies for National Renewal, The Report of the Commission on Social Justice.* London: Vintage.

CSO (Central Statistical Office) (1995). *Social Trends 1995.* London: HMSO.

EDC (Edinburgh District Council) (1996). http://www.efr.hw.ac.uk/EDC/Edinburgh.html

ENGLISH, J. (1979). 'Access and deprivation in local authority housing', in C. Jones (ed.), *Urban Deprivation and the Inner City,* 113–35. Beckenham, UK: Croom Helm.

FORD, J., and WILCOX, S. (1994). *Affordable Housing, Low Incomes and the Flexible Labour Market.* London: NFHA.

FORREST, R., and MURIE, A. (1988). *Selling the Welfare State.* London: Routledge.

GOODMAN, A., and WEBB, S. (1995). *The Distribution of UK Household Expenditure, 1979–92.* London: Institute for Fiscal Studies.

GORDON, D., and PANTAZIS, C. (eds.) (1995). *Breadline Britain in the 1990s.* Aldershot: Ashgate.

HAGUE, C. (1993). 'The restructuring of the image of Edinburgh: the politics of urban planning in a European Arena'. Paper presented at: *Proceedings of the 9th Urban Change and Conflict Conference*. Sheffield, UK: University of Sheffield.

HAMNETT, C. (1984). 'Housing the two nations: socio-tenurial polarisation in England and Wales, 1961–81'. *Urban Studies*, 21: 389–405.

——(1994). 'Social polarization in global cities—theory and evidence'. *Urban Studies*, 31: 401–24.

HENDERSON, J., and KARN, V. (1987). *Race, Class and State Housing: Inequality and the Allocation of Public Housing in Britain*. Aldershot: Gower.

HILLS, J. (1995). *Inquiry into Income and Wealth*, 2. York, UK: Joseph Rowntree Foundation.

HMSO (Her Majesty's Stationery Office) (1982). *Family Expenditure Survey: 1980*. London: HMSO.

——(1992). *Family Spending*. London: HMSO.

——(1993). *Households Below Average Income: A Statistical Analysis*. London: HMSO.

——(1994). *Social Trends*, 24. London: HMSO.

——(1995). *General Household Survey*, 24. London: HMSO.

HOWARTH, C., KENWAY, P., PALMER, G., and STREET, C. (1998). *Monitoring Poverty and Social Exclusion: Labour's Inheritance*. York, UK: Joseph Rowntree Foundation.

MALPASS, P., and MURIE, A. (1994). *Housing Policy and Practice*. London: Macmillan.

MURIE, A. (1994). *Cities and Housing after the Welfare State*. Amsterdam: Amsterdam Study Centre for the Metropolitan Environment, University of Amsterdam.

——, NINER, P., and WATSON, C. (1976). *Housing Policy and the Housing System*. London: Allen & Unwin.

NFHA (National Federation of Housing Associations) (1992). *Housing Associations After the Act*. London: NFHA.

OPCS (Office of Population Census and Surveys) (1981). *Small Area Statistics*. London: OPCS.

——(1991). *Small Area Statistics*. London: OPCS.

PAGE, D. (1993). *Building for Communities*. York, UK: Joseph Rowntree Foundation.

PAHL, R. (1975). *Whose City? And Further Essays on Urban Society*. Harmondsworth, UK: Penguin.

PHILPOTT, J. (1994). 'The incidence and cost of unemployment', in A. Glyn and D. Miliband (eds.), *Paying for Inequality: The Economic Cost of Social Injustice*, 130–44. London: Institute of Public Policy Research.

PRESCOTT-CLARKE, P., ALLEN, P., and MORRISSEY, C. (1988). *Queuing for Housing: A Study of Council Housing Waiting Lists*. London: HMSO.

——CLEMENS, S., and PARK, A. (1994). *Routes into Local Authority Housing*. London: HMSO.

REX, J., and MOORE, R. (1967). *Race, Community, and Conflict*. Oxford: Oxford University Press.

ROBSON, B. (1969). *Urban Analysis*. Cambridge: Cambridge University Press.

SASSEN, S. (1991). *The Global City: New York, London, Tokyo*. Princeton: Princeton University Press.

SEU (Social Exclusion Unit) (1998). *Bringing Britain Together: A National Strategy for Neighbourhood Renewal*. London: Cabinet Office.

WALKER, C. (1996). 'The feminisation of poverty: women and social welfare', in C. Booth, J. Darke, and S. Yeandle (eds.), *Changing Places: Women's Lives in the City*, 32–47. London: Paul Chapman.

WINCHESTER, H. P., and WHITE, P. E. (1988). 'The location of marginalised groups in the inner city'. *Environment and Planning: D*, 6: 37–54.

WILMOTT, P., and MURIE, A. (1988). *Polarisation and Social Housing*. London: Policy Studies Institute.

5

Towards Partitioned Cities in the Netherlands? Changing Patterns of Segregation in a Highly Developed Welfare State

Ronald van Kempen

Introduction

Dutch society in general and Dutch cities in particular are quite unlike those of many other western European countries and the United States. In the Netherlands, long-standing state policies in the field of welfare, social security, and housing have blurred the relation between household income and one's place of residence. Especially in the large cities, socially homogeneous areas are rare, certainly at the lower end of the scale. Ethnically homogeneous neighbourhoods do not exist in the Netherlands, nor do neighbourhoods without a substantial number of Dutch natives. Areas with a large social housing stock are not inhabited exclusively by low-income households. This suggests that the concept of the dual city does not apply to the Dutch situation today. We have to agree with Murie (1994), who takes issue with Winchester and White's (1988) contention that any group characterized by economic marginality will be constrained in their residential location and will occupy the poorest sections of the housing stock. Murie considers that assertion to be an oversimplification based on the situation observed in American and Australasian cities. That assertion certainly does not apply to the situation in the Netherlands.

The Dutch welfare state is in retreat today. Nonetheless, the state still shields people from all kinds of social risks (illness, unemployment, bad housing conditions). The advanced welfare system still serves as a buffer in times of economic downturn for many different groups (Engbersen and Snel 1996). Moreover, according to Engbersen and Gabriëls (1995), state institutions like

The author wishes to thank Jack Burgers, Frans Dieleman, Robert Kloosterman, and Jan van Weesep for their comments on an earlier version of this chapter.

schools, public housing agencies, police, and social work are still effective in areas with relatively high concentrations of low-income groups (compare, e.g., Chapters 11 and 12).

Has the retreating welfare state affected the spatial configuration of different types of households in Dutch cities? This chapter investigates how patterns have changed and offers some explanations for these changes. We want to find out if there is a tendency towards more partitioned cities in the Netherlands and, if so, why. The changing role of the state is central, but other factors— such as changing economic, demographic, and socio-cultural variables— should also be taken into account.

Income Policy in the Netherlands

The Netherlands is one of the most developed welfare states in the western world. This is evident in the high living standards in many fields. During the past forty years, the national government has adopted a range of programmes aimed at providing all households with a decent income, irrespective of their position in the labour market. Working people enjoy the benefits of minimum-wage laws and protection against the financial effects of sickness, disability, and unemployment. Those who cannot work, or are no longer working, receive welfare, social security, or help through a host of other programmes (Van Weesep and Van Kempen 1993: 179). Those without a job (the unemployed, the disabled, the elderly) receive a benefit; compared to other western European countries, these benefits are high (Tweede Kamer 1990). Moreover, subsidies are ubiquitous—housing, education, health, leisure, and culture. In the field of housing, the Netherlands is famous for its extensive social rented sector of relatively high quality (see, e.g., Dieleman 1994).

In the Netherlands, public administration has, historically, been decentralized, giving the provinces and the municipalities a strong position. The expansion of the welfare state, however, has curtailed the constitutional and financial autonomy of these lower tiers of government (Dieleman and Kloosterman 1997). The dominant role of central government is clearly illustrated by its intervention in the fields of income and housing. These two policy fields have had a major impact on present-day patterns of social and spatial segregation in the Netherlands.

Proportional representation and political pluralism have created a tradition of coalition governments in the Netherlands. In addition, the Dutch political model is essentially corporatist. This means that advisory boards composed of representatives of all sorts of social organizations influence the making of policy. Consequently, while the numerous political parties may have divergent philosophies concerning all aspects of policy-making, there is normally a fair degree of continuity of policy. But this does not rule out new policies.

Many post-Second World War cabinets gave high priority to the promotion of income equality. During the 1950s, the post-war reconstruction period, the economy was booming, wages were centrally negotiated, and everyone had a share in the growing affluence. In the 1960s, the welfare system was greatly expanded, and a minimum wage was set. At the end of this period, the taxes for lower incomes were reduced. Despite these trends, the income distribution in the Netherlands was not considered fair. Therefore, in the 1970s, the government increased expenditures in respect to welfare.

But since the middle of the 1980s, all western European welfare states, including the Netherlands, have been retreating. This tendency reflects a new philosophy, which calls for more individual initiatives and less state influence, but it was also prompted by declining state resources. The consequences were immediately evident: many households—especially those without a job—have to make do with decreasing incomes, and it has become more difficult to obtain certain benefits and subsidies. This means that newcomers—among them young people and immigrants—have trouble starting a working and housing career or consolidating their present positions in either the labour or the housing market.

For most of the 1980s, the country was governed by a Christian/liberal coalition. The greater income inequality achieved over that decade was partly a result of the government's policy of increasing the difference between wages and unemployment benefits. For example, while people used to have the right to 80 per cent of their wage as unemployment benefit or workman's compensation, this was cut back to 70 per cent; the minimum benefits were not indexed to reflect wage increases for the working population; and the benefits for young people were drastically reduced (Uitterhoeve 1990). Obviously, the retreat of the welfare state affected the income position of households. Compared to other countries, however, these arrangements are still relatively generous.

The elaborate welfare state arrangements in the Netherlands have not prevented a large income difference from arising between those with and those without a job. In 1993, the mean income was Nfl62,300 a year for civil servants and Nfl54,000 for people in other employment. For those who received an unemployment benefit and those on welfare, the mean income was around Nfl27,000 (Trimp 1994). Between 1984 and 1994 (earlier figures are not available), and especially in the second half of this period, purchasing power rose among all income categories. Nonetheless, income inequality expanded as higher-income households' buying power increased. Between 1984 and 1994, the top quarter of the incomes in the Netherlands had a 30 per cent increase in purchasing power, while the lowest quarter had no more than a 10 per cent increase. Especially those who already were or just became active on the labour market (i.e., those with a job) saw their purchasing power rise. This partly explains the relatively low increase among the bottom quarter of incomes, because that is where the unemployed, the elderly, and other non-working persons are concentrated (Trimp 1996). People who are dependent on welfare state provision (pensioners, the unemployed) are becoming increasingly worse off.

In the Netherlands, the income differences between the Dutch and several minority ethnic groups are significant. Turks, Moroccans, Surinamese, and Antilleans are more likely to live below the poverty line than nationals. The proportion of these groups with an income below 95 per cent of the social minimum wage is three to four times as large as among Dutch nationals (Tesser, Van Dugteren, and Merens 1998).

Housing and the Role of the State

Welfare state arrangements influence the income positions of different household types. In the Netherlands, they thus also affect the housing market positions of different types of households. A brief outline of the Dutch housing system is therefore appropriate here.

Governments across western Europe intervened in their housing markets after the Second World War, establishing a wide range of social measures, including rent control and a variety of subsidies (Lundqvist 1992). In addition, almost all countries created a social rented sector. The Netherlands went the farthest in this respect (Dieleman and Van Kempen 1994). The large proportion of social housing units within the existing stock (42 per cent) is indicative of this policy. Until the beginning of the 1990s, the number of newly built social and subsidized dwellings has consistently outstripped the number of new non-subsidized dwellings (Van Weesep and Van Kempen 1993). This is also the case in urban renewal areas in large Dutch cities. Generally, dwellings were renovated within the social rented sector. When demolition was considered necessary, the new dwellings replacing the demolished units were again in the social rented sector. In this way, the population of the area was not forced to move away. This policy of 'building for the neighbourhood' was especially popular in the 1970s.

Circumstances changed drastically in the 1990s as the field of housing was feeling the impact of a retreating government. In 1989, when the Secretary of State for Housing published his White Paper 'Housing in the Nineties' (Ministerie van VROM 1989), the Dutch started to pursue a market-oriented housing policy. Basically, it implied that the social rented sector should provide shelter for households with a low to modal income. The number of newly built non-subsidized dwellings was slightly larger than the number of new subsidized dwellings in 1993, but by 1994 the gap had widened significantly (38,000 subsidized, 49,000 non-subsidized; Directoraat-Generaal 1995). In 1997, only 17 per cent of the 92,000 new dwellings built that year were in the inexpensive rented sector (Directoraat-Generaal 1998). This is clearly a direct effect of the retreating welfare state.

Another important element of Dutch housing policy is the provision of demand-side housing subsidies. In addition to the enormous brick-and-mortar subsidies that had been extended since the end of the Second World War, the government introduced a system of individual housing allowances in the 1970s as part of the expansion of the welfare state (Dieleman 1994). This system was supposed to give households with low incomes the opportunity to move into dwellings that were new, of good quality, and (consequently) relatively expensive. During the second half of the 1980s, rents rose sharply while incomes remained stable, causing the numbers of housing allowance recipients to swell enormously. In 1979, only 395,000 households had received an individual housing allowance; ten years later, this number had risen to 918,000. After 1992, the number of households receiving this type of subsidy decreased by a few thousand per year, but since 1995 the numbers have again been increasing. At the last count, in 1999, more than 1 million households were eligible for this type of subsidy. But the increasing number of people with an individual housing allowance does not tell the whole story. In fact, housing costs are rising for everyone: tenants as well as owner-occupiers, subsidy recipients as well as those without any subsidy. For all tenants, the rent as a proportion of income increased from 18 per cent in 1986 to more than 24 per cent in 1998 (Ministerie van VROM 1998).

A new policy of urban restructuring has been in force since 1997. Building more expensive dwellings in predominantly low-rent neighbourhoods is one of its main objectives. The underlying idea is that restructuring is needed there because the concentrations of low-income households are too large. Demolition and upgrading of the existing stock, selling off rented dwellings, and building new housing are ways to diversify the population of these areas. At the same time, these measures should improve the quality of the local housing stock (Ministerie van VROM 1997).

The Social Rented Sector in the Netherlands

The social rented sector in the Netherlands is huge. It comprises 36 per cent of the country's total housing stock; in cities like Amsterdam and Rotterdam, more than 60 per cent of the stock belongs to this sector. In contrast, the private rental sector is relatively small (13 per cent of the total stock) and has been declining since the Second World War. In almost all western European welfare states, the owner-occupied sector has expanded. As of 1999, more than half of the total housing stock in the Netherlands is owner-occupied. This is clearly an effect of a changing housing policy. It is consistent with the deliberate retreat of the welfare state and the simultaneous promotion of the role of the market in housing production since the end of the 1980s (Ministerie van VROM 1989; see also Van Kempen and Priemus 1999).

The social rented sector has a mixed tenant profile. It is mixed not only according to age, household situation, and social status, but also in respect to income. The Dutch social rented sector accommodates many households with relatively high incomes, both young and old (Dieleman 1994; Van Kempen,

Table 5.1. Percentage of each income decile living in the social rented sector in the Netherlands (1981 and 1994)

Decile	1981	1994
1 (lowest)	40.2	48.9
2	49.9	65.9
3	49.4	60.8
4	49.6	57.1
5	48.2	47.9
6	44.3	38.7
7	39.3	32.6
8	34.2	26.2
9	26.9	18.4
10 (highest)	17.2	10.1

Source: Van Kempen, Schutjens, and Van Weesep (2000); Housing Demand Surveys (selected years).

Schutjens, and Van Weesep 2000). Because of tenant protection laws, higher-income households have the opportunity to remain in an inexpensive dwelling.

Since the beginning of the 1980s, the percentage of higher-income house-holds in social rented dwellings has been declining. Meanwhile, an increasing number of lower-income households have been accommodated in the social rented sector (Table 5.1). The retreating welfare state—specifically, the change in housing policy outlined in the memorandum 'Housing in the Nineties'—has already begun to have an effect. It is clear that income is playing a larger role in the housing market, determining where people can and cannot live. Declining opportunities are the result, especially for lower-income households.

Economic Development in the Netherlands

Before discussing the spatial patterns within Dutch cities, some background information on economic and demographic developments is appropriate.

For the first two decades after the Second World War, the Dutch economy had a relatively high proportion of labour-intensive industries compared to other western European countries. Therefore, the expanding economy and a consequent shortage of labour in the 1960s demanded a relatively large number of new workers. Labour migration was considered necessary. In those years, the government and employers alike thought the additional labour would be needed only temporarily. The concept of the 'guest worker' was invented. The migrants were given work permits and housing permits for only a year or a few years at most.

The situation changed drastically in the 1970s, and the impact of these changes continued to be felt in the 1980s. Demand for labour decreased as the economy went into recession. The number of jobs dwindled, especially in manufacturing and construction, but also in agriculture and the service sector. Increasingly, routine manual tasks were mechanized. When the demand for low-skilled labour fell, Elfring and Kloosterman (1989) reported that the manufacturing sector in the Netherlands shed 100,000 jobs between 1979 and 1986. Many former guest workers lost their jobs. In the same period, however, the service sector expanded by over 500,000 jobs. Specific tertiary industries, such as producer services, showed an increase in high-wage positions. These new jobs tended to be concentrated in the largest cities. Elfring and Kloosterman (1989) also noted a relative decline in intermediate-level employment in manufacturing in the Netherlands. In the service sector, low-paying occupations grew vigorously, especially in the cities of Amsterdam and Rotterdam (Kloosterman 1996). This did not mean that people who lost their job in manufacturing could easily transfer to the service sector: the workers sought in the service sector are not necessarily of the same calibre as the redundant industrial workers. The job descriptions differ and other skills are required (Dijst and Van Kempen 1991).

The service sector is not homogeneous. One part consists of lower-level jobs such as cleaning, security, and catering. The increase in these types of jobs leads to a rising employment rate among low-educated men and women. However, many of these newly created positions are 'dead-end' jobs—low wages, no contracts, no career opportunities, and no collective bargaining agreements. Another part of the service sector consists of specialized jobs in financial, services, insurance, real estate, and banking, requiring a high level of education. Both segments of the service sector are expanding in the Netherlands. This bifurcation may lead to an increasing income polarization (Harrison and Bluestone 1988; Kloosterman 1996).

In 1994, almost 10 per cent of the Dutch labour force (around 486,000 individuals) were unemployed. By 1999, this figure had declined to less than 3 per cent. The new millennium started with less than 200,000 unemployed in the Netherlands, which is as low as the number in 1980. The famous Dutch 'polder model' seems to play an important role in that respect. Basically, the 'polder model' is a set of arrangements and agreements between government, employers' organizations, and trade unions. The most important agreement is that trade unions will not demand high wage increases, thus facilitating the creation of more jobs. These agreements were made in 1982 at the Wassenaar Conference.[1]

Some groups did not profit significantly from the economic upturn. Unemployment is still high among immigrants, such as the former guest workers and those from the former colonies of Surinam and the Dutch Antilles. Plummeting industrial employment can be seen as the main reason for rising unemployment among these groups at the beginning of the 1970s (Dieleman 1993). A complex set of interacting factors was responsible for the continuous high rates of unemployment. This includes economic and demographic developments, the lack of qualifications of the immigrants themselves, their job search strategies, and discrimination on the part of employers (see Tesser 1993).

On the other hand, it is clear that some people did profit significantly from economic restructuring. In particular those with a university degree in computer science or management had no trouble finding a job with a good salary. Economic development in the Netherlands clearly coincides with diminished equity (Van Weesep 1996), and the state is not very eager to counteract that tendency.

Demographic and Socio-cultural Developments in the Netherlands

The total population of the Netherlands reached 16 million in 2000. By 2005, the Netherlands will probably have a total of 16.5 million inhabitants (Direc-toraat-Generaal 1995). In 1982, there were only 5 million households in the country. By 1995, this number had increased to almost 6.5 million. According to the latest forecasts (middle variant), the number of households will have increased to over 7.3 million in 2010.

One of the crucial qualitative changes in the demography of the Netherlands is its increasingly multicultural character. The growth of the ethnic population is an important dimension of the increasingly pluralistic Dutch society. The colonial legacy, as well as international labour migration, have made the country's population increasingly diverse. During the 1950s, many Dutch citizens of mixed ethnic stock were repatriated from Indonesia, accompanied by some 20,000 ethnic Moluccans. The economic boom of the 1960s prompted labour immigration, first from countries like Spain and Italy and later from more remote countries like Morocco and Turkey, where the labour pool was even larger than in the northern Mediterranean countries. In the mid 1970s, a relatively high number of people from Surinam, then still a Dutch colony, came to the Netherlands.

Legal labour migration to the Netherlands virtually came to a halt by the end of the 1970s, in the wake of the economic recession (Blauw 1991). Official recruitment in Mediterranean countries had already ended by 1976. This did not mean that the number of Mediterraneans in the Netherlands stabilized or declined. From the beginning of the 1980s, family reunification and a relatively high fertility rate were responsible for the continual growth of the number of Turks and Moroccans in the Netherlands. Many northern Mediterraneans, such as Spaniards and Italians, returned to their respective mother countries in the 1970s and 1980s. This probably was due to the more promising economic development in these countries compared to those such as Turkey and Morocco.

Table 5.2. Minority ethnic groups[a] in the four largest Dutch cities and in the Netherlands (percentages of total population of the cities, January 1998[b])

Ethnic group	Amsterdam	Rotterdam	The Hague	Utrecht	Netherlands
Turks	4.4	6.4	5.5	4.5	1.8
Moroccans	7.1	4.7	4.2	8.2	1.5
Surinamese	9.8	8.2	9.3	2.9	1.8
Other[c]	4.8	7.4	4.1	3.5	1.7
Total (%)	26.1	26.7	23.1	18.8	6.8
Total population	718,175	590,573	442,674	232,737	15,567,000

[a] People belonging to minority ethnic groups are those born in specified countries outside the Netherlands (see below) or who have at least one parent who was born in one of these countries.
[b] Figures for the Netherlands as a whole are for 1997.
[c] Greeks, Italians, persons from the former Yugoslavia, Cape Verdians, Portuguese, Spaniards, Tunisians, and refugees (comprising Vietnamese, Iraquis, Iranians, Somalians, Ethiopians). For Rotterdam and the Netherlands as a whole, refugees are not included in the figure.
Source: CBS (1998); Verweij *et al.* (1999).

Out of a total of 15.6 million inhabitants in the Netherlands in 1997, there were 280,000 Turks and 233,000 Moroccans (defined as such according to an individual's country of birth or the country of birth of one of the parents). Compared to these figures, the number of persons from former Yugoslavia (60,800), Italians (32,000), and Spaniards (29,000) is still relatively small (CBS 1998). Those of Surinamese ethnic origin, however, outnumber Turks and Moroccans: 287,000 Surinamese live in the Netherlands, almost a quarter of them in Amsterdam. Most Surinamese in the Netherlands are Dutch citizens. Moroccans outnumber Turks in Amsterdam and Utrecht. Both Rotterdam and The Hague have more Turks than Moroccans (Table 5.2). In the cities, minority ethnic groups make a far larger share of the total population than they do in the Netherlands as a whole. Later in this chapter their concentration patterns within the cities are described.

The Randstad

Within the Netherlands, differentiation is usually made between the urbanized western part of the country and the less urbanized regions in the east, north, and south. Within the western part, the Randstad has long been a focal point for policy but also an object of study in the social and geographical sciences. This horseshoe-shaped polynuclear urban region covers an area of roughly 80 square kilometres and houses about 6.5 million inhabitants.

After the Second World War, the Randstad became a problematic area. It was said to be too congested, having attracted too many companies and too many people, sometimes at the expense of the other parts of the country. And it was said to pose a threat to the Green Heart, a rural area in the middle of the

Randstad. Several measures have been taken to spread more evenly the country's economic growth and population. One of the main measures was the growth centre policy. During the 1960s and early 1970s, this policy channelled the population overspill from the major cities to some new towns. At the same time, the growth of other towns and villages was restricted by planning legislation.

Since the 1980s, the Randstad has no longer been seen as a problematic area; rather, it is said to be the engine of the Dutch economy. Two sites within the Randstad—Schiphol airport near Amsterdam and the port of Rotterdam— were labelled as the economic 'main ports' of the country. Indeed, they account for a large share of the country's economic growth in terms of output as well as labour (Ministerie van VROM 1990). Rotterdam is still the largest port in the world in terms of throughput. Almost 300,000 jobs are affiliated with the port, which amounts to 6 per cent of all jobs in the country (Kreukels and Wever 1996). Dutch planning policy in the 1980s increasingly sought to guide urban development towards locations within the existing cities. More recently, development has been steered to new areas adjacent to these cities. The four largest cities in the Netherlands are located in the Randstad. Of the 'big four', Amsterdam (the capital) is the largest (currently 720,000 inhabitants), followed by Rotterdam (595,800 inhabitants), The Hague (the seat of government, 444,300 inhabitants), and Utrecht (234,300 inhabitants).

As pointed out above, a considerable, though declining, number of higher-income households live in social rented dwellings, indicating that this is a mixed-income sector. In fact, their presence in this sector is even more pronounced in the cities (Table 5.3). This is largely due to the structure of the housing stock. In the cities, more than half of the stock consists of

Table 5.3. Percentage of each income decile living in the social rented sector for the four largest cities in the Netherlands (1981 and 1994)

Decile	1981	1994
1 (lowest)	43.5	50.1
2	51.6	68.5
3	48.4	69.1
4	50.4	64.0
5	48.9	54.9
6	44.9	49.0
7	43.7	51.1
8	45.4	44.9
9	37.6	35.4
10 (highest)	27.9	21.8

Source: Van Kempen, Schutjens, and Van Weesep (2000); Housing Demand Surveys (selected years).

low-rent dwellings, compared to just 22 per cent in the rest of the country. Also, owner-occupied dwellings make up less than 20 per cent of the dwelling stock in the cities, compared to over 50 per cent in the rest of the country. This means that many middle-income and even some higher-income households who want to live in the city are more or less forced into the (social) rented sector.

Both in the cities and in the country as a whole, the share of higher-income households living in the social rented sector declined throughout the 1980s and the first half of the 1990s. Apparently, more higher-income households were able to move from the rented to the owner-occupied sector. This is partly due to their rising incomes. But the increasing number of owner-occupied dwellings in the housing stock of the cities and their metropolitan areas is probably a more influential factor. The changing government policy, which promotes the private (owner-occupied) sector and places less emphasis on building in the (inexpensive) social rented sector (see earlier in this chapter), has obvious effects.

Spatial Segregation by Income in Dutch Large Cities

The data presented in the previous sections suggest at least two possible spatial outcomes. First, since not all low-rent dwellings in the cities are inhabited by low-income households, we might expect that spatial segregation along the lines of income will not be as high as it is in many other cities of the western world. In other words, we expect low-rent neighbourhoods to not only accommodate low-income households but also to be inhabited by higher-income households as well. Second, as of the mid 1980s, we might expect to see an increasing degree of spatial segregation. That expectation is based on the declining role of welfare state provisions and the ensuing moves of persons with relatively higher incomes. Under those circumstances, more and more households will have to live in dwellings that match their income level. In other words, in neighbourhoods that are characterized by low-rent dwellings, we may expect to find more and more low-income households, while other areas will have increasing numbers of high-income households.

As Musterd and Ostendorf (1997) point out, it is not only low-income households who live in neighbourhoods with low-rent housing. In all kinds of low-rent neighbourhoods (pre-war, early post-war, urban renewal areas), the population is characterized by a mix of income groups. Segregation indices (SI: lowest-income quintile v. the rest, using grids of 500 square metres as measurement areas) indicate a clear income mix in the cities of Amstredam (SI = 18.9 in 1996) and Utrecht (SI = 20.3). Figures for Rotterdam (SI = 23.6) and The Hague (27.1) are slightly higher (CBS 1999). On the other hand, as Engbersen and Snel (1996) indicate, we can also find urban neighbourhoods where a majority of the population is dependent on some form of welfare bene-fit. Although Engbersen and Snel argue that welfare reliance is not automati-cally related to poverty and marginalization, it is clear from their data that some neighbourhoods are inhabited by a majority of people who are relatively poor. (In these figures, the elderly, who sometimes make up more than 20 per cent of the population of the area, are not taken into account.)

Are those neighbourhoods that are characterized by a majority of low-rent dwellings increasingly inhabited by low-income households? Engbersen and Snel (1996) found that the number of neighbourhoods with a majority of welfare recipients decreased between 1989 and 1994, but they also found an increasing segregation of welfare recipients in the same period, resulting in an increasing concentration in some low-rent areas. While these findings seem to be contradictory, they can be explained by the fact that the total number of welfare recipients fell somewhat in this period (probably as a conse-quence of an expanding economy and stricter enforcement of welfare payment rules).

Dual Cities in the Netherlands?

The concept of the 'dual city' has been criticized for various reasons. It is a muddy concept: it is either incorrect or woefully incomplete, and its use does more political harm than good (Marcuse 1989).[2] According to Marcuse, there are at least seven things wrong with it. Eva van Kempen (1994) brings up some other drawbacks to add to this list. She notes that it is a problem of scale (do we have to look at the central city or at the level of the conurbation?); it is a ques-tion of dynamics (is it a static or dynamic concept?); and it is a problem of sev-eral presuppositions. One of the basic presuppositions is the direct relation between the income one earns and the place where one lives. This relation is clearer in some countries than in others.

In the Netherlands, the relation between income and the location of the home is rather weak. Moreover, although impoverished enclaves do exist in Dutch cities, they are relatively small and they never wholly lack social and commercial services. Dutch cities do not have such sharp contrasts between poor and rich areas as is found in American cities (between the ghettos and slums on the one hand and areas like New York's Upper East Side on the other; see, e.g., Fainstein 1996). Therefore, we conclude that the concept of the dual city is very difficult to apply to the Dutch situation. We should bear in mind the statement Fainstein, Gordon, and Harloe made in 1992 (p. 13): 'If the concept of "dual" or "polarized" city is of any real utility, it can serve only as a hypoth-esis, the prelude to empirical analysis, rather than as a conclusion' (see also Hamnett 1996; Kloosterman 1996). This may mean that we will never find a 'real' dual, quartered, or polarized city in the real world, not in the Netherlands, and not anywhere else.

Ethnic Segregation and Concentration in
Large Dutch Cities

As mentioned earlier in this chapter, many former immigrants have low incomes, and they are disproportionately affected by unemployment, and this is especially true of Turks and Moroccans. For this reason, we focus our analysis of ethnic spatial segregation in Dutch cities on these two minority ethnic groups. Southern Europeans (i.e., Spaniards, Italians, Greeks, Portuguese, and people from former Yugoslavia) and Surinamese are included in the discussion for the sake of comparison.

Does spatial segregation along ethnic lines exist in Dutch cities? If so, how have the spatial patterns developed[3] since the beginning of the 1980s? Table 5.4 shows the segregation index (SI)[4] for the selected groups. If this index has a value of 100, there is complete segregation. This means that all the members of that particular group reside in areas in which no other groups live. A few conclusions may be drawn from this table. First, the SI values are relatively low, especially when compared to the values of the indices for blacks in the United States (see, e.g., Clark 1986). However, it is more appropriate to compare the Netherlands with other European countries. For Turks and Moroccans, the SI is roughly comparable to that of Turks and Moroccans in, for example, Brussels, and higher than in the German cities of Frankfurt and Düsseldorf (Breebaart, Musterd, and Ostendorf 1996; Kesteloot, De Decker, and Manço 1997).

Second, segregation increased for Turks and Moroccans between 1983 and 1993, except in The Hague. This means that the groups tend to concentrate more in some urban areas than previously. Apparently, they have not been able to disperse over the city in the decade between 1983 and 1993. We return to this point below. Between 1993 and 1998, however, the figures for Turks and Moroccans declined (slightly) in three of the four cities; Amsterdam was the exception.

Third, there are considerable differences between cities. This may be a result of the different sizes of the neighbourhoods in the respective cities, although this factor certainly does not explain all the differences. For example, the neighbourhoods in Utrecht are on average much smaller than those in Amsterdam and Rotterdam. This might lead to higher SI values in Utrecht (see Woods 1976). It is clear from Table 5.4 that this is not necessarily the case, however.

Fourth, southern Europeans have low degrees of segregation compared to Turks and Moroccans. Apparently they have been able to find homes in many different neighbourhoods. This is probably connected with their overall better economic position in Dutch society. According to the literature, the generally lower degree of segregation found among the Surinamese, compared to Turks and Moroccans, is due to a combination of factors: their willingness

Table 5.4. Segregation index (SI) for different ethnic groups[a] in the four largest cities of the Netherlands (1983, 1993, and 1998)

Ethnic group (date)	Amsterdam	Rotterdam	The Hague	Utrecht
Moroccans (1983)	35.3	49.5	57.3	40.3
Moroccans (1993)[b]	38.8	49.9	53.2	42.7
Moroccans (1998)	41.2	44.2	48.6	44.5
Turks (1983)	35.7	50.7	65.1	35.7
Turks (1993)[b]	40.9	53.8	60.4	44.5
Turks (1998)	42.3	49.9	53.0	43.1
Southern Europeans (1995)[c]	15.9	25.2	16.7	20.4
Surinamese (1995)	34.8	28.6	40.2	24.0
Surinamese (1998)	34.2	26.2	38.7	23.4

[a] Individuals belong to one of these groups if they or one of their parents was not born in the Netherlands.
[b] Data for The Hague refer to 1992.
[c] Data for Amsterdam refer to 1994 and for The Hague to 1992.

Source: Municipal Statistical Offices; Tesser *et al.* (1995); Bolt and Van Kempen (2000).

to pay more for housing; a willingness to accept rent subsidies more readily; and, on average, a better standing *vis-à-vis* the labour market (see Van Kempen 1992).

An Explanation of the Patterns

To understand the development through time and the differences between Dutch cities, we have to look more closely at the changing pattern of spatial concentration. Here, the focus is on Turks and Moroccans. Which types of neighbourhood are the main concentration areas[5] for Turks and Moroccans? In The Hague and Rotterdam, Turks and Moroccans are relatively overrepresented in 19th-century neighbourhoods, and in areas built in the first decades of the 20th century. The low number of Turks and Moroccans in the early post-Second World War areas of Rotterdam and The Hague explains a large part of the higher segregation indices in these cities. They concentrate in a few, relatively older parts of the city and hardly penetrate into the early post-war areas, at least not before the second half of the 1990s.

In all Dutch cities, the dwellings dating from the 19th and early 20th century often belong to the worst of the urban housing stock, and as a consequence they have relatively low rents. Many dwellings are small (only one or two rooms) and are owned by private landlords. Various types of households live in these areas, but not all have low incomes. They are also attractive neighbourhoods for young starters in the urban housing market. Most of these neighbourhoods are now undergoing urban renewal. In the 1970s and 1980s, many demolished dwellings were replaced by new, somewhat more expensive social housing units or were renovated. The early post-war neighbourhoods were built between 1945 and 1959. The predominantly three- and four-room dwellings were initially meant for Dutch family households. Although the dwellings generally have a higher quality than the pre-war dwellings and, in any event, have more facilities, their rents are generally low. The increasing segregation found for Turks and Moroccans in Utrecht and Amsterdam (as indicated by the SIs in Table 5.4) can be explained by the increasing concentration of these groups in the early post-war neighbourhoods of these cities.

The decreasing segregation of Turks and Moroccans in the second half of the 1990s is to a large extent the result of an increase of these groups in the early post-war areas. It is not easy to explain why Turks in Rotterdam and The Hague did not penetrate into these areas before. The availability of suitable dwellings in the older areas certainly plays a role. To find an affordable dwelling with four or more rooms, they did not have to move to newer areas in these cities. But also the settlement patterns and preferences of the native population form part of the explanation. Especially in Rotterdam's early post-war areas, people, especially older households, were generally highly satisfied with their housing situation and their neighbourhood. Many have lived there for decades. By the end of the 1990s, the ageing Dutch population was gradually declining. As elderly people move to special homes for the elderly or die, their dwellings become available. Because these dwellings are suitable for (small) families, part of the new population comprises Turkish and Moroccan households. It remains unclear if forms of discrimination also play a role in the explanation.

In Utrecht, the early post-war neighbourhoods have been the most important concentration areas for both immigrant groups, but especially for Moroccans, for a much longer time. Although Turks and Moroccans in Amsterdam are still overrepresented in the neighbourhoods built in the early decades of the 20th century, the early post-war areas are the main growth areas for these groups.

From the descriptions above it becomes clear where Turks and Moroccans do not live. The neighbourhoods built after 1960 play almost no role in housing these former guest worker groups. Some of these newer areas do contain significant numbers of social housing, but the prices are generally higher. The higher prices of the dwellings in these areas, compared to other (older) areas, probably play a significant role. This is even true of the areas built in the 1960s, which are partly characterized by large, often monotonous high-rise complexes.[6] Areas built in the 1970s are often characterized by single-family houses, which are often too expensive for low-income non-indigenous households. Recently built dwellings are also too expensive. Since about 1990, even dwellings built in the social rented sector are considered to be too expensive for households with structurally low incomes.

From the above data, it is not yet clear how we should evaluate the patterns. We should be prudent in interpreting the spatial patterns in terms of ghetto-like developments. Engbersen and Snel (1996) conclude that the Dutch aspect of advanced marginality differs in many respects from the situation in jobless areas, as described by Wilson (1987), or the hyperghetto described by Wacquant (Chapter 11). Dutch cities do not have neighbourhoods that are only inhabited by the long-term unemployed, welfare recipients, poor households, and the elderly. In the Dutch situation, it is more appropriate to speak of a residential mix, albeit one with an increasing concentration of low-income and minority ethnic households in low-rent areas and some enclave formation by higher-income households.

Conclusions

Despite the high number of affordable social rented dwellings in many urban neighbourhoods, a social and ethnic mix is common in Dutch urban neighbourhoods and socially or ethnically homogeneous areas are not. The state has played a significant role in the development of this pattern. One way it has affected the pattern is through income policy. For a long period after the Second World War, the promotion of income equality has been high on the political agenda. Although this did not prevent high and even increasing income differences between various categories (e.g., the employed and the unemployed), it does mean that most households have experienced a general rise in purchasing power. Compared to other countries, welfare benefits are relatively high in the Netherlands. Moreover, the role of the state in housing has been immense since the Second World War. The large number of affordable social rented dwellings in the Netherlands as a whole, but specifically in the urban areas, and the existence of individual rent allowances are important facets of this policy. Extensive spatial segregation has also been prevented by the fact that middle- and higher-income households were willing—and allowed—to live in the social rented housing areas. The attractiveness of social rented dwellings, but also the lack of alternatives, were important factors in this pattern.

But what about the future? Will cities become more partitioned in the Netherlands? Future developments are important but not always easy to predict. Economic developments may change abruptly (as after the 1973 oil shock). Even demographic developments may suddenly take unexpected turns (e.g., as a result of increasing immigration of refugees). On the other hand, the present situation will continue to play a role in the future. Within ten or twenty years, we will not have a totally new division of urban space; the future is rooted in the cities' history in many ways.

As Van Weesep (1996: 11) states: 'The spatial effects of polarization can only be controlled as long as the equity policies of the waning welfare states remain on the books'. This will probably not happen. Increasingly, low-income households will be relegated to low-rent neighbourhoods because of a further retreat of the welfare state. There are no indications that this retreating tendency will change. The equitable society that has been pursued by public policy in the Netherlands has been crucial in buffering the negative effects of economic hardship. But at the moment it is clear that households that depend on transfer payments, such as welfare, will have a hard time in the next decade. The same applies to those receiving a minimum wage, their incomes will decline, at least relatively. Those dependent on the state and on social solidarity will also experience difficulties in the near future. This specifically holds for the earlier immigrants, such as the Turks and Moroccans, because they are among the hardest hit by unemployment. Declining income means a declining number of choices in the housing market.

Also in the field of housing, the positive influence of the state is declining. Although the individual rent subsidy system will remain in place, further restrictions are likely and will promote spatial segregation. The share of subsidized, and therefore affordable, dwellings in construction programmes will continue to dwindle. Those dwellings that are constructed in the social rented sector are far more expensive than social rented dwellings built previously. In fact, this means that newly built dwellings will not be accessible to households with a minimum income or to welfare recipients, not even with the help of a rent subsidy. Moreover, this means that those households are relegated to the existing stock in older neighbourhoods, like those built between the two World Wars and those built in the period just after the Second World War (1945–60). This obviously will foster the spatial concentration of low-income households. The concentration process will be reinforced by the outflow of higher-income households from these areas to the newly created, attractive areas with single-family owner-occupied units.

There is one tendency in the field of housing provision that might, at least at first sight, run counter to the increasing process of concentration. In many cities, local governments plan to build more expensive dwellings in low-rent areas, partly as a result of a new national policy of urban restructuring that was initiated in 1997 (some cities had applied this policy years before). In this way, they hope to keep higher-income households who move from low-rent dwellings to more expensive alternatives within the same neighbourhood and even attract new higher-income households to those areas. A further concentration of low-income households would then be inhibited. However, this implies that these low-income households will have to look for a home in other places. This may very well result in an increasing concentration in other neighbourhoods, where new developments have not (yet) taken place.

The retreating welfare state thus may very well prove to be the most influential factor in explaining future processes of segregation and concentration in Dutch cities. But other factors should not be forgotten. They also work in the direction of increasing segregation and concentration. It is expected that, despite a generally expanding economy, in the next decade the employment opportunities for people with a low level of education will decline further. The growth will be in jobs for which people with an intermediate and higher level of education ('urban professionals') are required. This means that many will not be able to take advantage of the employment growth. Inequality will increase, especially between those households with no earner (and state dependency) and those households with two earners (both with a relatively high income).

Moreover, the number of new entrants and people seeking to re-enter the labour market will continue to expand (SCP 1994). The imbalance between supply and demand will result in persistent structural unemployment. Immigrants—and among them especially Turks and Moroccans—will probably suffer most from these developments. In the Netherlands, of all the Turks and Moroccans with a job, no less than 85 per cent do unskilled or low-skilled work (Penninx 1989). More than 75 per cent of the Turks with a job perform elementary tasks, compared to less than a quarter of the Dutch (Tesser 1993). There are no indications that this will change very rapidly. Many of these low-skilled immigrants will have to live on state support. Increased partitioning is the likely social and spatial consequence of a retreating welfare state.

Notes

1. It is important to realize that this low number of the (officially) unemployed masks a large number of individuals who make use of a programme (called WAO) targeted to those who are either physically or mentally disabled and are unable to work. Over 900,000 (!) people derive an income from WAO: most do not have a job, but some work part-time. The remuneration from WAO is generally higher than that of social security benefits, because (at least temporarily), it is linked to the recipient's earnings in the previous job.
2. (1) it is a vague and shapeless metaphor; (2) it suggests a continuum along a single axis (consumption) and does not indicate structural dividing lines; (3) it is ahistorical; (4) it ignores the fact that most of the inhabitants in developed economies are neither very rich nor very poor; (5) it is based on the division of society in an 'underclass' and an 'overclass'; (6) it supports the idea that redistribution is the solution, rather than changes in the causes of the distribution; (7) it may lead to wrong kinds of policies.
3. Earlier spatial patterns are not considered here, because in previous periods the pattern was strongly influenced by the 'guest worker' status of the Turks and Moroccans. This meant that they lived in areas with many boarding houses, barracks, and (old) dwellings with very low rents. They lived there because they wanted to send as much money as possible to their mother countries and did not want to spend much of their income on rent.
4. The segregation index is calculated on the basis of neighbourhoods in the cities. Within a city the size of the neighbourhoods varies. Also between the cities, the average size of the areas varies, which means that comparisons between cities require great care. The average number of inhabitants of neighbourhoods used in the analysis of Amsterdam and Rotterdam is around 8,500. For Utrecht, the average number is only 2,400.

5. If an area (neighbourhood) shows an overrepresentation of a certain group, we speak of a 'concentration area' for that group (Van Amersfoort 1980). The overrepresentation is measured in comparison with the city as a whole: when, for example, the population of the city as a whole comprises 5 per cent Chinese, a neighbourhood with 10 per cent Chinese is considered as a concentration area (of course, it is a subjective matter if the urban average or, for example, twice this average, is taken as the breaking point). This definition implies that a concentration area may also house many members of other groups. For instance, a single neighbourhood may show an overrepresentation of Turks, as well as Moroccans, Surinamese, elderly, unemployed, etc.

6. An infamous area built in the 1960s is the Bijlmermeer in Amsterdam. High-rise dwellings predominate here. Although this area houses a high number of (legal and illegal) immigrants from all over the world, Surinamese, Antilleans, and migrants from different countries in Africa are the main non-native groups. Very few Turks and Moroccans live here. This probably has to do with the high price of housing and the relatively long distance to the older parts of the city.

References

BLAUW, W. (1991). 'Housing segregation for different population groups in the Netherlands', in E. D. Huttman (ed.), *Urban Housing Segregation of Minorities in Western Europe and the United States*, 43–62. Durham/London: Duke University Press.

BOLT, G., and VAN KEMPEN, R. (2000). 'Concentratie en segregatie in Nederlandse steden', in R. van Kempen (ed.), *Segregatie, mogelijke effecten en beleid*, 11–37. The Hague: Rijksplanologische Dienst, Ministerie van VROM.

BREEBAART, M., MUSTERD, S., and OSTENDORF, W. (1996). *Etnische segregatie en beleid; een internationale vergelijking*. Amsterdam: Amsterdam Study Centre for the Metropolitan Environment.

CBS (Centraal Bureau voor de Statistiek) (1998). *Allochtonen in Nederland 1998*. Voorburg: CBS.

——(1999). *Jaarboek welvaartsdeling*. Voorburg: CBS.

——(1992). *Nederland in drievoud; een scenariostudie van de Nederlandse economie, 1990–2015*. The Hague: SDU uitgeverij.

CLARK, W. A. V. (1986). 'Residential segregation in American cities'. *Population Research and Policy Review*, 5: 95–127.

DIELEMAN, F. M. (1993). 'Multicultural Holland: myth or reality?', in R. King (ed.), *Mass Migration in Europe: The Legacy and the Future*, 118–35. London: Belhaven.

——and KLOOSTERMAN, R. C. (1997). *Room to Manoeuvre; Governance, Post-industrial Economy, Housing Provision in Rotterdam*. Unpublished paper.

——and VAN KEMPEN, R. (1994). 'The mismatch of housing costs and income in Dutch housing'. *Netherlands Journal of Housing and the Built Environment*, 9: 159–72.

DIJST, M. J., and VAN KEMPEN, R. (1991). 'Minority business and the hidden dimension: the influence of urban contexts on the development of ethnic enterprise'. *Tijdschrift voor Economische en Sociale Geografie*, 82: 128–38.

DIRECTORAAT-GENERAAL VAN DE VOLKSHUISVESTING (1995). *Volkshuisvesting in cijfers 1995*. The Hague: Ministerie van VROM.

——(1998). *Volkshuisvesting in cijfers 1998*. The Hague: Ministerie van VROM.

ELFRING, T., and KLOOSTERMAN, R. C. (1989). *De Nederlandse 'Job Machine'; de snelle expansie van laagbetaald werk in de dienstensector, 1979–1986*. Amsterdam: Economisch Geografisch Instituut, Universiteit van Amsterdam.

ENGBERSEN, G., and GABRIËLS, R. (1995). *Sferen van integratie: naar een gedifferentieerd allochtonen-beleid*. Meppel: Boom.

——and SNEL, E. (1996). 'The rise of social security neighborhoods in the Netherlands'. Paper presented at the conference: *Globalization and the New Inequality*, Utrecht, 20–21 November.

FAINSTEIN, S. (1996). *The Egalitarian City: Images of Amsterdam*. Amsterdam: Amsterdam Study Centre for the Metropolitan Environment.

——GORDON, I., and HARLOE, M. (eds.) (1992). *Divided Cities: New York and London in the Contemporary World*. Oxford: Blackwell.

HAMNETT, C. (1996). 'Social polarisation, economic restructuring and welfare state regimes'. *Urban Studies*, 33: 1407–30.

HARRISON, B., and BLUESTONE, B. (1988). *The Great U-turn: Corporate Restructuring and the Polarizing of America*. New York: Basic Books.

KESTELOOT, C., DE DECKER, P., and MANÇO, A. (1997). 'Turks and housing in Belgium, with special reference to Brussels, Ghent and Visé', in A. Ş. Özüekren and R. van Kempen (eds.), *Turks in European Cities: Housing and Urban Segregation*, 67–97. Utrecht: European Research Centre on Migration and Ethnic Relations.

KLOOSTERMAN, R. (1996). 'Double Dutch; an enquiry into trends of polarization in Amsterdam and Rotterdam'. *Regional Studies*, 30: 467–76.

KREUKELS, T., and WEVER, E. (1996). 'Dealing with competition: the port of Rotterdam'. *Tijdschrift voor Economische en Sociale Geografie*, 87: 293–309.

LUNDQVIST, L. J. (1992). *Dislodging the Welfare State? Housing and Privatization in Four European Nations*. Delft: Delft University Press.

MARCUSE, P. (1989). '"Dual city"; a muddy metaphor for a quartered city'. *International Journal of Urban and Regional Research*, 13: 697–908.

MINISTERIE VAN VROM (Volkshuisvesting, Ruimtelijke Ordening en Milieubeheer) (1989). *Volkshuisvesting in de jaren negentig*. The Hague: SDU uitgeverij.

——(1990). *Vierde nota over de ruimtelijke ordening Extra*. The Hague: SDU uitgeverij.

——(1997). *Nota stedelijke vernieuwing*. The Hague: Ministerie van VROM.

——(1998). *Monitoring woonuitgaven*. The Hague: Ministerie van VROM.

MURIE, A. (1994). *Cities and Housing after the Welfare State*. Amsterdam: Amsterdam Study Centre for the Metropolitan Environment.

MUSTERD, S., and OSTENDORF, W. (1997). 'Socio-spatial Segregation in Amsterdam'. Paper presented at: *COST-CIVITAS Conference*, Oslo, 5–7 June.

PENNINX, R. (1989). 'Ethnic groups in the Netherlands; emancipation or minority group formation?', in Ph. J. Muus (ed.), *Migration, Minorities and Policy in the Netherlands: Recent Trends and Developments*, 27–44. Amsterdam: Instituut voor Sociale Geografie, Universiteit van Amsterdam.

SCP (Sociaal en Cultureel Planbureau) (1994). *Sociaal en cultureel rapport 1994*. Rijswijk: SCP.

TESSER, P. T. M. (1993). *Rapportage minderheden 1993*. Rijswijk: Sociaal en Cultureel Planbureau.

TESSER, P. T. M., VAN PRAAG, C. S., VAN DUGTEREN, F. A., HERWEIJER, L. J., and VAN DER WOUDEN, H. C. (1995). *Rapportage minderheden 1995: concentratie en segregatie*. Rijswijk: Sociaal en Cultureel Planbureau.

——VAN DUGTEREN, F. A., and MERENS, J. G. F. (1998). *Rapportage minderheden 1998*. Rijswijk: Sociaal en Cultureel Planbureau.

TRIMP, L. (1994). 'Inkomensverdeling 1993'. *Sociaal-Economische Maandstatistiek*, 12: 13–15. Voorburg: Centraal Bureau voor de Statistiek.

TRIMP, L. (1996). 'Tien jaar koopkrachtveranderingen: 1984–1994'. *Sociaal-Economische Maandstatistiek*, 1: 21–5. Voorburg: Centraal Bureau voor de Statistiek.

TWEEDE KAMER DER STATEN-GENERAAL (1990). *Inkomensbeleid 1990*. The Hague: SDU Uitgeverij.

UITTERHOEVE, W. (ed.) (1990). *De staat van Nederland*. Nijmegen: SUN.

VAN AMERSFOORT, J. M. M. (1980). 'Woonsegregatie, gettovorming en de overheid', in P. W. Blauw and C. Pastor (eds.), *Soort bij soort; beschouwingen over ruimtelijke segregatie als maatschappelijk probleem*, 113–38. Deventer: Van Loghum Slaterus.

VAN KEMPEN, E. (1994). 'The dual city and the poor; social polarisation, social segregation and life chances'. *Urban Studies*, 31: 995–1015.

VAN KEMPEN, R. (1992). *In de klem op de stedelijke woningmarkt? Huishoudens met een laag inkomen in vroeg-naoorlogse en vroeg-20ste-eeuwse wijken in Amsterdam en Rotterdam*. Utrecht: Stedelijke Netwerken.

——and PRIEMUS, H. (1999). 'Undivided cities in the Netherlands: present situation and political rhetoric'. *Housing Studies*, 14: 641–57.

——SCHUTJENS, V. A. J. M., and VAN WEESEP, J. (2000). 'Housing and social fragmentation in the Netherlands'. *Housing Studies*, 15: 505–31.

VAN WEESEP, J. (1996). *Urban Restructuring and Equity*. Stockholm: Nordplan.

——and VAN KEMPEN, R. (1993). 'Low income and housing in the Dutch welfare state', in G. Hallet (ed.), *The New Housing Shortage; Housing Affordability in Europe and the USA*, 179–206. London: Routledge.

VERWEIJ, A. O., LATUHERU, E. J., RODENBURG, A. M., and WEIJERS, Y. M. R. (1999). *Jaarboek 1998 Grote-Stedenbeleid*. Rotterdam: ISEO.

WILSON, W. J. (1987). *The Truly Disadvantaged; The Inner City, the Underclass, and Public Policy*. Chicago: University of Chicago Press.

WINCHESTER, H. P. M., and WHITE, P. E. (1988). 'The location of marginalised groups in the inner city'. *Environment and Planning: D*, 6: 37–54.

WOODS, R. I. (1976). 'Aspects of the scale problem in the calculation of segregation indices: London and Birmingham, 1961 and 1971'. *Tijdschrift voor Economische en Sociale Geografie*, 67: 169–74.

6

The Shifting Meaning of the Black Ghetto in the United States

Peter Marcuse

Introduction

The clearest divisions of urban space in the United States today are at the extremes: the segregation of the poorest, overwhelmingly black, in ghettos, and the self-isolation of the rich, in citadels. Both have changed significantly over time, with the state playing a major role in the form and content of each division. This chapter traces the history of the ghetto in the United States, highlighting its changing character and the influence state policies have had in shaping it.[1]

'Ghetto' has not always meant the same thing in United States history, either to its residents or to those, social scientists and others, writing about it; the term has changed significantly in character and meaning over time. We may distinguish three periods in which both from within and from without it was regarded quite differently, reflecting real changes in its nature and composition:

• A period of *Imposition*, running from the end of the 19th century to the Second World War, including periods of rapid urbanization, during which the black ghetto was essentially seen as 'normal'. It was accepted as inevitable, if not indeed healthy, by much of mainstream social science, condemned but seen as a part of a long-term historical process by more critical writers, including most African-American (Negro, in general usage) commentators, and widely recognized as a fact of life (if not uncritically) and used as a source of solidarity and strength by many of its residents.

In the cities, during this period, while black migrants to the cities clustered together for mutual help, the continued maintenance of black neighbourhoods and the walls separating them from the surrounding neighbourhoods were hardly entirely voluntary. The state, responding to but helping implement this, played a major role in the maintenance of the walls that confined blacks to the pervasive urban ghettos.

• A period of *Confrontation*, running from the beginning of the Second World War through the civil rights movement and the ghetto revolts of the 1960s to the mid 1970s, in which a major effort was made to contest the state structures of segregation, achieve integration of blacks (the preferred usage in this period) economically, socially, politically—and spatially. The goal was opening of the suburbs, with opposition to gilding the ghetto.

In the cities, many of the formal state structures of segregation were dismantled in this period, both through judicial and legislative action, but that state action was limited, and the realities of the segregation of blacks remained obdurate, working both through market and through racist social practices only marginally affected by the new laws and court decisions. Nor was all state support for segregation eliminated.

• A period of *Empowerment*, from the early 1970s on, coming with realization of how intractable structures of segregation are. Efforts at improvement emphasized the solidarity existing in the ghetto, in part derived from structures of partition, and moved from opposition to the gilding of the ghetto to efforts at empowerment of its residents and recognition of its history, traditions, and strengths. A renewed emphasis on an African heritage led to the preferred usage becoming African-American.

It is too early to tell how spatial development in cities will develop in the future. Ghettoized areas may develop as ethnic enclaves did, so that a degree of clustering and solidarity is combined with a general freedom of movement and significant subsequent spatial dispersion. Or the unique history of race and racism in the United States may continue to limit a substantial part of the black population to a structurally maintained ghetto, however empowered. State policies, by and large, are implicitly tending to acceptance of the continued existence of the ghetto, and the goals of desegregation and certainly of integration are playing an increasingly smaller role.

The contrast among black, immigrant, and Jewish areas of spatial concentration is striking: while the black ghetto follows the pattern suggested above, the immigrant enclave is presumed to go from strong concentration to milder concentration, internally and culturally driven, with substantial dispersion, while the Jewish pattern goes from ghettoization to enclave formation to dispersion, again with some remaining spatial concentration, largely internally and culturally driven.

This chapter begins with a brief review of the treatment of the Jewish ghetto in the earliest full discussion of ghettoization in the United States, and then details the history and the meanings assigned to the specifically black ghetto as they have changed over the periods described above. It concludes with a very generalized formulation of the contrast between the three types of spatial partitioning.

Definitions

In this chapter certain terms will be used with very specific meanings (see, e.g., the discussions following the publication of Wacquant 1997):

A *ghetto* is an involuntarily spatially concentrated area used by the dominant society to separate and to limit a particular population group, externally defined as racial or ethnic,[2] and held to be, and treated as, inferior.[3]

An *enclave* is a voluntarily spatially concentrated area in which members of a particular population group, self-defined by ethnicity or religion or otherwise, congregate as a means of protecting and enhancing their economic, social, political, and/or cultural development.

An *area of spatial concentration* is the generic term covering any concentration of members of a particular group, however defined, in space, at a scale larger than a building.

(In many cases areas of spatial concentration share some attributes both of a ghetto and of an enclave.)

Clustering is the generic term for the formation of any area of spatial concentration.

Segregation is the process of formation and maintenance of a ghetto.

Desegregation is the elimination of barriers to free mobility for residents of a ghetto.

Integration is the positive interaction among different groups in residential space.

Further: I use the word 'black' in general here, rather than 'African-American', even though the two terms (as well as 'Negro') arose at different times and have somewhat different social and political implications. While 'African-American' emphasizes a positive ethnic identity linked to a country or continent of origin,[4] and thus establishes a basis for identity and a claim for equality of treatment that has strong positive value, the issue here is rather the relationship with the dominant group(s).[5] For that purpose, colour remains the critical factor. The shift in terminology from Negro to black to African-American is discussed below.

Background: The Ghetto in the Social Science Literature

Two streams of work first brought attention to the issue of the ghetto in the United States. One was the work of social science researchers, largely black, concerned with analysing the position of blacks in American society at the beginning of this century. In that work patterns of residential concentration of blacks were found in many major cities, and their locational pattern described in some detail. The term 'ghetto' was rarely used in the early studies, for instance in W. E. B. DuBois' *The Philadelphia Negro* (1899); its context is the wider experience of blacks in the post-slavery United States in general. The subsequent work in this stream includes specific concerns with the black ghetto that took off with Gunnar Myrdal's *American Dilemma* and runs through Drake and Cayton's *Black Metropolis* (1945), Robert Weaver's *Negro Ghetto* (1948), Charles Abrams' *Forbidden Neighbors* (1955a), the Taeubers' *Negroes in Cities* (1965), Kenneth Clark's *Dark Ghetto* (1965), to Goldsmith and Blakely's *Separate Societies* (1992) and Massey and Denton's *American Apartheid* (1993). This rich body of evidence and analysis will be the main source for our discussion below.

Running parallel to this line of investigation, however, but largely uncon-nected to it (Louis Wirth's *The Ghetto* is not referenced in a single one of the works mentioned above), was the examination in what was to be mainstream sociology of the social nature of spatial patterns of distribution of population groups in large cities. The work of Louis Wirth, in particular, and the publica-tion of his *The Ghetto* in 1928, brought attention to the concept, in the context of the ecological theories of Park and Burgess and the Chicago School. Wirth's picture focuses on the story of the Jewish ghetto, and in broad outlines traces its origins to the expulsion of Jews from Palestine, forcing them to cluster together voluntarily and for self-protection, continues with the imposition of walls and legal separation on Jewish residents in the medieval ghetto, then fol-lows Jewish immigrants to the United States where, free from discrimination, they clustered together shortly after arrival. But then over time they dispersed, to the disappointment of some seeking to preserve Jewish culture and tradi-tion, in part by revitalizing the vestiges of the old settlement left behind in ear-lier migrations. In *The Ghetto*, the black experience played a very subordinate role; Wirth's work focused on the Jewish ghetto, and Park and Burgess, under whose influence he worked, by and large treated the black ghetto as simply another example of the natural clustering of ethnic groups in large cities. In Wirth's words,

. . . these new ghettos [in the United States today] do not need a wall or gates to keep the various species of man apart. Each seeks his own habitat much like the plants and animals in the world of nature; each has its own kind of food, of family life, and of amusement.   (Wirth 1928: 284)

Wirth's account in *The Ghetto* is the beginning of a long line of substantial research concerned with the trajectory of ethnic clustering (enclave formation) originally built on urban ecology approaches but now often quite unrelated to it, such as Harvey Zorbaugh's *The Gold Coast and the Slum* (1929) and includ-ing works as diverse as Gerald Suttles' *The Social Order of the Slum* (1974) Glazer and Moynihan's *Beyond the Melting Pot* (1963), Herbert Gans' work on second-generation immigrants (1996) and Alejandro Portes' detailed current work on immigrant enclaves (1993, 1996). The point here is not to criticize either Wirth or the more sophisticated work that followed his, but rather to highlight how it contrasts with the line of enquiry dealing with the specifically black ghetto in the United States.

Wirth's work projects an interesting view of ghetto formation and evolution. It pictures the evolution of the Jewish ghetto as one moving in the sequence:

Enclave → Ghetto → Enclave

and sees that progression as a 'natural' one, applicable to any ethnic cluster. The argument in this chapter differentiates the black ghetto sharply from this view. The picture painted here is rather of a ghetto, formed deliberately as a result of state action (rather than naturally) in the period of Imposition, moving to an attempt to dissolve the ghetto in the period of Confrontation, that effort largely giving way to the attempt to change the ghetto to an enclave in the period of Empowerment, again with state action as a necessary element in that change. Throughout, the reality suggests a striking difference between the clustering of blacks in the United States and the history of other ethnic clusters here and in other countries. For the black ghetto, the sequence is in the direction (if not yet completed):

Imposed ghetto → Confronted ghetto → Empowered ghetto

We turn then to the history of the forms of spatial concentration of blacks in the United States.[6]

The Immediate Aftermath of Slavery

In the years immediately after slavery, the black population of the United States lived predominantly in the South and on farms; even in 1910, 89 per cent of the black population was Southern and 73 per cent of that was rural. Figure 6.1 shows the figures nationally from 1880 to 1970. The urban pattern varied significantly between North and South. In general, in the urban centres in the South blacks often lived in close proximity to whites, although in much inferior housing. The spatial relations were not that different from the period of slavery: thus servants lived in inferior housing adjacent to the homes of their employers.

If the criterion of urbanity is the mixture of classes and ethnic groups, in some cases including a mixture of blacks and whites, along with dense living and crowded streets and the omnipresence of all manner of business near the homes in every quarter, then the cities of the United States in the years between 1820 and 1870 marked the zenith of our national urbanity . . . Only a primitive specialization in respect to urban land existed, and the neighborhoods and districts of the big cities were highly mixed in their activities, ethnicity and class. (Warner 1972: 62, 82)

It was an unstable pattern, however, as cities grew and industrialization progressed, and did not hold in the North. In New York City, for example,

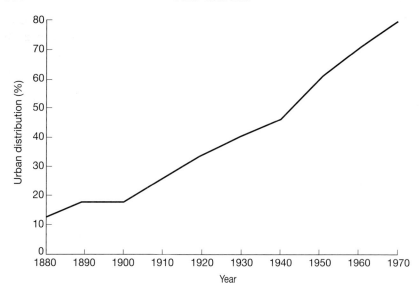

Fig. 6.1. Distribution of the black population in the United States (1880–1970)

Source: US Department of Commerce, Bureau of the Census, 1975

immigrant quarters developed after the Civil War, and by the 1890s became a cause of concern for many involved in New York City's housing and planning issues. By 1911, the New York City Commission on Congestion of Population (the Commission's appointment was a consequence of the work of the private Committee on Congestion of Population, founded by Benjamin Marsh in 1907) proposed a campaign to encourage the immigrants to become farm labourers and to discourage the segregating of immigrants in congested sections of the city.

For immigrants, the concern was that their segregation posed a threat to the surrounding community (see the similar argument made by David Gordon 1984); no similar concerns led to proposals for their integration. In the North, small areas of concentration developed, for example, at the site of the future Pennsylvania Station and in parts of Brooklyn in New York City, often where freedmen had settled before the Civil War, and sections of the shantytowns in what was to become Central Park were black-occupied (Blackmar and Rosenzweig 1992). In the draft riots of 1863, the attacks on blacks had easily identifiable areas as targets,[7] and similarly in 1900 a race riot found its black target concentrated in the Hell's Kitchen (now Clinton) section of Manhattan (Johnson 1968: 127 cited in Abu-Lughod 1999). Within these areas of black concentration, there was a mix of classes, notably in Harlem at its inception,[8] but also more than fifty years earlier within Greenwich Village, then known as 'Little Africa'.[9] Black movement out of such areas met major obstacles, including legal restrictions in many of the southern states. This was not the 'succession' of the Jewish ghetto that Wirth described, where Jews moved out as they prospered, leaving vacant units behind; it was rather displacement of those less able to pay by those somewhat better able to pay. But the process was generally seen as one of restriction of movement rather than of ghetto formation. Blacks simply wanted better housing than was available in the areas to which they were confined, and a particular relationship to such areas was not perceived as important, negatively or positively.

Interestingly enough, one might argue that in the United States the ghetto as recognized ghetto did not arise until the claim by the former slaves to full 'common citizenship' had become a widespread phenomenon. As Gunnar Myrdal pointed out in his landmark study, the patterns of segregation were quite different in the *ante-bellum* South than in the post-Civil War North:

Southern whites do not want Negroes to be completely isolated from them: they derive many advantages from their proximity . . . there is also segregation, but the segregation is based on what we may term 'ceremonial' distance rather than spatial distance. (Myrdal 1944: 621; see also the careful study of Atlanta and other Southern cities in the historical sections of Silver and Moeser 1995)

What Myrdal calls the 'racial etiquette' of the South, understood by both blacks and whites, was sufficient to maintain the relationships of subordination and domination. When that understanding breaks down, when the claim to equal treatment, equal access, equal rights, becomes prevalent among blacks, the necessity for ghettoization in its classic forms arises. Richard Morrill, for instance, argues that:

During the nineteenth century the American Negro population, in this country from the beginning but accustomed to servitude, remained predominantly southern and rural, and those who did move lived in small spatial concentrations about the cities. *The Negro ghetto did not exist.* Even in southern cities the Negroes, largely in the service of whites, lived side by side with the white majority. Rather suddenly, with the social upheaval and employment opportunities of World War II, Negro discontent grew, and large-scale migration began from the rural south to the urban north . . .   (Abrams 1955a: 19, citation in original; for a discussion of the parallel impact of migration from the rural South to the urban North after the Second World War, see Piven and Cloward 1974a: 200 ff.)

Morrill neglects the significant changes that occurred in the period of Imposition, with the new role of the state in ghetto formation, but his description rings true of the earlier and later periods.

A detailed study of Cincinnati between 1870 and 1880 bears out Morrill's picture: the lower the economic level, the greater the integration, although on a building by building basis three-quarters of all blacks lived in all-black buildings (Lammermeier 1971: 26). The pattern is more one of congregation than of ghettoization. David Goldfield puts the pattern in the South somewhat differently: as many small segregated clusters, in areas of environmental disamenity, rather than fewer large ghettos, as in the North (Goldfield 1997). The year 1917 is suggested as the symbolic breakpoint between this period and the next, as it marks the Supreme Court decision which declared specific municipal zoning ordinances enforcing racial discrimination in housing illegal (U.S. Supreme Court 1917). From then on the *de jure* claim to freedom from racial segregation, as well as its *de facto* implementation, underlay the development of racial patterns in the urban centres of the United States.

Massey and Denton summarize:

There was a time, before 1900, when blacks and whites lived side by side in American cities. In the north, a small native black population was scattered widely throughout white neighborhoods. Even Chicago, Detroit, Cleveland, and Philadelphia—cities now well known for their large black ghettos—were not segregated then. In southern cities such as Charleston, New Orleans, and Savannah, black servants and laborers lived on alleys and side streets near the mansions of their white employers. In this lost urban world, blacks were more likely to share a neighborhood with whites than with other blacks. In most cities, to be sure, certain neighborhoods could be identified as where blacks lived; but before 1900 these areas were not predominantly black, and most blacks didn't live in them. No matter what other disadvantages urban blacks suffered in the aftermath of the Civil War, they were not residentially segregated from whites. (Massey and Denton 1993: 17)[10]

The change from the pre-history to the period of Imposition, which we may date roughly to the 1920s, can be seen from the available figures shown in Fig. 6.2. Specific city studies bear out this scenario; in Chicago, for instance:

In the late nineteenth century, while most Negroes lived in certain sections of the South Side, they lived interspersed among whites; there were few all-Negro blocks. By 1915, on

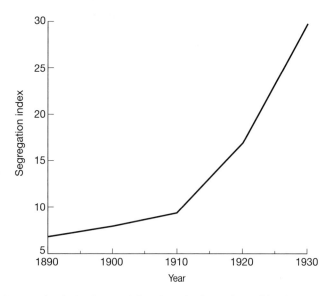

Fig. 6.2. Segregation index by wards in selected US northern cities (1890–1930)

Source: Lieberson (1980: 266, 288, cited in Massey and Denton 1993: 24)

the other hand, the physical ghetto had taken shape; a large, almost all-Negro enclave on the South Side, with a similar offshoot on the West Side, housed most of Chicago's Negroes. (Spear 1967, reprinted in Wakstein 1970: 269)

The Period of Imposition

The black ghetto, properly so called, did not come about by accident in the inter-war years; it was created, imposed from the outside, by a range of forces, the real estate industry prominent among them, and the instrument of that imposition was the state. The usefulness of division between whites and blacks for some employers, the economic advantage of some whites, the racist individual patterns of behaviour by whites engendered by decades of slavery, the continued disadvantages suffered by the victims of those decades, were all causative elements in the creation of the ghetto. But indispensable to its creation was the ability of those benefiting from segregation to use the instrumentalities of government to impose and enforce patterns of separation on blacks.

Only a brief account is necessary to show the role of government in fostering ghettoization:

• In city after city, local governments enacted zoning ordinances that explicitly provided that certain areas should be occupied exclusively by whites. While the practice of zoning using race as a formal criterion was finally ruled unconstitutional in *Buchanan* v. *Warley* in 1917, 'the construction of the ghetto continued apace despite Buchanan, and levels of black-white segregation in U.S. cities rose steadily' (Massey and Denton 1993: 188).

• Zoning has remained a major device for excluding blacks and restricting their alternatives to living in ghettoes. Devices include large-lot zoning, prohibiting multi-family construction or limiting areas available for it, or retaining discretionary powers in a local zoning board to permit or reject applications for construction (Abrams 1955a is an early but still excellent account).

• Courts, the third branch of government in the United States' federal system, provided judicial enforcement for restrictive covenants (i.e., agreements incorporated in deeds of transfer of real property, in this case restricting subsequent transfers to persons not of the Caucasian race), for many years a major device by which blacks were excluded from large parts of cities and confined to areas of already black residence. Although the practice violated the Civil Rights Act of 1866 (Massey and Denton 1993: 188), it was not until 1948 that the practice was declared unconstitutional by the United States Supreme Court (U.S. Supreme Court 1948; for the history, see Abrams 1955a: 212–22).

• City planning has in the past contributed significantly to limiting the opportunities for the location of residences for blacks. Designs for 'neighborhood unit' developments, the location of boulevards and major roadways, the location and timing of infrastructure provision, often conformed to essentially racist patterns (Thomas and Ritzdorf 1997). Robert Moses' biases, as Construction Coordinator for the City of New York and in multiple other public roles, to preserve existing segregated racial patterns and uses, and in fact to accentuate them through disproportionate displacement of blacks through public works, have been extensively documented (Caro 1974; Caro's research has recently been called into question, but the basic outlines he has presented have held up).

• The bulk of private single-family housing built in the last fifty years has been built with Federal government mortgage assistance, largely in the form of insurance through the Federal Housing Administration (FHA). Appraisal by the FHA of the value of a home was essential to get that assistance. In that appraisal, the FHA Manual for Underwriters stated: 'important among adverse influences . . . are . . . infiltration of inharmonious racial or nationality groups . . .'. It further favoured '. . . recorded deed restrictions . . . [to] include the following: . . . prohibition of the occupancy of properties except by the race for which they are intended' (the most detailed account of the FHA's discriminatory policies is in Jackson 1985).

• The Federal public housing programme, adopted in the United States Housing Act of 1937, provided for the construction of social housing in what is still the nation's major programme for government construction of housing. At the outset, and until the 1950s, such housing was uniformly constructed on a segregated basis: separate, and rarely equal. Public housing projects are today often at the heart of the black ghetto in major cities (for examples of the extensive literature on this subject, see Bauman 1987; Hirsch 1983; Marcuse 1986).

• The urban renewal programme, adopted under Title I of the Housing Act of 1949, was the basis for slum clearance and redevelopment in the United States, and became quickly known as a programme for Negro removal. Although coupled in the same piece of legislation with public housing, it destroyed more housing than it created in its early years, with a widely disparate impact on black housing, forcing black residents from often integrated areas desired for 'higher' uses into areas already of minority concentration.

• The Federal highway construction programme, massively subsidized with Federal funds after 1954, was a *sine qua non* for the development of the sprawling and all-white suburbs of the post-war years (the best account is perhaps Gelfand 1975; see also Jackson 1985). A significant part of the motivation for moves to the suburbs was to escape the inner cities, relying on these highways and leaving the inner cities, in turn, to house ever larger concentrations of black residents. The movement of employers and jobs to the suburbs aggravated the impact on segregation of blacks.

Between the two World Wars, and perhaps briefly thereafter, areas of concentration of blacks shared some of the attributes of a ghetto and some of an enclave. The clustering of blacks drew attention; already in 1913 Edmund Haynes, a Fisk University sociologist, wrote: 'New York has its "San Juan Hill" in the West Sixties and its Harlem district of over 35,000 within about eighteen city blocks; Philadelphia has its Seventh Ward; Chicago has its State Street; Washington its Northwest neighborhood, and Baltimore its Druid Hill' (Haynes 1913: 109). But the formation of the major areas of spatial concentration of blacks in central cities began only after the First World War. This was a period of rapid migration of blacks from the South to the North, and in the North to their metropolitan areas, and in those areas to their central cities; Fig. 6.1 provides the figures.

The positive side of clustering was as often adumbrated as the negative; the process was one of congregating as well as of being segregated. The attitude towards Harlem of the writers of the Harlem Renaissance, the elation Malcolm X describes on his first arrival there, the proud characterization of Harlem as the capital of black America, all suggest a strong positive association with it. There is a positive description of Harlem in, for instance, the biographies of Adam Clayton Powell.[11] And James Weldon Johnson spoke of the black situation in New York City in 1930 in almost thoroughly optimistic terms:

The Negro in New York . . . still meets with discrimination and disadvantages. But New York guarantees her Negro citizens the fundamental rights of citizenship and protects them in the exercise of those rights. Possessing the basic rights, the Negro in New York ought to be able to work through the discriminations and disadvantages. (Johnson 1968: 284 quoted by Abu-Lughod 1999: 451, fn.78; see also Johnson 1968: 146—the book is almost lyrical in its description of black Harlem)

New York's '. . . ghettos contained the well-to-do as well as the poor. The middle and upper classes resided in well-defined sections of the ghettos—such as Striver's Row or Sugar Hill in Harlem' (Bracey, Meier, and Rudwick 1971: 3). In Chicago, Bronzeville was an area of cultural pride in the 1920s, and 'the black ghetto . . . was still a functioning community as late as 1966. Blacks still provided most of the community services, they still owned the small shops and businesses, and black professionals still provided help to black citizens. There was a vertical integration . . .' (Wood 1992: 3). After that period the Chicago ghetto becomes the example William Wilson uses for the socially destructive ghetto (Wilson 1987: 3).

That the spatial pattern was that of a ghetto is, however, beyond doubt. Black belts existed in most Northern urban centres, and their expansion was violently resisted by their white neighbours, often with bombs (Johnson 1968: 156).

Negative characteristics of the ghetto are also, of course, recognized in this period of Imposition: run-down housing, overcrowding, inadequate sanitary facilities, dilapidation. But these were seen as attributes of slum housing, not confined to black areas, and the solutions were general ones addressed to such housing. Where later 'urban renewal' becomes synonymous with 'black removal', this was not the case before the Second World War; when slums were cleared on the Lower East Side or in Brooklyn to make way for public housing in New York City in the 1930s, the issue of race did not even come up. Black organizations simply demanded equal treatment for Harlem, and the construction of Harlem River Houses, although from the outset designated as an all-black project, was a response to the demands of the Harlem community. Williamsburg Houses, built contemporaneously by the New York City Housing Authority, was all-white; the protest against that was not so much that it was all-white, but that blacks in Harlem did not have an equivalent project in their community. The demand was for equality, not for integration.

Henry Louis Gates Jr. comments on the paradoxical nature of feelings about Harlem in his description of the attitude of leading black intellectuals in the 1920s and 1930s:

What *does* seem curious to me about the Harlem Renaissance . . . is that its creation occurred precisely as Harlem was turning into the great American slum. The death rate was 42 per cent higher than in other parts of the city. . . . The unemployment rate . . . was 50 per cent. There was no way to romanticize these conditions, but Locke [a leader of the black Harlem Renaissance movement] and his fellows valiantly attempted to do so . . . to create the fiction of Harlem as a model of civility and black bourgeois respectability, rather than as an example of the most heinous effects of urban economic exploitation and residential segregation. [James Weldon] Johnson continued, 'Harlem is not merely a Negro colony or community, it is a city within a city, the greatest Negro city in the world. It is not a slum or a fringe, it is located in the heart of Manhattan and occupies one of the most beautiful and healthful sections of the city'. (Gates 1997: 11)

In general, there was little objection to the continuation of the black ghetto in the period of Imposition; objections were, if any, to conditions within that ghetto, not to the existence of an area of spatial concentration for blacks as such. In fact, some may have seen the existence of the ghetto, whatever its origins, to move in the direction of Booker T. Washington's push for separation and independence of the black community from its white surroundings (Massey and Denton 1993: 115 speculate along these lines). The analogy to immigrant enclaves, the focus on cultural identity and pride, was widespread. The analogy, in terms of felt experience, was perhaps more to Wirth's 'voluntary Jewish ghettos' of the first millennium than to the imposed Jewish ghettos of the late Middle Ages, even though the facts were quite different. Inadequate housing conditions were seen as not confined to the ghetto. Particularly during the Depression, slums existed throughout the city, and blacks in the ghetto had no reason to feel uniquely confined to slum conditions.

The imposed character of the black ghetto is not visible either in the mainstream sociological studies of the period. In the pioneering work of the Chicago School of the 1920s, segregation is equated to clustering, with no emphasis on whether it is voluntary or not, and little distinction between immigrant, cultural, black, Jewish, or other areas of spatial concentration. In

Park, Burgess, and McKenzie's leading study (Park, Burgess, and McKenzie 1967), the sum of the references to issues of the black ghetto are the following:

Personal tastes and convenience, vocational and economic interests, infallibly tend to segregate and thus to classify the populations of great cities . . .   (Park, Burgess, and McKenzie 1967: 5)

In the city environment the neighborhood tends to lose much of the significance which it possessed in simpler and more primitive forms of society . . . On the other hand, the isolation of the immigrant and racial colonies of the so-called ghettos and areas of population segregation tend to preserve and, where there is racial prejudice, to intensi-fy the intimacies and solidarity of the local and neighborhood groups. Where individu-als of the same race or of the same vocation live together in segregated groups, neighborhood sentiment tends to fuse together with racial antagonisms and class interests . . .   (Park, Burgess, and McKenzie 1967: 10)

The slums are also crowded to overflowing with immigrant colonies—the Ghetto, Little Sicily, Greektown, Chinatown—fascinatingly combining old world heritages and American adaptations. Wedging out from here is the Black Belt, with its free and disorderly life . . .   (Park, Burgess, and McKenzie 1967: 56)

Chicago, like other large cities, has its cultural communities, each of which has, if not a local area, at least a local center. Hobohemia, Bohemia, Philistia, the Ghetto, and the Gold Coast are cultural communities.   (Park, Burgess, and McKenzie 1967: 150)

The confusion in these passages does not stem simply from a reading 70 years later under other conditions. The 'so-called ghettos' seem to incorporate all areas of concentration, yet 'The Ghetto' is only the Jewish ghetto, once paral-lel to other ethnic areas, the second time parallel to other cultural communities, with race and class weaving in and out, and the Black Belt as one ghetto among many others.

Read Louis Wirth's description of the ghetto, which he takes to apply equally to the black ghetto, in the context of the official state actions that shaped the black ghetto in the period of Imposition:

The ghetto . . . indicates the ways in which cultural groups give expression to their own heritage when transplanted to a strange habitat; it evidences . . . the forces through which the community maintains its integrity and continuity . . . the spatially separated and socially isolated community seemed to offer the best opportunity for following their religious precepts, their established ritual and diet, and the numerous functions which tied the individual to familial and communal institutions . . . The ghetto . . . was a self-perpetuating group to such an extent that it may be properly called a closed com-munity . . . it is . . . a cultural community [and] can be completely understood only if it is viewed as a sociopsychological, as well as an ecological phenomenon: for it is not merely a physical fact, but also a state of mind.   (Wirth 1928)

Wirth, of course, had in mind the immigrant concentrations of cities like Chicago, and in this sense was talking more of enclaves than of ghettos. But that very fact is noteworthy. By the time he was writing, Harlem had already achieved international recognition as a—the—centre of black life, and the South Side of Chicago was clearly Negro. 'By the outbreak of World War I, the larger centers of Negro population in the North had established segregated community facilities of various types . . . Black Belts had appeared' (Weaver 1948: 3). By 1925, densities of black areas in Chicago were twice the density of whites, in Philadelphia almost four times, in Manhattan one and a half times (Woofter 1928: 79, cited in Weaver 1948: 35). Yet Wirth did not deem it necessary to pay attention to the differences between the classic immigrant enclaves he describes and the black ghettos of these cities. And in mainstream white discussions of segregation along these lines, this comparability of black conditions with those of immigrants is general.[12]

And indeed this assumption that black ghettos are a subcategory of immigrant ghettos is not far removed from many black views. Langston Hughes wrote in 1938:

> I am the poor white, fooled and pushed apart,
> I am the Negro bearing slavery's scars.
> I am the immigrant clutching the hope I seek—
> And finding only the same old stupid plan
> Of dog eat dog, of mighty crush the weak.
> O, let America be America again—
> The land that never has been yet—
> And yet must be—The land where *every* man is free.
>
> Quoted by Hochschild 1995: 225

The belief that, as the black experience paralleled that of immigrants, the black ghetto would likewise be expected, and should, follow the 'natural' life cycles of areas of immigrant concentration, characterizes some of the thinking of the following period of Confrontation as well, although now in full recognition of the force of state imposition and opposition to it. Absent state imposition, the thinking would be, the black ghetto would 'naturally' go the way of the Jewish or the immigrant enclaves. It is only towards the end of the period of Confrontation that the uniqueness of the black experience takes centre stage in black views of the future of the ghetto.

The Period of Confrontation

The widespread view accepting the 'naturalness' of the black ghetto did not outlast the Second World War. Wartime experiences created claims, among black veterans and in black communities, for both a better and an unsegregated life, one without restrictions on mobility imposed from the outside; claims to a freer life, not just a more equal one. Such claims, combined with the also war-engendered new and fuller sense of having a formal right to full participation, produced a new militancy, willing to confront rather than adapt to the conditions of the ghetto.

State action reflects, parallels, and partially implements the post-war surge of claims to freedom and formal equality. One can trace the shift in the direction of public policies, and realize their importance on the ground, from a recitation of the key public measures adopted between 1945 and the mid 1970s, starting with the Second World War and peaking with the reactions to the civil rights movements and the ghetto rebellions of the mid to late 1960s. (In general, 'low-income' is tightly correlated with 'black' in the politics of housing policy in the United States.)

• The first formal governmental action directly affecting discrimination in housing was at the local level: the passage in New York City of the Sharkey-Brown-Isaacs law prohibiting discrimination in a broad range of housing activities in that city.

• The opening shot in the courts may taken as the decision in *Shelley* v. *Kramer* in 1948, holding racial restrictive covenants unenforceable as a matter of public policy.

• The Federal Housing Administration formally abandoned its policy of racial red-lining, refusing mortgages in areas of minority concentration, in 1949.

• The landmark decision on the road to judicial attacks on racial discrimination was however not in the housing area, but in education: the Supreme Court's *Brown* v. *Board of Education* decision outlawing separate but equal schools in 1953 added impetus and tools, a new approach developed to the issue of spatial segregation (for a detailed study of the change in three cities—Memphis, Atlanta, and Richmond—see Silver and Moeser 1995).

• President Kennedy issued Executive Order 11063 prohibiting discrimination in federally assisted housing in 1962.

• Title VI of the Civil Rights Act of 1964 made statutory the prohibition against discrimination in federally assisted housing.

• Title VIII of the Civil Rights Act of 1968 called for 'the achievement of fair housing', and was interpreted by Senator Mondale, one of the sponsors of the legislation, 'to replace the ghettos by truly integrated and balanced living patterns' (Congressional Record 1968; see also Polikoff 1986: 47 ff.).

• *Jones* v. *Mayer* in 1968 held that the 1866 Civil Rights Act bans all racial discrimination, public or private, in the sale or rental of housing.

• The Mt. Laurel decision of the New Jersey Supreme Court was the most far-reaching state court decision dealing with discrimination in the suburbs ever to be handed down; it held that local zoning ordinances have to make provision for housing in such a way as to provide opportunity for lower income residents to live in each community.

• In a series of rulings in the Gautreaux case, beginning in 1967, the courts required the Chicago Housing Authority to provide housing for public housing eligible households outside Chicago (i.e., in the suburbs), and that decision had wide ramifications in Federal policy, leading up to the issuance finally by the Department of Housing and Urban Development of regulations ordering the 'disestablishment' of racially dual public housing in 1983, extending its ruling to a direct espousal of the goal of eliminating racial segregation in public housing in 1985 (see Goering 1986: 197–8). For the internal opposition to such policies starting at least in 1980, see below.

• The Housing and Community Development Act of 1974, the last major piece of pro-integration legislation adopted by Congress, strengthened the government's commitment to 'avoid undue concentrations of lower income persons through Federal housing programs'.

And the numbers changed dramatically: between 1940 and 1960, the black population of central cities in the large metropolitan areas increased by 4,230,000 (Hauser 1971: 43). By 1959, George A. Nesbitt, in the official journal of the National Association for the Advancement of Colored People, wrote '. . . few indeed are the Negroes who would answer the question ['break up the black ghetto?'] other than with a resounding affirmative'. Going on to discuss the vested interests that had a stake in the preservation of the ghetto for business reasons, Nesbitt concluded: 'Negroes ought to help usher out the black ghettos in which they suffer and not be beguiled by the few who wax fat on its drippings' (Nesbitt 1959: 48–50, 52).

    This sense of being artificially separated spatially from that of which they are a part economically and socially can be seen in Robert Weaver's definition, given at the beginning of what was perhaps the last period that full integration of blacks into United States society seemed a practical goal, immediately after the end of the Second World War:

The modern American ghetto is . . . not, as the ghetto of old, an area which houses a people concerned with perpetuation of a peculiar (and different) culture. It is no longer composed of black people almost all of whom are too poor to afford decent shelter. The Negro ghetto of today is made up of people who are American to the core, who are a part of the national culture and who share a common language with the majority of Americans. . . . Its inhabitants are better prepared and more anxious than ever before to enter the main stream of American Life. Residential segregation, more than any other single institution, is an impediment to their realization of this American Dream. (Weaver 1948: 7)

Weaver thus implicitly argues that two of the three reasons Myrdal gave for the existence of black ghettos—poverty, ethnic attachment, and imposed segregation (Myrdal 1944: 619)—no longer existed: its only reason for continued existence, after the Second World War, was pure segregation.

In an ironic and sad illustration of the difference in outlook between the days Weaver entered the fray against racial discrimination and today, he concluded, in 1944:

If, instead of restrictions on account of race, creed, and color, there were agreements binding property owners not to sell or lease except to single families, barring excessive roomers, and otherwise dealing with the *type* of occupancy, property would be better protected during both white and Negro occupancy. This would afford an opportunity for the Negro *who has the means* and the urge to live in a desirable neighborhood. It would protect the 'integrity of the neighborhood'. (Weaver 1944: 191, cited in McKenzie 1994: 77)[13]

The fact of confinement was the focus of extensive civil rights agitation in the post-war years; the central concepts were equality of opportunity and freedom of choice. The cold war antagonism to the Soviet Union was used to further legitimate the struggle; in the words of Charles Abrams, one of the earliest and most vigorous advocates of integration,

it will awaken all minorities who now suspect the West to a new faith in the democratic principle. (Abrams 1955*b*: 388–9)

Positive aspects could indeed still be attributed to the ghetto, but as responses to an undesirable and hopefully dwindling reality: the racism of white society. Thus Drake and Cayton present the ghetto as a place where black people can 'escape from the tensions of contact with white people', a tension that is itself the subject of attack and is hoped will disappear (Drake and Cayton 1945). Even Kenneth Clark, in his later and very pessimistic view of the ghetto, says that 'there is considerable psychological safety in the "ghetto"; there one lives among one's own and does not risk rejection among strangers' (Clark 1965). That is not presented as any reason to preserve the ghetto, however; its dissolution remains the objective (see Boal 1981: 47). The tradition is that of the original Park and Burgess discussion, in which all ethnic groups in American cities were seen as passing through a series of stages from contact and competition to conflict to assimilation as the ultimate (and positively valued) end result, all as part of a natural and 'organic' development process (Park, Burgess, and McKenzie 1967). The 'social disorganization' of the ghetto was seen as 'evidence of the difficulty migrants had adjusting to the urban North' (Wolcott 1997: 49; Wolcott lists some of the key literature that contributed to this 'ghetto school' view of American urban history).

This two-sided approach to the ghetto—resistance to confinement within it, yet not questioning its positive attributes and even expecting its continuation as a cultural phenomenon, also exists in the writing of such perceptive critics as Jane Jacobs, with intimations of the pessimistic view that is to come:

The effective breaking down of residential discrimination outside a slum, and the less dramatic self-diversification within an unslumming slum, proceed concurrently. If

America has now, in the case of Negroes, reached an effective halt in this process and in general entered a stage of arrested development—a thought I find both highly improbable and quite intolerable—then it may be that Negro slums cannot effectively unslum in the fashion demonstrated by slums formed by other ethnic populations . . . (Jacobs 1961)[14]

'Unslumming' the ghetto is not destroying it; it is not the spatial concentration of blacks in itself that is the problem, but the conditions under which it occurs. The ghetto still has enclave-like properties. But the sense that the continued and unwanted existence of the ghetto may be both possible and ominous is already there.

Kenneth Clark's description of the ghetto seventeen years after Weaver's presents a more sombre picture:

The dark ghetto's invisible walls have been erected by the white society, by those who have power, both to confine those who have no power and to perpetuate their power-lessness. The dark ghettos are social, political, educational, and—above all—economic colonies. Their inhabitants are subject peoples, victims of the greed, cruelty, insen-sitivity, guilt, and fear of their masters. (Clark 1965: 11)

Clark wrote of the ghetto presciently, just at the point when its character was beginning to change. Powerlessness was no part of the feeling of Weaver's ghetto—and certainly not of James Weldon Johnson's Harlem of the period of Imposition, Harlem, the capital of black America in the 1920s (see Johnson 1925, and the last chapter of Osofsky 1968, with its warning against romanti-cizing the picture). It became characteristic of pictures of the ghetto by the late 1960s, but still in an integrationist context. Clark had after all given key support for the plaintiffs in the school desegregation cases that outlawed legal segregation in public schools in 1953. The colonies are linked to the colonizers, the masters have an interest in, profit from, the work of the subject peoples, and an appeal can be made that integration is in everyone's best interest.

It is that which has changed in the post-Fordist city. Those in today's black ghettos are not productive for their masters; their masters get no benefit from their existence. Their residents are outcasts; as far as the dominant society is concerned, they are only a drain on public and private resources, a threat to social peace, fulfilling no useful social role. They are outcasts; hence an outcast ghetto. That is the character of the ghetto in the period of Empowerment which is to follow. It is not of course in fact true of all residents of the ghetto, but it is its perceived character in the dominant politics.

The civil rights movement itself always had two quite distinct threads, an integrationist and a separatist or black power voice—Martin Luther King Jr. as contrasted with Stokely Carmichael. Opening the suburbs was one thread, 'gilding the ghetto', later more positively called 'community economic development', was the other. The integrationist view dominated in the 1950s and 1960s. By the end of the 1960s, the contrary voice was already beginning to be heard. In 1967, Stokely Carmichael and Charles V. Hamilton wrote:

'Integration' as a goal today speaks to the problem of blackness not only in an unrealistic way but also in a despicable way . . . 'integration' is a subterfuge for the maintenance of white supremacy.   (Carmichael and Hamilton 1967)

The success of the civil rights movement gave rise to a hope that was perhaps more immediate, more powerful, more emotional, than anything that had gone before. The limitations encountered in the real world produced a swing in the opposite direction. Jennifer Hochschild speaks of '. . . a transformative moment . . . for many African Americans [in] the late 1950s and early 1960s . . . but the sense of rebirth into a new world has diminished, and even curdled, for many' (Hochschild 1995: 245; word order changed slightly). By the mid 1970s, the change in orientation was clear. Integration as a goal recedes from the picture, whether because defeated and judged unrealistic, and/or undesired, and/or opposed for racial reasons.

The Period of Empowerment

The crucial political turning point in the United States is probably what with hindsight might be considered the defeat of the civil rights movement of the 1960s and the election of Nixon as president in 1968.[15] Two parallel quotations with a clock metaphor neatly illustrate the point (both are cited in the revised Banfield 1974: 2; Banfield essentially supports the Nixon position— it represents the conservative version of the perceived permanence of the ghetto).

President Johnson, August 1965, immediately after the Watts riots and at the height of civil rights militancy, declared:

. . . the clock is ticking, time is moving . . . we must ask ourselves every night when we go home, are we doing all that we should do in our nation's capital, in all the other big cities of the country.

Compare this to President Nixon, March 1973:

A few years ago we constantly heard that urban America was on the brink of collapse. It was one minute to midnight, we were told . . . Today, America is no longer coming apart . . . The hour of crisis is passed.

Nixon's comment ushered in an era in which governments at all levels abandoned those efforts at desegregation and their mild espousal of the goal of integration, recounted above, retreated from the positions already taken, and undermined the implementation of whatever efforts had been begun. Again, the list of governmental actions is telling:

• Neither Federal Fair Housing/Civil Rights legislation nor court decisions produced integration in housing. '. . . the systematic removal of . . . enforcement provisions . . . meant that [their goals] were virtually guaranteed to remain unrealized' (Massey and Denton 1993: 195).

• The United States Department of Justice took a firm position against the use of 'race-conscious' policies to achieve integration in housing, and filed lawsuits against policies establishing benign quotas for that purpose (*United States* v. *Starrett City*, see Marcuse 1962)

• Efforts to implement stated Federal policies for desegregation of public housing were consistently undercut within the Executive Branch and under-funded by Congress (Goering 1986: 198ff.). As a result, public housing has remained (with the partial exception of housing for the elderly) over-whelmingly minority-occupied.

• Enforcement of Federal fair housing legislation has always been sluggish. Regulations were not adopted till four years after the Act was passed. The Department of Housing and Urban Development had no enforcement powers until the Fair Housing Amendments Act of 1988, which put discrimination against handicapped or households with children present on the same plane as discrimination based on race and added enforcement provisions, which how-ever remained badly underfunded. The affirmative marketing provisions earli-er worked out for housing were essentially vitiated with governmental support (Massey and Denton 1993: 208).

• Title VIII of the Civil Rights Act of 1968 was interpreted in 1984 by the Assistant U.S. Attorney for Civil Rights in the Department of Justice as only prohibiting racial bias in housing, not promoting integration (Polikoff 1986: 49).

• The Reagan administration (1980–7) was properly accused of 'systemat-ically assaulting the very structure of the federal civil rights machinery'. (Com-ment of the American Civil Liberties Union, quoted by Vernarelli in Goering 1986: 230.)

• The 1988 Fair Housing Amendments Act strengthened the language of the 1968 Act. Passed partly in reaction to the excessive conservative subversion of the 1968 Fair Housing Act, it was perhaps the last positive move of govern-ment in the direction of integration, but its effects have, overall, been trivial. Funding has been grossly inadequate, and the scale of the effort is no match for the size of the problem.

• President Bush, in 1991, attempted to eliminate the U.S. Commission on Civil Rights (*New York Times* 1991), a governmental commission established to press the case for civil rights but progressively weakened through budget cuts and conservative appointments through successive administrations since 1980.

• Blacks trying to obtain mortgages to buy their own homes face discrimina-tion from mortgage-lending institutions (see, officially most recently, U.S. Department of Housing and Urban Development 1999). Yet the bulk of such institutions operate under governmental (Federal and state) charters, and legislation is on the books with the avowed purpose of ending such discrimination.

• The major urban initiative of the Clinton administration, its empowerment zone legislation, provides subsidies for activities located within empowerment zones only (which are by and large the ghettos in major cities); integration outside of the ghetto is no part of their goal (Marcuse 2000).

• HOPE VI projects, the major initiative in public housing in recent years (begun in 1992) envisages income mixing in public housing, but without the parallel provision aiming at equivalent housing for those displaced outside of existing areas of concentration of such housing. It requires all new investment to be in the site of the old projects, overwhelmingly in 'racially impacted areas', dropping an earlier ban on such investment.

A whole coterie of conservative commentators supported an anti-integration position and gave ideological cover to the rejection of integration as a goal of public policy (see Banfield 1974, as well as Moynihan 1970; Lowry 1987; and Salins 1987). Under its cover, the War on Poverty ran out, and the fight for integration became the pursuit of empowerment (Manning Marable is explicit in the formulation, but hardly the only one; see Marable 1996: 132–3). Not that discrimination was considered by civil rights advocates any more acceptable than it had been during the 1960s civil rights movement, but that the resiliency of segregation was acknowledged as having been underestimated. What amounted to an implicit strategic decision was made to build on the strengths existing segregated patterns might afford even while continuing the campaign for full equality. The negative side of the assessment that led to that strategy is illustrated in book titles such as *The Myth of Black Progress* (Pinkney 1984); the positive was prefigured in an iconoclastic article by Frances Piven and Richard Cloward in 1966 (Piven and Cloward 1966), and explicitly stated in their 'the case against urban desegregation' (Piven and Cloward 1974b: 200ff.; in this work they also publish the strong pro-integration arguments of two major black leaders, Whitney M. Young, Jr. and Clarence Funnyé. Cornel West speaks of 'the murky waters of despair and dread that now flood the streets of black America' (West 1994: 18). Perhaps the earliest formulation of that despair—Gates and West call it 'militant despair'—came from W. E. B. DuBois:

I just cannot take any more of this country's treatment. We leave for Ghana October 5th and I set no date for return . . . Chin up, and fight on, but realize that American Negroes can't win.   (Quoted in Horne 1986: 345; cited in Gates and West 1996: 111)

Recently, Leonard Steinhorn and Barbara Diggs-Brown, professors at American University's School of Communication—one African-American, one white, believing that 'integration is an ideal both of us would prefer to see realized in our lifetimes', produced a book arguing that real integration (as opposed to desegregation) simply will not happen (Steinhorn and Diggs-Brown 1999). They concluded 'the integration of blacks and whites is not working and may never work . . . We must conclude, regrettably, that integration is an illusion borne of hope and desire, that our very devotion to the ideal ironically helps us avoid a real reckoning on race, and that for our nation to move beyond today's racial endgame we must relinquish the hope of ever reaching the racial Promised Land . . .' (Steinhorn and Diggs-Brown 1999). In a set of commentaries on their book, the Poverty and Race Research Action Council heard from civil rights activists and researchers, by and large along the lines of the comments of Herbert Gans, who argued, in the most simple formulation, that racial equality must have priority over integration, and is likely a condition for it (Gans 1999; many others could be cited along the same lines, for instance, Orfield 1988). Desegregation (as defined above), or the 'defeat of racism' (Early 2000: 5–6), was posed as the goal by most, and even those who maintained the possibility/necessity of 'integration' essentially equated integration with the rejection of segregation, or desegregation (Roisman 2000: 4–5). One contribution was bluntly titled: 'No one even knows what integration is' (Woodford 2000: 11).

The cultural/ideological correlative of these developments lies in the use of the concept of empowerment to represent the goals of those pushing for ghetto-related public policies. This is not the optimistic and aggressive 'Black Power' slogan of the later stages of the civil rights movement, nor the self-help bootstrap strategy of, in different ways, Booker T. Washington and Marcus Garvey, and later W. E. B. DuBois in the 1930s, but a more defensive acknowledgment of relative powerlessness with the hope of piecemeal change with government assistance. It may be in part what has been called, in a somewhat ambivalent formulation, 'the excluded building pride in their excluded identity' (Castells 1997: 274).[16]

Little of the recent writing on the subject has focused on the qualitative change that the ghetto in the United States has undergone in the transition from the Fordist to the post-Fordist city, under the pressure of accelerated globalization. In two of the best recent books, the focus is more on the persistence and intensity of segregation and ghettoization than on changes in its character (Massey and Denton 1993 and Goldsmith and Blakely 1992; an exception is Vergara 1995, a graphic description that focuses on the contemporary ghetto, not the classic one of the past). Most see the ghetto in the United States as strictly a phenomenon of African-American residence;[17] others link the ghetto with the Latino barrio (Goldsmith and Blakely 1992); but that there have been recent changes in the relative role of African-American and other spatial concentrations of ethnic/racial groups is little explored. Thus, Massey and Denton say,

. . . no ethnic or racial group in the history of the United States, except one, has ever experienced ghettoization, even briefly. For urban blacks, the ghetto has been the paradigmatic residential configuration for at least eighty years.   (Massey and Denton 1993: 18–19)

Adding 'hyper-' to ghetto, as some current commentators do, might indeed suggest that something new is happening; hypersegregation might be thought of as referring to a new stage in the development of the United States ghetto. But that is not how it has generally been used. It has rather come into use to differentiate, in purely quantitative terms, areas of extreme differentiation on one or more scales from areas of lesser differentiation (see the complex definition of Massey and Denton 1993: 74, and their discussion in Massey and Denton 1989; see further Jencks and Peterson 1991). The worsening patterns that Massey and Denton demonstrate and discuss do however lend credence to the belief, which also comes through in their careful study, that something new is happening.

William Wilson has focused attention on changes in the character of the ghetto around the 1970s,[18] and in a detailed but somewhat neglected portion of his major study pointed to their deeper causes in the economic changes of the middle of the post-war period. The debates he generated, however, focused more on short-term issues, and here Wilson laid stress on the out-migration of middle class blacks from older areas of racial concentration in the 1970s as a result of the fair housing successes of the civil rights movement of the 1960s, arguing that that left behind a new form of ghetto that produced what he first called the 'underclass' and more recently the 'ghetto poor'. Thus, although Wilson begins his explanatory account of the new ghetto with the major economic and social changes that are often characterized as the advent of post-Fordism, he also directs explanation for changes in the role of the ghetto to narrower issues of demographics and population movement. And that has unleashed its own controversy, for some have argued that the out-migration he references is largely a chimera, and that middle class blacks remain segregated within black ghettos as much as poor blacks (see Fainstein 1993, for instance, or Massey and Denton 1993: 8). The debate is an important one, and the figures are not conclusive, but the weight of the evidence seems to be that there was indeed an out-migration of middle class blacks from the centres of the ghettos, but that segregation (at the edge or outside, in predominantly black suburbs) remains a major factor, resulting in an increasing concentration of blacks within the ghettos of those too poor to move out (see Silver and Moeser 1995, regarding Atlanta for instance).

The post-Fordist ghetto of the period of Empowerment is new[19] in its perceived permanence. It has now become what I have called elsewhere an outcast ghetto (Marcuse 1996), a ghetto of the excluded, rather than of those dominated and exploited but still marginally useful.[20] It is certainly not the multiclass ghetto of earlier periods. The outcast ghetto adds a new dimension to the classic ghetto, a specific relationship between the particular population group and the dominant society: one of economic as well as spatial exclusion.

Data tell part of the story. In the area designated as an Empowerment Zone in Harlem and the Bronx in New York City, for instance, 42 per cent of all residents lived below the poverty level; 18 per cent were officially counted as unemployed. Thousands more were discouraged and not even looking for jobs: only 51 per cent were actually in the labour force. 27 per cent of all households were headed by a single woman, more than one-third of all households were receiving public assistance, the death rate was much higher than in the city as a whole; black men living in Harlem were less likely to reach the age of 65 than men in Bangladesh.[21] New York City is hardly alone: a solid recent study of Philadelphia, for instance, shows that, in 1980, 47.5 per cent of blacks living in the ghetto were on public assistance; 17 per cent of men aged 25–44 were unemployed, 33.3 per cent were not in the labour force (Jargowsky, in Jencks and Peterson 1991: 248). 44.3 per cent of black families had single parents (Jargowsky 1997: 246). Similarly distressing figures on rates of incarceration through the judicial system, on victimization by crime, on drug abuse, or limited education, could be cited endlessly.

But, beyond the figures, the composition of the outcast ghetto differs from its predecessors, and from immigrant and ethnic enclaves, in the crucial area of social organization. Loïc Wacquant has described some of the key characteristics of the new ghetto in this period: he speaks of,

lack of social potency . . . low organization density . . . the massive inferiority of its resident institutions . . . de-solidarizing effects . . . an impossible community, perpetually divided against [itself] . . .   (Wacquant 1997; he warns, properly, against converting this description to a normative one, arguing that the ghetto has indeed a 'specific social order', but a 'socio-fugal' one: 372, n. 15)

Outcast ghettos have existed before, perhaps; the squatters in the area that was to become Central Park in New York City might be considered a 19th-century analogy. But there were means of survival available to them that are no longer available today—a marginal self-sufficiency, based in significant part on agricultural activities: pig raising, bone boiling, wood foraging, self-built housing (see Blackmar and Rosenzweig 1992: 65–77).

A peculiar irony accompanies this latest phase in the evolution of the ghetto. As its residents are increasingly cast out, marginalized, unemployed, and unwanted by the dominant forces in society, their internal cohesion is weakened, but the importance of place to them may be strengthened. As real economic bonds, bonds of a common and viable education, cultural life, work and community building, are eroded, the bonds a common residential area increase. Thus, even if the formal internal organizational structure of Harlem appears weakened, its residents' turf allegiance is strengthened—defensively, it is true, and as a last resort, perhaps, but nevertheless strengthened. Displacement from a neighbourhood was not a concern in the early slum clearance projects of the 1930s; slums became fiercely contested terrain just as their internal coherence and strength weakened.[22]

A parallel ambiguity exists as to the economic life of the ghetto today. The ghetto of course has an economy; its residents would not survive without an extensive network of economic activity. It is sometimes characterized as part of the informal economy, but the description is misleading. Some parts of the ghetto are indeed involved at the margins of the primary economy, in very low-paid jobs, in part-time or occasional labour, in illegal activities linked to the mainstream market, as with drug dealing. But the characteristic of the economy of the outcast ghetto is its separation from that mainstream. Merchants on 125th street in Harlem sell to residents of Harlem; livery cab services are used primarily north of 110th street, largely by law; trade and services are directed at the African-American market. It is not an inconsequential market; the Department of Housing and Development is promoting investment in inner cities by publicizing the size of the 'untapped' (by mainstream firms) buying power of residents in it. But it is largely a separate market. Unlike in earlier times, Harlem is not a magnet for middle class African-Americans who may live elsewhere; it is isolated. The painful aspect of this development appears in the discussions of economic development in the ghetto (Marcuse 2000): the best hope for increased incomes for many in the ghetto often appears to lie precisely in the development of those activities and enterprises that rely on the very separation from the mainstream to establish their markets.

The ghetto in the present period is an 'ethclass' ghetto, combining a subordinate ethnicity with a subordinate class, in a way in which neither the earlier black ghetto nor the classic immigrant ghetto was an ethclass ghetto.[23] Frequently, ethnicity is defined as a division cross-cutting the divisions of class; each intersection may be defined as an ethclass (see Glazer and Gordon 1964, especially at p. 53). Then 'each ethclass has the potential for residential segregation from other members of the same social class on the basis of ethnic differences, and from other members of the same ethnic group on the basis of social class' (Boal 1981: 55). The outcast ghetto is new and unique in that it is negatively differentiated *both* horizontally and vertically, with both divisions being sharp ones, race perhaps as before, but class in a new sense, connected with the exclusion that contemporary organization of the economic system has produced for a significant part of the population (for this argument, spelled out in the South African context, see Marcuse 1995).

Conclusions

So the black ghetto has changed as the society and as the state organs which created it and in which it is embedded have changed. The periodization suggested here is of course only true in broad terms; there are no clear cut-offs where one period ends and another begins, and characteristics of the contemporary ghetto and its predecessors exist in each of them. As the country moves from early capitalist industrialization to full industrialization to post-Fordist forms, the spatial concentration of blacks has also taken different forms, with different consequences for its residents, responding to different directions of state policy. (For a discussion of the relationship between globalization and the ghetto, see Marcuse and Van Kempen 2000, and particularly Goldsmith 2000 therein.)

State action is inextricably interwoven with this history of the ghetto, and the reactions to it. Ghettos are not the pure product of social attitudes or economic developments; they could not have been created without state action, their form and meaning has been dominated by the impact of state policies, and their continued existence is only possible with state tolerance. The state cannot be neutral on matters of urban partition. Its policies—that is to say, the policies of those individuals and groups who are decisive in determining the direction it takes—have in the past fostered growth of the ghetto in the United States, and today bring dismay to those who would contest its continued existence. The state is neither the source of racism not an independent actor dealing with racial issues; it is subject to a wide variety of pressures, and its political leaders inevitably respond to initiatives from others as much as they initiate policy themselves. Nor can state action by itself end racism; private individual actions and attitudes must be involved too. But the institutions of the state play major roles in determining what private actions will be permitted, supported, enforced, or outlawed, and in the area of land use (including the components of ghettoization) are the essential steering mechanism used to determine outcomes. Thus a focus on state action is appropriate for those seeking to understand and to influence patterns of ghettoization in society.

The form of today's black ghetto, with its perceived permanence, the outcast ghetto, is the most disastrous of all the manifestations racial separation has taken over the last hundred and thirty years in the United States. Whether it represents the future, or whether it, like other but different forms of segregation in the past, can be overcome, will be decided by conflicts not yet resolved.

Notes

1. This chapter continues an exploration begun in Marcuse (1997) and developed further in Marcuse (1998). The term 'citadel' was introduced in this context by John Friedmann, and has received—and deserves—further extended treatment, not possible here (see Friedmann and Wolff 1982).

2. Other characteristics may lead to ghetto formation, or to enclaves, as here defined: for instance, by sexual preference, or by language. Race and ethnicity constitute the most widespread, visible, and invidious bases for ghetto formation.

3. 'Institutionalized' is added to the definition by Van Amersfoort: a ghetto is 'an institutionalized residential area in which all the inhabitants belong to a single ethnically, racially or religiously defined group and all members of this group live in this area . . .', 'institutionalized' means that the inhabitants did not choose their dwelling or residential area themselves: 'they were to some degree coerced

by society . . . by law or . . . by subtle discrimination' (Quoted in Van Kempen, 1994: 3). It is thus apparently intended to be synonymous with 'involuntary', and an important, if self-evident, addition to the definition. Were it to mean either 'with its own institutions' or 'created by formal institutions of the dominant society' it would raise other important questions.

4. Although the steps from Africa to the United States may go through intermediate countries, which may also be important in establishing position in the United States: in New York City, as of 1996, one-quarter of the city's black population was foreign-born, primarily from the Caribbean, and the line of distinction between Caribbean-born and United States-born among African-Americans plays a significant role in social and political, as well as in economic, life (New York City Department of City Planning 1996: 29).

5. I thus follow Gans' logic: '. . . African-American . . . is a term that seems to me to emphasize an ethnic heritage, and thus to de-emphasize, if not intentionally, the racial issues inherent in the term black' (Gans, 1991: x). Further, 'African-American' differentiates from other black people of African descent (e.g., those from the Caribbean). The precise position of such non-'native' groups is complex. My judgement is that they are treated substantially like African-Americans in residential patterns, with significant but limited differences in terms of jobs and economic progress.

6. In a fascinating paper which I saw after the bulk of this chapter was written, but which deserves more attention, David M. Cutler, Edward L. Glaeser, and Jacob L. Vigdor (1999), using quantitative data on segregation and isolation and prices paid by blacks and whites for housing, argue for a very similar periodization of the history of the ghetto: 1890–1940, 1940–70, and 1970–90 (and presumably continuing). They suggest however the difference between the period of Imposition and the period of Empowerment is a shift from centralized discrimination to decentralized discrimination, the former being legally imposed, the second resulting from market actions of whites.

7. So say Janet Abu-Lughod (1999: 83–4) and Iver Bernstein (1990). But at this point there were only about 15,000 blacks altogether in New York City (Johnson, 1968: 19, 39–44).

8. A small black population was located in Harlem from its beginnings, and 'gradually increased in size in the late 19th century as coloured servants worked in homes of the wealthy who moved into the neighborhood' (Osofsky, 1968: 83–4, cited by Abu-Lughod, 1999: 84). By 1900, there were 60,000 blacks in the New York City area.

9. Apparently including, somewhat surprisingly, some black former slave-owners (Abu-Lughod, 1999: 83, citing Wilson, 1994). Blacks were replaced by Italians in Greenwich Village in the second half of the 19th century, and formed new areas of concentration in the Tenderloin district and Hell's Kitchen in Manhattan.

10. 'Share' might not be the most appropriate term here. The authors point out that, of course, 80 per cent of black Americans did not live in cities at the time; large-scale urbanization was to come some decades later.

11. A parallel change, but of a quite different complexion, was going on in many immigrant enclaves at the same time. Compare, for instance, Michael Gold's (1928) picture of the Lower East Side with Janet Abu-Lughod's (1993).

12. Thus, when Lewis Mumford crusades for diversity in urban life, he is railing against the homogeneity and monotony of the suburbs: '. . . a sort of green ghetto

dedicated to the elite. The city, on the other hand, by its nature is a multi-form non-segregated environment. Little groups may indeed form social islands within a city . . . as people from a Greek or a Polish village might form temporary nests together in the same block in Chicago or New York. But the metropolis was a mixture of people who came from different places, . . . meeting and mingling, co-operating and clashing, the rich with the poor, the proud with the humble' (Mumford, 1961: 493). The black ghetto is not different from other 'social islands'.

13. McKenzie comments '. . . homeowner associations and restrictive covenants shifted their emphasis to class discrimination, which is legal, from race discrimination, which is not, and . . . this approach inevitably contributes to continuing racial segregation' (1994: 78).

14. It is a striking paragraph. She adds: 'In this case, the damage to our cities might be the least of our worries; unslumming is a by-product of other kinds of vigor and other forms of economic and social change' (Jacobs 1961: 284). This was written in 1961!

15. An interesting argument is made in Von Eschen (1996). The author argues that the cold war forced black anti-colonialists to drop the international focus of their efforts, in effect moderating the civil rights movement and breaking its confrontation with what might now be called incipient processes of globalization. The argument might follow that, without that confrontation, in particular on the economic front, the advances to be made shrank, accounting for the subsequent confrontation with the difficulties of achieving integration and shift in attitude towards the ghetto.

16. Elsewhere, he speaks, I believe with substantial exaggeration, of the Milllion Man March of Louis Farrakhan as 'the reflection of a disappearing identity' (p. 58), but the defensive characterization is the same.

17. Massey and Denton, for instance, define the ghetto in such a way that they can say: 'no ethnic or racial group in the history of the United States, except one, has ever experienced ghettoization, even briefly' (Massey and Denton 1993: 19).

18. The evidence in support of a turning point at about this date is substantial; see, for instance, Rose (1971: 49): 'It is becoming increasingly evident that the ghetto is evolving into a configuration devoid of meaningful employment opportunities, and at the same time is becoming the place of residence of persons with limited employment potential'.

19. The term is hardly precise; we are concerned here with specifying more precisely what is new, and why. Camillo Vergara, in a number of writings, has used the term to denote a ghetto created by government, in part through the concentration of public actions locating specific groups (e.g., the homeless, drug-dependent populations), in concentrated areas which become ghettos even more than they were before. His point is valid and useful, but I use the term 'new' here in the broader sense of the outcast ghetto. See Vergara (1991).

20. Christian Kesteloot suggests, in an interesting paper, that 'the growing importance of exclusion over marginalization' is a key characteristic of the present phase (Kesteloot 1994). The exclusion phenomenon is clearly an international one, although in most other countries not coupled with 'race', as in the United States. See, for instance, the description of the slum Villa Paraiso, in Cospito, Argentina, which Javier Auyero describes today: 'Villa Paraiso, once the place of the new-born working class, is now the space where the unpopulation (unemployed and unedu-

cated) survives . . . the functional links that used to tie the slum to larger society . . . have been severed. . . . Today, poverty in the slum exists in a context of deindustrialization and the generalized downward mobility of formerly large middle classes. As a consequence, slum poverty ceases to be perceived as transitory; social or economic mobility is unthinkable. Both perceptions mark a real difference from past beliefs . . .' (Auyero 1999: 58, 63, 64). The historical evolution Auyero describes parallels quite closely the account given here for the United States ghetto's change from the period of Confrontation to the period of Empowerment.

21. All figures are from the Empowerment Zone application filed with the U.S. Department of Housing and Urban Development in 1995 (New York City 1995).

22. Of course, the absence of turf resistance to displacement in the 1930s has something to do with Depression conditions, and stable and strong communities in the 1950s in New York, for instance, also resisted Moses' axe-like intrusions on their turf vigorously, so the logic suggested in the text runs along more complicated lines. Desperation is not the only reason people oppose displacement. See Marc Fried's (1963) path-breaking argument.

23. A qualification is needed here, although tangential to our main argument: the evidence is that blacks leaving the ethclass ghetto may well form middle class areas of concentration that are overwhelmingly black in the suburbs. But these are more akin to enclaves, in our sense. Andrew Hacker (1998: 28) quotes Alan Wolfe: 'In most cases, the rise of a black middle class produces black middle-class suburbs, distinct from white ones'. DeKalb county outside Atlanta is 54 per cent white, 42 per cent black. But within DeKalb, the towns of Gresham Park and Pantherville are both 95 per cent black, Tucker and Dunwoody are 90 and 94 per cent white (see, in general, Logan and Schneider 1984).

References

ABRAMS, C. (1955*a*). *Forbidden Neighbors.* New York: Harper.

——(1955*b*). 'Public housing myths', *The New Leader*, 25 July.

ABU-LUGHOD, J. (ed.) (1993). *From Urban Village to 'East Village': The Battle for New York's Lower East Side.* Oxford: Blackwell.

——(1999). *New York, Chicago, Los Angeles: America's Global Cities.* Minneapolis: University of Minnesota Press.

AUYERO, J. (1999). '"This is a lot like the Bronx, isn't it?" Lived experiences of marginality in an Argentine slum'. *International Journal of Urban and Regional Research,* 23(1): 45–69.

BANFIELD, E. C. (1974). *The Unheavenly City Revisited.* Boston: Little, Brown.

BAUMAN, J. F. (1987). *Public Housing, Race, and Renewal: Urban Planning in Philadelphia, 1920–1974.* Philadelphia: Temple University Press.

BERNSTEIN, I. (1990). *The New York City Draft Riots: Their Significance for American Society and Politics in the Age of the Civil War.* New York: Oxford University Press.

BLACKMAR, E., and ROSENZWEIG, R. (1992). *The People and the Park: A History of Central Park.* Ithaca: Cornell University Press.

BOAL, F. W. (1981). 'Ethnic residential segregation', in H. Johnston (ed.), *The Geography of Housing*, 41–77. London: Aldine.

BRACEY, J. H., MEIER, A., and RUDWICK, E. (eds.) (1971). *The Rise of the Ghetto.* Belmont, CA: Wadsworth.

CARMICHAEL, S., and HAMILTON, C. V. (1967). *Black Power: The Politics of Liberation in America.* New York: Random House.

CARO, R. A. (1974). *The Power Broker: Robert Moses and the Fall of New York.* New York: Alfred A. Knopf.

CASTELLS, M. (1997). *The Information Age: Economy, Society and Culture: Vol. II. The Power of Identity.* Oxford: Blackwell.

Citizens Commission in Civil Rights (1983). *A Decent Home: Report of the Citizens Commission On Civil Rights.* Washington, DC: United States Government Printing Office.

CLARK, K. (1965). *Dark Ghetto: Dilemmas of Social Power.* New York: Harper & Row.

CONGRESSIONAL RECORD (1968). Vol. 114, 20 February.

CUTLER, D. M., GLAESER, E. L., and VIGDOR, J. L. (1999). 'The rise and decline of the American ghetto'. *Journal of Political Economy*, 107(3): 455–506.

DRAKE, S. C., and CAYTON, H. (1945). *Black Metropolis: A Study of Negro Life in a Northern City.* New York: Harcourt, Brace.

DUBOIS, W. E. B. (1899). *The Philadelphia Negro.* Philadelphia: University of Pennsylvania. Reprinted in 1967. New York: B. Blom.

EARLY, J. (2000). 'What is the question: integration or defeat of racism?'. *Poverty and Race Research Action Council: Poverty and Race*, January/February: 5–6.

FAINSTEIN, N. (1993). 'Race, class, and segregation: discourses about African Americans'. *International Journal of Urban and Regional Research*, 17(3): 384–403.

FRIED, M. (1963). 'Grieving for a lost home: psychological costs of relocation', in L. J. Duhl (ed.), *The Urban Condition: People and Policy in the Metropolis*, 151–71. New York: Basic Books.

FRIEDMANN, J., and WOLFF, G. (1982). 'World city formation: an agenda for research and action'. *International Journal of Urban and Regional Research*, 6: 309–44.

GANS, H. J. (1991). *People, Plans, and Policies: Essays on Poverty, Racism, and Other National Urban Problems.* New York: Columbia University Press.

——(1996). 'Second generation decline: scenarios for the economic and ethnic futures of the post-1965 American immigrants', in N. Carmon (ed.), *Immigration and Integration in Post-Industrial Societies: Theoretical Analysis and Policy-Related Research*, 65–87. New York: St. Martin's Press.

——(1999). 'An integration scenario or ending the illusion'. *Poverty and Race*, November/December: 6–7.

GATES, H. L. (1997). 'Harlem on our minds'. *Critical Inquiry*, 24(1): 1–12.

——and WEST, C. (1996). *The Future of the Race.* New York: Alfred A. Knopf.

GELFAND, M. (1975). *A Nation of Cities: The Federal Government and Urban America, 1933–1965.* New York: Oxford University Press.

GLAZER, N., and GORDON, M. M. (1964). *Assimilation in American Life.* New York: Oxford University Press.

——and MOYNIHAN, D. P. (1963). *Beyond the Melting Pot: The Negroes, Puerto Ricans, Jews, Italians, and Irish of New York City.* Cambridge, MA: MIT Press.

GOERING, J. M. (1986). *Housing Desegregation and Federal Policy.* Chapel Hill: University of North Carolina Press.

GOLD, M. (1928). *Jews Without Money.* New York: Harcourt Brace.

GOLDFIELD, D. (1997). *Region, Race and Cities: Interpreting the Urban South*. Baton Rouge: Louisiana State University Press.

GOLDSMITH, W. W. (2000). 'From the metropolis to globalization: the dialectics of race and urban form', in P. Marcuse and R. van Kempen (eds.), *Globalizing Cities: A New Spatial Order?*, 37–55. Oxford: Blackwell.

——and BLAKELY, E. (1992). *Separate Societies: Poverty and Inequality in U.S. Cities*. Philadelphia: Temple University Press.

GORDON, D. (1984). 'Capitalist development and the history of American cities', in W. Tabb and L. Sawers (eds.), *Marxism and the Metropolis*, 2nd edn, 21–53. New York: Oxford University Press.

HACKER, A. H. (1998). 'Grand Illusion'. *New York Review of Books*, 11 June.

HAUSER, P. (1971). 'Demographic factors in the integration of the negro', in J. H. Bracey, A. Meier, and E. Rudwick (eds.), *The Rise of the Ghetto*, 40–3. Belmont, CA: Wadsworth.

HAYNES, G. E. (1913). 'Conditions among Negroes in the City'. *Annals of the American Academy of Political and Social Science*, 49 (September): 105–19.

HIRSCH, A. (1983). *Making the Second Ghetto: Race and Housing in Chicago, 1940–1960*. New York: Cambridge University Press.

HOCHSCHILD, J. L. (1995). *Facing Up to the American Dream: Race, Class and the Soul of the Nation*. Princeton: Princeton University Press.

HORNE, G. (1986). *Black and Red: W.E.B. DuBois and the Afro-American Response to the Cold War*. Albany: State University of New York Press.

JACKSON, K. (1985). *Crabgrass Frontier: The Suburbanization of the United States*. New York: Oxford University Press.

JACOBS, J. (1961). *The Death and Life of Great American Cities*. New York: Random House.

JARGOWSKY, P. A. (1997). *Poverty and Place: Ghettos, Barrios, and the American City*. New York: Russell Sage.

JENCKS, C., and PETERSEN, P. E. (1991). *The Urban Underclass*. Washington, DC: Brookings Institution.

JOHNSON, J. W. (1925). 'Harlem, Mecca of the New Negro'. *Survey*, 1(March): 635–9.

——(1930/1968). *Black Manhattan* [reissue]. New York: Da Capo Press.

KESTELOOT, C. (1994). 'Three Levels of Socio-spatial Polarization in Brussels'. Paper presented at: *ISA International Congress*, Bielefeld, Germany.

LAMMERMEIER, P. J. (1971). 'Cincinnati's black community: the origins of a ghetto, 1870–1880', in J. H. Bracey, A. Meier, and E. Rudwick (eds.), *The Rise of the Ghetto*, 24–8. Belmont, CA: Wadsworth.

LIEBERSON, S. (1980). *A Piece of the Pie: Blacks and White Immigrants since 1880*. Berkeley: University of California Press.

LOGAN, J. R., and SCHNEIDER, M. (1984). 'Racial segregation and racial change in American suburbs, 1970–1980'. *American Journal of Sociology*, 89: 874–88.

LOWRY, I. S. (1987). 'Where should the poor live?', in P. Salins (ed.), *Housing America's Poor*, 90–110. Chapel Hill: University of North Carolina Press.

MARABLE, M. (1996). *Speaking Truth to Power: Essays on Race, Resistance, and Radicalism*. Boulder: Westview Press.

MARCUSE, P. (1962). 'Benign quotas', in A. F. Westin (ed.), *Freedom Now*, 193–200. New York: Basic Books. Reprinted, in revised form, in C. Abrams and P. Marcuse (eds.) (1965), *Equality*, New York: Pantheon.

MARCUSE, P. (1986). 'The beginnings of public housing in New York'. *Journal of Urban History*, 12(4): 353–90.

——(1995). *Race, Space, and Class: the Unique and the Global in South Africa.* Occasional Paper Series. Department of Sociology, University of Witwatersrand, Johannesburg.

——(1996). 'Space and race in the post-Fordist city: the outcast ghetto and advanced homelessness in the United States today', in E. Mingione (ed.), *Urban Poverty and the Underclass*, 176–216. Oxford: Blackwell.

——(1997). 'The enclave, the citadel, and the ghetto: what has changed in the post-Fordist U.S. city'. *Urban Affairs Review*, 33(2): 228–64.

——(1998). 'Space over time: the changing position of the black ghetto in the United States'. *Netherlands Journal of Housing and the Built Environment*, 13(1): 7–24.

——(2000). 'Federal urban programs as multicultural planning: the empowerment zone approach', in M. Burayidi (ed.), *Urban Planning in a Multicultural Society*, 225–34. Westport, CT: Praeger.

——and VAN KEMPEN, R. (eds.) (2000). *Globalizing Cities: A New Spatial Order?* Oxford: Blackwell.

MASSEY, D., and DENTON, N. A. (1989). 'Hypersegregation in U.S. metropolitan areas: black and Hispanic segregation along five dimensions'. *Demography*, 26: 373–91.

————(1993). *American Apartheid: Segregation and the Making of the Underclass.* Cambridge, MA: Harvard University Press.

MCKENZIE, E. (1994). *Privatopia: Homeowner Associations and the Rise of Residential Private Government.* New Haven: Yale University Press.

MOYNIHAN, D. P. (1970). *Maximum Feasible Misunderstanding: Community Action in the War on Poverty.* New York: The Free Press.

MUMFORD, L. (1961). *The City in History: Its Origins, its Transformations, and its Prospects.* New York: Harcourt, Brace.

MYRDAL, G. (1944). *An American Dilemma.* New York: Harper & Brothers.

NESBITT, G. A. (1959). 'Break up the black ghetto?' *Crisis*, 56: 48–50, 52.

New York City (1995). *Application for Empowerment Zone.* Washington, DC: Department of Housing and Urban Development.

New York City Department of City Planning (1996). *The Newest New Yorkers.* New York: The City of New York.

New York Times (1991). 13 October, sec. 3: 9.

ORFIELD, G. (1988). 'Race and the liberal agenda: the loss of the integrationist dream, 1965–1974', in M. Weir, A. S. Orloft, and T. Skocpol (eds.), *Politics of Social Policy in the United States*, 313–55. Princeton: Princeton University Press.

OSOFSKY, G. (1968). *Harlem: the Making of a Ghetto: Negro New York, 1890–1930.* New York: Harper & Row.

PARK, R. E., BURGESS, E. W., and MCKENZIE, R. D. (1925/1967). *The City.* With an Introduction by Morris Janowitz. Chicago: University of Chicago Press.

PINKNEY, A. (1984). *The Myth of Black Progress.* Cambridge: Cambridge University Press.

PIVEN, F. F., and CLOWARD, R. A. (1966). 'Desegregated housing: Who pays for the reformers' ideal?' *New Republic*, 155 (27 December): 17–21.

————(1974a). *The Politics of Turmoil.* New York: Vintage Books.

————(1974b). 'The case against urban desegregation', in R. A. Cloward and F. F. Piven (eds.), *The Politics of Turmoil*, 177–200. New York: Vintage Books.

POLIKOFF, A. (1986). 'Sustainable integration or inevitable resegregation: the troubling questions', in J. M. Goering (ed.), *Housing Desegregation and Federal Policy*, 43–70. Chapel Hill: University of North Carolina Press.

PORTES, A. (1996). *Immigrant America: A Portrait*. Berkeley: University of California Press.

——and STEPICK, A., and FERNANDEZ KELLY, P. (1993). *City on the Edge: The Transformation of Miami*. Berkeley: University of California Press.

ROISMAN, F. W. (2000). 'Is integration possible? Of course . . .'. *Poverty and Race Research Action Council: Poverty and Race*, January/February: 4–5.

ROSE, H. (1971). *Black Ghetto*. New York: McGraw Hill.

SALINS, P. (1987). 'Conclusion', in P. Salins (ed.), *Housing America's Poor*, 175–93. Chapel Hill: University of North Carolina Press.

SILVER, C., and MOESER, J. V. (1995). *The Separate City: Black Communities in the Urban South, 1940–1968*. Lexington: University Press of Kentucky.

SPEAR, A. H. (1967). *Black Chicago: The Making of a Negro Ghetto, 1890–1920*. Chicago: University of Chicago Press.

STEINHORN, L., and DIGGS-BROWN, B. (1999). *By the Color of Our Skin: The Illusion of Integration and the Reality of Race*. New York: Dutton.

SUTTLES, G. D. (1974). *The Social Order of the Slum: Ethnicity and Territory in the Inner City*. Chicago: University of Chicago Press.

TAEUBER, K. E., and TAEUBER, A. F. (1965). *Negroes in Cities: Residential Segregation and Neighborhood Change*. Chicago: Aldine.

THOMAS, J., and RITZDORF, M. (eds.) (1997). *Urban Planning and the African American Community: In the Shadows*. California: Sage.

U.S. Department of Commerce, Bureau of the Census (1975). *Historical Statistics of the United States, Colonial Times to 1970*. Washington, DC: United States Government Printing Office.

U.S. Department of Housing and Urban Development (1999). *What We Know About Mortgage Lending Discrimination in America, 1999*. Washington, DC: United States Government Printing Office.

United States Supreme Court (1917). *Buchanan vs. Warley* 245 U.S. 60, 38 S.Ct. 16, 62 L.Ed. 149.

——(1948). *Shelley vs. Kramer* 334 U.S. 1.

VAN KEMPEN, R. (1994). 'Spatial segregation, spatial concentration, and social exclusion: Theory and practice in Dutch cities'. Paper presented at: *European Network for Housing Research Workshop*, Copenhagen, May.

VERGARA, C. (1991). 'Lessons learned, lessons forgotten: rebuilding New York city's poor communities'. *The Livable City*, 15(1): 3ff.

——(1995). *The New American Ghetto*. New Brunswick, NJ: Rutgers University Press.

VON ESCHEN, P. M. (1996). *Race Against Empire: Black Americans and Anti-colonialism, 1937–1957*. Ithaca: Cornell University Press.

WACQUANT, L. (1997). 'Three pernicious premises in the study of the American ghetto'. *International Journal of Urban and Regional Research*, 21: 341–53.

WAKSTEIN, A. M. (ed.) (1970). *The Urbanization of America: An Historical Anthology*. Boston: Houghton Mifflin.

WARNER, S. B. (1972). *The Urban Wilderness: A History of the American City*. New York: Harper & Row.

WEAVER, R. C. (1944). 'Race restrictive housing covenants'. *Journal of Land and Public Utility Economics*, 20(3): 183–93.

——(1948). *The Negro Ghetto*. New York: Harcourt, Brace.

WEST, C. (1994). *Race Matters*. New York: Vintage Books.

WILSON, S. (1994). *New York City's African Slaveholders*. New York: Garland.

WILSON, W. J. (1987). *The Truly Disadvantaged: The Inner City, the Underclass, and Public Policy*. Chicago: The University of Chicago Press.

WIRTH, L. (1928). *The Ghetto*. Chicago: University of Chicago Press.

WOLCOTT, V. W. (1997). 'The culture of the informal economy: number runners in inter-war black Detroit'. *Radical History Review*, 69: 46–75.

WOOD, C. N. (1992). *The Critical Chasm between Racism and Poverty in Present-day America*. Chicago: The Human Relations Foundation of Chicago, May.

WOODFORD, J. (2000). 'No one even knows what integration is'. *Poverty and Race Research Action Council: Poverty and Race*, January/February: 11.

WOOFTER, T. J. (1928). *Negro Problems in Cities*. New York: Garden City.

ZORBAUGH, H. (1929). *The Gold Coast and the Slum*. Chicago: University of Chicago Press.

7

Economic Restructuring and Urban Segregation in São Paulo

Sueli Ramos Schiffer

Introduction

The spatial changes in the São Paulo Metropolitan Area can be assessed in terms of its economic development from the late 1800s, when coffee production spurred the city's emergence as Brazil's economic centre, through the 1990s, when the nation had to restructure the whole of its economy to fit into today's patterns of economic globalization.

The main factor determining São Paulo's current form is the nature of Brazilian society. In Brazil, an 'elite society' controls the nation's economy by employing a process of 'hindered accumulation', designed to restrain the development of productive forces and to control the production of space through the ongoing association of the nation's elite with foreign capital.

Although immigrants (mainly Italian, Japanese, Jewish, German) formed ethnic clusters in the first decades of the 20th century, the most significant urban segregation in São Paulo is segregation by class. The urban pattern that developed alongside post-industrialization (i.e., after 1950) preserved a radial form expanding out from the colonial nucleus, and is characterized by the settling of lower-income groups in the outskirts of the city.

During the 1990s, the elite society maintained economic control, guaranteed by the country's ability to adapt to global economic patterns. Although new economic measures have been introduced and changes in the role of the state have been called for, there have not been structural changes, a fact that has resulted in a continuing imbalance in Brazilian society. This is strongly reflected in the urban space of the São Paulo Metropolitan Area.

As Brazil's main economic centre, this metropolis today demonstrates increasing urban segregation. Simultaneous to the expansion of advanced economic activities and the flourishing of expensive leisure activities and shops in upper-class districts has been unemployment and a great increase in violence, primarily in the outlying, lower-income areas. The sizeable growth of people living in slums and *favelas* occurs side by side with an expansion of high-income housing clusters, in the form of gated communities. This contrast makes urban class segregation even more visible than in the past.

Controlling the Production of Space in São Paulo

The São Paulo Metropolitan Area, created in 1973, comprises an area of 8,051 km², and includes 39 municipalities, subdivided into 137 districts. It is populated by 16,583,234 inhabitants, according to the 1996 official population survey. The municipality of São Paulo, the state's capital, is the largest municipality in both size (1,509 km² containing 96 of the total 137 metropolitan districts) and population (9,839,436 inhabitants in 1996, representing 59.3 per cent of the total metropolitan population). It is the largest Brazilian city.

The recent urban and socio-economic changes in the São Paulo Metropolitan Area cannot be attributed essentially to the present stage of internationalization of the economy, although the effects of internationalization can clearly be observed in the arrangement of metropolitan space. To understand the prevalent shape of urban form and the social relations that comprise it, we have to look back to the foundations of Brazilian society, in particular to the control it exerted on the production of national space and the development of urban agglomerations.

As mentioned by Préteceille (1997: 67), most studies since the mid 1980s that address the dynamics of urban change in world metropolises emphasize international processes as a main determinant. He claims that increasing international integration in trade and financial markets tends to overpower national economies, weakening the influence of their historically unique national socio-economic processes.

In our view, in developing countries at least, one cannot deny the importance of states as mediators between international capitalists and domestic economies at each stage of development, including that of the present. In fact, state intervention in Brazil serves the ultimate interests of dominant national groups. The consequential effects on the nation, in terms of both economy and space, are a result of how these interests interconnect with the historical process underway during a certain period of time. Referring to Latin America, Fernandes (1973: 59–60, 96) attributes,

the continuing and constant renovation of [its] subordination to foreign patterns through a very complex type of interconnection (partially spontaneous and partially planned, guided and controlled) between economies, societies and cultures of unequal development . . . However, what connects them is an internal decision of the bourgeoisie, which has the autonomy to choose alternative solutions, and the power to impose their will. To this end, they are able to capture national interests and to use the State to attain their goals . . . At the same time that dependent capitalism imposes heteronomous economic, social and political standpoints, it also offers major privileges to the high and middle classes as a primary mechanism of self-defense and of preservation of the internal basis for dominating relations.

According to Fernandes (1973), this is how an elite society is formed.

Interpreting this process, Deák (1999) proposes that the material basis for the reproduction of the national elite is a 'process of hindered accumulation', reminiscent of the colonial period. This process is designed to control the development of productive forces, to restrain them whenever their advance represents a force antagonistic to the prevalent economic model. Deák (1999: 31) stresses that,

on the level of social relations, the form of capitalism characterizing Brazilian society differs from other forms because it is an elite society, distinct from the bourgeoisie society, where the reification of social relations is not complete . . . since the principle of generalization of the commodity form does not predominate. Regarding the organization of production, the same prerequisites apply to ranking surplus expatriation over domestic accumulation . . .

The guarantee of effective control over the domestic economy offered by the national elite facilitates partnerships with foreign capital.

Based on these premises, we can argue that the Brazilian economy has been dictated by the relations between national and foreign capital, designed to maintain domination by the elite through a process of hindered accumulation. These relations were made possible by the state, which implements economic and legal measures internally, organizes public investments, and disseminates ideology, all in order to assure an ongoing economic process.

One of the central mechanisms used by the Brazilian elite to ensure its internal dominance is to control the intensity and nature of the national production of space, creating homogeneity by installing the infrastructure needed to allow the flow of capital, goods, and labour (Deák 1999), while simultaneously recreating urban and regional inequalities.

Focusing on cities, Villaça (1998: 148) attributes spatial segregation to disputes within localities, either between social groups (in the case of ethnic segregation) or between social classes. In regard to social classes, these disputes imply struggle, insofar as class segregation in urban space is 'a necessary process for the exercise of political domination and for the unequal appropriation of spatial resources, understood as the product of human work and the determinant force of the urban structure' (Villaça 1999: 221). Although this process can been considered universal, in developing countries the socio-economic contrasts in urban space are much deeper, expressing powerful inequities, exposing both unacceptable misery and absurd wealth.

In this sense, we can argue that the control of economic development by the ruling classes also requires that spatial segregation be shaped in a distinct manner. The range of spatial differentiation among segregated areas, whether regional or urban, in both physical and social terms, is determined by the particular stage of development of society, as measured by political and socio-economic, rather than macro-economic, indicators. It also means that the current process of urban segregation in the São Paulo Metropolitan Area cannot be understood without examining the historical development of its economy and spatial organization.

Historical Development of the São Paulo Metropolitan Area

Founded in 1554 on the site of a Jesuit church, São Paulo City lies on a plateau. For about three centuries, it was a small commercial depot into which state agricultural produce from inland regions en route to the port of Santos was channelled. The city saw sweeping expansion and economic ascent following the introduction of coffee plantations and the production of coffee in the state in the second half of the 19th century. The construction of a railroad network[1] centred on São Paulo City resulted in the city's economic prominence and its position at the core of the Brazilian economy. The railroad network enabled the transport of coffee through the port of Santos, replacing the traditional port of Rio de Janeiro.

Another important factor in the economic consolidation of São Paulo was the introduction of salaried labour for coffee production, as opposed to the slave labour[2] that was used in sugar cane production in the Northeast. For more than three hundred years, sugar cane had been Brazil's main export commodity. As the pace of coffee production quickened, both the opening of virgin land and a greater number of workers to work the land were required. The need for additional workers was filled by a large contingent of European immigrants, initially mostly Italians.

According to Matos (1958: 89), the urban form of São Paulo was reshaped just after 1880–90, with growing diversification of urban functions. The rapid expansion of the small colonial nucleus at that time led to spatial segregation. Workers' districts and higher-income residential areas started to be built at a distance from each other. Spatial class segregation was illustrated by Petroni (1958: 105), who noticed sometime in the first decade of the 20th century 'what could be observed as an interspersing of manufacturing plants, mostly of small and medium size, among worker homes' in manufacturing areas, predominantly along the railways.

It was at this time that two of the factors most determinant in the structuring of the Brazilian metropolis (particularly São Paulo) came into play: the location of manufacturers and the location of high-income housing areas (Villaça 1998: 140).

By 1910, segregation had definitely had an effect on urban form:

The city was divided into two major areas, and the Tamanduateí river acted as the divider between the two . . . Both areas were interconnected [at the Northeast side of the city], but only by a few roads. The two areas grew into two distinct cities, into twin cities . . .On one hand, there was the downtown area and the West, Southwest and South districts [mainly occupied by the higher-income groups]. On the other hand, there was the neighbourhood of Brás and its extension toward the East side of the city where the workers settled and where the manufacturing district was established. (Petroni 1958: 115)

Coffee production also attracted national and foreign immigration to São Paulo City, to such an extent that its population almost doubled in ten years, totalling 1,046,530 inhabitants in 1934. During the first three decades of the 20th century, growth of the city also meant greater urban segregation. This was reinforced by the uneven installation of public infrastructure and transport, as reported by Petroni (1958: 130–6). He observed that the first-provided and best-served areas were those occupied by higher-income groups and the down-town, which housed local businesses. This pattern emerged because the installation of a basic public infrastructure, including water, electricity, sewage, streetcars, and telephones, was governed by the logic of profit. These public services were provided by private companies through legal concessions. Since the public service contracts involved only the legal urban area,[3] remarkable differences in land prices resulted between this primary area and the un-served neighbouring rural areas (Rolnik 1999), a fact that eventually had major implications for the local real estate market.

The higher-income housing areas expanded towards the Southwest side of the city, after the construction, in 1891, of Avenida Paulista, a development with a complete infrastructure, built by private capital (Rolnik 1999). Here, coffee plantation owners settled and built their mansions. The so-called 'gar-den district' residential areas were developed, also toward the Southwest, for the upper class after 1915, mainly during the 1930s. The first was named Jardim América (American Garden); others followed. They were planned and built by a British real estate company, 'Companhia City':

The City [Company] bought 12 million m² of land, mainly in the South and West sides of the city. The success of the enterprise, however, was guaranteed by an association of interests of three parties: the City [Company], an English capital company, the Brazilian Light and Power company, which at that time had a streetcar transport and electric power monopoly in [São Paulo] City, and the São Paulo Municipal government. When the Garden district was opened, it guaranteed residents streetcar transport, water and power. (Leme 1999: 300)

Villaça (1998: 227) points out that the lower-income groups, composed mainly of production workers and former plantation household servants that had moved into town, 'participated in producing two types of lower income hous-ing areas . . .: the downtown area, frequent in the second half of the 19th cen-tury, and the outskirts, first settled in the early 20th century, when the lower classes were expelled from the historical centre. Until today, the outskirts are the major loci of the poor.' Today, the outskirts consist mostly of precarious, self-built homes. When the upper class began abandoning the downtown area during the 1960s, the central area again became the loci of lower-income housing, much of it occupied by squatters.

Foreign immigration also had a role in the spatial organization of São Paulo City. Immigration peaked around 1920 and continued at different intensities until just before 1950. Italians and other newcomers, such as Japanese, Germans, Jews, and Arabs, were involved in urban activities such as commerce, specialized manual work, and manufacturing. They occupied specific low-cost areas around the historical centre. During the second half of the 20th century, the ethnic ghettos gradually dispersed and were replaced by a spatial organization based on class segregation. Today, the only exception is what remains of the Japanese centre; most immigrants were integrated into the urban fabric according to their income levels.

In the early 20th century, coffee production profits were gradually and continuously transferred to the manufacturing sector,[4] so that by the late 1940s, coffee was no longer the predominant source of revenue in São Paulo State.

The urban expansion that would soon shape Greater São Paulo accompanied the rapid growth of the manufacturing industry along the railways, especially along the line to the port of Santos, whose terminal was located at the Southeast side of the city. The industrialization of peripheral cities began around 1940 in the neighbouring municipalities of São Caetano do Sul and Santo André to the south east, Guarulhos to the north east, and Osasco to the west.

Between 1955 and 1960, a major influx of foreign capital, mainly in the automobile industry, strengthened the economic primacy of the São Paulo Metropolitan Area; indeed, its share of national manufacturing value-added rose to over 50 per cent by 1960. The axis of industrialization then revolved around the main state highways, especially those leading to Rio de Janeiro (Presidente Dutra) and to the port of Santos (Via Anchieta). The latter reinforced the industrialization of the Southeast, which became one of the nation's largest manufacturing centres, including the municipalities of Santo André, São Bernardo, São Caetano, and Diadema (EMPLASA 1994).

A pronounced process of urban expansion, encompassing most of the small suburban centres and the already high-density built-up area has been the general pattern since the late 1940s. It was sparked primarily by the occupation of empty lots within the consolidated urban area and also by the vertical growth of residential districts (Langenbuch 1971: 179). Somekh (1997: 24) indicates that rising vertical expansion between 1940 and 1956 can be attributed largely to the demand for small flats, such as studio apartments. With the introduction of legislation that established building guidelines that constrained construction by the end of the 1950s, vertical growth was seen mostly in the higher-income areas. This represented an important element in the segregation of the city: 79 per cent of the districts with the greatest increase in vertical building in 1979 were concentrated in the Southwest side of São Paulo City, an area largely occupied by higher-income groups (Somekh 1997).

After 1960, the local real estate market for middle- and high-income groups quickly developed,[5] creating opportunities for profit from vertical growth or the development of new commercial areas (sometimes involving gentrification) which were moving away from the traditional downtown area towards the Southwest side of the city (Villaça 1998). This process was led by the upper classes in order to bring most of the dynamic economic activities and government institutions closer to their newly established residential areas, and has been ongoing ever since.

Since the mid 1970s, the São Paulo Metropolitan Area's manufacturing industry has been undergoing decentralization. This process can be attributed more to the strengthening of the local trade unions than to disadvantages arising from agglomeration. In the late 1970s, the unions achieved salary gains by striking. This caused an upheaval in the wage control system used by employers (Storper 1984). Although the transfer of manufacturing plants to other cities was intense, the process cannot be interpreted as one of de-industrialization. Notwithstanding, most head offices have remained in this region (Lencioni 1996), and the São Paulo Metropolitan Area's share of national manufacturing value-added was still about 21 per cent as late as 1996.

In fact, the São Paulo Metropolitan Area became a tertiary-oriented region, a process similar to that experienced by most major cities of developing countries in the period before 1990. So the predominance of the tertiary sector in both the city and the metropolis has not followed the same route as job distribution. Although the tertiary sector labour force has increased more than the manufacturing sector labour force, this difference in growth has been much higher than the production performance of these two sectors, strongly impacting job offers, as shall be discussed later.

In addition, the economic crisis faced by Brazil since the early 1980s has taken its toll on the labour market. The most evident result is the increase in informal jobs and other forms of non-legal job contracts, which do not offer official guarantees, such as paid vacation, social security, etc., to employees. This process marked the 1990s to an even greater extent, as discussed below.

The immediate impact was a decline in the population growth rate in both São Paulo Metropolitan Area, and more intensely, in the city of São Paulo. According to the official census, this growth rate averaged 1.9 per cent per annum and 1.2 per cent per annum from 1980 to 1991 in the metropolitan area and the city, respectively, as compared with 4.5 per cent per annum and 3.7 per cent per annum from 1970 to 1980.

The consequence for the urban form was a new process of occupation emerging during the 1980s, an invasion of mostly public land and the creation of new *favelas*. 'What is new in this process is that the lower-income groups do not need to pay for the land anymore' (Villaça 1998: 235). The predominant area of invasion was the city's South side, since it was relatively close to the city's wealthiest area (the Southwest), where informal jobs could be obtained.

Since the mid 1970s, there has been an increase in average density, which has been spreading from central to peripheral areas. The increase in average density in the central area was due to the expanding vertical growth of the wealthiest districts, whereas the increase in average density in the periphery was mostly due to high low-income housing congestion. Both aspects are further detailed in the following section, in which the metropolis' recent spatial form is discussed.

Alongside these local processes, São Paulo has had to deal with shifts in the world economy, particularly after the early 1990s, when Brazil introduced strong institutional and economic measures to ensure its inclusion in the globalized economy, as discussed in the following section. These measures have had major impacts on the city, both spatially and socio-economically.

Trends in the Brazilian Economy During the 1990s

The economic stagnation of leading countries began in the early 1970s, characterized by a decreasing per capita GNP growth rate and the downgrading of industrial production. According to the editors of the *Monthly Review* (1992/9) these were the driving forces behind the introduction of new rules for international accumulation, an effort to seize new opportunities for capital profitability. The new set of competitive bases introduced since then has enhanced 'the freedom of markets and the spirit of cooperation, presumably developing among ruling classes of different nations, in consonance with higher levels of globalization' (*Monthly Review* 1992/10).

The Brazilian ruling class has seen in the new international economic order an opportunity to preserve its internal hegemony, which has been weakened by the economic crisis that has persisted since 1981.[6] 'Globalization patterns' were firmly introduced into the Brazilian economy during the 1990s, using an ideological approach. That is, national development was enhanced by attracting foreign capital, either to provide direct investments or to force the modernization of national industry's technology and management in order to meet new competitive standards.

In the previous period, particularly between 1950 and 1980, the Brazilian state acted as a monopolistic supplier of infrastructure services and controlled most heavy industry. During the 1990s, discourse regarding the development of an ideal state was based on liberal precepts, despite the fact that strong state intervention was actually crucial to attain 'market' goals.

Two great historical challenges had to be met—huge price inflation that soared to almost 80 per cent a month by late 1989 and the promotion of a general opening of the economy—as prerequisites for Brazil's integration into prevalent international financial and trade markets.

Some of the key measures taken in this period can be summarized as follows:

1. Abrupt reduction of the import tax on a long list of products.
2. Deregulation of specific sectors to allow for the greater inflow of foreign capital, either in the financial sector (stock market, commercial and investment banks), or in the production sector.
3. Implementation of the 'Plano Real' in July 1994, designed to control inflation, which introduced high annual interest rates.
4. Privatization of state-owned heavy industry, and later, of the telecommunications industry, and concessions for private operation of electric power and highway systems.
5. Reorganization of the state structure, justified by claiming historical inefficiency and lack of resources due to a government fiscal imbalance.

The sudden introduction of most of the measures stated above, especially the opening of the economy, has had important effects on both the overall performance of the manufacturing sector and the labour market. Soares (1998: 272) concludes that 'the indiscriminate deregulation of imports . . . had an enormous destructive potential. Whole segments of our [i.e., the Brazilian] economy were dismantled, with all the well-known economic and social side effects, for instance, the de-engagement of part of the labour force'.

Overall, despite the effects of this dubious economic transition, Brazil's economic performance since the early 1990s has been marked by persisting hindered accumulation, based once more on a recessive economy, and coming at the expense of social investment. This process has also impacted urban and regional development and planning.

Brazil's ongoing 'liberal' restructuring has focused on the role of municipalities,[7] as both national and regional approaches to forming urban policies have been abandoned. This has been justified by the argument that it is more appropriate for municipalities to address 'local problems' and community demands. Municipalities have also been privileged targets for official financing, including financing from the World Bank. This new source of financing reflects an important change from previous trends of financing the state. This approach entails more than a mere substitution of the 'urban planning' concept for the 'local management' concept, as it prevents any possible action to address structural problems, which can be solved only at the federal level. Although issues like income distribution, structural unemployment, social exclusion, etc., are local political matters, it is not the duty of the municipality to address them.

It is worth noting the spread of the following ideological doctrine: namely that, today, because of the recurrent 'fiscal imbalance' of the state, jobs are mostly created through direct foreign investment, particularly in the manufacturing sector. This belief has provoked an overall tax war among the federal states, with the involvement of municipalities as well, entailing offers of special privileges to new investors. In addition to the public installation of required infrastructure at no cost to private capital, local (or state) governments offer long-term tax subsidies to guarantee the profitability of private invest-ments. Based on the assessment of a number of case studies, Piancastelli and Perobelli (1996) concluded that the direct and indirect financial benefits offered by the states and municipalities fell far short of providing a positive return on investment, even considering the prospective new jobs or the (doubtful) agglomeration effects that could ensue.

Some local efforts to rechannel new investments in Brazil have been success-ful, particularly those aimed at attracting manufacturing assembly lines. The general trend, however, is an increasing concentration of capital and the expan-sion of advanced services and businesses in São Paulo. The city continues to attract a more diversified supply of leisure and cultural events, as well as private investments geared to the higher-skilled labour force. These tendencies have left their mark on the spatial configuration of the city's metropolitan area, reshaping the urban form according to the political and socio-economic processes underway.

The Recent Spatial Form of the Metropolis

The São Paulo Metropolitan Area, as Brazil's leading economic centre, has reacted more quickly than other areas to broad national efforts to adapt to the recent increase in the internationalization of the economy. Its reaction has been characterized by two opposing trends. On one hand, the city of São Paulo has attracted an increasing concentration of specialized and technologically ad-vanced activities, including financial services, business conferences, 'designer' international shops, and diversified leisure activities (Schiffer 2001). It has also accumulated the benefits of heftier investments, namely direct and infrastruc-ture ventures, and has built up its skilled labour force. On the other hand, it is the locus of social dislocations resulting from greater globalization, such as growing unemployment and informal employment, increasing violence, and expanding urban squatter settlements.

It can be assumed that the urbanization process in the state of São Paulo, which was partially responsible for the intense metropolitan population growth rate, especially from 1950 to 1980, has ended: an official survey by the FIBGE (1996) reports that just 6.9 per cent of the whole state population was classified as rural in 1996. The decline in the population growth rate as of 1980 indicates an end to the status of the São Paulo Metropolitan Area as the region's main destination of immigration. Nonetheless, it is remarkable that despite even lower growth rates from 1991 to 1996 (1.4 and 0.4 per cent per annum for the São Paulo Metropolitan Area and the City, respectively) than during the previous decade the population increased from 1980 to 1996 (in absolute numbers) by 3,961,448 in Greater São Paulo and by 1,318,550 in the city proper. This population growth creates considerable demand for housing, jobs, and public services. This is exacerbated by the fact that the geographical distribution of population growth within the metropolitan area is quite irregular, as indicated in Figs 7.1(a) and (b), with negative growth rates in the more established areas, where the higher-income population lives, and positive rates in the outskirts, where there are already serious deficiencies in the social and urban infrastructure, particularly in transport and telecommunications.

Overall, during the 1990s, the duality of the urban structure of the metropolis has intensified. Characterizing this duality is the existence of districts well served by advanced infrastructure alongside districts with scarce basic infrastructure; high levels of unemployment and unskilled employment contrasting with employees paid the highest wages in the nation; luxurious buildings equipped with all sorts of advanced electronic technology to serve the business-oriented international economy coexisting with the *favelas* that house an increasing number of people.

Changes in the Labour Market

Ever since the mid 1970s, the metropolitan manufacturing sector has been undergoing a pronounced process of assembly line and management restructuring aimed at increasing productivity. In practice, this has led to a huge decrease in job offers. The national economic changes of the 1990s, as previously discussed, had even greater impacts on the metropolitan labour market.

According to research conducted by Cacciamali (1991, 1998), the main changes in the composition of the metropolitan area's labour market between 1985 and 1995, were: (i) a growth in the number of non-registered and unlicensed workers and informal jobs;[8] (ii) an increasing number of sole proprietorships and small companies; (iii) a drop in average wages in all economic sectors and job levels; (iv) an increase in total unemployment; and (v) a growing predominance of tertiary sector jobs (including informal jobs) over manufacturing sector jobs.

In respect to economic performance, following the world trend of the last few decades, the metropolitan area has increased its value-added related to the tertiary sector from 20.5 per cent of total value-added produced in 1985 to 37.7 per cent in 1995. At the same time, the value-added share for the manufacturing sector fell from 75.7 per cent to 58.0 per cent. This trend has been more intense in São Paulo City, where there has been a dramatic shift in the sectoral composition of value-added, with an increase from 28.8 per cent to 46.2 per cent in the tertiary sector, and a decline from 69.1 per cent to 49.1 per cent in the manufacturing sector in the same period (FSEADE, tables selected from the website, May 1999).

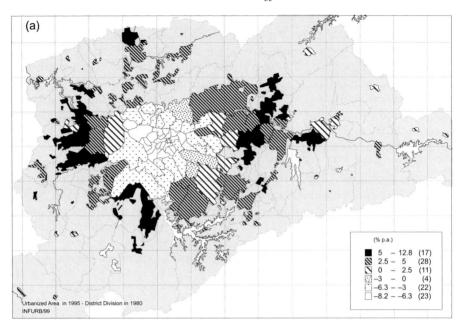

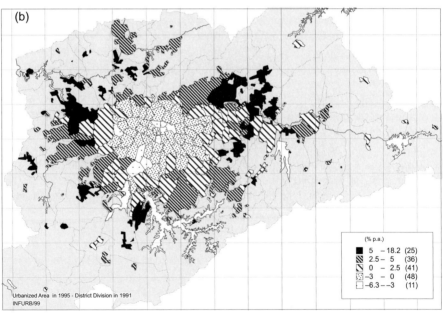

Fig. 7.1. The São Paulo Metropolitan Area. (a) Population growth rate (1980–91); (b) Population growth rate (1991–96)

Sources: FIBGE Demographic Census, 1991 and Population Survey, 1996

Meanwhile, the correlated increase in tertiary jobs did not make up for the jobs lost in the manufacturing sector, resulting in a sharp rise in the unemployment rate, which has been increasing substantially ever since 1989. In March of 1989, the unemployment rate was 7.5 per cent for São Paulo City and 7.7 per cent for the Metropolitan Area; by March of 1999 it had soared to 16.8 per cent and 18.1 per cent, respectively. Unemployment is slightly higher in the municipalities surrounding São Paulo City, mainly because these areas are predominantly occupied by manufacturing sector workers, and consequently have been most affected by the restructuring of this sector. Taking March 1988 as base 100 for the metropolitan job level in the manufacturing sector, by March 1999 the level had declined to 67.5. In addition, the portion of the working-age population in informal jobs has also climbed, from 12.2 per cent in 1989, to 14.7 per cent in mid 1996 (Montagner and Springer 1997).

Especially noteworthy is the fact that the spatial distribution of tertiary jobs within the metropolis indicates a high concentration in the wealthiest areas, as shown on Fig. 7.2. These data also provide a clear picture of spatial segregation, especially when compared to the spatial distribution of household incomes (Figs 7.3a and b).

Salaries in all income brackets have been affected by the current Brazilian economic recession and the performance of the metropolitan economy, a fact with major repercussions for the average household income. Although this is higher in São Paulo City than in the São Paulo Metropolitan Area, a general decline was observed between 1989 and 1996: from R$2,654 to R$1,681 in the

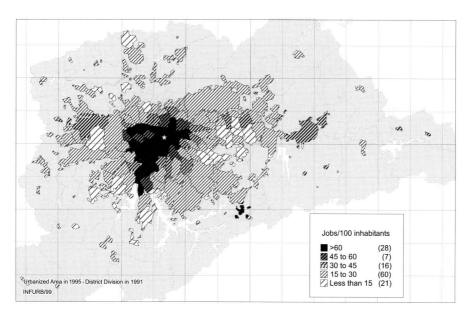

Jobs/100 inhabitants	
■ >60	(28)
▨ 45 to 60	(7)
▨ 30 to 45	(16)
▨ 15 to 30	(60)
▨ Less than 15	(21)

Urbanized Area in 1995 - District Division in 1991
INFURB/99

Fig. 7.2. São Paulo Metropolitan Area. Tertiary sector employment rate (1997)
Source: FIBGE, METRÔ Origin–Destination Survey, 1997

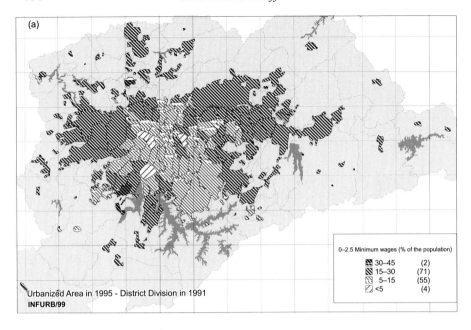

(a)

0–2.5 Minimum wages (% of the population)

▨ 30–45 (2)
▧ 15–30 (71)
▨ 5–15 (55)
▱ <5 (4)

Urbanized Area in 1995 - District Division in 1991
INFURB/99

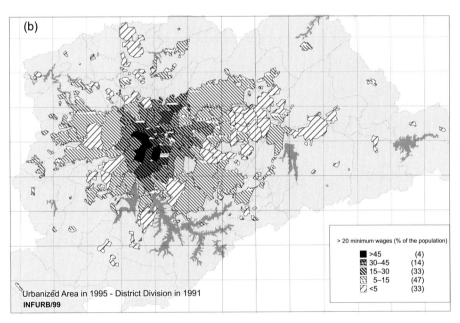

(b)

> 20 minimum wages (% of the population)

■ >45 (4)
▨ 30–45 (14)
▨ 15–30 (33)
▨ 5–15 (47)
▱ <5 (33)

Urbanized Area in 1995 - District Division in 1991
INFURB/99

Fig. 7.3. (*a*) São Paulo Metropolitan Area. Predominance of household incomes up to 2.5 minimum wages* (1997). (*b*) Predominance of household incomes over 20 minimum wages* (1997)

Note: *1 minimum wage = US$ 80 (December 1999)
Source: FIBGE, METRÔ Origin–Destination Survey, 1997

city, and from R$2,491 to R$1,507 in the metropolitan area (figures for June 1997, FSEADE 1999).

Growing unemployment and the fall of average real wages, on one hand, and the concentration of capital within São Paulo City, on the other, have had an important spatial impact on urban segregation, particularly in the housing sector.

Housing Segregation

Although the São Paulo Metropolitan Area has maintained a radial form and has never adopted the peripheral upper-class model associated with urbanization in the United States, the establishment of elite residential areas towards the Southwest resulted in a very exclusionary urban pattern, since the benefits of unequally installed modern infrastructure favoured the wealthiest areas. This pattern can readily be seen in Figs 7.3a and b, showing the lowest and highest household incomes. In fact, the spatial distribution of the income brackets essentially replicates the distribution found within the metropolis of most social indicators, such as public health and education, transport facilities, and location of squatter settlements.

The physical and legal constraints on urban occupation, in addition to the high price of land at the core of São Paulo City, have led to a pattern of peripheral low-income housing occupation. After the mid 1970s, this process crossed over city boundaries, and the lower-income population was literally pushed into the neighbouring municipalities, to such an extent that by 1996, Guarulhos had became the second largest city (in terms of population) in the state of São Paulo, behind only São Paulo City itself. Concurrent with the great increase of land invasions in the inner city (as described above) was an increase in the inhabitants per room index (Fig. 7.4) for lower-income homes in the metropolitan peripheral areas and vertical growth in the inner districts. These processes together have reorganized urban density among the metropolitan districts, tending to lessen the differences between districts (Fig. 7.5). The precariousness of most peripheral occupation in the metropolitan area, assessed by the number of inhabitants per room, reveals a very dense and inadequate housing situation.

In the metropolitan area, there has been a growing aggravation of housing problems, with a sharp decrease in the supply and financing of housing for low-income groups, following the restructuring of the federal system for housing funding in 1986. This has resulted in a greater portion of the population living in *favelas*. Whereas the FIPE/SEHAB survey counted 1.1 per cent of the population living in *favelas* in São Paulo City in 1987, the percentage soared to 19.3 per cent in 1993, a percentage that represents almost 2 million people (FIPE/SEHAB, Cadastro de Favelas 1987 and 1993). The *favelas* are unequally distributed within the urban environment, as indicated on Fig. 7.6, with a high concentration in the outskirts and a lower concentration in areas of more developed infrastructure.

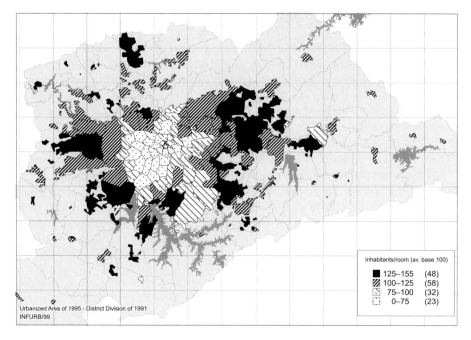

Fig. 7.4. São Paulo Metropolitan Area. Housing congestion index (1991)
Source: FIBGE, Demographic Census, 1991

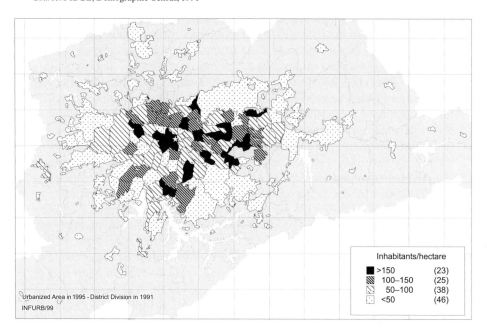

Fig. 7.5. São Paulo Metropolitan Area. Net density (1997)
Source: FIBGE, METRÔ Origin–Destination Survey, 1997

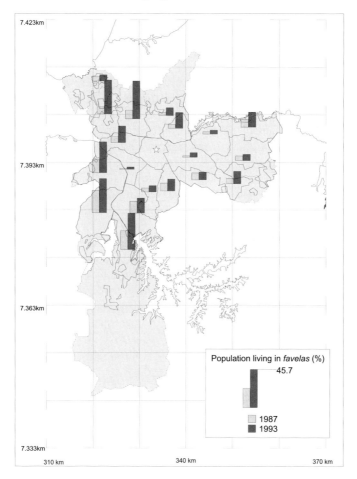

Fig. 7.6. São Paulo City. Population living in *favelas* (1987–93)
Source: FIPE/SEHAB, *Cadastro de Favelas*, 1987, 1993

As for the number of slum-dwellers in the municipality of São Paulo, Taschner (1997) estimates the figure at close to 6 per cent of the population in 1993. This represents less than 600,000 inhabitants. There is no information on the geographical dispersal of slum-dwellers. Although the number of homes in the *favelas* has increased sharply in recent years, Taschner (1997) observes that a great number of these homes have improved in terms of construction quality and household appliances.

The most apparent problem of the peripheral settlement pattern is the invasion of the reservoir area by illegal housing settlements, particularly in the South side of São Paulo City, around the Guarapiranga basin, and in the Southwest side of the metropolis along the Billings basin. The Billings and the Guarapiranga are the two main regional reservoirs.

Most of the areas situated to the extreme south and north east of the metropolitan area belong to the protected water reservoir region, in which economic development is restricted. The control of settlements around the water reservoir is regulated by a special state law (1172/76) of 1976, which established that illegal settlements have no right to water, energy, and sewerage facilities, in addition to stipulating penalties and fines. In 1997, a new state law,[9] designed to prevent further environmental degradation in these areas, allowed the government to implement emergency interventions, such as the provision of infrastructure, particularly water, energy, and sewerage facilities, and the containment of erosion in the more densely invaded areas (FSP, 11-2-98).

Two central issues emerging after the country's accumulation stage in the 1960s were resolved as early as the 1980s, benefiting practically the entire central metropolitan area and almost 80 per cent of the peripheral areas. These issues were: access of the population to treated water and electric power, required by Health Sanitation, and to the growth in overall paid consumption, which included the expansion of basic infrastructure. Nonetheless, the quality and frequency of these services still remain unequally distributed among the districts. The distribution is even more unequal for more technologically advanced infrastructures, such as telecommunications (especially fibre optics).

Data from the Official Municipality Real Estate Register, compiled to collect taxes for road maintenance and cleaning (Cadastro de Taxa Predial de Conservação e Limpeza: TPCL) in 1990 and 1995, show significant growth in new (legal) construction in the central districts, which are precisely those for which the demographic growth rate was negative. Taking 1995 as an example (even though an Official Municipality Register aiming at tax collection could be considered a precarious source for obtaining data on the non-legal areas), these data indicate that the districts of highest vertical growth, as well as those districts housing more commercial buildings, largely coincide with those of higher income. Moreover, recent manufacturing construction still predominates in the same districts as before, mainly along the Pinheiros and the Tiete rivers. Figure 7.7, compiled after the Official Municipality Register (1995), shows the predominance of land use measured in terms of built-up areas, with high-income horizontal and vertical housing, commerce, lower-income housing, and manufacturing areas within São Paulo City.

The Creation of 'New' Centres

The tendency of the São Paulo elite to periodically create new centres for modern business or leisure activities has contributed to the sharpening contrast between districts where dynamic sectors (mostly connected with 'global' activities) are established and those districts on the outskirts of the city.

According to Villaça (1999: 230), 'the process of abandoning a traditional centre and creating a "new centre" is initiated by the real estate market. More highly valued "central" locations are created in areas settled by high-income

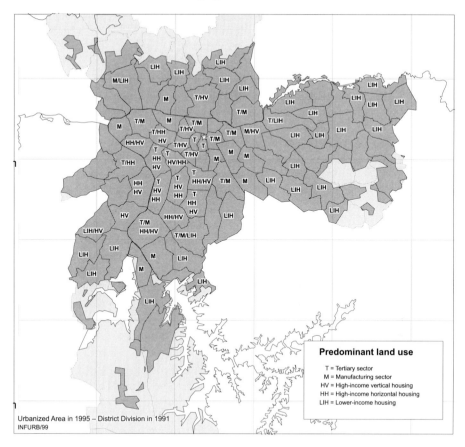

Fig. 7.7. São Paulo City. Predominant land use (1995)
Source: Prefeitura Municipal de São Paulo. *Cadastro TPCL*, 1995

housing, following the move to a "New Centre". By controlling the real estate market, the dominant class controls not only the growth (or the lack of growth) of the traditional centre, but also the form (continuous or discontinuous) and the direction of this growth.' This process can be assessed by real estate market values within the metropolitan area (Fig. 7.8). Today, the most visible outcome of this process, whereby the elite controls the creation of 'new centres', is the existence of four main economic centres within São Paulo City. As reported by Villaça (1998: 264), by the end of the 1950s, the traditional centre of São Paulo was already divided into two sides by the Anhangabau Valley: the Southwest side, home to prestigious offices, restaurants, and shops, and the Northeast side, housing lower-income shopping and leisure activities.

A second centre was developed during the late 1960s along Paulista Avenue, where modern buildings replaced coffee plantation mansions. This 'new' centre did not completely replace the traditional one. Rather, it became a centre for

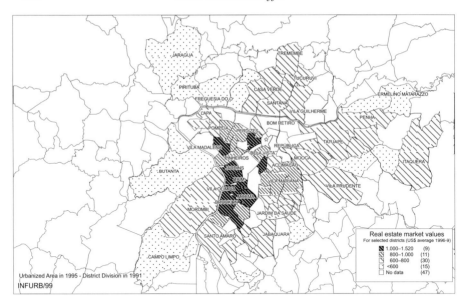

Fig. 7.8. São Paulo Metropolitan Area. Values set by the real estate market for selected districts (1996–8)

Source: EMBRAESP Annual Report, 1999

activities engaged in specifically by the elite, housing an array of movie theatres, designer shops, bank head offices, and specialized services. At this time, scattered sub-centres on streets located in non-elite residential areas also began to emerge to serve the low- and middle-income population, in contrast to the elite activities performed in the 'new city centre'.

A third centre, Faria Lima, was formed in the 1970s, at the foot of and south west of the Paulista Ridge, along Brigadeiro Faria Lima Avenue. Here, offices were built in the vicinity of the oldest shopping mall in town, which had been erected in the previous decade. Most of the sophisticated shops moved to this mall as well as to others later built in the highest-income housing areas. The area around Faria Lima mainly housed offices, bank branches, mid size stores, and luxury apartment buildings, following a pattern similar to the occupation along and around Paulista Avenue; both were described by Villaça (1998: 266) as 'extended centres'.

The newest centre, which was developed after the 1980s along Luiz Carlos Berrini Avenue, is also an extended centre. This centre has essentially become the venue for multinational corporations operating in the manufacturing and financial sectors in connection with globalized activities. Even the architectural pattern predominant in this centre is very similar to the new buildings located in the central business districts (CBDs) of New York City or London. Most of these newer office buildings were designed by prestigious foreign architectural firms and built by transnational investors, a signal that the process of de-location of the real estate sector in São Paulo is ongoing and that it is following a process described by Beauregard and Haila (1997: 335) as being common to primary world cities. This fourth centre was recently connected to the third centre (Faria Lima) by a new avenue, called Nova Faria Lima, along which office buildings, providing space for the self-employed, general contractors, and other service-rendering professions catering to the growing outsourcing market.

The emergence of each 'new' elite centre usually leads to a process of gentrification, which, although conducted mainly by private capital, is largely dependent on considerable state and/or municipal investment, such as the installation of telecommunications and other direct core business-related infrastructure services, and the construction of new access facilities, such as roads and tunnels. This infrastructure modifies previous traffic flows and mobility rates, and, most importantly, changes the value of land in the metropolitan districts by increasing the value of the renewed areas and their surroundings.

The Increase in Violence and the Formation of Upper-class Urban Clusters

As Costa (1999: 237) argues, data from European and Latin America countries indicate that violence has been increasing worldwide. Particularly alarming in Brazil, and especially in the São Paulo Metropolitan Area, is the rise in homicides. Cardia (1999: 1) indicates that the homicide rate in the São Paulo Metropolitan Area grew from 14.6 per 100,000 inhabitants in 1981 to 55.8 in 1998, which was almost twice as high as the national rate.

The spread of violence in the metropolis over the last two decades can be attributed to structural and local factors, related to the economic development of both the country and the metropolis. At the national level, monetary and fiscal policies have been prioritized at the expense of social policies. The ceiling for and duration of welfare benefits remain low. There was a shortfall in social housing construction and financing during the 1980s. Three particular local factors can be mentioned. First, average household income decreased dramatically, mostly affecting low-wage earners. Second, and most importantly, industrial restructuring has led to unemployment. Third, state intervention is too weak to improve the poorest peripheral areas or to re-urbanize the *favelas*, a particular aspect of the general inadequacy of state social intervention.

Maricato (1996: 80) also points out that 'the emergence of organized crime and the drug trade, vigilante groups, and the killing of children and adolescents are facts that gained new dimensions after the 80's'.

Although surveys show that violence is the most evident urban problem for all classes and ages, it affects different urban areas and different genders in various ways. Cardia (1999: 3) stress that violence mainly 'victimizes young males living in the poorest areas of cities (the deprived areas on the outskirts of the cities developed and made habitable by the people themselves), where now-existing public services arrived precariously after people had settled the area'.

Such patterns have roots in metropolitan spatial segregation, expressed in the unequal distribution of social facilities (such as public schools and sport or leisure areas) and effective policing, as well as other basic services that the poorest areas are denied. Other factors promoting the spread of violence include the growing unemployment, the alarming increase in the number of homes in the *favelas* since the mid 1970s, and the spiralling rate of inhabitants per room in the poorest districts. The association of growth in the *favelas* with that of violence can be easily established by comparing the geographical distri-

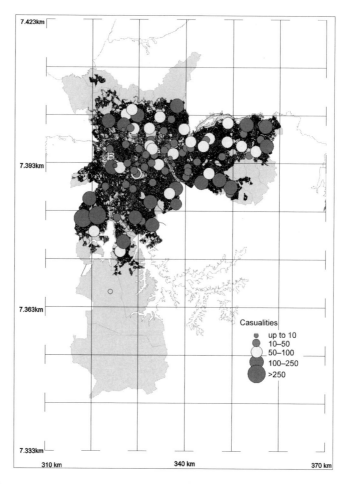

Fig. 7.9. São Paulo City. Number of homicides (1997)

Source: Secretaria da Seguranca Pública do Estado de São Paulo, 1997

bution of *favelas* shown in Fig. 7.6 and data on the homicide rate (Fig. 7.9) in São Paulo City, 1997. The figures show clearly that homicides are much more frequent in the outskirts.

The reaction of the upper classes to climbing levels of violence has been to develop shopping and residential urban clusters. The flourishing of several malls for the middle or upper classes in the metropolitan area since the late 1970s has resulted in mall shopping replacing most street shopping. The construction of high walls enclosing single dwellings, as well as the hiring of private security guards to protect a group of homes, has become very common. However, the newest trend of the last two decades has been the rapid spread of fortified 'citadels', to use Marcuse's term (1997: 311) for the American example: urban gated communities that house luxury apartment buildings or a group of homes, communities serviced by private security guards, and electronic equipment to control visitor entrances and exits.

Although we can find some existence of the 'edge city' pattern in the São Paulo Metropolitan Area, mainly in western metropolitan limits where over ten high-income housing condominiums have been built since 1970 (including several gated communities serviced by private security), the most valuable real estate today consists of fortified enclaves within the higher-income districts of São Paulo City. These enclaves combine proximity to upper-class leisure, shopping, and private schools with greater access to workplaces, since, as discussed earlier, the local elite traditionally attracts advanced economic activities and skilled jobs to its new residential areas.

These urban clusters are not just the supreme expression of spatial segregation among classes, but also represent upper-class segregation from the city itself. The city no longer represents a place where members of the elite live; a place characterized by a distinct landscape of contrasting geography and land use patterns. The city, except for the particular gated areas that house elite activities, becomes an unknown (violent) space, towards which the elite feels no commitment.

Conclusions

Spatial segregation was introduced in the São Paulo Metropolitan Area during the last decade of the 19th century, following its economic rise as a depot for coffee, produced in the interior of the state, en route to the port of Santos.

Although much economic restructuring has taken place in Brazil since, the basic structure of the national accumulation process has not shifted from the paradigm of colonial times. In that period, an elite society was formed, the particular nature of which was to impose a process of hindered accumulation internally through periodic associations with foreign capital, aimed at maintaining the security of its hegemony. These associations were historically orchestrated in such a way that benefited both foreign capital and the national elite: foreign capital could exert control over advanced industries in Brazil, and the national elite could control the development of the productive forces through the means of the state.

Control over the production and alteration of national space is one of the central mechanisms used by the Brazilian elite to ensure its internal dominance. Another feature of this society is its creation of high-income segregated areas, either for housing or for skilled employment, in which all types of urban facilities and infrastructure are installed by the state.

Urban segregation in most Brazilian cities, particularly in the São Paulo Metropolitan Area, is a result of class segregation, although up until the 1940s, ethnic segregation due to (newcomer) immigrant clusters could be seen in the spatial structure of cities.

Today, the metropolitan spatial form reflects two processes. The first is the historical local process, which basically began with the growth of industrialization after 1955, which was eventually followed by economic restructuring during the mid 1970s, particularly in the manufacturing sector. The second, subsequent process brought about economic adjustments resulting from the accommodation of current international accumulation patterns.

As a main economic outcome of both the historical and the internationalization processes in the São Paulo Metropolitan Area, the metropolis has evolved from a manufacturing-oriented to a tertiary-oriented economy. Characterized by a high concentration of advanced services and financial industries, the metropolitan area is home to head offices of national and foreign corporations, located in the municipality of São Paulo, the state's central city and Brazil's leading economic centre.

At the same time, negative side effects, such as growing unemployment, massive growth in the number of *favela* inhabitants, the spread of upper-class clusters, and social violence have threatened the quality of life of the whole population. These deficiencies jeopardize the functional attractiveness of the city, and challenge urban managers and the ruling class to revise the elitist approach to the development of the built environment, an approach that has historically led to high levels of social and urban segregation.

Notes

1. The first railroad was completed in 1868, connecting the city of São Paulo to the port of Santos. Another line was built in 1872, connecting São Paulo to the main coffee plantation regions around the city of Campinas. The railroad network in São Paulo State expanded speedily as new coffee plantation areas sprouted throughout the landscape; by the late 19th century, its total length was 3,375 km. (Matos 1958: 68).
2. Slavery was officially abolished in Brazil in 1888, but international traffic in slaves was forbidden earlier, in 1850.

3. The urban perimeter is delimited by municipal law in Brazil.
4. This transfer was a result of aggressive state policies introduced in about 1900, remaining in effect until the mid 1930s. These policies favoured the domestic elite (the coffee plantation owners) who strove to sustain international coffee prices, mainly by buying (and stocking) practically the entire supply at elevated prices. This generated profits that had to be channelled to other activities in the face of the mounting international supply of coffee.
5. Villaça (1998) stresses that one of the three mechanisms used by the ruling class to control the production of the built environment is the control of the real estate market.
6. The economic crisis in Brazil was postponed until the early 1980s thanks to a specific government plan (II PND–II National Development Plan), implemented between 1974 and 1976, and designed to provide new guidelines for Brazil's inclusion in the world economy. The plan was abruptly suspended because further implementation depended on substantially raising the general level of productive forces, a step interpreted by the national elite as a threat to its dominance. For further assessment of the economic and political impact of the Plan, see Schiffer (1992).
7. Partly at the root of the municipality-oriented restructuring is the National Constitution of 1988, which increased municipalities' share of total tax revenue controlled by the federal government.
8. The definition of informal jobs used here is based on the International Labour Organization's (ILO) classification: independent workers (not including those who work for just one firm with more than five employees), workers in firms with less than five employees, unregistered workers, owners of a family business with less than five employees, and family members who work in a family business and are not paid a salary.
9. State Decree 43022/98 that regulated State Law 9866/97.

References

BEAUREGARD, R. A., and HAILA, A. (1997). 'The unavoidable incompleteness of the city'. *American Behavioral Scientist*, 41: 327–41.

CACCIAMALI, M. C. (1991). 'O ajustamento do mercado de trabalho na década de oitenta'. Paper presented at the proceedings of the seminar: *Reestruturação do espaço regional e urbano no Brasil*. Ouro Preto: ANPUR/CEDEPLAR/IPPUR.

——(1998). *O mercado de trabalho na região metropolitana de São Paulo no fim do século XX*. São Paulo: INFURB-USP.

CARDIA, N. (1999). *Urban violence in São Paulo*. São Paulo: Núcleo de Estudos da Violência da Universidade de São Paulo. Discussion paper.

COSTA, M. R. (1999). 'Violência e ilegalidade na sociedade brasileira', in M. A. Souza *et al.* (eds.), *Metrópole e globalização. Conhecendo a cidade de São Paulo*, 237–44. São Paulo: CEDESP.

DEÁK, C. (1999). 'Acumulação entravada no Brasil e a crise dos anos "80"', in C. Deák and S. R. Schiffer (eds.), *O processo de urbanização no Brasil*, 19–48. São Paulo: FUPAM/EDUSP.

EMBRAESP (Empresa Brasileira de Estudos de Patrimônio S/C Ltda.) (1999). *Informativo imobiliário: relatório anual de 1998*. São Paulo: EMBRAESP.

EMPLASA (Empresa Metropolitana de Planejamento da Grande São Paulo SA) (1994). *Plano Metropolitano da Grande São Paulo: 1994/2010.* São Paulo: EMPLASA.

FERNANDES, F. (1973). *Capitalismo dependente e classes sociais na América Latina.* Rio de Janeiro: Zahar.

FSEADE (Fundação Sistema Estadual de Análise de Dados) (1999). *PED: Pesquisa Emprego Desemprego.* São Paulo: FSEADE.

FIBGE (Fundação Instituto Brasileiro de Geografia e Estatística) (1991). *Censo demográfico.* Rio de Janeiro: IBGE.

——(1996). *Contagem da população.* Rio de Janeiro: IBGE.

FIPE/SEHAB (Fundação Instituto de pesquisas Econômicas / Secretaria da Habitação da Prefeitura de São Paulo) (1987 and 1993). *Cadastro de favelas.* São Paulo: FIPE/SEHAB.

FSP (Folha de São Paulo) (1998). *Procon alerta sobre lotes em mananciais* (11-2-1998: 5).

LANGENBUCH, R. J. (1971). *A estruturação da Grande São Paulo.* Rio de Janeiro: FIBGE.

LEME, M. C. DA S. (ed.) (1999). *Urbanismo no Brasil: 1895–1965.* São Paulo: Studio Nobel/FUPAM.

LENCIONI, S. (1996). 'Restruturação urbano-industrial no Estado de São Paulo: a região da metrópole desconcentrada', in M. Santos *et al.* (eds.), *Território. Globalização e fragmentação,* 198–210. São Paulo: HUCITEC/ANPUR.

MARCUSE, P. (1997). 'The ghetto of exclusion and the fortified enclave. New patterns in the United States'. *American Behavioral Scientist,* 41: 311–26.

MARICATO, E. (1996). *Metrópole na periferia do capitalismo. Ilegalidade, desigualdade e violência.* São Paulo: HUCITEC.

MATOS, O. N. DE (1958). 'São Paulo no século XIX', in A. Azevedo (ed.), *A cidade de São Paulo. Estudos de geografia urbana,* Vol. II, 49–100. São Paulo: Brasiliana.

METRÔ (Companhia do Metropolitano de São Paulo) (1997). *Pesquisa origem-destino (O/D).* São Paulo: METRÔ.

MONTAGNER, P., and SPRINGER, P. (1997). 'Evolução das inserções ocupacionais na Região Metropolitana de São Paulo, 1988/96'. Paper presented at the IPEA, International Workshop: *O setor informal revisitado: novas tendências e perspectivas de políticas públicas,* Brasília, July.

Monthly Review, Editorial. (1992). 'Globalization—to what end?' Parts I and II. *Monthly Review,* 43(9 and 10).

PETRONI, P. (1958). 'São Paulo no século XX', in A. Azevedo (ed.), *A cidade de São Paulo. Estudos de geografia urbana,* Vol. II, 101–65. São Paulo: Brasiliana.

PIANCASTELLI, M., and PEROBELLI, F. (1996). *ICMS: evolução recente e guerra fiscal.* Brasília: IPEA.

Prefeitura Municipal de São Paulo (1990 and 1995). *Cadastro TPCL: Taxa Predial de Conservação e Limpeza.* São Paulo: PMSP.

PRÉTECEILLE, E. (1997). 'Cidades globais e segmentação social', in L. C. Q. Ribeiro and O. A. Santos jr. (eds.), *Globalização, fragmentação e reforma urbana. O futuro das cidades brasileiras na crise.* 2nd edn, 65–89. Rio de Janeiro: Civilização Brasileira.

ROLNIK, R. (1999). 'Para além da lei: legislação urbanística e cidadania. (São Paulo 1886–1936)', in M. A. Souza *et al.* (eds.), *Metrópole e globalização. Conhecendo a cidade de São Paulo,* 102–29. São Paulo: CEDESP.

SCHIFFER, S. (1992). *A territorialidade revisitada. Brasil pós II PND.* São Paulo: Faculdade de Arquitetura e Urbanismo da Universidade de São Paulo.

—— (2001). 'São Paulo: Articulating a Cross-Border Region', in S. Sassen (ed.) *Cities and Their Cross-Border Networks.* London: Routledge (forthcoming).

SOARES, L. T. R. (1998). *Ajuste neoliberal e desajuste social na América Latina.* Rio de Janeiro: Anna Nery/UFRJ.

SOMEKH, N. (1997). *A cidade vertical e o urbanismo modernizador.* São Paulo: 1920–1939. São Paulo: Studio Nobel/EDUSP.

STORPER, M. (1984). 'Who benefits from industrial decentralization? Social power in the labour market, income distribution and spatial policy in Brazil'. *Regional Studies,* 18: 143–64.

TASCHNER, S. P. (1997). 'Núcleos de habitação informal', in INFURB, *Avaliação dos Instrumentos de Planejamento e Gestão do Uso do Solo na Região Metropolitana de São Paulo.* Research Report for IPEA. Brasília. IPEA.

VILLAÇA, F. (1998). *Espaço intra-urbano no Brasil.* São Paulo: Studio Nobel/ FAPESP/Lincoln Institute.

—— (1999). 'Efeitos do espaço sobre o social na metrópole brasileira', in M. A. Souza *et al.* (eds.), *Metrópole e globalização. Conhecendo a cidade de São Paulo,* 221–36. São Paulo: CEDESP.

8

Residential Segregation among Social and Ethnic Groups in Budapest during the Post-communist Transition

János Ladányi

Introduction

Socio-economic residential segregation has increased in Budapest since the post-communist transition. Higher social status groups have started to move toward new suburbs. The physical condition of buildings in the slum belt that surrounds the inner parts of Pest is deteriorating faster than ever before. A massive invasion of underprivileged social and ethnic groups into this slum belt is on its way. Budapest is splitting into two parts. Parts of the city inhabited by higher status social groups look more and more like similar areas in western Europe. By sharp contrast, other parts, inhabited by the losers of post-communist transition, tend to resemble parts of cities of the Third World.

There have been two characteristic explanations to this development. Below we present the two explanations in an ideo-typical form:

• According to what we refer to as an 'anti-communist' interpretation, it is the state socialist regime that is responsible for all the problems the city presently has. Advocates of this view argue that the inner parts of the city are declining, higher social status groups are moving to the suburbs, and neighbourhoods of old state-owned apartment houses are deteriorating as a consequence of the urban and housing policy of state socialism. These developments were the consequences of the cancellation of the regulation of the prices of building plots, neglect of the maintenance of state-owned apartment houses, and the state redistribution of resources from the construction of houses and apartments.

• According to another explanation, which we refer to as 'new leftist', the increase in residential segregation, the deterioration of the inner districts, the escape of higher status social groups to the suburbs, the splitting of the city into two parts, etc., are necessary consequences of emerging capitalism. Proponents of this view argue that, now that the state socialist urban and housing policy—which strongly limited the forces of the market—has been abandoned, no one should be surprised to see that the spatial and social inequalities have become emphasized in Budapest.

My view is that there are elements of truth in both of the above explanations, but neither is correct on its own. The key point, however, is to try to analyse precisely what is happening, and what can be done about it today. The simple truth is that both the state socialist system as well as the capitalist system have produced segregation, but of quite different forms. Today, unfortunately, the two different forms do not cancel each other out, but rather reinforce each other.

Below are summarized the most important components of this chapter.

• The level of residential segregation in Budapest under state socialism was not lower than that in Vienna at the same time. Vienna is a capitalist city that best offers itself for comparison because of a common historical past and similarities in cultural traditions and urban spatial patterns.

• The patterns of spatial allocation of the highest and lowest social status groups in Budapest were similar to corresponding patterns of western European cities, also towards the latter part of the state socialist era in Hungary.

• State socialist urban policy and housing policy could not eliminate the significant residential segregation in Budapest. The level of segregation did not subside between the early 1950s and the late 1980s, namely in the period when the institutions of state socialist urban and housing policy were established. In fact, residential segregation increased.

• The decline into slums of some of the inner parts of Budapest, ghettoization along ethnic lines, and the escape of higher social groups into the suburbs started in the late 1960s, as market policies began to be allowed, but well before the collapse of state socialism.

• The state socialist system was not able to stop the socio-spatial consequences of Fordist and post-Fordist changes of the city. What happened instead was a delay in, and a direction into, a 'state socialist channel'. This turned out to be a 'dead-end' after the collapse of state socialism.

• The process of the city splitting into two parts gained momentum in the post-communist era because of the combination of this dead-end development and the newer introduced process of post-Fordist capitalist change. Today, Budapest has to grapple with the difficulties of both post-communist and post-Fordist transformation.

• State policies may influence the patterns of segregation, and specific policies can be envisaged that would be effective to decrease it. However, adoption of these kinds of policies does not seem likely.

János Ladányi

I will first summarize the main results of my research carried out on the changes of spatial segregation of different socio-economic groups in Budapest. I shall analyse the changes in the patterns and intensity of residential segregation in the inter-war and post-Second World War periods. I will then discuss the characteristics of the spatial segregation of the lowest-status population and of the lowest-status ethnic group in Budapest. This is followed by an analysis of recent trends of ghettoization and suburbanization. In conclusion, I will examine the possibilities of a post-communist welfare state in handling the problems of increasing polarization, ghettoization, and the emerging underclass.

Changing Patterns of Socio-economic Segregation

Table 8.1 shows the large-scale summary of changes in socio-economic segregation in Budapest in the period 1930–90 based on the Hungarian census. Despite all difficulties of comparison,[1] the basic tendency is clear: residential segregation slightly increased between 1930 and 1939. After this it decreased, probably due to the great social changes of the second half of the 1940s. These changes included the collapse of the inter-war conservative-authoritarian

Table 8.1. Segregation indices (SIs) of economically active workers in Budapest (1930–80)

	A	B	C	D	E
1930	21.2	--	19.6	--	--
1939	23.3	--	22.8	--	--
1949	--	--	--	--	16.8
1960	--	15.1	--	17.8	16.2
1970	--	16.9	--	21.0	17.2
1980	--	18.9	--	20.9	15.9
1990	--	--	--	--	14.7

Note: Columns A, B, C, D, figures are for manual workers with economically active owners and tenants as the comparison group. Column E, figures are for manual workers with economically active earners as the comparison group. When calculating the data for the first three columns, we used the 14 districts which existed during the 1930–9 period, while for the period 1949–80 we computed the indices on the basis of the present 13 districts, which cover the area of Small-Budapest (built before 1950). When calculating the data for column A, we took the categories of that time ('workers', 'civil servants', 'market women', 'stallkeepers and vendors', and 'commercial employees'), economically active owners and tenants into account. When calculating the data for column C, we computed the data of 'tradesmen', in addition to those for column A (economically active owners and tenants). Data for columns D and E refer to the present 22 districts of Budapest.

Source: Census of different years.

regime, followed by the emigration of a significant part of the political and economic elite, and, later, the emergence of the democratic regime in the period 1945–8, and the inauguration of an entirely new state regime in 1949. The difference is so very marked that differences in the source of the data are not very likely to have had a vital influence on it. The decrease slowed down noticeably in the 1950s and gradually turned into an increase in residential segregation in the 1960s. It continued to fluctuate within a narrow band in the 1970s and 1980s. The above picture is practically the same as that reported in the literature about the social mobility of this period (Andorka 1982). We have more detailed figures for the period 1970–90 (Tables 8.2a–c). These data show a relatively stable situation for this period, with a slight decline for blue-collar workers.

Table 8.2a. Dissimilarity indices (DIs) and segregation indices (SIs) of economically active wage earners in Budapest by occupational group (490 census tracts) (1970)

Group	DIs[a]						SIs (all groups)
	1	2	3	4	5	6	
1. College-educated	--	--	--	--	--	--	32.9
2. Other white-collar	22.9	--	--	--	--	--	12.6
3. Total white-collar	17.4	5.6	--	--	--	--	23.3
4. Skilled workers	37.2	16.0	20.7	--	--	--	11.1
5. Semi-skilled and unskilled workers	41.4	21.2	25.8	7.1	--	--	18.1
6. Total skilled and semi-skilled workers	39.3	18.5	23.3	3.7	3.4	--	23.3

[a] Horizontal numbers correspond to the vertical numbers in the first column.

Source: Csanádi and Ladányi (1992: 106).

Table 8.2b. Dissimilarity indices (DIs) and segregation indices (SIs) of economically active wage earners in Budapest by occupational group (490 census tracts) (1980)

Group	DIs[a]						SIs (all groups)
	1	2	3	4	5	6	
1. College-educated	--	--	--	--	--	--	28.3
2. Other white-collar	21.0	--	--	--	--	--	7.1
3. Total white-collar	14.2	6.8	--	--	--	--	20.4
4. Skilled workers	32.1	12.6	18.5	--	--	--	11.7
5. Semi-skilled and unskilled workers	35.9	17.4	23.1	7.1	--	--	17.0
6. Total skilled and semi-skilled workers	33.7	14.6	20.4	3.3	3.8	--	20.4

[a] Horizontal numbers correspond to the vertical numbers in the first column.

Source: Csanádi and Ladányi (1992: 107).

Table 8.2c. Dissimilarity indices (DIs) and segregation indices (SIs) of economically active wage earners in Budapest by occupational group (490 census tracts) (1990)

Group	DIs[a]						SIs (all groups)
	1	2	3	4	5	6	
1. College-educated	--	--	--	--	--	--	27.0
2. Other white-collar	21.4	--	--	--	--	--	13.2
3. Total white-collar	12.3	9.7	--	--	--	--	19.9
4. Skilled workers	28.6	9.6	17.4	--	--	--	12.0
5. Semi-skilled and unskilled workers	34.5	18.3	24.9	12.7	--	--	18.9
6. Total skilled and semi-skilled workers	30.7	12.8	19.8	5.5	8.0	--	19.9

[a] Horizontal numbers correspond to the vertical numbers in the first column.

Source: Csizmady (1995: 42).

The decrease of spatial segregation among the different social groups took place at a time when the structural characteristics of the previous system had already disintegrated, but the new ones, typical of state socialism, had not developed completely. It was a time when previous privileges had already disappeared, but the new system had not yet developed and strengthened its own system of inequalities. The lower level of segregation cannot be explained by the prevalence of egalitarian objectives characteristic of the urban and housing policies of eastern European socialist societies, because segregation decreased substantially only in the period when this system was still developing, with increases apparent in the period 1960–70, and a mixed pattern within a narrow range thereafter.

In discussing the analysis of spatial segregation of lower-status socioeconomic groups, we have to draw attention to the fact that the shape of the segregation curve characteristically differs from the shape commonly used in the literature. It expresses itself in the phenomenon that—no matter what the number, size, and delineation of our territorial units is—the segregation curve has a J-shape instead of the common U-shape, as the indices of the lower-status social groups were significantly lower than those of the higher-status ones. After analysing this phenomenon, we had to conclude that the irregular shape of the segregation curve could not be explained by the results of state socialist urban and housing policy. In Budapest, on the one hand, the 'irregular' shape of the segregation curve can be substantiated for the fifty-year period (Ladányi 1989). On the other, research carried out by others for various European cities also establishes the 'irregular' shape of the segregation curve (Belleville 1962; Kaufmann 1978; Gisser 1969; Hamnett 1976; Dangschat 1987).

In less technical terms, the segregation pattern in Budapest (and in other European cities) can be explained as follows. Whereas high-status social groups have the opportunity to be concentrated in those parts of the city where they want to be, low-status groups can only relocate when they have the means to do so and only if they are permitted. Therefore, high-status groups concentrate in specific areas of the city, and are able to develop advantageous systems of subsidies, high-quality educational and service networks, etc. for themselves, and exclude others by various tactics. In contrast to this, low-status social groups can only live in those parts of the city where nobody wants to live—yet or already. These groups can only 'choose' among the wide variety of the most unfavourable living conditions. As a consequence of these factors—at least in European cities—there is a tendency for higher-status groups to be clustered in fewer, usually larger and spatially coherent area(s), whereas lower-status groups are usually segregated in several, smaller, spatially non-coherent 'micro-segregates'. It is not the extent, but the nature of their segregation that is basically different.

These tendencies are characteristically different in North American cities (Duncan and Duncan 1955; Uyeki 1964; Roof and Van Valey 1972). There, not simply different social and occupational groups, but primarily different ethnic groups are segregated. Social and ethnic differences are closely related to each other in American cities, and the vast majority of the most underprivileged social and occupational groups comes from among African-Americans. As the most underprivileged ethnic groups, besides their unfavourable social position, they are also afflicted by a whole series of ethnic prejudices and discrimination. The spatial segregation in North American cities compared to that in Europe is thus not only stronger, but also has a different pattern. Thus in North American cities low-status groups are segregated in similarly few, large, and spatially coherent areas as the high-status groups.

Changing Patterns of Residential Segregation in Budapest

Today, patterns of residential segregation are in the process of fundamental change in Budapest. Since the 1930s, the lowest-status areas can increasingly be found in sporadic micro-segregates of different size in the various parts of the city, but especially on the Pest (east) side, while the majority of highest-status zones are increasingly situated on the hilly parts of the Buda side in spatially contiguous and gradually expanding areas.

Changes in the above pattern were noticeable around the early 1970s. As a result of the massive construction of new housing estates consisting of high-rise blocks of flats, the vast majority of state housing projects was increasingly concentrated in the outer regions of the city, whereas the areas in inner Pest, mostly the belt around the city centre with apartment houses, increasingly deteriorated. Until the mid 1970s, most of the apartments in the new housing estates were allocated to 'medium to high-status' young families. At the same time, central Pest became increasingly the location of an ageing population, whose average status became gradually lower (because of higher-status families moving outwards). Rapid construction of condominiums on the Buda side had very similar influences. Especially since about the mid and late 1960s, the move of high-status families to the green belt on the Buda side accelerated.

Evidently, deterioration of areas dominated by state-owned flats took place in almost every part of the city. Indeed, the Pest side of the city was particulary affected, because here the vast majority of apartment houses was located. The decline of neighbourhoods of state-owned apartment houses can be explained by the facts that—as it is well known from Szelényi's analysis for many years—the heavily subsidized rents were insufficient to cover renovation of the existing housing stock, let alone for building new state-owned apartment houses (Szelényi 1983).

However, the pattern of residential segregation did not only change for the above reasons. According to our data, the fundamental change of the pattern of residential segregation in Budapest was primarily caused by the rapid shift of Gypsies into the state-owned flats in the much deteriorated belt of apartment houses of inner Pest during the last two decades.[2] In 1986, already 46 per cent of the Budapest Gypsies lived in these areas of the capital city, and this proportion has increased to well over 50 per cent since then. According to 1971 school statistics, the proportion of Gypsy pupils among the elementary school-children was 1.2 per cent in Budapest, while 2.7 per cent were already in the 6th, 7th, 8th, and 9th districts. By 1986, this proportion had more than tripled, and reached 8.3 per cent in the 6th–9th districts, whereas it only doubled (2.4 per cent) in Budapest. These data refer to relatively large areas. However, because of high residential concentration and school segregation, in some elementary schools the proportion of Gypsy pupils is more than thirty times higher than the Budapest average. Moreover, there are some schools where more than two-thirds of the pupils are Gypsies. In contrast, in the 2nd and 12th districts, where the highest-status people of Budapest live, only 0.2 per cent were Gypsy schoolchildren in 1986. More recent data show the continuity of these tendencies and increasing residential and school segregation in this part of the city (Ladányi 1992).

Consider what can be expected in Budapest if the migration of Gypsies does not only continue, but accelerates (which is very likely). And what can be expected if—as the beginnings of it can already be observed—also a large number of non-Gypsy poor migrate to Budapest?

Ghettoization and Suburbanization

On the hilly Buda side of the city and in the suburbs, a large and highly homogeneous, high-status zone of condominiums developed, where high-status social groups are concentrated to an extent uncommon even in most of the cities of the world. However, in the inner parts of Pest, where deteriorated apartment housing is typical, an expanding, increasingly homogenous zone of slums is developing, which more and more concentrates the Gypsy population (Ladányi 1992).

An increasing ghettoization in the inner parts of Pest started several years before the collapse of state socialism. Under the conditions of post-communist transition, this process picked up speed. In fact, one of the most surprising consequences of the early years of post-communism was a demographic turnabout: for the first time since 1948–9, the population of cities in Hungary, including that of Budapest, declined. Since 1990, the number of people settling in rural areas was each year higher than that of those leaving the villages. Part of this process can be ascribed to *suburbanization*, that is, the exodus from the city of the middle and the upper-middle class because of air pollution and an increasing crime rate. Another aspect of this process can be attributed to the escape from the cities to rural villages in *areas beyond the suburbs*. People involved in this process include major groups of Gypsies, who have a low level of education, lost their jobs in the cities, and originally come from rural areas. (See Ladányi and Szelényi 1998, for more information.) Both processes are elaborated below.

The acceleration of *suburbanization* is a principal factor of the decrease of population in the cities. As a reminder for the reader: in Hungary after the Second World War a state socialist, centralized model of redistribution was introduced. Under state socialism, little attention was paid to the development of the residential infrastructure. Urban development was drastically underfinanced, revenues generated locally were channelled to other sectors of the economy, and repeated attempts were made to hamper isolated local examples of urban growth. After the collapse of the central redistribution system, however, a highly dynamic development began in these suburban areas despite the recession or stagnation of other sectors of the economy. In recent years, a spectacular development has occurred in Hungarian suburban settlements with regard to the supply of tap water, sanitation, and piped gas. The telephone network, which used to be on a very low, almost Third World level, has also undergone rapid development.

More importantly, a transition started from a specific state socialist model of suburbanization to another model that is more typical of post-industrial societies. What we call the state socialist model of suburbanization has the following characteristics: heavy taxes are imposed on the rural settlements, various subsidies and credits are only available for certain types of buildings, groups of owners, and construction arrangements (Ladányi and Szelényi 1998). As a consequence, under state socialism the 'suburbs' emerged within the boundaries of metropolitan areas, in Budapest mainly on the hilly areas on the Buda side, and they mostly consisted of condominiums and single-storey villas. Their residents were sociologically homogeneous, mostly of a high social status, who had access to various covert and overt state subsidies.

As far as *areas beyond the suburbs* were concerned, they were not populated by people of a high social status, but by 'post-peasants' who ingeniously combined farming and industrial pursuits, and by people who had an industrial job in the city but lived in the countryside. The latter group had no hope of becoming the tenant of a state-owned home and were therefore forced to commute to work.

Once the prohibitions of the former regime were cancelled, many people of higher social status decided to leave the metropolitan areas for adjacent areas which were more favourable. This process was augmented by the fact that, compared to the level of the country's economic development and especially the state of the stock of dwellings, the ratio of weekend cottages was very high, and the major part of them were to be found in the vicinity of metropolitan areas. By now, these areas have also started out on the road to become suburbs.

Because of the decline in living standards, the rise of rents and prices of utilities, large groups of poor people have also decided to move from metropolitan areas to nearby settlements in the countryside. Some of these poor people are forced to move even further away from the cities, where rents and property prices are lower. Unemployment is rampant among these people and they are thus eager to rent or buy a plot of land where families can produce at least some of their food.

In addition, a considerable number of the former users of workers' hostels have decided to return to their home villages. In most cases, they have lost their jobs and the hostels no longer operate. A new type of community is emerging on the peripheries of Hungarian settlements: the rural ghettoized village. In previous decades, the population of these villages fell drastically, in fact, everybody left who was able to leave. The only residents there today are the infirm elderly, young 'drop-outs', and new settlers who cannot strike roots anywhere else. With the exception of the village teacher—if there is one—the mayor and two or three persons who do public work, all the residents of such villages are unemployed. The proportion of Gypsy families is very high.

This recent type of settlement attracts a new social category: the 'rural underclass' (Ladányi and Szelényi 1996). It is a new phenomenon because until now the relevant literature only mentioned the emergence of the underclass exclusively for the case of ghettoized neighbourhoods of metropolitan areas. Moreover, the term 'underclass' does not simply refer to the unemployed and/or poor or very poor people. In the case of the Hungarian countryside it carries an entirely new meaning. Normally, even poor people have a role to play in the social and economic division of labour, even if this role is marginal and subordinated. By contrast, the 'rural underclass' mentioned here consists of people who, due to social and economic change, have become completely redundant in the emerging division of labour.

In the case of Hungary, the major change that unleashed this process was the end of the almost unlimited demand of state-owned factories for unskilled labour. To make a bad situation worse, next to nothing has so far been done to arrange retraining or alternative employment for these workers. The members of this underclass are the principal losers in the transition from communism to a free market economy. They have found themselves on the periphery and are likely to remain there for quite some time. They and their children—in the event that the present trends continue—will not get a proper job, social security, and a pension during their lifetime. The emergence of this underclass means that although Hungary is about to join the European Union and is linked to the rest of the world with sophisticated telecommunications, the Third World has appeared in impoverished rural regions of the country—and also in the heart of its capital.

Bearing the above thoughts in mind, it can be concluded that the increasing integration of the world market is offering new opportunities and challenges for Hungarian society. Provided the decline of the impoverished regions in Hungary continues and the rate of people actually out of work remains at a high level, provided a substantial part of those out of work become unemployed for long periods or even for their entire lifetime, provided school opportunities will further deteriorate for children of unfavourable social background, in other words, provided the split of society continues, then a con-siderable section of Hungarian society will either be unable to enjoy the oppor-tunities offered by integration or can only do so at the level of producing and consuming the shoddiest of goods. It is an illusion to believe that when eco-nomic recession is replaced by recovery, these problems will be resolved. No economic recovery can ensure a solution for the problems of poverty and marginalization (Ladányi and Szelényi 1997).

Not all impoverished households migrate to the countryside. There are also those who move from the countryside to the cities. Budapest has always been the principal destination for poor Gypsies and non-Gypsies who sought to resettle from their rural homes. This tendency is already posing serious prob-lems in the capital, even though a really large influx of the poorest into the metropolitan areas has not yet started. Let us examine the causes why the influx has not been greater until now.

In the most deprived regions of the country, especially in small villages, which under the previous regime were destined to disappear gradually, the radical decline of the population began some decades ago. Property prices are therefore very low in such areas and even the poorest can live under relatively favourable living conditions and can produce some food for their families. If, however, the impoverishment of these regions continues, and no jobs are gen-erated there, when economic recovery arrives many households will attempt to resettle in Budapest in the hope of finding a job. Their most likely destination will be inner parts of Pest, specifically the ghettoized areas.

I have serious doubts whether a lasting economic recovery can begin, even in Hungary's more fortunate regions, and among better off social groups, if the state fails to launch soundly based programmes of investment in human cap-ital. Today, culture, the sciences, education, and technical innovation—whose development was largely ignored under state socialism—are growth industries. While in the 1930s and 1940s the Hungarian economy gathered impetus by constructing new roads and encouraging the spread of automobiles, today, the spread of the 'information superhighways' are the engine of economic growth. However, international experience shows that governments that pursue a liberal economic policy in market economies of a medium level of development or in semi-peripheral situations are unable to upgrade their countries' human capital and adequately spread high technology. It is unlikely, therefore, that a country like Hungary, which exactly fits this description, can take a radical step forward unless it spends proportionately more on the maintenance and upgrading of its human capital than those European countries with which it aspires to catch up.

In our view, a new phase has started in Budapest. Until recently, middle class families tended to move to homes of higher quality in the same districts, even if these districts showed a decline in overall residential quality. However, the upwardly mobile families nowadays tend to leave such areas, and they have large houses built in the outskirts of Budapest or in regions outside the Budapest metropolitan area. In the increasingly distressed districts of the city, the ratio of Gypsy families is increasing, which brings with it the danger that there will be no social group of substantial economic background that would be available to fill the vacuum. As a consequence, the concentration of the most destitute Gypsy families is likely to grow in the poorest quarters. This is likely to accelerate ghettoization.

It is evident that the means at the disposal of the economic and administrative management of Budapest are insufficient to prevent the unfavourable effects of these tendencies. But it is also clear that regeneration of the most deprived districts could slow down or even stop ghettoization. Policies aimed at improving these areas are, however, inconceivable without effective coordination by the Budapest municipality and cooperation by the district-level municipalities.

Conclusions: A Role for the State?

As we have seen, ghettoization in the inner parts of Pest is the consequence of the structural problems of the country as a whole. Therefore, the limited resources at the disposal of the municipalities concerned are insufficient to tackle these problems. It is essential that the post-communist welfare state should also assume a role here, even though it strives to reduce its involvement and expenditures. It is an area where the resolute intervention of the state is essential. Provided such action is taken, the trends described above can be halted. Certain results may be achieved provided the following steps are taken: planning is carried out in a circumspect manner, the peripheral regions, especially the small villages, are given more resources for development, no time is wasted before the inner parts of Pest are regenerated, the currently ineffective social welfare net is made more efficient, and major efforts are made to reintegrate the urban and the rural 'underclass' into the post-communist welfare state.

However, I have little hope that these steps will actually be taken because Hungary's politicians and opinion-forming professionals are currently captivated by the self-regulated market and are wary of planning of any sort, including urban or regional planning, and of welfare institutions, which they dismiss as hangovers from communism. This attitude is even more alarming because there are signs that Budapest faces the danger that the 'under-urbanization' of state socialism will turn into its opposite (Ladányi and Szelényi 1998). It is feared that, in the form of a thrust of 'overurbanization', typical of the Third World, inner parts of the city from where middle class residents have fled will be occupied by an underclass of poor Gypsies and non-Gypsies who migrate from deprived small villages and declining urban areas.

The trends of socio-spatial changes in Hungary reflect that post-Fordist transformation began in the country well before the collapse of the state socialist regime. Under the state socialist milieu, this transition was delayed and followed a controversial, in many respects dead-end course of development. This is why the consequences of post-Fordist transformation and post-communist crisis are strengthening each other, resulting in serious social conflicts. The end of autarkic state socialist economy and the collapse of large socialist enterprises are coinciding with the decline of traditional manufacturing industries and a traditional working class in eastern Europe. The new workplaces generated in the fast-developing service sector cannot absorb unemployment, which has been created by closures in manufacturing industries and a decline in the agricultural sector. Compared to 1989, the number of jobs in Hungary in 1996 had declined by more than one-third. The growing polarization of society and the increasing importance of ethnic boundaries have resulted, among other things, in an increasing social division in Budapest. As a spatial consequence of these developments, the bulk of the inner areas of the city have become slums. The higher-status groups only aggravate this problem by leaving these areas and finding new homes in suburban regions and beyond. Signs of 'gentrification' of the inner districts of the city have so far failed to appear.

Notes

1. As is well known, segregation indices are sensitive to the number of spatial units and their internal homogeneity. See the note below Table 8.1 for particular differences with respect to calculations.
2. The proportion of this group in the capital city was about 1.3 per cent in 1971 and about 2.4 per cent (44,000 persons) in 1994, which was about half the Hungarian average.

References

ANDORKA, R. (1982). *A társadalmi mobilitás változásai Magyarországon*. Budapest: Gondolat.

BELLEVILLE, G. (1962). *Morphologie de la population active a Paris. Etude des catégories socio-professionelles par arrondissements et quartiers*. Paris: Centre d'Etudes Economiques.

CSANÁDI, G., and LADÁNYI, J. (1992). *Budapest térbeli-társadalmi szerkezetének változásai*. Budapest: Akadémiai Kiadó.

CSIZMADY, A. (1995). *A lakótelep, mint szegregációs típus Budapest*. Unpublished manuscript.

DANGSCHAT, J. (1987). 'Sociospatial disparities in a "socialist" city—the case of Warsaw at the end of the 1970s'. *International Journal of Urban and Regional Research*, 11(1): 37–60.

DUNCAN, O. D., and DUNCAN, B. (1955). 'Residential distribution and occupational stratification'. *American Journal of Sociology*, 60: 493–503.

GISSER, R. (1969). 'Ökologische Segregation der Berufsschichten in Großstädten', in L. Rosenmayr and S. Hollinger (eds.), *Sociologieforschung in Österreich*, 199–219. Wien: Verlag Hermann Bohlhaus.

HAMNETT, C. (1976). 'Social change and social segregation in inner London, 1961–1971'. *Urban Studies*, 13: 261–71.

KAUFMANN, A. (1978). *Sozialräumliche Gliederung der österreichischen Großstadtregionen*: I–II. Wien: Institut für Stadtforschung.

KONRÁD, G., and SZELÉNYI, I. (1972/1977). 'Social conflicts of under-urbanization', in M. Harloe (ed.), *Captive Cities*, 157–74. Chichester, UK: Wiley.

LADÁNYI, J. (1989). 'Changing patterns of residential segregation'. *International Journal for Urban and Regional Research*, 13: 555–72.

——(1992). 'Gondolatok a középsõ Józsefváros rehabilitációjának társadalmi összefüggéseirõl'. *Tér és Társadalom*, 3 and 4: 75–88.

——and SZELÉNYI, J. (1996). *The Making of the Rural Underclass—The Rural Ghetto of Poor Gypsies and Csenyéte*. Unpublished manuscript.

————(1997). 'Chancen für einen postkommunistischen "New Deal"'. *Österreichische Zeitschrift für Soziologie*, 21: 30–65.

————(1998). 'Class, ethnicity and urban restructuring in post-communist Hungary', in G. Enyedi (ed.), *Social Change and Urban Restructuring in Central Europe*, 67–86. Budapest: Akadémiai Kiadó.

ROOF, W. C., and VAN VALEY, T. L. (1972). 'Residential segregation and social differentiation in american urban areas'. *Social Forces*, 51: 87–91.

SZELÉNYI, I. (1983). *Urban Inequalities under State Socialism*. Oxford: Oxford University Press.

UYEKI, E. S. (1964). 'Residential distribution and stratification 1950–60'. *American Journal of Sociology*, 69: 491–8.

9

From Egalitarian Cities in Theory to Non-egalitarian Cities in Practice: The Changing Social and Spatial Patterns in Polish Cities

Grzegorz Węcławowicz

Introduction

This chapter forms part of a set of contributions on the spatial effects of the post-communist transformation in former eastern Europe (see also Węcławowicz 1992; 1996). The concern here is with the effects on the urban areas in Poland. The main issue is the pattern of disparities formed in urban space under communism and in the post-communist period after 1989. It is shown here how the inherited pattern of the socialist city, together with the new processes introduced by the post-communist transformation became the sources for the formation of a new intra-urban pattern in Poland. While the legacy of the past is still the most important explanatory element of current socio-spatial disparities, the new market forces are rapidly gaining importance, resulting in a growing polarization between different areas within the city in terms of income. Under communism the scale of intra-urban disparities was much smaller than in comparable cities of western Europe. The current internationalization of the Polish economy and the return to a western European orientation will inevitably lead to a new partitioning of the city.

In this chapter, the contemporary social and spatial disparities in Polish cities are described and the origins of these disparities indicated. It has become clear that Polish society and the spatial patterns within cities during the communist period were egalitarian in theory: in practice, however, they were not egalitarian at all. It has also become clear that Polish cities in the 1990s (the post-communist period) have also become partitioned, but on the basis of a different set of variables than hitherto.

The chapter is organized as follows. A brief introduction to the background of the socialist city is followed by a description of the formation of such a city.

A section on the internal division of the socialist city follows. The most important developments since 1989 are described, together with the intra-urban effects of these developments. The chapter concludes with some comments about other cities in eastern Europe.

The Political Roots of Socio-spatial Differentiation of Urban Areas under Communism

During most of the 20th century, the reduction of regional inequalities was one of the principal aims of Polish governments. The idea of egalitarianism and spatial justice gained particularly wide acceptance after the Second World War, with the imposition of communism in Poland. While definite successes in the reduction of regional inequalities could be recorded, the implementation of such policy was not always successful. In particular, the concept of equal spatial allocation of productive forces to achieve regional equalization of living standards proved to be inadequate. One of the key factors behind this inadequacy was the subordination of regional policies to economic planning in the command economy in the communist era. In general, economic goals came first.

Further industrialization of the Polish economy has been a goal of successive Polish communist governments. The increasing importance of industry went hand in hand with increasing urbanization: Poland changed from a rural to an urban society. In the 45 years of communism, the proportion of people living in urban areas increased from 31.8 per cent in 1946 to 62 per cent in 1999 (GUS 1999). Urban growth has been concentrated in the industrialized and other large cities. At present, more than 50 per cent of the total urban population live in cities with more than 100,000 inhabitants.[1]

Under communism, industry became the most important economic function of most of the cities in Poland. The development of a city without an industrial economic base would not have been contemplated. A new industrial plant was constructed first, followed by housing for the labour force, constructed as a patron estate or company town. This was particularly the case for the new industrial regions, where huge industrial plants were located in proximity to small towns or medium-sized cities. Examples include: Płock, Tarnobrzeg, Puławy, Lubin, Legnica, Konin, Bełchatów, Kędzierzyn-Koźle (see also: Kaltenberg-Kwiatkowska 1982).

Many industrial cities were located in new mining areas (coal, copper, or sulphur ores). Other new cities were constructed as dormitory satellites of already existing larger cities: Nowe Tychy and Jastrzębie Zdrój in the Upper Silesian coalfields; Legnica and Głogów in the copper region of Lower Silesia. Nowa Huta is an illustration of extensive housing construction. Administratively, this industrial city was incorporated into Cracow. Its homogeneous working-class character was partly diluted by the preservation of the national and cultural elite of Cracow.

The political leaders quickly adopted Modernism in a specific way. Modernism became a tool for the communist leaders to make decisions in the name of society regarding the form and planning of cities and the living conditions of the population. The Modernist idea also became the theoretical background for the overfunctionality of urban spaces, particularly with respect to the creation of enormous mono-functional housing estates. Under communism, additional developments such as infrastructure (roads and public transport), shops and other facilities, including schools, were only constructed after years or even decades of delay; these mono-functional housing estates entailed inadequate living conditions for the residents.

Although many households would have liked to move, most were unable to do so. During the communist period, housing was a scarce commodity. Even the construction of mass public housing in the 1960s and 1970s, invariably consisting of large apartment blocks, failed to satisfy the increasing demand. Housing became the object of competition among particular social groups. The location and conditions of the housing of particular social groups became an indicator of their political strength. Attractive housing in favourable locations was for the powerful, while those with fewer resources were relegated to less desirable accommodation.

The part played by housing allocation was important. Official housing allocation policy had been undergoing constant modification according to the needs of the ruling strata. An understanding of the influence of housing policies on the shaping of the cities' socio-spatial structure requires an acknowledgement of the fundamental significance of two contradictory processes: the egalitarian distribution of housing conditions; and the selective housing policy granting privileges to certain social and professional groups.

During the post-war period the following criteria for access to housing were in force. They had a significant influence on the socio-spatial differentiation in Polish cities:

• The social value of the labour force in relation to the nature of the profession exercised and the actual job performed. The current value of the labour force was often determined via the labour market, but more frequently by a political decision. Apartments were more easily obtained by people whose professions were in short supply at a given stage in a city's development.

• The hierarchical position in the political, economic, or administrative bureaucracy; this cannot be considered separately from the system of informal connections and access to information.

• The previous housing conditions and the number of family members.

• The financial situation of the family.

• The length of period of residence in a given city and the waiting time for a new apartment.

As stated above, the egalitarianism of communist society is clear in theory, but has not been fulfilled in practice. This gap between theory and practice gradually widened throughout the communist period.

The Formation of the Socialist City

Before the Second World War, the majority of Polish cities had a socio-spatial structure similar to that of other western European cities, although with numerous elements of pre-industrial structures. Despite wartime destruction, resettlement, and political transformation this structure has not totally disappeared. It is still possible to trace inherited historical patterns and spatial differentiation. The implementation of communist rule, with its concomitant process of industrialization and housing allocation rules, had decisive consequences for the internal spatial structure of many Polish cities.[2] For the ruling communist group, the new industrial cities served as a model for future socialist cities.[3]

The most significant features of the type of socialist city developed in Poland under communist rule which differentiated it from western European capitalist cities were as follows (Węcławowicz 1996):

• The industrial production sector dominated employment, with the consequence of large numbers of industrial workers and a low percentage of middle class households, so that the population of cities consisted mainly of the working class (proletariat). In theory, communist society held to the egalitarian principle of class homogeneity within cities and a low level of wealth differentiation. In practice, the principles were relatively easily modified and a comprehensive system of privileges and prices based on political and ideological criteria was introduced.

• The centrally arranged allocation of housing often obliged citizens to live in undesirable social surroundings shaped by the communist ideal of socially mixed neighbourhoods. This artificial social mix, together with the organization of the social life of urban dwellers around their place of work, diminished the opportunity for creating local communities.[4]

• The city was totally dependent on central government for its finances and was organizationally divided. The centralized authoritarian system split off different decision-making bodies for the city, each of which came from different government departments and, at lower levels, from the authorities of particular cities. The mayor represented the interests of the central state to the citizens rather than the other way round. Even the elected city councils stood for the central government and its policies, not local interests. Municipal offices were mere units subordinated to state admin-istration.

• The Modernist ideas of the communist governments resulted in a uniform-ity of architecture and urban landscapes. The focus on developing new areas led to the deterioration of the old quarters of cities (with the exception of some cultural heritage areas). A principal government objective imposed on plan-ners and builders was to provide housing for the (industrial) labour force in the quickest possible way. So construction of large, homogeneous housing estates in many cities, frequently inhabited by more than 100,000 people, became a significant part of the spatial order of cities. The supply of adequate service facilities usually lagged behind, because of constant investment shortfalls.

• Ignorance of land value, particularly in central locations, resulted in empty spaces in areas of extensive use, even in districts with a good technical infra-structure. Ignorance of the environmental problems caused by industry and urban development created situations of ecological catastrophe in some indus-trial regions. There was an attempt at the redistribution or elimination of the visible presence of non-communist symbols from the city. There was also an attempt to control the inflow of people to the city. The authorities only approved the influx of people needed in the labour force and those social cat-egories acceptable from an ideological point of view (members of the Commu-nist Party). Following industrialization, a high level of immigrants from rural areas with no experience of urban life came to live in the cities. For many of them, adaptation to an urban life style proved to be difficult.

Internal Division in the Socialist City

During the process of industrialization, new housing estates were added to already existing villages or medium-sized cities, like Puławy, Płock, Bełchatów, Łęczna, and Tarnobrzeg. The new estates were physically isolated from the existing buildings. They represented the socialist city, although the new and older parts of a city were functionally interdependent. For example, new hous-ing estates would be inadequately equipped with respect to services, so the residents had to depend on services located in the older part of the city. The two parts differed, however, in numerous ways.

The older part would be inhabited by a population with an urban tradition, with a balanced, possibly older demographic structure including a substantial share of service sector employees, craftsmen and industrial workers, and rem-nants of the pre-war intelligentsia. Social activities and social life were concen-trated around the local community. Housing in the old part of the city was owned by the communal administration (usually a nationalized former private property) or remained private, with a dilapidated or underdeveloped technical infrastructure.

The new part of the city would be inhabited by younger immigrants, usually of rural origin and without urban experience, employed in industrial jobs. Most of their social activities would be organized around their place of work (often an industrial plant). Housing in the new part of the city was invariably in monotonous apartment blocks with a complete communal infrastructure and standard equipment, owned by cooperatives or an industrial complex.

This dual old/new character is still to be seen in most Polish cities. Strong egalitarian tendencies did not prevent the operation of further differentiation processes after the 1970s, with a clear acceleration in the 1980s and 1990s.

An Additional Characterization of the Urban Socio-spatial Structure of the Socialist City

The urban socio-spatial structure of the Polish socialist city can be character-ized by concentrations of higher-level socio-economic categories within the central parts of cities. Island-like locations of dilapidated buildings together with socially degraded areas within these central parts disturb this general pattern. These islands accommodate representatives of the lower social categories: the elderly, and the socially and economically deprived.

The appearance of these two groups in the central areas, and their small-scale spatial separation within these areas, is the result of the mosaic pattern of apartment quality. Some parts of the central areas were reconstructed rela-tively rapidly after the war, but some were not. Considerable differences arose in the quality of the apartments in different parts of the same area. In the 1950s, many apartments in the central areas were still being inhabited by the lower social groups. During the 1960s and 1970s, the reconstructed apartments were gradually taken over by people from economically viable groups. These people were not interested in the new monotonous housing estates being con-structed far away from the city centres with their inadequate transport and poor services. They did not take over the apartments that had not been recon-structed: these remained the homes of the people already living there.

While many central areas can be characterized as housing areas for econom-ically viable categories with islands for the weaker groups, the opposite is gen-erally the case in the peripheries. Here, the share of lower socio-professional groups is generally much higher, but the pattern is significantly disrupted by island-like locations of estates with higher standards of housing, single-family housing areas, areas with better transport accessibility, or of higher natural and environmental value.

The spatial distribution of socio-professional position takes on a concentric pattern in the central areas, becomes radial with sectors at increasing distances from the centre, and may even turn partially polycentric in the peripheries. This general picture is disrupted by the scattering of small spatial units with a socio-professional composition distinctly different from that of the surrounding areas, so that an overall impression of a mosaic or patchwork socio-spatial pattern is created. This picture applies principally to the large cities. The physical structure of small cities is often bipolar in nature. Medium-sized cities develop in a more multi-dimensional way and display more complex physical patterns.

Finally, it should be mentioned that there was not only a spatial division of socio-economic groups in the Polish socialist city; demographic variables were also important. A typical example is provided by the higher proportions of small households and the elderly in the central parts of cities, specifically in older apartments with lower equipment standards. As distance from the centre increases and housing estates become newer, the proportions of younger, professionally active people, and children also increase. Given low intra-urban mobility, mainly a result of the shortage of new housing, it used to be quite common for inhabitants to age together with their apartments. Consequently, in some of the various stages of the life cycle through which families pass, their housing conditions could not satisfy their changing needs.

The Social, Political, and Economic Transformation after 1989

The increase in spatial polarization is one of the most frequently described consequences of the transformation from a socialist economy to one that is moving in the direction of a market-oriented economy (see also Kovács 1998; Ladányi, Chapter 8). The increase in social disparity, the evolution of the housing market, and the political consequences of the reintroduction of local self-government can be seen as the most significant causes of this increasing spatial polarization.

The Increase in Social Disparity

One of the tendencies in Polish society with most influence on the changing socio-spatial structure has been the substantial fall in the dominance of the working class. The number of workers in the productive sector has declined, while the number of those employed in the service and specialist sectors has increased. Many specialists are self-employed. The reduction of the working class and the increase in self-employment are two opposite, complementary social tendencies.

This significant change in the labour market was caused to some extent by the economic recession and the economic deactivation of the population, but primarily by the expansion of the private sector after 1989. New, well-paid highly skilled jobs in business, banking, and financial institutions have emerged. The expansion of the private sector has also created a demand for skilled jobs as vendors, clerks, financial staff, and secretaries and also for semi-skilled labour. In the private sector, employees are more efficient and better paid than their counterparts in the public sector. The shadow economy has also played an important part in the transformation of urban locations in terms of employment and production. This shadow economy is not just a mass of street vendors and illegal markets; it should also be seen as a large (although how large is difficult to estimate) share of all trade and production.

The emerging new social structure is based on elements of the social structure formed under communism and even on some surviving elements of pre-war structures. Słomczyńzski (1994) identifies the following classes in the late stage of socialism: managers, first-line supervisors, experts and professionals, office workers, state factory workers, petit bourgeoisie, farmers, and private enterprise workers. The new categories emerging in the period of transformation are the capitalist class and the unemployed. According to Wesołowski (1994), the latter transformation indicates the resumption of the Weberian class scheme with the return of the importance of economic resources, power, and knowledge as elements determining position in the class structure, with a declining direct role played by the state.

It seems that in the country as a whole and in the largest urban areas of Poland, the process of the formation of three large social groups is under way: the elite, the middle class, and a poverty class. The elite group comes from the former communist elite or nomenclature members, part of the former anti-communist opposition, and part of the intelligentsia. In very rare cases, members of the former working class or peasants may be seen as belonging to this elite. Part of the elite group has become the new capitalist class. It consists of several components (Węcławowicz 1996).

The middle class group is derived from the former communist upper and middle grade nomenclature, in part from the anti-communist opposition leaders, and in part from the intelligentsia. A lack of capital resources, low skills, adherence to passive attitudes, dependence on the state, and a lack of political will on the part of their leaders sets limits to the upward mobility of the majority of the working class. The intelligentsia has become the main recruitment group for the middle class, because the continuing deterioration in their prospects has encouraged them to move into the private sector.

A poverty group is emerging from the social categories losing out from the transformation. It consists of the unemployed, some unskilled workers, and even some of the lower-level intelligentsia. A large segment of the unskilled working class will also be among these losers, as are the majority of elderly people.

The poverty group in Polish cities is further augmented by the enormous share of poorly paid people employed in administration or otherwise dependent on the state budget. For them, the cities, particularly the large cities, have become very expensive places in which to live. It is remarkable, however, that the proportion of poor households (below the relative poverty line) is lower in larger cities (4.9 per cent) than in smaller cities (10.7 per cent; Ochocki and Szukiełojć-Biekuńska 1996). The existence of a niche in the informal sector of the economy is a probable explanation for this.

The Evolution of the Housing Market

The transformation to the market economy finally solved the constant ideological problem of the two conflicting tendencies of socialist housing policy: egalitarian versus selective allocation. Under the new market conditions the only housing allocation criterion that remains is the individual's financial situation. For those who have a choice, personal preferences can operate. Access to housing has become regulated by the market mechanism. While under the communist regime an individual's political position was the main criterion, economic criteria now determine the rules of spatial allocation.

Not only have allocation procedures changed, but also the nature of housing supply. New housing construction is of substantially better quality. One indicator is the size of dwellings: in Warsaw, the average floor space of new housing increased from $69\,m^2$ in 1991 to $82\,m^2$ in 1994. Consequently, this housing was more expensive and was therefore allocated to the higher-income groups. Generally, the increase in housing quality meant that the new housing stock ceased to be accessible to households with average or below-average incomes.

Meanwhile, the construction of inexpensive housing subsidized by the state ceased. The most dramatic changes occurred in the building of cooperatives, which are still responsible for 72.4 per cent of total housing construction in Warsaw. The cooperatives were no longer able to produce inexpensive housing following the withdrawal of state subsidies. New cooperative housing is therefore only accessible to 10–12 per cent of a cooperative's long-term members. As a result, the new tenants of the new cooperative housing represent the social category of a newly emerging middle class with well-above-average incomes. Thus, cooperative housing moved from a sector that was accessible to low-income groups to a housing segment that is only accessible to those with above-average incomes. However, people with high incomes are not always interested in living in this sector, so new apartments stand empty and await tenants, a phenomenon not seen in Warsaw since the end of the Second World War. Meanwhile, the waiting list for members of the cooperative remains very long.

Another important new factor influencing the socio-spatial structure of Polish cities is rent reform, a process that has yet to be completed. This reform has brought rent increases in cooperative and municipal dwellings as a result of the partial withdrawal of direct and indirect subsidies. The Renting of Residential Properties and Housing Allowances Act which came into force at the end of 1994 has affected the lower socio-economic categories. For many families, declining incomes have precipitated the problem of rent arrears.

An important effect of rent reform and the privatization of the housing stock has been the process of sub-letting, especially by the elderly, and particularly in the central areas of the larger cities. The motivation for sub-letting is usually financial: it provides an additional source of income, sometimes even the only source. Those who sub-let generally move from prestigious, centrally located areas to the periphery—to their children, or to cheaper accommodation. Figures are not available, but it is a clear process of a new partitioning of urban space as a consequence of a new social structure and new rules on the housing market.

The Struggle for the Control of Urban Space (Old and New Actors)

As a result of political transformation, after 1989, central government control of urban affairs and urban space shifted to local government. An important consequence of this shift has been the opportunity for newly formed social groups to press their demands on their democratically elected representatives in local government. This has enabled residents to identify with the environment in which they live. However, it has to be said that not all social groups have become self-aware social interest groups. Long-term imposed passivity has left some people unable to articulate their own interests adequately.

The increasing importance of the introduction of local government has had positive consequences for most urban areas. One of the very few negative results was the splitting up of Warsaw into seven independent communes with inadequate coordination of the responsibilities for the city as a whole. The newly created government authorities first turned their efforts to local interests and the inherited poor infrastructure. Consequently, the strategic development of the city as a whole has been neglected.

Under socialist conditions, the attention of urban authorities was concentrated on the production function. The factories and the state as employers were frequently the only organizers of social and cultural life and the only providers of food and services. Rejection of the socialist ideology in the 1990s has redirected (local) government attention from the place of work to the place of residence. Now, the main arena of social activity has to a large extent become the local community associated with the place of residence. Social life is organized more by the private sector and individual initiatives.

The rapid shift from central to local control of urban space created many problems in the beginning. The new government was not prepared to deal with the emergence of numerous new actors (mostly from the private sector) competing for space. The spontaneous development of street markets and other commercial activities has been the first visible element of economic transformation. The struggle of these emerging social categories for space for their activities challenged planning regulations and led to a partial appropriation of public space.

Some changes in the use of space have a symbolic character. The central square in Warsaw, previously used for political demonstrations, has now become a huge marketplace. The Warsaw Stock Exchange is housed in the former headquarters of the Central Committee of the Communist Party. A former stadium was transformed into a market and later into the largest wholesale area in the city. Around these kinds of activities new social categories and interest groups are starting to emerge. Sometimes they turn into pressure groups and have specific demands, such as more sanitary facilities.

A radical increase in the intensity of land use runs parallel to the functional transformation of space. Numerous previously empty spaces have now become major development areas for commercial purposes, such as hotels, banks, trade and business centres, offices, in buildings of new architectural design. Large numbers of new restaurants, shops, kiosks, and street markets are leading to a further intensification of urban land use in Warsaw. This process of the intensification of land use started in 1989 in a highly chaotic manner. Then, street trade meant nothing more than people selling from the pavement, or from their outstretched hands as they stood by the side of the street. Later, street traders were located in places equipped for informal retailing; they gradually moved to more permanent small shops or shopping centres. This private retail trade practically eliminated the problem of the supply of everyday products, even in the large new housing estates where the provision of goods and services had previously been so poor.

The most rapid transformation occurred in areas with good transport connections and a tradition of private sector development. The lack of commercial facilities in the best locations resulted in strong competition for available space and also contributed to the price differentiation of land. Generally, the central areas of the cities and suburban areas with good transport connections to the city centre now have the highest commercial values.

The latest developments however, particularly those imposed by the new left-wing government since 1993, include a gradual limitation of the early 1990s shift of power over space from central to local government. Also, a political polarization can be detected between different parts of the city. In Warsaw, for example, the inhabitants of the central area of the city usually support left-wing, democratic or liberal parties, whereas the inhabitants of the periphery tend to support right-wing or conservative parties (Węcławowicz 1995).

Spatial Effects of the Transformation

From the previous sections certain political and economic processes can be listed that have had an impact on the transformation of urban space in the Polish post-socialist city:

(1) the return of the market mechanism and particularly the emergence of the importance of land rent;
(2) the changes in the ownership structure of land from not strictly defined or state ownership to local government or private ownership;
(3) the shift of control over space from central to local levels, mostly through the return of local government and the formation of new local interest groups;
(4) the radical increase in the number of actors competing for particular locations in urban space;
(5) the changing rules of spatial allocation for people and economic activities from political to market criteria;
(6) the transformation of the employment structure from domination by the production sector (mostly industry) to the service sector; and the formation of a new social structure generated by the shift in employment structure.

Despite these changes, however, from the beginning of the transformation in 1989 until the present, no explicit urban policies have been formulated, not even at the local government level.

As a consequence of these developments, Polish cities are in various degrees beginning to distance themselves from the principal features of the socialist city. The spatial consequences can be described, first of all, as an increase in socio-spatial differentiation. Second, a substantial transformation of the urban landscape and a new architecture have become visible. Third, the spatial consequences are present in the demise of some features and the reassessment of other aspects of urban spaces, mostly in the form of the replacement of communist symbols by historic and national symbols. Communist street names have been replaced by the pre-war names, for example. Fourth, the function and intensity of land use, particularly in centrally located areas, have changed frequently from administration or political functions to a commercial function. Fifth, the spatial behaviour of inhabitants has been modified, for example by new patterns of shopping behaviour and commuting to work.

The most rapid formation of a new socio-spatial structure has taken place in the central areas of the cities. New elite enclaves have been formed in redeveloped parts within or adjoining deteriorating neighbourhoods and housing inhabited by the poor and elderly. The increasing scale of social and wealth contrasts creates a special kind of dual city where the rich and the poor live together in the same areas (e.g., in the same apartment block, particularly in city centres), but use very different spaces: the rich go to the streets with the luxury designer shops, the poor patronize the street markets; the rich drive private cars, the poor use public transport; they have different places of work.

Lifting the administrative restrictions for settlement in the largest cities opened them up, in principle, to uncontrolled immigration. This did not happen, however: cities became administratively open, but economically closed. For many citizens they have become too expensive to live in. The cities have become virtually inaccessible to new poor immigrants, unless they accept poorly paid jobs and poor housing in emerging slum areas. Parallel to this is the inflow of wealthy people who are able to pay for their accommodation. On the other hand, for the poor who do live in the city, there is no chance of leaving, because of the housing shortage and poor employment prospects elsewhere. Increasingly, therefore, Polish cities show a development to a dual socio-spatial structure consisting of poor people who do not have the opportunity to move out and people with good positions and prospects in the labour market.

The changes, however, are highly differentiated regionally. The most radical evolution has occurred in the region of western Poland and in the larger agglomerations. The process of transformation is far from complete: it is in an advanced stage in the largest cities and prosperous regions, and in the initial stage in most of the smaller cities and less prosperous regions. The employment structure, particularly the availability of well-paid jobs in the service sector, is the most important differentiating factor in the prosperity of cities. Relatively good situations in this respect can be found in Warsaw, Poznań, Wrocław, Cracow, and Trio City (Gdańsk-Sopot-Gdynia) and some other cities. Other large cities, particularly those with a specialized industrial structure, such as Łódź and Katowice, or mono-functional medium-sized cities like Mielec and Wałbrzych, now have substantial problems.

Towards Globalization: A Challenge for Polish Cities

The political and economic transformation has created a new challenge for the Polish urban system. Securing a place in the emerging urban hierarchy of Europe was recognized by the Polish government as being a major goal. A successful outcome of the competition would contribute cogently to the prospect of all cities in Poland in the new century. The development of the national economy and the political structure of the country can be seen as two other important factors.

The polycentric urban system in Poland, with the existence of several large urban centres and agglomerations, will probably result in the differential development of various cities and their urban regions. As capital city and an important economic centre, Warsaw exerts a considerable influence on the diffusion of the modernization process into the eastern region of the country. This influence has been substantially increased by the rapid development of the private sector. The city has, however, never developed as a typical major city, despite its significant domination in the social, economic, and administrative domains. In addition, in the 1990s, the pre-eminent position of Warsaw was challenged by Cracow on the grounds of cultural, scientific, and spiritual values, by Gdańsk on the grounds of political power, and by Poznań on the grounds of economic leadership in the transformation. Moreover, Warsaw's regional location has become a sort of ballast. The city is located in one of the underdeveloped regions of Poland, so that one of the basic conditions of Warsaw's future development is the reduction of the economic imbalance between the city and its surrounding region.

Increasing integration of the Polish urban system with western Europe is inevitable. While in the past economic cooperation was mainly between Warsaw and other Polish cities, new opportunities for economic cooperation have emerged as a consequence of European integration and the declining influence of the national central government. For example: Gdańsk could become a partner with Copenhagen; Wrocław with Prague; Cracow could establish closer ties with Vienna and Budapest. With improving faster transport systems, a Polish city could even fulfil a suburban function for a western metropolis within close proximity: Bratislava could have this function for Vienna, while Poznań, Szczecin, and Wrocław could become suburban areas for Berlin. The challenge for Warsaw will be to become more attractive than other large Polish cities, because the alternative would be to result in merely being the capital of eastern Poland.

At the moment, the most obvious winners in the transformation are Warsaw and its region, accumulating a large majority of total foreign investment in Poland, Poznań, Gdańsk, and Cracow. At the regional level, the winners are the cities along the western border. The lifting of many border constraints resulted in booming economic developments connected with international activities. This prosperity is in sharp contrast with the economic stagnation and continuing high unemployment along the eastern border with the former Soviet Union. The potential prosperity of eastern border regions is still constrained by the unstable political situation and deteriorating economies in Belarus, the Ukraine, Lithuania, and Russia. The majority of industrial cities, particularly those connected with the military (Mielec, Dêbica, Radom) and the traditional heavy industry in Upper Silesia (Łódź and the Katowice agglomeration) can also be counted among the losers.

Conclusions

The type of socialist city that developed in Poland after the Second World War can only be classified in very general terms as a version of the industrial city that developed in western Europe in that period. Compared with the west, the socialist type of industrialization process in Poland resulted in cities with a relatively low level of social and spatial differentiation. Polish cities were also characterized by low-quality services and inefficient organizational and physical structures.

The political and economic transformation since 1989 has strongly influenced the intra-urban patterns. Gradually, the specific socialist pattern started to disappear. Rationalization of the use of space, a substantial improvement of the service sector and the quality of housing, and a more efficient organization of urban life can be ranked among the positive effects of this transformation. A negative development is an increasing social segregation and polarization of urban society. Clearly, this does not mean that cities are increasingly characterized by spatial segregation between rich and poor. Mixed neighbourhoods are currently more usual. The dual structure of Polish cities cannot be read from the residential patterns in the cities, but can be found in the differential character and location of the activity patterns of the rich and the poor in the cities.

The transformation of the socialist city into the post-socialist city will probably follow a path comparable to the evolution of the capitalist industrial cities to post-industrial cities. Openness to international influences will probably lead to the immigration of people from countries worse off than Poland, including the countries of the former Soviet Union. This immigration would contribute to the introduction of ethnic differentiation and ethnic segregation. It is not difficult to predict that the local elites of the cities, mainly those who have found steady, well-paid jobs in the new service sector, would try to form enclaves. The present mix in different neighbourhoods can only be seen as a remnant of the socialist state that is soon to disappear. The native poor would be displaced, especially from the most attractive residential areas. Together with the impoverished immigrants, the native poor will probably find themselves in the least attractive parts of the city or the agglomeration. The high-rise apartment blocks are a case in point. Although not all these complexes are poorly maintained, badly located, and amenity-poor, those that are might be seen as potential post-socialist slums.

The capitals of the former communist countries have all been centres of command and control, but unlike many western European, American, or Asian cities, the socialist capitals were only centres on the regional scale, separated from the rest of the world by a strict political curtain. Only Moscow was different: this city had unquestionable supremacy over the other socialist capitals and could be seen as the only global city in the communist world until the end of the 1980s. The collapse of communism will inevitably lead to the reintegration of the former communist countries (particularly those in central Europe) with the world economy. While the position of Moscow is already sliding downwards, the other post-communist capitals are struggling for an advantageous position in the European urban hierarchy.

The size of the Polish national urban system and its geopolitical location are important assets in this struggle. Berlin is a challenge and an opportunity for more rapid economic development in the western part of Poland. In the central region of the country, the substantial improvement of urban infrastructure in the Warsaw, Łódź, and Poznań agglomeration can possibly create a counterweight for Berlin's dominance in this part of the continent.

Notes

1. The western region of the country is the most urbanized, but the largest urban agglomerations can be found in the central and southern regions. However, the presence of extensive regions of low urbanization in the central and eastern parts of the country indicates the continuing importance of the traditional rural way of life there.
2. Not all Polish cities have been affected by the industrialization process. Some have maintained elements of their historical patterns. Some large, old cities could not be so readily transformed and adapted to the new ideological system. Cracow is a good example (Piotrowski 1966; J. Kaczmarek 1996; S. Kaczmarek 1996).
3. The best sociological analysis of a new industrial city totally formed under communism has been provided by Szczepański (1991) for the Upper Silesian city of Nowe Tychy.
4. The centrally arranged allocation could also easily lead to the opposite: forced segregation and the concentration of professionally or politically homogeneous groups.

References

GUS (Główny Urząd Statystyczny) (1999). *Rocznik Statystyczny 1996*. Warszawa: GUS.

KACZMAREK, J. (1996). *Dzienna ścieżka życia mieszkańców Łodzi a warunki życia w mieście*. Łódz: Łódzkie Towarzystwo Naukowe.

KACZMAREK, S. (1996). *Struktura przestrzenna warunków zamieszkiwania w Łodzi*. Łódz: Łódzkie Towarzystwo Naukowe.

KALTENBERG-KWIATKOWSKA, E. (1982). *Społeczno-przestrzenne zróznicowanie miasta. Fakty i opinie. Płock, Społeczeństwo miejskie w procesie uprzemysłowienia*. Warszawa: KiW.

KOVÁCS, Z. (1998). 'Ghettoization or gentrification? Post-socialist scenarios for Budapest'. *Netherlands Journal of Housing and the Built Environment*, 13(1): 63–81.

OCHOCKI, A., and SZUKIEŁOJĆ-BIEKUŃSKA, A. (1996). 'The methods of poverty measurement applied to household budget surveys in Poland', in *Poland '96: Habitat and Human Development*, 11–18, Warsaw: UNDP, Foundation for Social Security.

PIOTROWSKI, W. (1966). *Społeczno-przestrzenna struktura m*. Łodzi/Wroclaw: Studium ecologiczne/Ossolineum.

SLOMCZYŃSKI, K. (1994). 'Class and status in Eastern European Perspectives', in M. Alestelo, E. Allardt, A. Rychard, and W. Wesołowski (eds.), *The Transformation of Europe—Social Conditions and Consequences*, 167–90. Warsaw: IFiS.

SZCZEPAŃSKI, M. S. (1991). *'Miasto socjalistyczne' i świat społeczny jego mieszkańców. Rozwój regionalny—Rozwój lokalny—Samorząd terytorialny, 32*. Warszawa: Uniwersytet Warsaw.

WĘCŁAWOWICZ, G. (1992). 'The socio-spatial structure of the socialist cities in East-Central Europe. The case of Poland, Czechoslovakia and Hungary', in F. Lando (ed.), *Urban and Rural Geography*, 129–40. Venice: Department of Economic Sciences, University of Venice.

——(1995). 'The electoral geography in the national, regional and intra-urban scale', in B. Gałczyńska and G. Węcławowicz (eds.), *Urban and Regional Issues in Geographical Research in Poland and Italy*, 59–70. Conference Papers 24. Warsaw: Institute of Geography and Spatial Organization, Polish Academy of Science.

——(1996). *Contemporary Poland, Space and Society*. London: UCL Press.

WESOŁOWSKI, W. (1994). 'Procesy klasotwórcze w teoretycznej perspektywie'. *Studia Socjologiczne*, 1: 19–35.

10

A Metropolis at the Crossroads: The Changing Social Geography of Istanbul under the Impact of Globalization

Murat Güvenç and Oğuz Işık

Introduction—Geographers Trapped

To the casual onlooker Istanbul is a city with many and, more often than not, conflicting faces. It may appear, to those who are not familiar with the peculiarities of urban development in Turkey, as a puzzling collage of not too closely related fragments, a city where social landscapes from earlier periods seem to coexist with those of today in particular ways without an apparent combining logic. This depiction of Istanbul as a city without order is further reinforced by the everyday images one can see in the media. A city ruled by an Islamic fundamentalist mayor since March 1994; a city where in March 1995 nearly twenty people were killed in severe clashes between the police and the residents of the Gazi district known to be occupied largely by Alevis; a city which was a candidate for the 2000 and 2004 summer Olympic Games; a city which hosted the Habitat II meeting in June 1996 and the OSCE summit in November 1999, allegedly the last summit of the 20th century; a city in which the tradesmen of the Laleli district, a shopping centre for tourists mostly from the ex-eastern bloc countries, provided generous financial support to the election campaign of Boris Yeltsin; a city where according to the latest reports a large number of Romanians work illegally especially in the construction sector—Istanbul is a city where the global dynamics seem to have articulated with the contingencies of local history and politics in peculiar ways. At first glance, Istanbul is a city where the contingency has overruled the necessity, and the unpredictability of agency has generated outcomes that are hardly likely to be found elsewhere.

This multi-faceted and elusive character of Istanbul finds its clearest expression in recent academic accounts. There are, at one extreme, those studies that describe it as a global city in the making.[1] For the proponents of this view, Istanbul is on the way to become a truly multi-cultural city where '. . . a new type of cosmopolitanism is at its gates' (Göle 1993: 23). It is in the process of transformation '. . . from a tired city whose glory resided in the past into a metropolis full of promise for the twenty-first century' (Keyder and Öncü 1993: 29). For them 'income and employment polarization' brought about by globalization 'in the short to medium run' (Keyder and Öncü 1993: 37) is the undesirable but manageable outcome of this process. At the other extreme are those accounts which see Istanbul not as a site for a new cosmopolitanism but as an arena of encounter for increasingly hostile identities and groups (Aksoy and Robins 1993, 1994). 'What may be emerging in reality are new forms of segmentation and cleavage among different groups in the urban population' (Aksoy and Robins 1994: 64). In their view what has been happening in Istanbul is not the unfolding of global dynamics, but simply the return of the '*suppressed Istanbul*'. While it is disharmony to which the latter approach draws attention, it is for the first view harmony that prevails in the case of Istanbul. What is implicit in the writings of the advocates of the *globalization thesis* is that the everyday events taking place in Istanbul can be seen as the unfolding of an omnipresent and omnipotent logic: the logic of globalization. On the contrary, the Istanbul depicted by the proponents of the *confrontation thesis* is a city where unplanned, spontaneously created landscapes are juxtaposed with no apparent reason, and chaos and disorder prevail.

Divergent though they certainly are in their political implications and especially in the degree of optimism about the future of the city, these two approaches exhibit striking similarities in terms of their methodologies. They are both *totalizing* and *idealizing* stances that rule out attempts for alternative formulations. The first one is an overgeneralizing stance, tending to spot a ubiquitous regularity with little room left for particularities. The second approach is one that pushes its emphasis on particularism to its logical limits, to the point of chaos where no rule prevails. What is more important for our purposes is that these two approaches to Istanbul represent the polar ends of a growing *binarism* that seems to characterize the social sciences in the late 1990s. As noted by Soja (1996: 4) in his *Thirdspace*, this is a binarism between '. . . self-proclaimed postmodernists who interpret the epistemological critique as a license to destroy all vestiges of modernism' and '. . . a growing cadre of adamant anti-postmodernists' who associate the postmodern critique '. . . exclusively with nihilism, with neo-conservative empowerment, or with a vacuous anything-goes . . . philosophy'.

This chapter is an attempt to interpret, from what we prefer to call an *in-between position*, the social landscapes of Istanbul and cleavages among its population groups, and the attitude the state has taken towards these cleavages. Especially in studying the social segregation in Istanbul we are aware that modernist and postmodernist positions have different ontological assumptions. It is the *mutually exclusive* character of these positions that we wish to overcome.

Adapting an in-between ontological position has also crucially important implications as to the claims for distinctiveness in the study of particular localities. We believe that the dynamics shaping the city of Istanbul are to a large extent distinct from those one can observe in the case of, say, western metropolises. In arguing for the distinctiveness of Istanbul, however, we wish to keep at a critical distance from postmodern approaches that push such claims to the point of uniqueness. While rightly criticizing the overarching generalizations of modernist geographers, postmodern geography has argued for the uniqueness of localities and thereby paved the way for modes of political action that may lead, intentionally or not, to parochialism and fragmented identity politics. It is therefore not only the ontological assumptions but also the likely political outcomes of these polarized approaches in contemporary geographical thought that we wish to go beyond.

Our insistence on an in-between position also originates from our belief that Istanbul is not a city that can be explained with the help of binary oppositions that dominate western social thinking. This of course does not mean that in studying Istanbul we have nothing to learn from categorizations developed for western societies. The overall picture of Mediterranean cities depicted by Leontidou (1993), for example, has striking similarities with that of Istanbul. We simply wish to emphasize that the unquestioned use of western categories may be misleading in the particular case of Istanbul. Istanbul is a city that has always been evolving, a city where transformation seems to be the rule; in short, a reality in which theories with fixed reference points are destined to fail even at the outset. One can safely argue that the sense of destruction that western scholars have experienced with the advent of postmodern critiques has long been familiar to the students of urbanization in Turkey who have had to make sense of the world from within a never-ending process of destruction and creation.

The following section is a brief summary of the research aiming to decipher the social geography of Istanbul with the aid of 1990 population census data. Here, we introduce a composite *status-tenure index* which, given the lack of spatial data on household income, is certainly capable of measuring social differentiation with regard to income. Figure 10.1 is a map derived from this methodology and the conclusions obtained are also discussed. The third section in this chapter (p. 209) summarizes the changes that seem to have taken place in the social landscapes of Istanbul since 1990, with particular emphasis on courses of action taken by different urban groups.

The Social Geography of Istanbul

Studying social segregation in a city like Istanbul is complicated by a number of factors. The first difficulty stems from its unique geographical setting. Built on

two continents with a seaway (the Bosphorus) between and two geographically distinct areas on the European side separated by the Golden Horn, Istanbul
is indeed divided into three geographical units.[2] A second difficulty originates
from the fact that it is a city that is literally *on the move.* Even a cursory look at
the following population figures may reveal this fact. In the forty-seven-year
period between 1950 and 1997 Istanbul's population has grown more than
sevenfold (see Tables 10.1 and 10.2). Not only does nearly one-fifth of the
urban population of Turkey live in Istanbul today, but also, according to
some estimates, Istanbul accounts for nearly one-third of all Turkey's national
product (Ergün 1997).

Table 10.1. The population of Turkey and Istanbul (1950–97)

	Turkey: total (A)	Turkey: urban (B)	Istanbul (C)	Index Turkey: total	Turkey: urban
1950	20,947,188	5,244,337	1,166,477	100.0	100.0
1955	24,064,763	6,729,343	1,533,822	114.9	132.1
1960	27,754,820	8,859,731	1,802,092	132.5	168.9
1965	31,391,421	10,805,817	2,293,823	149.9	206.0
1970	35,612,776	13,691,101	3,019,032	170.0	261.1
1975	40,347,719	16,869,068	3,903,650	192.6	321.7
1980	44,736,957	21,993,318	4,741,890	213.6	374.6
1985	50,664,458	26,865,757	5,475,982	241.9	512.3
1990	56,473,035	33,326,351	6,620,241	269.6	637.6
1997	62,610,252	40,882,357	8,180,319	298.9	779.6

Table 10.2. Turkey and Istanbul: annual growth
rate (1950–97)

Istanbul	Total	Urban	Istanbul	C/A[a]	C/B[a]
100.0	--	--	--	5.6	22.2
131.5	2.8	5.6	5.5	6.4	22.1
154.5	2.9	4.9	3.2	6.5	20.3
196.6	2.5	4.0	4.8	7.3	21.2
258.8	2.5	4.7	5.5	8.5	22.1
334.7	2.5	4.2	5.1	9.7	23.1
406.5	2.1	3.0	3.9	10.6	24.1
469.4	2.5	6.3	2.9	10.8	20.4
567.5	2.2	4.4	3.8	11.7	19.8
701.3	1.5	2.9	3.0	13.1	20.0

[a] A, Turkey: total; B, Turkey: urban; C, Istanbul.

Source: State Institute of Statistics, Population Censuses, various
years.

It is the nature of social segregation itself that seems to have posed the most enduring difficulty in the case of Istanbul. For Istanbul can be best defined with what may be termed a mild, or even a soft, social segregation. As far as the cleavages (class, ethnic, and otherwise) that exist among its population are concerned, Istanbul differs, for instance, from Los Angeles where spatial social divisions are more easily observable.[3] While the term that would best describe the nature of social segregation in Los Angeles is '*juxtaposition*', the metaphor that one should use in the case of Istanbul should be '*superimposition*'. In other words, the study of social divisions in Istanbul is complicated by the spatial superimposition of inherently different geographical attributes. One needs, therefore, a different method of analysis (*a layer-by-layer analysis*) in order to disclose the social divisions in Istanbul. Put more clearly, it is not only the degree of segregation but also the way in which different spatial geographical attributes coexist differ from most of the examples in the contemporary literature:[4] it is, to continue with the *superimposition* metaphor, a kind of *archaeological survey* that one needs to carry out to read the social cleavages in Istanbul.

Another major difficulty has its origins in the lack of adequate data. Above all, the dearth of area-coded data has been a significant problem for urban studies in Turkey. In fact, none of the five-year censuses from 1935 to 1985 had sub-district level area codes for urban areas. It follows that students of urban phenomena in Turkey have for a long time lacked the *sine qua non* condition of their studies. One had to wait until the 1990 census for a definitive solution of the problem. The inclusion, for the first time in Turkey, of neighbourhood level area codes in the 1990 population census represented in itself an important step forward for the issue of data availability.[5] The availability of geographically coded census data, however, does not constitute a solution on its own to the problem of deciphering social segregation.

Income-based social divisions are extremely difficult to detect since standard census questionnaires do not include entries for income levels. Under such circumstances the relevance and the discriminatory capability of most census categories are seriously impaired. For instance, students cannot differentiate by using the data on employment status between high-income wage earners, such as company managers, and low-income factory workers, both classified under the heading of 'wage earners'. Given the absence of a direct indicator for income level, we propose a new empirical construct, a status-tenure index, which, as we discuss below, is well capable of measuring social differentiation along the lines of income. This index is produced by cross-tabulating employment status by the tenure type of dwellings.

The construction of housing tenure types is fairly straightforward. The following four types of housing tenure can be distinguished:

1. *Tenure type 1*: Households who own at least two dwelling units.
2. *Tenure type 2*: Households who own only the housing unit they occupy (i.e., owner-occupiers).

3. *Tenure type 3*: Tenant households who own at least one dwelling unit elsewhere (i.e., high-income tenants).
4. *Tenure type 4*: Tenant households who rent a dwelling (i.e., low-income tenants).

A subsequent cross-tabulation of these housing tenure types by employment status (i.e., wage earners, employers, self-employed, and *'others'*)[6] yielded a total of sixteen *status-tenure* categories. Each of the 80,000 households in the 5 per cent sample data was then assigned to these composite categories to see their distribution amongst some 600 neighbourhoods of Greater Istanbul. A cursory examination of the resulting matrix suggests that neighbourhoods display rather complex status-tenure profiles. In fact, there is hardly any neighbourhood of Istanbul in which a particular status-tenure group is dominant. There are only places where some status-tenure groups show relative concentrations. When analysed by conventional indices, such as percentages, the picture of the distribution of status-tenure groups in Istanbul may be interpreted simply as a chaos in which each group seems to be everywhere in the metropolitan area.

This brings us back to a point we made at the beginning of this chapter: the need for new tools to study cities characterized by soft social segregation. In order to account for this type of segregation we have produced tables based on the *signed chi-square index* proposed by Gatrell (1985).[7] Thanks to its interesting methodological properties, this index yields important insights relative to the soft social segregation in Istanbul. Illustrative results are summarized in Table 10.3 for the three geographical units of the Istanbul metropolitan area.[8] Despite the fact that considerably larger units of observation are used, contrasts in status-tenure index values are striking, meaning that each geographical unit of the Istanbul metropolitan area has a distinct character of its own.

The results reveal a clear pattern of segregation between the geographical units of Istanbul as far as the status-tenure profiles of its inhabitants are concerned: the Istanbul side is characterized by the striking absence of the status category of *'others'* and the concentration of the relatively poor wage earners and the self-employed; the Beyoglu side is characterized by the near-to-expected levels of almost all categories and by the preponderance of low-income tenant *others* and the absence of owner-occupier wage earners; and the Anatolian side is characterized by the significantly high concentration of categories of A1–A3 and D1–D3, and the absence of all segments of the self-employed. These properties make this index particularly relevant for Istanbul. Our results also suggest that, although devised as an indirect estimate of income variation *within* given status categories, the status-tenure index is useful in detecting contrasts in terms of social and demographic properties as well (see Güvenç and Işık 1996).

The next step in our study was to classify the neighbourhoods of Istanbul according to their status-tenure profiles. The results of this exercise are

Table 10.3. Status-tenure profiles[a] of three geographical units of the Istanbul metropolitan area (*signed chi-square values*)

Geographical units	Status-tenure categories															
	A1	A2	A3	A4	B1	B2	B3	B4	C1	C2	C3	C4	D1	D2	D3	D4
Istanbul	-71.7	5.1	-11.5	105.9	-26.6	2.9	-14.2	-1.1	0.3	66.6	0.0	73.6	-120.1	-48.6	-19.2	-16.3
Beyoglu	-0.1	-25.3	0.5	0.1	4.9	1.0	0.8	0.0	0.0	-0.7	-0.2	-0.8	3.3	0.5	0.0	16.9
Anatolian	915.9	481.5	69.9	-1,256.2	21.9	-95.1	60.0	18.9	-27.4	-536	-3.2	602.2	557.7	394.9	94.2	-53.9

[a] A1, high-income wage earners; A2, owner-occupier wage earners; A3, high-income tenant wage earners; A4, low-income tenant wage earners.
B1, high-income employers; B2, owner-occupier employers; B3, high-income tenant employers; B4, low-income tenant employers.
C1, high-income self-employed; C2, owner-occupier self-employed; C3, high-income tenant self-employed; C4, low-income tenant self-employed.
D1, high-income *others*; D2, owner-occupier *others*; D3, high-income tenant *others*; D4, low-income tenant *others*.

Source: Güvenç and Işık (1996: 25).

summarized in the general status-tenure map of the Istanbul metropolitan area (see Fig. 10.1).[9] The resulting social landscape of Istanbul is made up of two components with distinct characteristics. The first component includes those neighbourhoods whose status-tenure profiles are unique and clearly different from the rest. The second component includes those neighbourhoods with homogeneous status-tenure profiles, namely those that were assigned to readily decipherable clusters.[10]

It is interesting to note that almost all the neighbourhoods in the first group exhibit striking concentrations of the high-income groups, regardless of their employment status. This means that the rich segments, with different tastes, lifestyles, etc., have come together to create a living space of their own isolated from other urban groups. Clearly cut off from low- and middle-income groups within the city, the neighbourhoods of the wealthy, nevertheless, contained within themselves a considerable degree of heterogeneity in that they housed

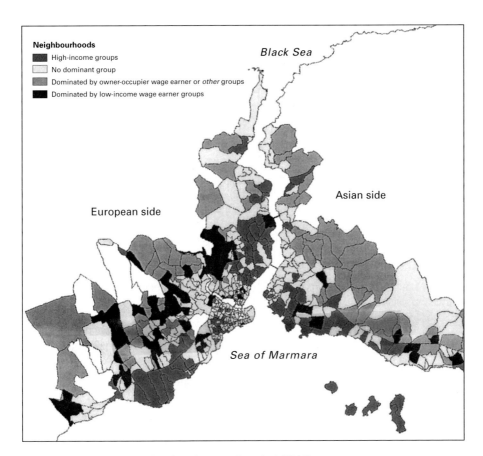

Fig 10.1. The social geography of greater Istanbul (1990).

rich segments of all employment categories. This implies that the rich had the ability to come together to form spatial coalitions regardless of their differences. We shall argue in the next section that this no longer seems to be the case as the high-income groups have become differentiated among themselves along several lines, including but not limited to their employment status, and have chosen to create more homogenous living environments after 1990. Also note that the concentrations of the wealthy are almost without exception on the sea coast (see Fig. 10.1).

The remaining group comprises two types of neighbourhoods. The first, mixed areas, covers neighbourhoods where none of the defined emerge as a predominant group, while the second consists of clusters where one status-tenure group is visibly dominant. *Neighbourhoods with no predominant groups* are those in which all the status-tenure groups are represented at levels that are close to the metropolitan average, where in technical terms the *signed chi-square values* for each status tenure category assume values near zero. Figure 10.1 shows that such mixed neighbourhoods constitute border areas between more homogeneous neighbourhoods occupied by the wealthy and squatter housing areas where tenant or owner-occupier wage earners are predominant. Most of them are former squatter neighbourhoods regularized through successive building amnesty laws or spaces adjacent to the first urban thoroughfare connecting the first bridge over the Bosphorus to the inter-city highways.

The neighbourhoods where one status-tenure group is visibly dominant, the more homogeneous neighbourhoods, are distinguished in the first place by the dominance of different tenure groups of wage earners. First, there are those neighbourhoods where owner-occupier wage earners are the dominant group. Figure 10.1 shows a concentration of such neighbourhoods on the Asian side of the metropolitan area, known to be specialized in capital-intensive Fordist business, such as pharmaceuticals, automotive and automotive spare parts, shipyards, general chemistry, glass and production of non-ferrous metals, paints and varnish, etc. These businesses with comparatively stable production levels, predictable employment strategies, and formal retirement schemes create relatively favourable conditions for home ownership. Hence, this unevenness in the geographical distribution of neighbourhoods is closely associated with the industrial geography of the Istanbul metropolitan area (Güvenç 1992*a,b*).

Second, there are neighbourhoods where low-income tenant wage earner households constitute the dominant group, the majority of which are squatter housing areas. Note that these areas are mostly concentrated on the European side of the metropolitan area where the central business district of Istanbul is located. This geographical unit of the metropolitan area is specialized in trades such as textiles, the garment industry, etc., where the bulk of production is realized within vertically disintegrated production complexes. In such trades flexible employment strategies are deployed. This leads to little or no job security and chronic fluctuations in household incomes, a fact which also accounts for the low levels of home ownership.

The high-income groups are concentrated in the relatively homogeneous coastal enclaves on each geographical unit of the metropolitan area and, with a few exceptions, the areas characterized by the predominance of wage earners are completely cut off from the sea. It is interesting to note that the mixed neighbourhoods with no predominant groups seem to act as a buffer between these two sectors (see Fig. 10.1). In fact, one can immediately see that the areas dominated by the wealthy have almost no common borders with the neighbourhoods inhabited by the relatively poor.

It is also worth noting that the areas occupied by the rich and the poor have indeed developed through entirely different processes. The seaside neighbourhoods occupied by the rich are older compared to their inland counterparts and, in most cases, subject to formal building regulations. Thus, a seaside location constitutes a guarantee against the negative externalities associated with the uncontrolled urban growth. On the other hand, inland neighbourhoods inhabited by the poor are subject to the control of patron/client type local networks and the so-called *real estate mafia*, a fact which in part accounts for the concentration of people with the same ethnic origin in particular parts of the metropolitan area.

Despite all its complexity the emerging picture of social segregation in Istanbul in the year 1990 is clear enough, with seaside locations occupied by the rich segments of several status groups, the fringes inhabited by the poor, and mixed neighbourhoods with no predominant groups acting as a buffer between the latter two. We shall see in the concluding section that this picture has changed significantly since 1990.

What Has Changed in Istanbul Since 1990?

Figure 10.1 can be viewed as a summary of the social divisions characterizing Istanbul in 1990 when, subsequent to the collapse of the eastern bloc, the processes of globalization started to unfold with greater impact. Istanbul was already a *divided city* in 1990 with little room left for the expansion of comparatively old neighbourhoods inhabited by the wealthy. What we now wish to do is to discuss how this picture has changed since 1990, and how it is likely to change in the years to come, with special emphasis on the course of action taken by different groups in the urban setting.

The year 1990 represents a turning point in the social and spatial history of Istanbul. It is a point in time when local dynamics came to interact with global forces in ways that had previously been unknown in Turkish society. The collapse of the eastern bloc came at a time when Istanbul was already amidst the process of a transformation induced, to a large extent, by the wider social and economic transformations that Turkish society had been undergoing since the late 1970s. Globalization further intensified the conflicts that had been building up for some time. The transformations that Istanbul has undergone in the last two decades need, therefore, to be explained in the context of a number of intertwined processes. The first has its origins in the economic and social transformations that Turkish society has experienced since the late 1970s, and the other in the changing position of the city within the global network in the late 1980s.

The scale of transformations that Turkish society has gone through in the last two decades is too great to be summarized in a few words.[11] During this period, the Turkish economy was transformed from an inward-oriented one producing for the local market to an export-led one producing for the world markets. The consequences of this restructuring process are well known and not unique to Turkey: the consolidation of a new growth model based on the consolidation of the working class; a dramatic income redistribution with massive declines in real wages; a radical transformation of political structures and class alliances that had been geared to the maintenance of a closed economy since the early days of the Republic.

The most tangible impacts of the global dynamics on Istanbul were felt after the collapse of the eastern bloc. Coupled with the growing importance of the city as a gateway to the Balkans and the Black Sea countries, the massive influx of tourists from the former eastern bloc countries prepared the ground for a major change in Istanbul's local economy. This influx has reached such dimensions that an airport is under construction solely for the tourists from the former eastern bloc countries. Such dynamics also led to a large-scale restructuring of Istanbul's economy. In the turbulent economic atmosphere of the five-year period between 1992 and 1997—a period marked by the 1994 fiscal crisis which was comparable in scope and effect to the Mexican crisis—no less than 4,000 plants were closed with almost the same number of new plants being established.[12] Most of the newly established plants are smaller in scale than their predecessors and concentrate on textile and clothing sectors serving mostly the demand from the former eastern bloc countries.

The combined effect of these intertwined processes on Istanbul has been the worsening of income distribution with a large-scale redistribution of wealth within the city. Income distribution statistics for Istanbul give a clear indication of this fact.[13] The available data suggest that the *gini coefficient*, a measure of the degree of inequality in income distribution, rose from 0.38 in 1978 to 0.48 in 1987 and finally to 0.59 in 1994. Similarly, when households are divided into ten income groups, the share in total urban income of the wealthiest 10 per cent increased from 28.9 per cent in 1978 to 39.2 per cent in 1987 and to 52.0 per cent in 1994, with the richest 1 per cent only receiving 29 per cent of all income in 1994. Not only do the gaps between different income groups seem to have widened, but also the entire income structure of the city has undergone a radical change. This is best evidenced in a drastic fall in the share of wages and salaries in the total urban income: from 57.9 per cent in 1978 to 32.9 per cent in 1987 and to 23.6 per cent in 1994. What is of equal importance is the increase in the share of wages in some high-income groups and thus the emergence of a new high-income wage-earning group employed mostly in the finance, insurance, and real estate sectors.

The forces of globalization thus further accelerated the income polarization process that had been at work in the society for some time, helping the 'winners' and the 'losers' become crystallized. The process of polarization has had clearly visible spatial consequences that are not much different in broad terms from the countries undergoing similar experiences.[14]

The rich, who had significantly increased their wealth in the last decade and who had earlier been concentrated in their dense enclaves along the coast, started to create new sites for themselves outside the built-up portion of the metropolitan area. Newspaper advertisements indicate that the new sites that are fashionable for the wealthy are on the previously uninhabited coasts of the Black Sea, in and around forests along the Bosphorus, or lakeside areas, with property prices as high as US$1 million in some instances. More often than not, these new islands of high consumption by the wealthy are literally walled, 'fortified territories' (Aksoy and Robins 1994: 68), access-controlled residential areas under the constant surveillance of private security agencies.[15] The marketing strategies of these new sites of the rich overtly stress the aim of providing their inhabitants with a secure environment, in fact a new lifestyle '. . . combining the amenities of urban living with the sense of community of the small town' (Aksoy and Robins 1994: 66). In some instances those who wish to buy a housing unit in such sites are asked to fill in questionnaires about their living styles and habits, which are then distributed to the residents who make the final decision as to whether or not to allow the dwelling unit to be sold (see Öncü 1997). Despite the obvious differences, however, the new spatial strategy of the wealthy has some similarities with the previous one: these new sites are not easily accessible for most of the urban groups and it is almost impossible for such areas to be surrounded in the near future by other groups, especially by the poor.

The wealthy segments of the populace have thus chosen to isolate themselves from the other groups. What is equally important is the fact that this rise of 'fortified enclaves' of the rich has been accompanied by the rise of a new elitist culture in Turkish society. The nascent urban elite have used the elements of global culture as a means to detach themselves from the rest of the society. The evidence is abundant: housing estates where, should you wish to do so, you can watch your child live on the internet while he or she plays with other children in the kindergarten; housing projects offering its residents a new lifestyle, among the components of which are recreational and sporting facilities and most importantly schools, a service that once used to belong to the public sector but which is now being rapidly privatized. It now seems to be the case that the rich and the poor use different modes of transport, send their children to different schools, use different health facilities, and so on. The result, on the part of the nascent elite, is an impermeable, caste-like culture in which the elements of the national culture are used as an asset in the globalization game.

On the other hand, the poorer groups that definitely seem to have lost in this game have not been passive witnesses. In some instances they have resisted in ways that have been open to themselves, and in others they have created new ways of action. In every case, however, they have adopted more aggressive survival strategies in the face of worsening economic conditions. The first strategy of the poor has been to play the 'card of the real estate market', in an attempt to offset what they had lost in the economic arena. They exerted pressure on national and local politics to obtain, initially, title deeds, and subsequently, additional development rights for the illegal settlements they had built. And thanks to the overtly populist-clientelist structure of Turkish politics,[16] they did succeed in most cases: in the mid 1980s four reconstruction amnesties were enacted. The impacts of these amnesties on urban areas have been enormous.[17] Squatter houses which, in previous phases of Turkish urbanization, were modest low-rise structures built directly for the use of migrants themselves, became valuable urban properties, creating pressures for a change in these areas. Soaring values of squatter houses encouraged their owners to pull them down to build multi-storey structures. The undeclared aim of these amnesties was to pave the way for the appropriation of ground rents by the immigrants. These four amnesties must therefore be regarded as one of the clearest examples of the state's long-known attitude towards urbanization and the urban poor: financing the whole urbanization process through the massive ground rents generated by rapid urban development and fuelling and then manipulating these ground rents as an income redistribution mechanism.

These amnesties brought with themselves some drastic results as far as the overall social structure of squatter areas is concerned, not to mention its environmental consequences. The newcomers were in most cases deprived of the means to build a multi-storey structure for themselves, since the practice of users building their squatter houses was already a thing of the past. They were forced, therefore, to live as tenants in the newly transformed squatter areas, accelerating the differentiation in these areas along the lines of housing tenure. In short, the transformation of previous squatter areas induced a process of diversification within the already existing squatter settlements.

Another strategy on the part of the urban poor has been to strengthen the networks they already had, or to set up new networks of solidarity among themselves.[18] It must be noted that the new networks migrants establish differ from those earlier ones in that the new ones seem to operate not merely on a job status or ethnicity basis. In other words, not only did the existing class and ethnic divisions sharpen, but also cultural, political, and even religious overtones were added to the existing societal divisions. These new divisions have not replaced existing class divisions as some have argued (see, e.g., Ercan 1996) but have articulated with them in unusual ways. These new divisions have also penetrated the informal job market, indicating that this has also become fragmented along the lines of ethnicity, politics, and culture. The divisions between Kurds and Turks, religious segments (Alevis and Sunnis), 'Islamic fundamentalists', and 'secularists' have become more spatially visible, with substantial population movements between parts of the city.

As far as the changing spatial strategies of the rich and the poor in the 1990s are concerned, it could certainly be asserted that the state has been more than a silent partner in both cases. The part played by the state not only in the recent developments of the 1990s but also in the overall urbanization process can best be described with reference to its clearly dominant role in land ownership in and around urban areas. Founded on the remnants of the Ottoman Empire, where all the land belonged to the 'sultan' and where private property rights were consolidated only in the second half of the 19th century, the republican state inherited from its imperial past vast tracts of land and is the largest landowner in contemporary Turkey.[19] Seen from this aspect, the urbanization process in Turkey is one whereby the state land around urban areas is appropriated and opened up for urban development by various groups. In the early stages of the urbanization process it was essentially the newcomers, the urban poor, who appropriated this land by means of spontaneous occupation. In the later stages, there arose an illegal land market where the state land around cities was subdivided and then sold by mafia-like groups to the newcomers. In both cases, however, the state land around cities has been opened up for urban development without any planning controls.[20]

The course of action taken by the state with respect to the appropriation of state land around cities has been of enormous importance for the overall manipulation of the urbanization process. It is clear that tolerating and subsequently providing, on the part of local governments, basic infrastructure to these mushrooming settlements on state land and enacting, on the part of the central government, successive building amnesties have been the most effective tool for urban populism in Turkey. In this sense, the post-1990 period has been no exception, a period in which urban populism was pushed to its limits with the state responding in most cases positively to various demands on the urban fringe. The attitude of the state towards the urban poor has not been much different in the last decade than inpreceding periods, in that it has paved the way for an extensive legalization of squatter settlements via amnesties, granting in addition some extra development rights. What makes the post-1990 period different is the attitude of the state towards the wealthy, who previously had not placed large-scale demands on the uninhabited state land. Most of the recently built enclaves of the rich in Istanbul are on former state land, obtained either through the privatization of forests or through special arrangements with central or local government. It is interesting to note that in most cases central government has intervened to facilitate the appropriation of virgin land around Istanbul for private developments. One example is the permit granted by central government, despite the opposition of the municipality, for the construction of one of the largest private universities along the Bosphorus.

Conclusions

Istanbul, at the beginning of the 21st century, is thus characterized by a growing split: on the one hand, the wealthy are increasingly isolating themselves from the rest of the society, retreating to their fortified enclaves outside the built-up area of the city, and promoting a closed culture with no element of compromise with the other urban groups. On the other, the urban poor, living in inward-looking communities, are watching from a distance the city they would like to be a part of. What the future may bring is far from being certain. One possibility is that the nation-state may manage to organize itself into a more democratic one and thus bring together the fragments of this increasingly hostile tug-of-war. A second scenario might be the rise of micro-authoritarianism in which community-based actions have a major role to play. In any case, however, Istanbul is literally at a crossroads. The fact that the population growth rate has somewhat slowed down and is likely to continue to fall in the first decades of the 21st century (TUSIAD 1999) might mean the end of populist-clientelist local politics which simply redistributed the benefits of rapid urban growth and hence the end of clientelist networks of solidarity. This means that the urban poor who were so far beneath the aegis of such networks may remain unprotected and unsupported in the future. This also implies the possibility for the emergence of an underclass excluded from any and all support networks. It is probably the case that Turkey will now have to face the urban environment and all that is associated with it.

Notes

1. For examples of such studies see especially Göle (1993), Keyder (1993), and Keyder and Öncü (1993 and 1994).
2. The barrier effect generated by the sea is too important to ignore and unlikely to be overcome through technological means (like new bridges) in the near future.
3. For the examples of studies on Los Angeles see, in particular, Soja (1989, 1996).
4. For the examples of studies on cities with relatively milder social segregation see Laquian (1996) and Winston (1996).
5. The research summarized in the pages that follow is carried out on the 5% sample drawn from the 1990 population census. In this census, Istanbul was divided into some 600 neighbourhoods with varying surface areas and population sizes.
6. The category '*others*' includes those household heads not included in the previous categories (i.e., the retired, unemployed, students, and *rentiers*).

7. These tables display data as *signed chi-square deviations* from an expected theoretical value computed separately for each neighbourhood. Since it is based on an expected value for each unit of observation, this index accounts for size variations in neighbourhoods and is therefore capable of bringing to light the relative concentrations that would otherwise remain hidden. While deriving the *signed chi-square index*, the first step is to calculate expected values for each neighbourhood assuming an absolutely homogenous distribution of the category in question. These expected values are then compared with the actual ones to find out in the end the deviation. Above-zero levels of the index indicate the concentration of the category in question, while below-zero levels refer to lower than expected amounts of the category. Therefore, the larger the absolute deviation, the larger the concentration or de-concentration of the category in the geographical unit of observation. Similarly, near-to-zero levels of the chi-square index mean that the category under consideration is close to the levels expected for the whole metropolitan area. For a detailed explanation of the method and results, see Güvenç and Işık (1996).

8. As we mentioned above, Istanbul is built on three separate geographical units: the Anatolian side on the Asian continent and two units on the European side. The northern part of the European side is referred to as Beyoglu, and the southern part as the Istanbul side.

9. The classification of Istanbul's neighbourhoods with respect to their status-tenure profiles through standard cluster analysis techniques has proved difficult because of the high level of variation among neighbourhoods. In fact, even if the number of clusters is set to an arbitrarily high level (say 50) one sees that no less than 20 of them are occupied by single neighbourhoods, while remaining neighbourhoods are forced into 30 clusters that remain available. Consequently, the attempts of classification of Istanbul's neighbourhoods through cluster analysis produced two types of clusters: (i) those comprising only a small number of neighbourhoods with distinctive status-tenure profiles; and (ii) those comprising a large number of neighbourhoods where the dominant characteristics cannot be easily deciphered. It is our contention that the characteristics of this landscape cannot be deciphered unless its constituent parts are *separately* studied. To this end it is sufficient to exclude those clusters with single or few neighbourhoods (i.e., those that appear unique), from the list. In this particular example six eliminatory runs sufficed to exclude all groups with single or few neighbourhoods.

10. The results are certainly not encouraging for those inclined to emphasize 'uniqueness', as the first component in Istanbul comprises only a handful of neighbourhoods. On the other hand, those aiming to detect an all-embracing homogeneity in Istanbul will be disappointed, as the neighbourhoods with readily decipherable characteristics constitute only a part of the social landscape. It follows that in the case of Istanbul ontological positions emphasizing uniqueness or generality do not in themselves yield fruitful outcomes (Güvenç and Işık 1997). Hence our insistence on the necessity to adopt an in-between ontological position.

11. For an excellent account of the transformation of Turkish society in the 1980s, see Keyder (1987) and Zürcher (1993).

12. These figures are taken from the Istanbul Chamber of Industry membership files.

13. All the data quoted in this paragraph concerning the income distribution in Istanbul are taken from SIS (1997).

14. See for instance Caldeira's analysis for São Paulo (Caldeira 1996).

15. See Caldeira (1996) for the rise of similar 'fortified enclaves' in the case of São Paulo, and Marcuse (1997).
16. As an instrument of political mobilization populism-clientelism has a long history in Turkish politics. See Ayata (1994) for an account of the roots of clientelism in Turkey and Tekeli (1994) for the part played by the patron–client relations in the urban economy.
17. See Işık (1996) for an analysis of the impact of reconstruction amnesties on urban areas.
18. On the urban informal networks see Erder (1996, 1997).
19. This accounts in part for the lack of a large-scale landowning class and the preponderance of small peasant farming and thereby the excessive fragmentation of private urban landownership in Turkey. See Keyder (1981) for an historical account of the transformation of landownership in Turkey.
20. Some estimate that almost as much as 60–65% of the total Istanbul population live in such areas. See Işık (1996).

References

AKSOY, A., and ROBINS, K. (1993). 'Ezilen Istanbul'un dönüsü: Reddedilen, bastirilan öteki kültürler' (The return of the suppressed Istanbul: Oppressed other cultures). *Istanbul*, 3: 13–18.
———(1994). 'Istanbul between civilisation and discontent'. *New Perspectives on Turkey*, 10: 57–74.
AYATA, A. (1994). 'Roots and trends of clientelism in Turkey', in L. Roniger and A. Ayata (eds.), *Democracy, Clientelism and Civil Society*, 49–63. London: Lynne Rienner.
CALDEIRA, T. P. (1996). 'Fortified enclaves: The new urban segregation'. *Public Culture*, 8: 303–28.
ERCAN, F. (1996). 'Kriz ve yeniden yapilanma sürecinde dünya kentleri ve uluslararasi kentler: Istanbul' (World city or international city: The case of Istanbul). *Toplum ve Bilim*, 71: 61–96.
ERDER, S. (1996). *Ümraniye: Istanbul'a Kaçak bir Kent Kondu* (Ümraniye: A squatter area in Istanbul). Istanbul: Iletisim.
———(1997). *Kentsel Gerilim: Enformel Iliski Aglari Alan Arastirmasi* (Urban Tension: A Field Survey on Informal Networks). Ankara: um:ag.
ERGÜN, H. (1997). 'Çeliskiler megapolisi' (A metropolis of contradictions). *Radikal Iki*, 8–9: 13.
GATRELL, A. C. (1985). 'Any space for spatial analysis?', in R. J. Johnston (ed.), *The Future of Geography*, 190–208. London: Methuen.
GÖLE, N. (1993). 'Istanbul's revenge'. *Istanbul* (English language edition), 1(2).
GÜVENÇ, M. (1992a). 'General industrial geography of Greater Istanbul metropolitan area: An exploratory study', in I. Tekeli *et al.* (eds.), *Development of Istanbul Metropolitan Area and Low-Cost Housing*, 112–60. Istanbul: Municipality of Greater Istanbul, IULA–EMME (International Union of Local Authorities–Section for the Eastern Mediterranean and Middle East).

GÜVENÇ, M. (1992*b*). *Introduction to structural landscape analysis: Overviews on the industrial landscapes of Greater Istanbul.* Unpublished Ph.D. dissertation, Ankara, Middle East Technical University, Department of City and Regional Planning.

——and IŞIK, O. (1996). 'Istanbul'u okumak: Statü-konut mülkiyeti farklilasmasina iliskin bir çözümleme denemesi' (Reading Istanbul: An essay on spatial differentiation with respect to employment status and housing tenure types). *Toplum ve Bilim*, 71: 6–60.

——————(1997). 'Istanbul'u okumak: II. Mahalle düzeyinde konut mülkiyeti-statü farklilasmasina iliskin bulgular nasil genellenebilir?' (Reading Istanbul: II. How to generalise findings on status-tenure differentiation at neighbourhood level). *Toplum ve Bilim*, 72: 153–64.

IŞIK, O. (1996). '1980 sonrasi Turkiye'de kent ve kentlesme' (Urbanization in Turkey after the 1980s), in *Cumhuriyet Dönemi Türkiye Ansiklopedisi*, 783–801. Istanbul: Iletisim.

KEYDER, Ç. (1981). *The Definition of a Peripheral Economy: Turkey—1923–1929.* Cambridge: Cambridge University Press.

——(1987). *State and Class in Turkey.* London: New Left Books.

——(1993). 'Istanbul'u nasil satmali?' (Marketing Istanbul), in *Ulusal Kalkinmaciligin Iflasi*, 66–78. Istanbul: Iletisim.

——and Öncü, A. (1993). *Istanbul and the Concept of World Cities.* Istanbul: Friedrich Ebert Foundation.

——————(1994). 'Globalization of a third world metropolis: Istanbul in the 1980s'. *Review*, 7: 151–74.

LAQUIAN, A. A. (1996). 'The multi-ethnic and multi-cultural city: An Asian perspective'. *International Social Science Journal*, 147: 43–55.

LEONTIDOU, L. (1993). 'Postmodernism and the city: Mediterranean versions'. *Urban Studies*, 30: 949–65.

MARCUSE, P. (1997). 'The ghetto of exclusion and the fortified enclave: New patterns in the United States', in H. Priemus, S. Musterd, and R. van Kempen (eds.), *Towards Undivided Cities in Western Europe: New Challenges for Urban Policy*: 7. *Comparative analysis*, 5–20. Delft: Delft University Press.

ÖNCÜ, A. (1997). 'The myth of "ideal home" travels across cultural borders to Istanbul', in A. Öncü and P. Weyland (eds.), *Space, Culture and Power: New Identities in Globalizing Cities*, 28–44. London: Zed Books.

SIS (State Institute of Statistics) (1997). *Results of Income Distribution Survey, 1994.* Ankara: SIS.

SOJA, E. (1989). *Postmodern Geographies: The Reassertion of Space in Social Theory.* London: Verso.

——(1996). *Thirdspace: Journeys to Los Angeles and Other Real-and-Imagined Places.* Oxford: Blackwell.

TEKELI, I. (1994). 'The patron–client relationship, land-rent economy and the experience of urbanization without citizens', in S. J. Neary, M. S. Symes, and F. E. Brown (eds.), *The Urban Experience*, 9–17. London: Spon.

TUSIAD (Turkish Industrialists' and Businessmen's Association) (1999). *Turkiye'nin Firsat Penceresi* (Turkey's Window of Opportunity). Istanbul: TUSIAD.

WINSTON, P. (1996). 'Managing a multi-ethnic and multi-cultural city: Leicester'. *International Social Science Journal*, 147: 25–33.

ZÜRCHER, E. J. (1993). *Turkey, A Modern History.* London: Tauris.

PART III

Conclusions

11

The Rise of Advanced Marginality: Notes on its Nature and Implications

Loïc Wacquant

Introduction

Over the past two decades, the self-image of First World societies as increasingly pacified, homogeneous, cohesive, and egalitarian—'democratic' in de Tocqueville's sense of the term, 'civilized' in Nobert Elias' lexicon—has been shattered by virulent outbreaks of public disorder, mounting ethnoracial tensions, and the palpable resurgence of inequality and marginality in the metropolis (Wacquant 1994a). As persistent joblessness, social deprivation, and ethnoracial conflict rose in unison in cities on both shores of the Atlantic, parallel debates developed in the United States and western Europe around the intersection of poverty, 'race' (or immigration), and urban decline.

With the accelerating dislocation and degradation of the metropolitan core, American social scientists and public policy experts have grown alarmed about the emergence and growth of a so-called black *underclass*, said to be entrapped in the urban core and increasingly isolated from the broader society.[1] In France and several other western European countries, a veritable moral panic has broken out over the rise of *'new poverty'*, the consolidation of *'immigrant ghettos'*, and the menace that these represent for national integration and public order, as working-class boroughs witnessed a deterioration of social conditions while former 'guest workers' and their children became an increasing, permanent component of their population.[2] On both sides of the Atlantic, the theme of the dualization, or polarization, of the city, has taken centre stage in the most advanced sectors of urban theory and research, as the extremes of high society and dark ghetto, luxurious wealth and utter

A preliminary version of this chapter was prepared for the Experts Meeting on Distressed Areas in Cities and Suburbs, OECD, Paris (March 1994), presented to the Seminar on Comparative Macrosociology, Department of Sociology, University of California–Los Angeles (January 1995), and published in *Acta Sociologica* (1996). Critical comments and reactions from both of these audiences are gratefully acknowledged. Specific suggestions by Janet Abu-Lughod, Peter Marcuse, Thomas Sugrue, Ronald van Kempen, Eric Wanner, and Bill Wilson were helpful, even when I chose not to heed them.

destitution, cosmopolitan bourgeoisie and urban outcasts, flourished and decayed side by side.[3]

Together, these developments would seem to point to an epochal transatlantic convergence in patterns of urban marginality. Yet close analysis of the ecology, structural location, composition, and organizational makeup of long-standing or newly emerging territories of exclusion in the Old and New Worlds suggests that European regimes of urban poverty are *not* being 'Americanized'. Contrary to first impressions and superficial, media-driven accounts, the changeover of the continental metropolis has not triggered a process of ghettoization: it is not giving birth to culturally uniform sociospatial ensembles based on the forcible relegation of stigmatized populations to enclaves where these populations evolve group- and place-specific organizations that substitute for and duplicate the institutional framework of the broader society, if at an inferior and incomplete level (Wacquant 1991).

A paired comparison between neighbourhoods of relegation in Chicago's 'Black Belt' and the Parisian 'Red Belt' shows that the declining French metropolitan periphery and the Afro-American ghetto remain two sharply distinct socio-spatial constellations. And for good reasons: they are heirs to different urban legacies, produced by different logics of segregation and aggregation, inserted in different welfare state and market frameworks—all of which result in markedly higher levels of blight, segregation, isolation, and distress in the United States ghetto. To put it crudely, 'exclusionary closure' (as formulated by Parkin 1978) and sociospatial relegation to the American Black Belt operate first and foremost on grounds of 'race'[4] bolstered by state structure and policies and aggravated by class divisions. Not so in the French Red Belt where socio-spatial extrusion is driven chiefly by class factors, partly exacerbated by colonial-immigrant status and partly alleviated by the (central and municipal) state. Correspondingly, the United States ghetto is a racially and culturally monotonous universe characterized by low organizational density and state penetration (and therefore high physical and social insecurity),[5] whereas its French counterpart is typically heterogeneous in both ethnonational and class recruitment with a comparatively strong presence of public institutions and far-reaching state penetration (Wacquant 1992*b*).

The differential 'stitching together' of colour, class, and place on both sides of the Atlantic does not, however, obviate the possibility that the recent transformations of the US ghetto, the French *banlieue*, and the British and Dutch 'inner cities' might herald the crystallization of a novel, still inchoate, yet distinctive *regime of urban marginality*, different from both America's traditional ghetto (Trotter 1993) and the 20th-century European 'workers' space' (Verret 1979; Thrift and Williams 1987). Viewed from this admittedly prospective angle, the 'return of the repressed' realities of extreme poverty and social destitution, ethnoracial divisions (linked to their colonial history) and public violence, and their accumulation in the same distressed urban areas, suggests that First World cities are now confronted with what we may call *advanced marginality*. Such new forms of exclusionary social closure and peripheralization have arisen—or intensified—in the post-Fordist metropolis as a result not of backwardness but of the uneven, disarticulating, mutations of the *most advanced sectors* of western societies and economies, as these bear on the lower fractions of the working class and on dominated ethnoracial categories, as well as on the territories they occupy in the divided city (Sassen 1991; Mingione 1991; Thrift 1993).

The qualifier 'advanced' is meant to indicate that those forms of marginality are not *behind* us and being progressively reabsorbed, whether by 'free market' expansion (i.e., further commodification of social life) or through the arm of the welfare state, but rather that they stand *ahead of us*. Novel forms of political intervention urgently need to be elaborated to check or redirect the structural forces that produce them, including polarized economic growth and the fragmentation of the labour market, the casualization of employment and autonomization of the street economy in degraded urban areas, mass joblessness amounting to outright deproletarianization for large segments of the working class (especially youth), and state policies of urban retrenchment if not outright abandonment. If new mechanisms of social mediation are not put in place to reincorporate excluded populations, one can expect that urban marginality will continue to rise and spread, and along with it the street violence, political alienation, organizational desertification, and economic informalization that increasingly plague the neighbourhoods of relegation of the metropolis in advanced society.

Some Distinctive Properties of 'Advanced Marginality'

An ideal-typical characterization of this new marginality *in statu nascendi* may be provisionally attempted by contrasting it with selected stylized features of urban poverty in the post-war era of 'Fordist' growth and prosperity (1945–75). Ideal-types, it may be recalled, are not purely analytical, 'synthetic constructs', but socio-historical abstractions of real instances of a phenomenon (Weber 1949: 86–92). They assist us in the process of hypothesis formation and comparison; they offer a baseline for identifying significant variations and their possible causes. As heuristic devices, however, ideal-types are not covered by criteria of truth or falsehood.

The summary characterization of 'advanced marginality' that follows is offered with reservation, knowing full well that, as Wittgenstein once warned (1977: 55), 'concepts may alleviate mischief or they may make it worse; foster it or check it'. Binary oppositions of the kind fostered by such conceptual exercise are prone to exaggerate differences, confound description and prescription, and set up overburdened dualisms that miss continuities, underplay contingency, and overstate the internal coherence of social forms. With these caveats in mind, six distinctive features of advanced marginality may be singled out for scrutiny.[6]

1. *Desocialization of wage-labour*: whereas in the decades of Fordist expansion or 'organized capitalism' (Lash and Urry 1988), the wage–labour relation offered an efficient solution to the dilemmas of urban marginality and social destitution, it appears that under the ascending new regime, it must be considered (also) part of the problem.

By becoming 'internally' unstable and heterogeneous, differentiated and differentiating, the wage–labour contract has turned into a source of fragmentation and precariousness rather than homogeneity and security for those held at the border zones of the employment sphere.[7] Witness, among other signs, the growth of part-time, 'flexible,' variable-schedule positions, with fewer benefits, negotiable extension and benefit clauses, revised wage scales, and the various avenues pursued to evade the standard, homogenizing effects of state regulation of wage-work (e.g., France's aborted attempt to create a sub-minimum wage for unskilled youth under the Balladur government in the spring of 1995). The resurgence of sweatshops, piecework and homework, the development of tele-work and two-tier wage scales, the outsourcing of employees and the individualization of remuneration and promotion patterns, the institutionalization of 'permanently temporary' work, not to mention the multiplication of 'make-work' formulas (such as 'workfare' forced labour in the United States and cheap, government-sponsored, 'public utility work' in France) imposed as condition of access to public assistance: all point to the rampant desocialization of wage-labour.

In addition to the erosion of the integrative capacity of the wage–labour relation, each of the elements of security granted under the Fordist-Keynesian social contract (Standing 1993) has been undermined or is under frontal attack: labour market security (efforts by the state to reach full employment), income security (through social provision, jobless benefits, and incorporation into unions), and employment security (the reduction of capitalist command over terms of hiring and firing). All in all, the structural roots of economic uncertainty and precariousness have ramified and extended in reach as well as depth.[8]

2. *Functional disconnection from macro-economic trends*: advanced marginality is increasingly disconnected from short-term fluctuations in the economy so that expansionary phases in employment and consumption have little durable effect upon it. Social conditions and life chances in neighbourhoods of relegation in Europe and the United States changed very little, if at all, during the boom years of the 1980s and early 1990s, but worsened noticeably during recessionary phases. Thus, youth joblessness kept rising in the Parisian Red Belt under the Rocard administration, breaking post-war records in one working-class municipality after another, even when strong growth had momentarily checked the onslaught of national unemployment. In Chicago, nearly 80 per cent of ghetto residents reported a deterioration of their financial

situation after four consecutive years of buoyant economic growth under Reagan and most felt that their neighbourhood was firmly set on the path to further dilapidation (Wacquant and Wilson 1989: 21–2).

Considering this asymmetric relation between national and even regional aggregate unemployment and labour market trends on the one hand, and neighbourhood conditions on the other, and given current levels of productivity increases and emerging forms of 'jobless growth', it would take miraculous rates of economic expansion to absorb back into the labour market those who have been durably expelled from it. This means that, short of actually guaranteeing employment, social policies premised on boosting the absorptive capacity of the labour market have every chance of being both costly and inefficient, since their benefits will 'trickle down' to the new urban outcasts last and only after every other more privileged group has benefited from growth.

3. *Territorial fixation and stigmatization*: rather than being diffused throughout working-class areas, advanced marginality tends to be concentrated in well-identified, bounded, and increasingly isolated territories viewed by both outsiders and insiders as social purgatories, urban hellholes where only the refuse of society would accept to dwell. A stigma of place thus superimposes itself on the already pervasive stigmata of poverty and (where applicable) of caste or colonial-immigrant origin, as these 'penalized spaces' are, or threaten to become, permanent fixtures of the city and as discourses of vilification proliferate about them (Wacquant 1993).[9] In every major First World metropolis, a particular urban district or township has 'made a name for itself' as that place where disorder, dereliction, and danger are said to be the normal order of the day. The South Bronx and Brownsville in New York City, Les Minguettes and Vaulx-en-Velin near Lyons, London's Brixton and East End, Gutleutviertel in Hamburg, Rinkebẙ on the outskirts of Stockholm, and Millinxbuurt in Rotterdam: the list gets longer by the year. On this level, whether or not those areas are in fact dilapidated, dangerous, and declining matters little: the prejudicial belief that they are suffices to set off socially detrimental consequences.

Living in the (sub)proletarian housing projects of the periphery of Paris creates a 'muted sentiment of guilt and shame whose unacknowledged weight warps human relations' (Pétonnet 1982: 148). People commonly hide their address, avoid having family and friends visit them at home, and feel compelled to make excuses for residing in an infamous locale experienced as inferiorizing and a blotch on one's self-image. 'I'm not from the *cité*, me myself,' insists a young woman from Vitry-sur-Seine, 'I live here because I have problems right now but I'm not from here, I have nothing to do with all those people from over here' (Pétonnet 1982: 149). Similarly, inhabitants of Chicago's ghetto deny belonging to the neighbourhood as a criss-crossing network of mutual acquaintance and assistance and they strive to distance themselves from a place and population they know are universally reviled: 'Hell, I don't know what people [around here] do, I guess I'm pretty much on my own. I don't sociate with people in the neighborhood' (Wacquant 1993: 369). All too often, the sense of social indignity can be deflected only by thrusting the stigma onto a faceless, diabolized, Other—the downstairs neighbours, the foreign family dwelling in an adjacent building, the youths from across the street who 'do drugs', or residents over on the next block that one suspects of illegally drawing unemployment or welfare benefits.[10]

4. *Territorial alienation, or the dissolution of 'place'*: the obverse of this process of territorial stigmatization is the dissolution of 'place', that is, the loss of a locale that marginalized urban populations identify with and in which they feel secure. Theories of post-Fordism intimate that the current reconfiguring of capitalism involves not only a vast reshuffling of firms, jobs, and people *in space* but a sea change in the organization and experience *of space* itself (see especially Harvey 1989; also Soja 1989 and Shields 1991). This is consistent with the changeover of both ghetto and *banlieue* from communal 'places' suffused with shared emotions, joint meanings, and practices and institutions of mutuality, to indifferent 'spaces' of mere survival and contest.

The distinction between these two conceptions or modes of appropriation of the extant environment may be put roughly thus: 'Places are "full" and "fixed", stable arenas' whereas '"spaces" are "potential voids", "possible threats", areas that have to be feared, secured or fled' (Smith 1987: 297). The shift from a politics of place to a politics of space, adds Smith, is 'encouraged by the weakening of territorially-based communal bonds in the city. It is also fostered by the tendency to retreat into the privatized household and by the strengthening of feelings of vulnerability arising in the course of the pursuit of fulfilment or security.'

One must be careful not to romanticize conditions in the proletarian neighbourhoods and segregated enclaves of yesteryear. There never was a 'golden age' when life in the American ghetto and the French *banlieue* was sweet and social relations therein harmonious and fulfilling. Yet it remains that the experience of urban relegation has changed in ways that make it distinctively more burdensome and alienating today.

To illustrate briefly: until the 1960s, the black American ghetto was still a 'place', a collective *oekoumène*, a humanized—though brutally oppressive—urban landscape with which blacks felt a strong positive identification, as expressed in the rhetoric of 'soul' (Hannerz 1968), and over which they desired to establish collective control—such was one of the goals of the Black Power movement. Today, the ghetto is a 'space', and space is no longer a common resource that Afro-Americans can use to shelter themselves from white domination. It has become, rather, a vector of intra-communal division and an instrument for the virtual imprisonment of the urban sub-proletariat of colour, a dreaded and hated territory from which, as one informant from Chicago's South Side tersely put it, 'everybody's tryin' to get out'.

Far from providing a measure of protection from the insecurities and pressures of the outside world, the space of the 'hyperghetto' is now a perilous battlefield (Wacquant 1994*b*) on which a four-corner contest is waged between organized and independent street predators (gangs and hustlers) who seek to plunder whatever riches circulate in it, local residents and their grassroots organizations (such as MAD, 'Mothers Against Drugs', on the West Side of Chicago, or block clubs and merchants' associations where they have survived) who strive to conserve the use- and exchange-value of their neighbourhood, surveillance agencies of the state entrusted with containing violence and disorder within the perimeter of the racialized urban core, and outside institutional predators (realtors in particular) for whom converting fringe sections of the Black Belt for middle class use can yield phenomenal profits.[11]

5. *Loss of hinterland*: adding to the erosion of place is the disappearance of a viable hinterland. In previous phases of modern capitalist crisis and restructuring, workers temporarily rejected from the labour market could fall back upon the social economy of their community of provenance, be it a functioning working-class borough, the communal ghetto, or a rural village in the backcountry or in the country of emigration (Kornblum 1974; Lipsitz 1989: chapters 1 and 3; Sayad 1991).

When they were dismissed from the factories and foundries, mills and car shops of Chicago where they toiled, because of a cyclical downturn in the industrial economy, residents of 'Bronzeville' relied on the support of kin, clique, and church. Most inhabitants were wage earners and a densely knit web of neighbourhood-based organizations helped to cushion the blow of economic hardship, while 'shady enterprises' ramifying across the class structure supplied precious stopgap employment (Drake and Cayton 1945/1993). By contrast, a majority of the residents of today's South Side are jobless; the area has been virtually emptied of its means of collective sustenance; and bridges to outside wage-work have been drastically shortened by the outright deproletarianization of large segments of the local population: sisters, friends, and uncles are hard pressed to help one find employment when they are themselves jobless.

Nowadays, individuals durably excluded from paid employment in neighbourhoods of relegation cannot readily rely on collective informal support while they wait for later work which, moreover, may never come. To survive, they must resort to individual strategies of 'self-provisioning', 'shadow work', underground commerce and quasi-institutionalized 'hustling' (Gershuny 1983; Smith 1986; Inchiesta 1986; Pahl 1987; EEC 1989; Wacquant 1994*b*; Bourgois 1995), which do little to alleviate precariousness since 'the distributional consequences of the pattern of informal work in industrial societies is to reinforce, rather than to reduce or to reflect, contemporary patterns of inequality' (Pahl 1989: 249). The character of the informal economy has also changed in many cities. It appears to be increasingly disjoined from the regular wage-labour sector and its parallel circuits offer fewer entry points into the 'legit' occupational world so that youth who engage in underground work often have every chance of becoming durably marginalized.

6. *Symbolic and social fragmentation*: advanced marginality also differs from its predecessors in that it develops in the context of class decomposition (Azémar 1992) rather than class formation or consolidation, and under the press of *de*proletarianization rather than proletarianization (Sugrue 1993). It therefore lacks a language, a repertoire of shared representations and signs through which to conceive a collective destiny and to project possible alternative futures. Ageing industrial labourers and lower-level clerks made expendable by technological innovations and the spatial dispersion of productive activities, human rejects of the social services and criminal justice systems, long-term recipients of public aid and the chronically 'homeless', disgruntled offsprings of the declining fractions of the working class faced with the unexpected competition of youth from racially stigmatized communities and new immigrant inflows: how to forge a sense of common condition and purpose when the press of social necessity is so diversely configured?

The absence of a common idiom by which to unify themselves symbolically accentuates the objective social dispersion and fragmentation of the new urban poor. The perennial organizational instrument of collective voice and claims-making for the urban proletariat, namely, trade unions, is strikingly ill-suited to tackle issues that arise and spill beyond the conventional sphere of regulated wage work and their traditional defensive tactics seem only to aggravate the dilemmas they face.[12] The nascent organizations of the dispossessed (such as unions of the unemployed, homeless defence groups, and grassroots associations protecting the rights of 'the excluded') are too fragile and have yet to earn recognition on the political stage to exert more than intermittent local pressure.

Implications for Urban Theory and Research

If a form of advanced marginality of a 'third kind', coterminous with, but different from, the marginality embodied by the historic American Black Belt and the traditional French Red Belt (or the British, Dutch, German, etc., 'problem neighbourhoods'), is indeed incubating in the post-Fordist city, two challenges arise, the one intellectual and the other political, that call for a serious *revamping of inherited modes of social analysis* and political action when it comes to issues of urban inequality.

For social research, each of the ideal-typical features of advanced marginality outlined above supplies a topic for empirical investigation.[13] In what ways exactly has the nature of the wage–labour relation and its effects upon life strategies changed, and for whom (Mingione 1991; Castel 1995)? How does the erosion of the 'social worker' relate to the internal diversification of the working class and to the distribution of socio-economic redundancy across groups and areas (Cross and Waldinger 1992)? How do aggregate trends in employment, flexibility, productivity, pay and benefits concretely reshape the labour market(s) faced by poor urbanites (Freeman 1993; Gordon and Sassen 1992)? Is it the case that economic growth is largely without repercussions in neighbourhoods of relegation and that the tightening of the labour market, when it does occur, does not '*re*proletarianize' their residents (Osterman 1991; Engbersen *et al.* 1993)?

Is territorial stigmatization simply a subtle modality of racial discrimination in disguise, or can one muster data demonstrating that it exerts real—and deadly—effects independently of, and in addition to, invidious ethnoracial or ethnonational distinctions, including *within* the same group (Wilkinson 1992; Bobo and Zubrinski 1995)? Is the loss of a sense of place in territories of urban exile an artefact of distant observation or a deeply felt reality, and if so, how does it differ from the experience of deracination in previous eras of working-class formation and transformation (Thrift and Williams 1987; Sayad and Dupuy 1995)? What languages do the new (sub)proletariat(s) of the dual city borrow from or forge anew to make sense of their situation and (re)articulate a collective identity (Bourdieu *et al.* 1993): one that reconnects them to the working class from which they issue, pits them against the state, or turns them onto one another? And how do state structures, policies, and ideologies impact on the social, spatial, and symbolic transformation of which neighbourhoods of relegation are the result?[14]

One of the main tasks of future research on advanced marginality will be to establish how each of these variables or processes specifies itself differently in different countries and/or types of urban environment. Note that these questions have immediate policy relevance in that it seems hard to tackle many of the concrete manifestations of the new marginality unless we first arrive at an empirical assessment of its distinctive features and of the ways in which these features render traditional modes of policy remediation inefficient, sometimes even counterproductive.

For social theorists, *fin-de-siècle* urban dualisms raise in a pointed manner the question of the adequacy of the concepts, theoretical frameworks, and approaches inherited from an era of capitalist organization that is drawing to a close. Should France's 'excluded' and America's 'underclass'— to the extent that these preconstructed categories have stable empirical referents[15]—still be considered part of a 'working class' when that class itself is agonizing, indeed fast disappearing in the form in which we have known it for much of the past century? Do they stand at the fringe of the service (sub)proletariat in an entirely new class constellation? Or are residents of neighbourhoods of relegation located 'outside' the class structure altogether, having fallen into a zone of social liminality wherein a specific social tropism operates that effectively isolates them from others around? Similarly, have not the categories of 'race', 'minority', and 'immigrant' been rendered analytically problematic, perhaps even obsolete in their current conformation, by the fact that their empirical contents have become internally differentiated, unstable, and dispersed, referring to widely dissimilar classification grids, social positions, and experiences across groups and over time?[16]

Finally, if *citizenship*, and not class, income, employment status, or 'race', is becoming the central pivot of exclusionary closure and basis for entitlement to transfers, goods, and services from the national collectivity, then we stand in dire need of an adequate sociological understanding of this institution, central to modernity yet still relatively marginal to social theory and research. Models of the new socio-spatial order of cities would gain greatly by drawing and building on recent sociological studies of citizenship that have laboured to revise the overly evolutionary, progressivist, and consensual model inherited from T. H. Marshall.[17] In turn, rethinking the mechanisms that link group membership and advanced marginality will require us to examine up close what 'mediating institutions' (Lamphere 1992) need to be invented to 'resolidarize' the city and beget the social integration that previously resulted from incorporation into a class or a compact ethnoracial community. All of which suggests the need to go beyond the rudimentary 'state-and-market' paradigm that implicitly undergirds much of current thinking in social science and social policy.

Towards a Revolution in Public Policy

At the political level, the onset and spread of advanced marginality poses formidable dilemmas and demands a radical questioning of traditional modes of state intervention. Bringing people into the labour market can no longer be safely relied upon to reduce poverty in the city, as is clearly indicated by the continuous inflation of the ranks of the 'working poor' in the United States as the labour force expands to record numbers along with substandard employment slots, because the wage-labour relation itself has become a source of built-in economic insecurity and social instability. Therefore, straightforward 'social democratic' modes of state intervention are doomed to stall, disappoint, and eventually undermine themselves.[18]

If it is true that the functional linkages between economic growth and employment, and between employment and individual and household subsistence strategies via the 'family wage', have been substantially loosened, nay severed (Offe 1993), then social policies aimed at combating advanced marginality will have to *reach 'beyond employment' and outside of the market paradigm* that upholds it for efficacious solutions (Offe and Heinze 1992). Because of the ever-tighter constraints of global interdependency, generalized 'reflation' of the economy is now beyond the means of any one country and jobs-creation schemes are clearly not sufficient to make a sizeable dent in structural and disguised unemployment (this much the French experience of the past decade has taught us). The low-level service jobs route taken by the United States promises only to spread poverty around and to generalize insecurity (Freeman 1993; Wacquant 1996*b*), as does the labour flexibility option favoured by employers the world over, for all too obvious reasons.

There seems to remain only one viable solution: in the short term, re-establish or expand state services so as to guarantee equal provision of basic public goods throughout urban areas and immediately alleviate the hardship created by the *social disinvestment* caused by the retrenchment, partial (in continental Europe) or wholesale (in the United States), of public institutions in territories of relegation in the past decade (Wacquant 1998). And, for the longer term, relax the obligation of wage-labour and enlarge social redistribution so as: (i) to reduce the supply of labour, and (ii) to restructure and stabilize anew the system of strategies of household reproduction and mobility.

Forsaking the highly dubious assumption that a large majority of the members of advanced society can or will see their basic needs met by formal employment (or by employment of members of their households), public policies designed to counter advanced marginality must work to facilitate and smooth out the severance of subsistence from work, income from paid labour, and social participation from wage earning that is already happening in a haphazard and uneven manner: 'If the labour market cannot generate income security, as presumed in the creation of the post-war social consensus, then, to allow the "labour market" to operate efficiently, social policy should *decouple income security from the labour market*' (Standing 1993: 57).

This can be done at once by instituting a guaranteed minimum income or '*basic income*' *plan*, that is, by granting unconditionally to all members of society on an individual basis, without means-test or work requirement, adequate means of subsistence and social participation. Rich capitalist societies have the means to do this; it only remains for them to develop the political intelligence and will.[19]

Whether it is done incrementally by piecemeal expansion of the reach of currently existing income support programmes, or through some 'big bang' creation *ex nihilo* of brand new sets of redistributive programmes, instituting a 'citizen's wage' is a tall order which requires a thorough revision of our accepted conceptions of work, money, time, utility, welfare, and justice. Van Parijs (1992: 7) rightly sees in it 'a profound reform that belongs in the same league as the abolition of slavery or the introduction of universal suffrage'. Yet, however unpalatable, costly, or unrealistic it might appear today, one thing is certain: as persistent and acute marginality of the kind that has plagued American and European cities over the past decade continues to mount, strategies for the 'government of misery' (Procacci 1993) will have to be reorganized in ways so drastic that they can hardly be foretold today. Before the French Revolution, the idea of overturning the monarchy was properly unthinkable, for how was a child-people to live without the guidance of their fatherly king (Hunt 1992)? And yet 1789 came, and came by storm. The institutionalization of a citizenship right to subsistence and wellbeing outside the tutelage of the market might well be the Bastille of the new millennium.

Notes

1. Notable studies on the topic include Glasgow (1981), Wilson (1987, 1993), Harris and Wilkins (1989), Katz (1989), Jencks (1991), Massey and Denton (1993), Devine and Wright (1993), and Moore and Pinderhughes (1993). For a critical analysis of the 'invention' of the demonic myth of the underclass, and of its ideological and political functions in the intellectual and political-journalistic fields, cf. Wacquant (1992*a*, 1996*a*). Perceptive discussions of its analytical and policy liabilities respectively are Marks (1991) and Gans (1991).

2. For example, Dubet (1987), LePuill and LePuill (1990), Paugam (1991, 1993), Jazouli (1992), Dubet and Lapeyronnie (1992), Lapeyronnie (1993), Brun and Rhein (1994), Vieillard-Baron (1994). See Wacquant (1992*b*) for an analysis of the diffusion of the 'moral panic' of *cités-ghettos* in France and its social bases and meaning. For a panorama of issues at the forefront of the broader European debate and transatlantic comparison, consult Rex (1988), Dahrendorf (1989), Negri (1989), Allen and Macey (1990), Leibfried (1991), Heisler (1991), Cross (1992), ADRI (1992), Guidicini and Pieretti (1993), Engbersen, Van der Veen, and Schuyt (1987, 1993), Silver (1993), Godard (1993), Hein (1993), McFate, Lawson, and Wilson (1995), and Mingione (1996).

3. For instance, Castells (1989), Davis (1990), Mollenkopf and Castells (1991), Fainstein, Gordon, and Harloe (1992) and, for caveats, Marcuse (1993).

4. Meaning the peculiar dichotomous 'black/white' opposition instituted in the United States as the historical legacy of slavery, a division admitting of no mediating term that is unique in the world for its rigidity and persistence (Davis 1991) and by reference to which the position of other groups (Latinos, Asians, Native Americans, persons of mixed descent, etc.) is defined.

5. With the notable ubiquitous presence and forceful intervention of the penal wing of the state (police, courts, corrections), which contribute powerfully to destabilizing the social structure of the ghetto.

6. These features comprise processes, trends, and outcomes as well as proximate causes and propitiating factors. This is by design. It would premature at this stage to attempt to separate those out. As Robert Merton is fond of saying, one must 'specify the phenomenon' before attempting to explain it.

7. And for growing numbers closer to the core: 'Since 1985', notes Paul Hirsch (1993: 144–5, 154–5), internal labour markets based on 'long-term reciprocal commitments, careers within companies, attractive wages, and job security' have 'come under attack from opinion leaders in both academe and the business press'. With the decline of such markets as the result of corporate downsizing (now christened 'rightsizing'), even the employment environment of 'the managerial class begins to look much more like [that of] labor.' And 'as the management class begins to see

itself as more and more like labor and less like capital, the polarization of society may increase'. For an analysis of the 'democratization of wage insecurity' as the basis of an incipient crisis of reproduction of the American middle class that explains the United States turn towards punitive policies against the poor, waning support for 'affirmative action', and rising anti-state sentiment, see Wacquant (1996*b*).

8. On the 'disorganization' of wage-labour, see Ebel (1985), Lash and Bagguley (1988), Pollert (1988), Boyer (1988), Burtless (1990), Beaud and Pialoux (1991), and Freeman and Katz (1994). McLeod (1995) draws a vivid, ground-level portrait of structural disorientation and dereliction in the new low wage-labor market in a northeastern American city.

9. For a more detailed analysis of the weight and effects of territorial stigmatization in neighbourhoods of relegation in France, see Pétonnet (1982), Avery (1987), Bachmann and Basier (1989), Paugam (1991), and Dulong and Paperman (1992).

10. Sad to report, social scientists have often added to the burden of urban disrepute by concocting pseudo-scholarly notions that dress up newer prejudices in analytical garb. Such is the case for instance with the prefabricated category (in the etymo-logical sense of *public accusation*) of 'underclass areas' (Ricketts and Sawhill 1988).

11. Two paradigmatic examples of external, profit-oriented, intrusions into the ghetto are perennial attempts by the City of Chicago to disperse and reconvert the Cabrini Green project on the Near North Side, within a stone's throw of the opulent Gold Coast, and efforts by the University of Chicago to close down and 'renovate' the dilapidated public housing concentrations of the adjacent areas of Oakland and 63rd Street in Woodlawn. The complexities of new struggles over turf in the fragmenting metropolis are brought out in full view in the Abu-Lughod *et al.* (1994) study of the transformation of New York's Lower East.

12. As when unions relinquish hard-earned collective rights to ward off mass lay-offs or concede the institution of two-tier wage systems as a means of protecting their eroding membership.

13. The few selective references that follow are inserted to indicate existing work providing possible models for further analysis or baselines and clues for compari-son and critique.

14. One particularly important variable here is the folk theories that state and urban elites develop to describe, explain, and control urban degradation—or those who are made to bear its burdens. Recent research on urban marginality is of little assis-tance here since it focuses almost exclusively upon the poor themselves. A notable and stimulative exception is Bourdieu *et al.* (1993: 219–47, 261–9, 927–39).

15. My position, it should be clear, is that they do not. These half-scholarly, half-common-sensical categories are what Kenneth Burke calls 'terministic screens': they hide more than they reveal and constitute yet another obstacle to an adequate understanding of the reconfiguring of marginality in the post-Fordist city.

16. Lest this be mistaken for a 'postmodernist' call to cast off the indispensible instruments of a critical and 'concrete science of empirical reality' (Weber 1949), and with them the *least imperfect* intellectual weapons we have at our disposal in our effort to understand and change the world: to recognize that the concepts of class and race should be revised and modified, perhaps even overhauled, to increase their cognitive potency, is not the same as saying that (1) they are worthless; (2) that objective class divisions and ethnoracial cleavages have suddenly vanished in thin

air; or (3) that they exist only in the guise of local, ever-changing, highly malleable, and almost fugitive 'discursive' achievements, as some radical (de)constructionist approaches would have it.

17. Among the many works that partake of the remarkable flowering of citizenship studies over the past few years, Heisler (1991), Turner (1992), Roche (1992), Brubaker (1992), Morris (1993), Janoski (1993), Soysal (1994), and the papers presented at the session on 'Citizenship: Conceptual Links to Racism and Ethnic Conflict' organized by Czarina Wilpert at the 1994 World Congress of Sociology in Bielefeld.

18. Conservative policies of laissez-faire and laissez-passer need not detain us here since *causes* of advanced marginality can hardly be counted upon to provide remedies.

19. The excellent collection of essays by Van Parijs (1992) argues the case for (and against) basic income on grounds of liberty, equality, economic efficiency (defined as the ability to reach a target goal or to foster growth), and community. See also *Theory and Society* (1985), Brittan and Webb (1990), and the research amassed by the Citizens Income Study Centre in London; and compare with assessments of the first three years of France's RMI, the (means-tested) national guaranteed minimum income plan, in Castel and Laé (1992) and Paugam (1993).

References

ABU-LUGHOD, J. *et al.* (1994). *From Urban Village to East Village*. New York and Cambridge: Blackwell.

ADRI (Agence pour le Développement des Relations Interculturelles) (1992). *L'inté-gration des minorités immigrées en Europe*. Paris: Editions du Centre national de la Fonction publique territoriale.

ALLEN, S., and MACEY, M. (1990). 'Race and ethnicity in the European context'. *British Journal of Sociology*, 41: 375–93.

AVERY, D. (1987). *Civilisations de La Courneuve. Images brisées d'une cité*. Paris: L'Harmattan.

AZÉMAR, G.-P. (ed.) (1992). *Ouvriers, ouvrières. Un continent morcelé et silencieux*. Paris: Autrement.

BACHMANN, C., and BASIER, L. (1989). *Mise en images d'une banlieue ordinaire*. Paris: Syros.

BEAUD, C., and PIALOUX, M. (1991). 'The slave and the technician'. Paper presented at: *Conference on Poverty, Immigration, and Urban Marginality in Advanced Societies*, Maison Suger, Paris, May.

BOBO, L., and ZUBRINSKY, C. (1995). *Prismatic Metropolis: Race and Residential Segregation in the City of Angels*. Working Paper 78. New York: Russell Sage.

BOURDIEU, P. *et al.* (1993). *La misère du monde*. Paris: Editions du Seuil.

BOURGOIS, P. (1995). *In Search of Respect: Selling Crack in El Barrio*. Cambridge: Cambridge University Press.

BOYER, R. (1988). *The Search for Labor Market Flexibility*. Oxford: Clarendon Press.

BRITTAN, S., and WEBB, S. (1990). *Beyond the Welfare State: An Examination of Basic Incomes in a Market Economy*. Aberdeen: Aberdeen University Press.

BRUBAKER, W. R. (1992). *Citizenship and Nationhood in France and Germany.* Cambridge, MA: Harvard University Press.

BRUN, J., and RHEIN, C. (eds.) (1994). *La ségrégation dans la ville.* Paris: L'Harmattan.

BURTLESS, G. (ed.) (1990). *A Future of Lousy Jobs?* Washington, DC: The Brookings Institution.

CASTEL, R. (1995). *Les métamorphoses de la question sociale.* Paris: Flammarion.

——and LAÉ, J.-F. (eds.) (1992). *Le revenu minimal d'insertion. Une dette sociale.* Paris: L'Harmattan.

CASTELLS, M. (1989). *The Informational City.* Oxford: Blackwell.

CROSS, M. (ed.) (1992). *Ethnic Minorities and Industrial Change in Europe and North America.* Cambridge: Cambridge University Press.

——and WALDINGER, R. (1992). 'Migrants, minorities, and the ethnic division of labor', in S. Fainstein, I. Gordon, and M. Harloe (eds.), *Divided Cities: New York and London in the Contemporary World,* 151–74. Oxford: Blackwell.

DAHRENDORF, R. (1989). *The Underclass and the Future of Britain.* Windsor: St. George's House Tenth Annual Lecture.

DAVIS, F. J. (1991). *Who is Black? One Nation's Definition.* University Park: Pennsylvaria State Press.

DAVIS, M. (1990). *City of Quartz: Excavating the Future in Los Angeles.* London/New York: Verso.

DEVINE, J. A., and WRIGHT, J. D. (1993). *The Greatest of Evils: Urban Poverty and the American Underclass.* Berlin: Aldine de Gruyter.

DRAKE, ST. C., and CAYTON, H. R. (1945/1993). *Black Metropolis: A Study of Negro Life in a Northern City.* Chicago: The University of Chicago Press.

DUBET, F. (1987). *La galère. Jeunes en survie.* Paris: Editions du Seuil.

——and LAPEYRONNIE, D. (1992). *Les quartiers d'exil.* Paris: Editions du Seuil.

DULONG, R., and PAPERMAN, P. (1992). *La réputation des cités HLM: enquête sur le langage de l'insécurité.* Paris: L'Harmattan.

EBEL, K. (1985). 'Social and labor implications of flexible manufacturing systems'. *International Labour Review,* 124: 133–45.

EEC (European Economic Community) (1989). *Underground Economy and Irregular Forms of Employment: Synthesis Report and Country Monographies.* Mimeo. Brussels: EEC.

ENGBERSEN, G., SCHUYT, K., TIMMER, J., and VAN WAARDEN, F. (1993). *Cultures of Unemployment: Long-Term Unemployment in Dutch Inner Cities.* Boulder: Westview Press.

——,VAN DER VEEN, R., and SCHUYT, K. (1987). *Moderne armoede: overleven op het sociaal minimum.* Leiden: H. E. Stenfert Kroese.

FAINSTEIN, S., GORDON, I., and HARLOE, M. (eds.) (1992). *Divided Cities: New York and London in the Contemporary World.* Oxford: Blackwell.

FREEMAN, R. B. (ed.) (1993). *Working Under Different Rules.* New York: Russell Sage Foundation.

——and KATZ, L. F. (1994). *Differences and Changes in Wage Structures.* Chicago: University of Chicago Press.

GANS, H. (1991). 'The dangers of the underclass: Its harmfulness as a planning concept', in *People, Plans and Policies: Essays on Poverty, Racism, and Other National Urban Problems,* 328–43. New York: Columbia University Press.

GERSHUNY, J. I. (1983). *Social Innovation and the Division of Labor*. Oxford/New York: Oxford University Press.

GLASGOW, D. (1981). *The Black Underclass*. New York: Vintage.

GODARD, F. (ed.) (1993). 'La ville américaine: futur de nos villes?' *PIR-Villes*, 2: 4–10.

GORDON, I., and SASSEN, S. (1992). 'Restructuring the urban labor market', in S. Fainstein, I. Gordon, and M. Harloe (eds.), *Divided Cities: New York and London in the Contemporary World*, 105–28. Oxford: Blackwell.

GUIDICINI, P., and PIERETTI, G. (eds.) (1993). *La residualita come valore: Poverta urbane e dignita umana*. Milan: Franco Angeli.

HANNERZ, U. (1968). 'The rhetoric of soul: Identification in negro society'. *Race*, 9: 453–65.

HARRIS, F., and WILKINS, R. W. (eds.) (1989). *Quiet Riots: Race and Poverty in the United States—The Kerner Report Twenty Years Later*. New York: Pantheon.

HARVEY, D. (1989). *The Condition of Postmodernity*. Oxford: Blackwell.

HEIN, J. (1993). 'Ethnic pluralism and the disunited states of North America and Western Europe'. *Sociological Forum*, 8: 507–16.

HEISLER, B. S. (1991). 'A comparative perspective on the underclass: Questions of urban poverty, race, and citizenship'. *Theory and Society*, 20: 455–84.

HIRSCH, P. (1993). 'Undoing the managerial revolution? Needed research on the decline of middle management and internal labor markets', in R. Swedberg (ed.), *Explorations in Economic Sociology*, 145–57. New York: Russell Sage Foundation.

HUNT, L. (1992). *The Family Romance of the French Revolution*. Berkeley: University of California Press.

INCHIESTA (1986). *Economie informale, strategie familiari e mezzogiorno*. Special Issue, 74.

JANOSKI, T. (1993). *Citizenship and Civil Society: Theoretical Frameworks and Processes of Rights and Obligations in Industrialized Countries*. Unpublished manuscript, Duke University.

JAZOULI, A. (1992). *Les années banlieue*. Paris: Editions du Seuil.

JENCKS, C. (1991). *Rethinking Social Policy: Race, Poverty, and the Underclass*. Cambridge, MA: Harvard University Press.

KATZ, M. B. (1989). *The Undeserving Poor*. New York: Random.

KORNBLUM, W. (1974). *Blue-Collar Community*. Chicago: The University of Chicago Press.

LAMPHERE, L. (ed.) (1992). *Structuring Diversity: Ethnographic Perspectives on the New Immigration*. Chicago: University of Chicago Press.

LAPEYRONNIE, D. (1993). *Individu et minorités*. Paris: PUF.

LASH, S., and BAGGULEY, P. (1988). 'Labour relations in disorganized capitalism: A five-nation comparison'. *Society and Space*, 6: 321–38.

——and URRY, J. (1988). *The End of Organized Capitalism*. Madison: University of Wisconsin Press.

LEIBFRIED, S. (1991). 'A comparative analysis of welfare regimes in Europe and the United States'. Paper presented at: *Conference on Poverty, Immigration, and Urban Marginality in Advanced Societies*, Maison Suger, Paris, May.

LE PUILL, G., and LE PUILL, S. (1990). *La décennie des nouveaux pauvres*. Paris: Messidor/Editions sociales.

LIPSITZ, G. (1989). *A Life in the Struggle: Ivory Perry and the Culture of Opposition*. Philadelphia: Temple University Press.

MARCUSE, P. (1993). 'What's so new about divided cities?' *International Journal of Urban and Regional Research*, 17: 355–65.

MARKS, C. (1991). 'The urban underclass'. *Annual Review of Sociology*, 17: 445–66.

MASSEY, D., and DENTON, N. (1993). *American Apartheid: Segregation and the Making of the Underclass*. Cambridge, MA: Harvard University Press.

McFATE, K., LAWSON, R., and WILSON, W. J. (eds.) (1995). *Poverty, Inequality, and Future of Social Policy: Western States in the New World Order*. New York: Russell Sage Foundation.

McLEOD, J. (1995). *Ain't No Makin' It*, 2nd edn. Boulder: Westview Press.

MINGIONE, E. (1991). *Fragmented Societies: A Sociology of Economic Life Beyond the Market Paradigm*. Oxford: Blackwell.

——(ed.) (1996). *The Underclass and the New Poverty*. Oxford: Blackwell.

MOLLENKOPF, J. H., and CASTELLS, M. (eds.) (1991). *Dual City: Restructuring New York*. New York: Russell Sage Foundation.

MOORE, J., and PINDERHUGHES, R. (eds.) (1993). *In the Barrio: Latinos and the Underclass Debate*. New York: Russell Sage Foundation.

MORRIS, L. (1993). *Dangerous Classes: The Underclass and Social Citizenship*. New York: Routledge.

NEGRI, N. (1989). *Povertà in Europa e trasformazione dello stato sociale*. Milan: Angeli.

OFFE, C. (1993). 'A non-productivist design for social policies', in Ph. van Parijs (ed.), *Arguing for Basic Income: Ethical Foundations for a Radical Reform*, 61–78. London: Verso.

——and HEINZE, R. G. (1992). *Beyond Employment: Time, Work, and the Informal Economy*. Philadelphia: Temple University Press.

OSTERMAN, P. (1991). 'Gains from growth? The impact of full employment on poverty in Boston', in C. Jencks and P. E. Peterson (eds.), *The Urban Underclass*, 122–43. Washington, DC: The Brookings Institution.

PAHL, R. E. (1987). 'Does jobless mean workless? Unemployment and informal work'. *Annals of the American Academy of Political and Social Science*, 493: 36–46.

——(1989). 'Is the emperor naked? Some questions on the adequacy of sociological theory in urban and regional research'. *International Journal of Urban and Regional Research*, 13: 709–20.

PARKIN, F. (1978). *Marxism and Class Analysis: A Bourgeois Critique*. New York: Columbia University Press.

PAUGAM, S. (1991). *La disqualification sociale. Essai sur la nouvelle pauvreté*. Paris: Presses Universitaires de France.

——(1993). *La société française et ses pauvres*. Paris: Presses Universitaires de France.

PÉTONNET, C. (1982). *Espace habités. Ethnologie des banlieues*. Paris: Galilée.

POLLERT, A. (1988). 'Dismantling flexibility'. *Capital and Class*, 34: 42–75.

PROCACCI, G. (1993). *Gouverner la misère. La question sociale en France, 1789–1848*. Paris: Editions du Seuil.

REX, J. (1988). *The Ghetto and the Underclass*. Aldershot: Avebury.

RICKETTS, E., and SAWHILL, I. V. (1988). 'Defining and measuring the underclass'. *Journal of Policy Analysis and Management*, 7: 316–25.

ROCHE, M. (1992). *Rethinking Citizenship*. Cambridge: Polity Press.

SASSEN, S. (1991). *The Global City: New York, London, Tokyo*. Princeton: Princeton University Press.

SAYAD, A. (1991). *L'immigration ou les paradoxes de l'altérité*. Brussels and Paris: De Boeck.

SAYAD, A. (with the collaboration of E. Dupuy) (1995). *Un nanterre Algérien, terre de bidonvilles*. Paris: Autrement.

SHIELDS, R. (1991). *Places on the Margins*. London: Routledge.

SILVER, H. (1993). 'National conceptions of the new urban poverty: Social structural change in Britain, France, and the United States'. *International Journal of Urban and Regional Research*, 17: 336–54.

SMITH, D. (1987). 'Knowing your place: Class, politics, and ethnicity in Chicago and Birmingham, 1890–1983', in N. Thrift and P. Williams (eds.), *Class and Space: The Making of Urban Society*, 277–305. London: Routledge & Kegan Paul.

SMITH, S. (1986). *Britain's Shadow Economy*. Oxford: Clarendon Press.

SOJA, E. R. (1989). *Postmodern Geographies: The Reassertion of Space in Critical Social Theory*. London: Verso Press.

SOYSAL, Y. N. (1994). *Limits of Citizenship: Migrants and Postnational Membership in Europe*. Chicago: University of Chicago Press.

STANDING, G. (1993). 'The need for a new social consensus', in Ph. van Parijs (ed.), *Arguing for Basic Income: Ethical Foundations for a Radical Reform*, 47–60. London: Verso.

SUGRUE, T. (1993). 'The structures of urban poverty: The reorganization of space and work in three periods of American history', in M. B. Katz (ed.), *The Underclass Debate: Views from History*, 85–117. Princeton: Princeton University Press.

Theory and Society (1985). 'Special issue on a capitalist road to communism'. *Theory and Society*, 15.

THRIFT, N. (1993). 'An urban impasse?' *Theory, Culture, and Society*, 10: 229–38.

—— and WILLIAMS, P. (eds.) (1987). *Class and Space: The Making of Urban Society*. London: Routledge & Kegan Paul.

TROTTER, W. J., JR. (1993). 'Blacks in the urban North: The "underclass question", in historical perspective', in M. B. Katz (ed.), *The Underclass Debate: Views from History*, 55–84. Princeton: Princeton University Press.

TURNER, B. S. (ed.) (1992). *Citizenship and Social Theory*. Newbury Park, CA: Sage.

VAN PARIJS, P. (ed.) (1992). *Arguing for Basic Income: Ethical Foundations for a Radical Reform*. London: Verso.

VERRET, M. (1979). *L'espace ouvrier*. Paris: Armand Colin.

VIEILLARD-BARON, H. (1994). *Les banlieues françaises ou le ghetto impossible*. Paris: de l'Aube.

WACQUANT, L. (1991). 'What makes a ghetto? Notes toward a comparative analysis of modes of urban exclusion'. Paper presented at: *Conference on Poverty, Immigration, and Urban Marginality in Advanced Societies*, Maison Suger, Paris, May.

——(1992a). 'Décivilisation et démonisation: la mutation du ghetto noir américain', in C. Fauré and T. Bishop (eds.), *L'Amérique des français*, 103–25. Paris: François Bourin.

——(1992b). 'Banlieues françaises et ghetto noir américain: de l'amalgame à la comparaison'. *French Politics and Society*, 10: 81–103.

——(1993). 'Urban outcasts: Stigma and division in the black American ghetto and the French urban periphery'. *International Journal of Urban and Regional Research*, 17: 366–83.

——(1994*a*). 'O retorno do recalcado: Violência urbana, "raça" e dualizaçâo em três sociedades avançadas'. *Revista Brasileira de Ciencîas sociaís*, 24: 16–30. (In English as: Working Paper 45, Russell Sage Foundation.)

——(1994*b*). 'The new urban color line: The state and fate of the ghetto in postfordist America', in C. Calhoun (ed.), *Social Theory and the Politics of Identity*, 231–76. Oxford: Blackwell.

——(1996*a*). 'L'"*Underclass* urbaine" dans l'imaginaire social et scientifique américain', in S. Paugam (ed.), *L'exclusion: l'état des savoirs*. Paris: La découverte.

——(1996*b*). 'La généralisation de l'insécurité salariale en Amérique: restructurations d'entreprises et crise de reproduction sociale'. *Actes de la recherche en sciences sociales*, 115: 65–79.

——(1998). 'Negative social capital: state breakdown and social destitution in America's urban core'. *The Netherlands Journal of the Built Environment*, 13: 25–40.

——and WILSON, W. J. (1989). 'The cost of racial and class exclusion in the inner city'. *Annals of the American Academy of Political and Social Science*, 501: 8–25.

WEBER, M. (1949). *Methodology of the Social Sciences*. Glencoe, IL: The Free Press.

WILKINSON, D. (1992). *Isolating the Poor: Work and Community in the Inner City*. Unpublished BA honors thesis, Harvard University.

WILSON, W. J. (1987). *The Truly Disadvantaged: The Inner City, the Underclass and Public Policy*. Chicago: University of Chicago Press.

——(ed.) (1993). *The Urban Underclass: Social Science Perspectives*. Newbury Park, CA: Sage.

WITTGENSTEIN, L. (1977). *Vermischte Bemerkungen*. Frankfurt: Syndicat.

12

'Poverty Pockets' and Social Exclusion: On the Role of Place in Shaping Social Inequality

Eva T. van Kempen

Introduction

Social segregation in cities can be considered both as a reflection and a cause of social inequality. In this chapter I will focus on the role of social segregation in shaping social inequality. The central question is whether and how the spatial concentration of poverty in certain areas or neighbourhoods enhances the process of social exclusion. I will use the term 'poverty pocket' in order to stress that the focus is on areas that clearly discern themselves from other areas by the predominance of poor households. The focus is on post-Fordist welfare states.

This view fits the continental tradition of social policy analysis. Two traditions dominate the recent poverty discussion in western Europe (Jordan 1996). The Anglo-Saxon tradition, using a liberal point of view, tends to deal with the poverty problem as a socially undesirable consequence of market interaction and hence, on the individual level as a lack of resources. The continental tradition focuses on the welfare state as an organizing principle for society and hence on citizenship.

Whereas the first tradition dominated the 'new poverty' debate, the latter tradition has got wider adherence with the introduction of the term 'social exclusion' as a main policy target (e.g., in the Action Programme to Combat Social Exclusion and to Promote Social Solidarity, of the European Commission in 1993). It represents a change of focus from distributional issues, prevalent in the Anglo-Saxon poverty discussion, to relational issues or in other words to problems regarding inadequate social participation, lack of social integration and lack of power (Madanipour, Cars, and Allen 1998; Room 1995). According to this line of thought, a low income is not a sufficient cause for being poor. Issues of membership and hence of 'access' and 'belonging' are also at stake. This turns the attention to the concept of 'social citizenship' as a concept that deserves a central place in the poverty discussion, next to labour market position or economic capital.

In the following I will first focus on the 'whys?' and the meaning of including social citizenship into the poverty debate and especially into the debate on poverty pockets. Then I will look at the role that can be attributed to 'place' and at the mechanisms that can be held responsible for the occurrence of so called 'locality effects'. In the argument presented in this chapter, the delivery of welfare plays an important role. Living in the Netherlands, many of the examples I have used are derived from the Dutch experience.

Poverty and Social Citizenship

There are three main reasons to reserve a central place for social citizenship in the discussion on poverty and social exclusion. The first one has to do with the basic characteristic of welfare states; that is their decommodifying capacity, or capacity to ensure individuals or households that they can uphold a socially acceptable standard of living independently of market participation (Esping-Andersen 1990: 21ff., 37). This implies that unearned incomes, whether in cash or kind (see Titmuss 1968), form an often taken-for-granted part of the subsistence of households. The amount of money involved is a good indicator for the national commitment to welfare state provisions and can be considerable. In this respect the Netherlands, for instance, comes to the fore as a highly committed welfare state with 41 per cent of the gross national product in 1997 spent on government consumption and on social insurance and social security. This is about 80 per cent of total government expenditure (CBS 1998: 95). Hence, a description of the poverty problem in welfare states in terms of money income and labour market participation tends to give an incomplete picture.

Besides, the dependency of households on welfare state provisions has grown considerably in the last decades. This is not only illustrated by the number of people who are dependent on a social security benefit, but even more so by the character of their involvement. De-industrialization and the globalization of the economy and the subsequent loss of lower-skilled jobs made a growing number of people dependent on unemployment and social security benefits. Although unemployment in the European Union on the whole has been decreasing during the last five years or so, the percentage of long-term unemployed is considered to be a restraint on a further decline. Half of the unemployed in 1998 in the European Union were unemployed for more than a year, a third of them were more than two years without a job. The situation in the Netherlands represents the Union average (CBS 1999: 178ff.). These long-term unemployed as well as the number of people with a disability benefit show the increased importance of social insurance and benefit schemes as a more permanent income source (in the Netherlands the number of people with a disability pension is particularly high; in 1997 the relation between people with a disability benefit and the working population was 1 in 7; CBS 1997*b*).

Another aspect of the changed role of social security is the interweaving of social security schemes and labour market developments. In the Netherlands, this is not only expressed in the linking of social benefits to the legally settled minimum wage or the dependence of the disability pension on the last earned income. It is also expressed in the way it enables the flexibilization and deregulation of the production process as part of economic restructuring. Temporary and part-time employment has become a common phenomenon in western countries (Den Broeder 1996; CBS 1999: 179; OECD 1996: 192; OSA 1996: 12). This implies that increasingly people are confronted with alternating periods of employment and state dependency.

A new form of structural economic insecurity seems to confirm the more general finding of the OECD (1996: 17), based on job studies, that temporary job spells are more likely than permanent ones to follow a spell of unemployment or another temporary job. This is aggravated by the bureaucracy of the welfare state. Alternate labour market participation and state dependency can lead to real hardship because of the bureaucratic entanglement such a situation implies and the presence of inadequate and insufficient rules, causing unforeseen income gaps (Kempson 1996: 81ff.; Engbersen, Snel, and Ypeij 1998). Hence, the capacity to find one's way through the bureaucracy and use the welfare state provisions to the utmost has become an important part of people's economic capital.

The second reason to focus on social citizenship is its importance in understanding the social construction of socio-spatial inequalities. Esping-Andersen (1990: 19–20) uses the term 'black box' to indicate that comparable state expenditures on welfare can hide different forms of redistribution, social organization, and social integration. The three types of welfare state regimes he discerns—on basis of the national commitment to decommodification and principles of social redistribution—can be seen thus as a plea for a contextual approach in studying social inequalities. The context implied here is the national context, but there are good reasons to focus on the local level as well.

Deregulation and decentralization have become catchwords in the debate about the character of the post-Fordist welfare state. Even in a centralized welfare state, such as in the Netherlands, the municipal discretion (and responsibility) in the field of social care and income policy have grown considerably. Local authorities are not only allowed to work out their own system of local tax exemptions, they are also made responsible for the interpretation and implementation of new as well as already existent welfare policies. On the implementation level the 'fight against poverty' policy announced by the national government is mainly a municipal affair, leading to a considerable difference between municipalities in the ways social policies are worked out (Van der Pennen and Hoff 1999).

The third argument to focus on social citizenship is of a more theoretical nature and regards the discrepancy between the idea of 'universality' inherent in the idea of citizenship and the idea of socio-spatial inequality. The seminal ideas of T. H. Marshall on citizenship are important in this respect (see also Rees 1996). Central to Marshall's concept of citizenship is the idea of participation. Social citizenship rights play an important part in his argument. In the wording of Marshall (1965: 88) they are intended to diminish inequality by 'creating an universal right to real income which is not proportionate to the market value of the claimant', to further social integration, and to provide full citizenship to those who were excluded before like the poor. They refer to the right to enjoy a minimum standard of living, according to the standards prevailing in one's society, including housing, health, education, welfare, and social security. Conceptualized in this way, social citizenship rights point to social exclusion as a condition that represents a standard of living below the agreed upon minimum, due to restricted or even barred access to social citizenship rights; a description that resembles the conceptualization of modern poverty by Peter Townsend (1987) in terms of 'relative deprivation'. Yet, unlike the idea of relative deprivation, which focuses on resources, the idea of social exclusion as described above focuses on membership.

Marshall himself already points to the existence of *uncertainties*, inherent to the conceptualization and delivery of social rights that undermine the idea of the equality of opportunity and the idea of full membership implied in the idea of social citizenship. For our argument they are especially important because they give room to spatial inequalities. The first uncertainty regards the definition of social rights. Marshall argues that social rights cannot be defined precisely by law because, especially in the provision of services, the qualitative element is too great. Housing offers a clear example. Even if the basic right of citizens to a dwelling is laid down in law and citizens can claim a roof over their heads, this claim can be met in a variety of ways. Legal regulations about what this roof should be are necessarily limited and make the implementation of the 'right on housing' prone to local discretion.

The second uncertainty also focuses on this latitude for normative interpretation in legal rights, now by the citizens or 'consumers'. Marshall (1965: 114) argues that the citizen assesses the service he or she gets not by his or her legal rights, but through a 'superstructure of legitimate expectations'. This sets the stage for social inequality, or rather, perceived social inequality. Whereas the superstructure of legitimate expectations is largely formulated at the societal level, the outcomes are, among other things, dependent on the place where one lives. Part of the problem comprises the material restrictions on achieving social rights for everyone at the same moment. It is to this aspect that Marshall mainly refers. But the legitimate expectations of individual citizens can also lead to local disparate outcomes. Legitimate expectations differ between citizens because of different frames of reference. Especially in the case of public provisions, the locality is important in shaping different frames of reference.

On the one hand, public goods and services are delivered locally, which make their availability prone to local demand. On the other hand, social expectations will also differ locally because of differences between local social structures and the different location of people with the same social position within them.

To these two uncertainties I would add a third one. This uncertainty turns on the way in which social rights are implemented. Formulated at the national level at least in a general sense, the specification and delivery occur in the end at the local level, often by local organizations. This makes the implementation process prone to local differences in population and funding. In addition, the indefiniteness of social rights already referred to makes the implementation process even more susceptible to local influences by giving room for interpretation. This interpretation will differ because of the different experiences, expectations and norms, or more generally the different frames of reference, of the officials responsible for the implementation process, in different localities.

The three uncertainties make it likely that even in centralized welfare states the provision of public services and goods will vary between localities. Sometimes these differences will be a consequence of deliberate policies. In the Netherlands, as stated before, deregulation and the striving for greater efficiency have led to a decentralization of powers to the local authorities in the field of social policies, increasing their discretion among others in the field of income policy and the fight against social disadvantage considerably. However, apart from these policies more hidden mechanisms also seem to lead to unintended, local differences in the quality of the services and non take-up (Engbersen, Snel, and Ypeij 1998; Schep and Bommeljé 1994). This turns the attention to the impact of local conditions and more specifically the impact of the conditions in poverty pockets on the implementation of social rights, or in more general terms to the role of place in shaping social exclusion.

The Role of Place

The role of 'place' in social life is a subject that is not easy to lay one's finger on. To begin with, what term should be used? Many names are going around in the scientific discussion on the role of place in social life of which place and community are the most well known. Yet, the term 'place' is rather indefinite and the term 'community' is loaded with emotional meaning. Therefore, within the context of the present argument, which focuses on local disparate life chances and hence on place in the sense of *a* place, I prefer to use the term *locality*, because of its more neutral, instrumental connotation, its local reference, and its anchoring in a social conception of space.

Locality I define as the local configuration of organizations and people and their relations and social practices, connected by residence in a particular area.

The term *configuration* points at the coincidental aspect that is present in area-based mingling of actors and hence at the specific distinguishing features of a locality. Practices stand for the cultural momentum and hence continuity.

From the above definition *specificity* comes to the fore as the core feature of the locality and hence as the basis for the explanation of local disparate outcomes of social processes. This idea is already present in the generally accepted idea of place as a setting of interaction (Agnew 1987: 26; Paasi 1991; Soja 1985: 148ff.; Storper 1985; Thrift 1983) and not only among geographers. Giddens, in developing his theory of social structuration, reserves an important role for place, or locale as he names it, by emphasizing its character of 'being a setting of interaction' (Giddens 1984: 375). He argues that locales cannot be described in terms of physical properties and human artefacts alone. Generally speaking, a locale only gets meaning by 'the modes of its utilization in human activity' (Giddens 1984: xxv, 118). The situated character of interaction in time-space, involving the setting of the interaction, the actors co-present and the communication between them, makes for the contextuality of social life and social institutions or, in other words, it gives social life and social institutions in different locales their specific character (Giddens 1984: 118, 132, 373).

This specific character not only means that social processes which take place on a macro-scale, such as the globalization of the division of labour, have locally distinct appearances and locally distinct outcomes (see also Cooke 1989: 10ff., 296; Massey 1994: 86ff.), but it also will generate locally specific relations and practices. Designated as *locality* or *concentration effects* (Duncan 1989: 236ff.; Wilson 1987), but outside the study of poverty known under such different names as contextual, structural, multi-level, neighbourhood, or compositional effects (De Vos 1997), these locally specific relations and practices form the kernel of the discriminating role of place. They refer to social patterns and behaviour that can only be explained by the specific local configuration of organizations and people and social structure of the local environment in which they evolve. Although poverty pockets themselves will differ in terms of history and societal context and thus can induce different locality effects, their resemblance in terms of social position allows us to ask the question whether poverty pockets are prone to the same kind of mechanisms, which by their interrelated, complementary character are responsible for the occurrence of locality effects, specific to poverty pockets.

The Spatial Concentration of Poverty as Part of the Poverty Problem

The question of whether the spatial concentration of poverty noticed in post-Fordist welfare society can be considered an inherent part of the poverty problem is in fact the question of whether the poverty pocket represents more than just a collection of poor people, marginalized by a restructuring economy and their position in the housing market. Wilson (1991: 12), for instance, in discussing the detrimental effects of ghetto life on the life prospects of its inhabitants, formulates the question as follows: 'The issue is not simply that the underclass or ghetto poor have a marginal position in the labour market similar to that of other disadvantaged groups, it is also that their position is uniquely *reinforced* [emphasis added] by their social milieu' (i.e., the ghetto or extreme poverty concentration area). Although the role of race is not very pronounced and rather different in the ethnically mixed poverty concentration areas of western Europe, the question is easily transferable to the European situation. It then becomes the question of the reinforcement of the exclusion from mainstream society, inherent in both the ideas of social exclusion and new poverty by living in areas of concentrated poverty.

The mechanisms Wilson mentions to explain the occurrence of concentration effects can be subsumed under two headings: '*a reduced access to the job market*' and '*socialization*'. Both mechanisms are neither mentioned for the first time, nor specific for the American ghetto. Also in European studies on poverty pockets these two mechanisms are frequently coming to the fore. This also reveals a third important, place related mechanism: '*stigmatization*' (see among others Morris 1994: 53ff.; Wacquant 1993). The three mechanisms have in common that they focus on how the poverty pocket poor are excluded from mainstream society and especially from the job market. Yet, they pass over the importance of social citizenship rights for 'social inclusion'. Hence, at least a fourth mechanism should be added that refers to the ways social rights can be realized in practice. In the following I will refer to this mechanism as '*a limited access to social rights*'.

Access to the Job Market

Reduced access to the job market in the poverty pockets of major western cities is mainly attributed to 'outside' processes on the labour and housing market such as the 'mismatch' and 'left behind' theses do. These theses play an important part in the discussion on the concentration of poverty and underemployment in inner cities.

The mismatch thesis focuses on economic participation and the poor as people being left out. This is attributed to two coinciding developments: (1) the increase in educational and skill demands of the urban economy that has outstripped the skills of an increasingly large segment of the urban population; and (2) the suburbanization of jobs that bereaved the inner cities from part of their economic base (Kasarda 1989, 1990; Thrift 1979).

The left behind thesis focuses on changes in the inner city population. The central argument is that mass suburbanization first of the affluent and later the middle classes drained the central cities of their more well-to-do and better-educated population, leaving the inner city to those who are not able to move out (Johnston 1984; Massey and Eggers 1993; Thrift 1979). Leaving aside the dispute about both theses, it is important for our argument that they contain the same message: structural developments in post-Fordist society should be held responsible for the unemployment problems in post-Fordist inner cities in the first place.

Although both theses, thus, acknowledge that economic restructuring affects local job opportunities differently in different places, they reserve a modest role for 'place'. In fact the role of place is restricted to the role of go-between. A change of focus from structural shifts in the supply of jobs to the ways people are introduced into jobs, however, shows that access to the job market does have a clear local component. Informal networks are reported to play an important part, especially in the case of the lower-skilled (Mingione 1991; Pahl 1985). Hence, the absence of informal, local networks in poverty pockets that can transmit information on job opportunities and requirements because of the lack of those who are gainfully employed comes to the fore as an important impediment to finding one's way on the labour market. Here, place appears as a generative factor of its own. In this respect it resembles the role that can be ascribed to place in socializing the poor.

Socialization

A key term in the discussion about the concentration of poverty and socialization is 'social isolation'. Yet, the content can be quite different, ranging from lack of social contacts and outdoor life in terms of non-participating in social clubs or cultural events to an interpretation of the social life of the poor in terms of an impediment to taking part in mainstream society. The latter approach meets the structural meaning the term has obtained in discussing the poverty problem in western society, an approach that finds its basis already in the classic study of Jahoda, Lazarsfeld, and Zeisl (1933) of the decline of social life in the poverty-stricken village of Mariënthal in Austria as a consequence of the closure of the one and only factory. In this respect, Wilson's interpretation of the concept of social isolation holds true also. Looking at the situation in the American black ghetto he defines the concept in a rather physical way: 'as the lack of contact or of sustained interaction with individuals and institutions that represent mainstream society'. The basic assumption here is that 'a person's patterns and norms of behavior tend to be shaped by those with which he or she has had the most frequent or sustained contact and interaction' (Wilson 1987: 60ff.). The question, thus, becomes whether, apart from the American ghetto, poverty pockets in welfare states form a main frame of reference and induce attitudes and behaviour that are deviant from mainstream society.

Various researchers in different countries record that poor households do have more restricted social relations and contacts (Hoff 1998; Jordan 1996;

Kempson 1996; Meert, Mistiaen, and Kesteloot 1997; Van Berkel, Brand, and Vrooman 1997). This is especially true of the long-term unemployed and long-term welfare recipients. Work-induced relations have been lost or did not have the chance to develop and there is no money to meet the costs of transport for regular visits to family or friends who are living elsewhere or to entertain them at home.

This reinforces the meaning of the locality as a social environment, despite the fact that many of the local contacts are functional or bear a latent character or, once manifest, tend to be restricted to one's own ethnic group. Research points at the importance of the locality as a frame of reference in dealing with the problem of inactivity and being poor in prosperous welfare states. Especially in poverty pockets where structural unemployment seems to have become endemic because of the cutting back or closure of the main industries, an attitude of resignation can be found. This attitude is characterized at the same time by minimizing the significance of economic activity and having a job and by a display of a thorough distrust of social agencies, which can be seen as a mechanism to defend one's independence despite one's welfare dependency (Engbersen, Snel, and Ypeij 1998; Van Berkel, Brand, and Vrooman 1997: 94ff.; Leibfried *et al.* 1995: 142ff.; SCP 1996: 208). In such a climate people resort to coping strategies, which not only embrace the question of making ends meet but also the question of self-esteem. The latter explains the high non take-up of means-tested provisions even in a situation where people have accepted their state dependency and are not ashamed of it.

A locally accepted and common strategy is informal work, sometimes balancing on the edge of being legal (Kroft *et al.* 1989: 85ff.; Renooy 1990: 113ff.; Rommelspacher and Oelschlagel 1989; Van Berkel, Brand, and Vrooman 1997). Informal work is undertaken to enhance the family income and thus is mostly not declared to the welfare agency, because its short term and fluctuating character means a lot of paperwork and red tape, and financial problems may arise if it is reported. Hence, informal work can be considered as a strategy that will stretch the limits set by the social security system and use it to the utmost.

This kind of strategy is not restricted to economic activities but can also take account of family life. In a situation where the awarding of social allowances is dependent on household structure, the very household structure becomes an asset. Not only in the American ghetto, but also in European countries, such as the Netherlands or Britain, common law marriage forms an accepted strategy to survive or to gain independence in poverty pockets (Anderson 1989; Sullivan 1989; Testa *et al.* 1989; Van Kempen and Teijmant 1990) and is an important factor in making women more prone to poverty.

Although defined as deviant by mainstream society, the above-mentioned attitudes and strategies can be seen as locally accepted and internalized adaptations to the specific circumstances of being poor in poverty pockets in welfare states. This observation is reminiscent of the controversial concept of the 'culture of poverty'. Although developed in quite another societal context, the initial idea of the existence of a 'culture of poverty' in poverty pockets also stresses the adaptive character of the cultural traits included in the concept of the culture of poverty. '. . . [M]any of the traits of the culture of poverty can be viewed as attempts at *local* [emphasis added] solutions for problems not met by existing institutions and agencies because the people are not eligible for them, cannot afford them, or are ignorant or suspicious of them', Lewis (1968: 188) states in reflecting on his idea of the culture of poverty. Although its connotations of undeservingness and predestination, developed in the poverty debates, are a solid reason to refute the term 'culture of poverty', they do not invalidate the idea represented in the above quotation that poverty pockets offer a favourable breeding ground for specific, but locally accepted behavioural strategies, deviating from mainstream society. Adapted to the particular conditions of the poverty pocket, these strategies gain a certain degree of permanency by their embedding in local norms and practices and contribute to the generally bad repute of poverty pockets.

Stigmatization

Strategies and behaviour that are considered as deviant by an outside world play an important part in providing neighbourhoods with a negative stigma. Once invoked, the stigma becomes a social given on its own. By its impact on the behaviour of the inhabitants it even can become a self-fulfilling prophecy and produce in the words of Wacquant (1993: 375) 'social atomism, community "disorganization" and cultural anomia'. The latter quotation refers to the reaction of the inhabitants to the stigma their neighbourhood has incurred or, in more general terms, to the impact of territorial stigmatization on social cohesion and solidarity in poverty pockets, in this case the French *banlieue*. Also, in the Netherlands people in such neighbourhoods are recorded as employing a variety of strategies of social distinction and withdrawal towards their neighbours and neighbourhood in order to escape the stigma that is attached to them by virtue of their living in that neighbourhood (Droogleever Fortuyn and Van Kempen 1998).

In more general terms this kind of behaviour can be considered as a reaction to the fact that people are socially positioned by the neighbourhood in which they live. In the social ordering of the city 'labelling' plays an important part. Territorial labels with their emphasis on socio-spatial segregation and separation serve social control and especially the exclusionary mode of social control with its practice of social isolation (Cohen 1985: 234). From this point of view territorial labelling is not merely a subjective appreciation of a deviant situation by mainstream society, but a social exclusionary instrument as well. This is consonant with the definition of deviance as 'the infraction of some agreed-upon rule' that is central to labelling theory. 'Social groups create deviance by making the rules whose infraction constitutes deviance, and by applying those rules to particular people and labelling them as *outsiders'* (Becker 1963: 9, emphasis added). According to this line of argument, territorial stigmas, thus, reflect both the powerless position of the inhabitants involved and a verdict to social exclusion by mainstream society. This 'verdict' makes the place where one lives a factor in its own right by affecting the attitudes and behaviour of important others, such as employers or officials who are responsible for the implementation of social rights.

Discrimination in the job market on the basis of one's address is a phenomenon frequently referred to, although it is hard to find sufficient evidence. Better documented is an example from the financial world. It concerns the practice of 'redlining', a practice by which inhabitants of certain neighbourhoods perceived as 'risky', are excluded from financial funding if they want to get a mortgage on a property in that neighbourhood (Goetze 1979: 32ff; Roscam Abbing 1999). Overall information on how stigmatization pervades allocation policies and impedes the access to goods and services, however, is scarce. It concerns a mechanism that is difficult to prove because of the social taboo that adheres to it and because of the fact that officials are generally reluctant to admit the practice. Nonetheless, also because of its interference with other mechanisms, stigmatization seems to be an important factor in the social exclusion process.

Access to Social Citizenship Rights

It has been argued that despite the claim of universality and continuity, social rights may differ across people and places. Until now, nothing has been said about the kind of differences meant. The three uncertainties mentioned before that are inherent to the definition and the implementation of social rights, have at least two main implications that tend to limit the access to social rights in poverty pockets.

The first implication is the most concrete one and concerns the impact of local conditions on the quality of the services offered. The scarce provision of poverty pockets with private goods and services may be no surprise because of the lack of spending power of the residents. In the case of public goods and services the impact is more complicated. Policies that are targeted on poor areas such as extra job-training programmes, the extra financing of schools, and the creation of local 'counters' to make welfare agencies more accessible are in fact extra provisions, meant to enhance the life chances of the people living there. It is at least questionable, however, if they can counterweight the negative effects of 'crowding'. Crowding occurs if too many people of the same signature or with the same kind of problems are going to use the same public provision. Public goods are especially prone to crowding; they manifest themselves as 'positional goods' (Hirsh 1977) because funding is restricted or lags behind. This implies that under conditions of crowding the quality of the good or service declines. Queuing and waiting in vain are experiences that are quite common for people living in poverty pockets.

Crowding also affects the access to public provisions because of its impact on the interpretation of officials of the local situation. This can lead to other than the effects wished for. The discretion local officials have been given in the implementation of welfare policies, for instance, does not seem to have resulted in a more individually geared approach as was intended in decentralizing the powers to the local level. The high demands officials face in poverty pockets impede the implementation of the individually tailored approach demanded of social schemes and stimulate a routine implementation of the rules. As a consequence the possibilities of the schemes are not sufficiently used.

Examples of routine behaviour come from the field of the regular employment exchange. Officials do not tend to be very inviting to welfare recipients looking for a job, like single mothers with small children who want to work but are not obliged to apply for a job. They tend to concentrate their efforts on people they consider likely to be more successful (Engbersen, Snel, and Ypeij 1998; Fleurke and De Vries 1997). This tendency to focus the efforts on people who are perceived as relatively promising or as more receptive to the proposals in a situation of crowding is also known from the field of housing. Here, it is one of the mechanisms that funnels people, who have the least choice, into poverty pockets (Henderson and Karn 1987; Van Kempen 1992).

The most discussed example comes from the field of education, however. In the Dutch situation the relatively poor performance of schools in poverty pockets cannot be explained by the lack of funds or the mere concentration of socially disadvantaged youth. Primary schools in poverty pockets have been subjected to positive discrimination since the early 1980s; they get extra funding from the national government. Since then, the 'poverty pocket schools' in the main cities not only have become more 'black' (41 per cent of the schools in the four main cities have more than 60 per cent ethnic minority students; CBS 1997*a*: 78), they also have again obtained extra facilities and more extra funding. Nonetheless, the conclusions about the effects of this 'Educational Priority Policy' are a source of worry. Looking at the performance of children in priority schools their achievements still lag behind and have barely improved (Dronkers *et al.* 1999; SCP 1998: 255).

The explanation for this disappointing result is sought in the home situation and the cultural background of the students, as well as in the scarce information exchange and contacts between the school and the home environment of the students. Secondary school counselling given at the end of primary school points at an underestimating of the students' possibilities, due to the low expectations of the teachers about the aspirations of the students, although 'over-advising' also occurs. But over-advising also gives way to detrimental effects; it is considered to be an important cause for the frequent, early drop-out of ethnic minority students from secondary education and their entering the labour market without any formal qualification (Clark, Dieleman, and De Klerk 1992; SCP 1998: 253; Tesser and Veenman 1997: 53ff., 154ff.; Veenman 1996: 33). Different as they are, both types of advice can be seen as a reaction to what is experienced locally.

The second implication has to do with the legitimacy problem and the way legal rights leave room for different evaluations by the public. Different frames of reference shape the actions of officials and by that the implementation process. Managers are not only prone to local influences by the signals they get from their street level workers. They also have to negotiate with the local authorities and to compete with other organizations for funds and qualifications and to take care of their output in such a way that it legitimizes the organization's existence (Bomley 1989). This can lead to an alignment of policies between local organizations and the formulation of formal rules and practices that turn to risk reduction away from the social aims of the organizations at stake.

Different frames of reference also shape the expectations of the individual consumers of the ways in which social rights apply to themselves. Here too, the local situation forms an important frame of reference because individuals tend to judge their prospects and attainments by what they see around them. This does not only concern local differences in the quality of the public goods and services provided, but also concerns how people perceive their situation compared to that of others. In this respect the location of people within local social structures is important. How people place themselves in these structures often interferes with the official views and criteria, on which welfare state policies are based. People falling within the same officially designated categories often do not experience themselves as in the same position. Hence, they do not find it fair that the 'others' get the same kind of treatment and benefits. Ethnic minorities form an evident example of such a contrasting frame of reference. In the Netherlands, people living in ethnically mixed neighbourhoods frequently comment that they have problems with the equal entitlements immigrants have to social services and goods which they themselves have worked for during their entire lives. Confrontations such as this frustrate people, whose feelings of legitimacy play an important role in causing feelings of deprivation, social resignation, and social withdrawal (Blokland-Potters 1998: 276ff.; Engbersen 1990: 218).

Conclusions

The emphasis laid on poverty pockets in the discussion about poverty and social exclusion in post-Fordist welfare states seems to be justified. Although poverty may be less visible and the effects of living in poverty pockets less tangible in western post-Fordist cities, this does not imply that the impact of living there on the life chances of people has disappeared. The bureaucratic entanglement of the poor in welfare states even seems to have added to their susceptibility for local influences.

Nonetheless, it is hard to provide a conclusive answer to the central question of this chapter, of whether living in a poverty pocket in a post-Fordist welfare state affects social exclusion, because evidence is still scattered and scarce. The existing evidence together with more theoretical insights on the meaning of 'place' for social life and on organizational attainments, however, points to the presence of locally derived mechanisms that affect the life chances of people living in poverty pockets in such a way that choices are restricted and the participation in mainstream society is impeded.

Against this negative view on the impact of the poverty pocket on the life chances of people, it may be argued that government programmes targeted on these areas represent opportunities that are not available for the poor elsewhere. As yet, these programmes do not seem to counterbalance the negative effects of living in a poverty pocket as the disappointing results of the Dutch Educational Priority and labour market activation programmes illustrate. The four mechanisms identified—reduced access to the job market, socialization, stigmatization, and limited access to social rights—that may affect the life chances in poverty pockets, have an enclosing character, also by their interrelatedness. They concern locally derived mechanisms that are a prerequisite for the occurrence of locality effects. This implies that many of the social and economic problems in poverty pockets owe their origin to the specific conditions of the local, social environment.

Furthermore, to understand the impact of the spatial concentration on the poverty problem itself in post-Fordist welfare states, the entanglement of welfare state provisions and the consequences of economic restructuring in terms of unemployment and the flexibilization of the labour market is important. Growing unemployment and flexibilization not only mean a growing dependency on the state but also a shifting involvement with the state bureaucracy for a growing number of people. Hence, the delivery of social rights and the ways people can claim them, have become an important aspect of the poverty problem. Uncertainties already inherent in the conceptualization of social rights and the susceptibility of the implementation and delivery process to local circumstances lead to local disparities in welfare outcomes, often not to the advantage of the people living in poverty pockets. Although there is certainly truth in the statement that 'unequal circumstances ask for unequal solutions', without the recognition of the mechanisms that are at work in poverty pockets these kinds of area-based policies will only exacerbate social exclusion.

References

AGNEW, J. (1987). *Place and Politics*. Boston: Allen & Unwin.

ANDERSON, E. (1989). 'Sex codes and family life among poor inner-city youths'. *Annals of American Academy of Political and Social Science*, 501: 59–78.

BECKER, H. S. (1963). *Outsiders. Studies in the Sociology of Deviance*. New York/London: The Free Press.

BLOKLAND-POTTERS, T. (1998). *Wat stadsbewoners bindt. Sociale relaties in een achterstandswijk*. Kampen: Kok Agora.

BOMLEY, N. K. (1989). 'Interpretive practices: the state and the locale', in J. Wolch and M. Dear (eds.), *The Power of Geography. How Territory Shapes Social Life*, 175–96. Boston: Unwin Hyman.

CBS (Centraal Bureau voor de Statistiek) (1997*a*). *Allochtonen in Nederland 1997*. Voorburg: CBS.

——(1997*b*). *Maandblad voor de sociale en economische statistiek*. Voorburg: CBS.

——(1998). *De Nederlandse economie 1997*. Voorburg: CBS.

——(1999). *De Nederlandse economie 1998*. Voorburg: CBS.

CLARK, W. A. V., DIELEMAN, F. M., and DE KLERK, L. (1992). 'School segregation: managed integration or free choice?' *Environment and Planning: C*, 10: 91–103.

COHEN, S. (1985). *Visions of Social Control. Crime, Punishment and Classification*. Cambridge: Polity Press.

COOKE, P. (1989). *Localities: The Changing Face of Britain*. London: Unwin Hyman.

DE VOS, S. (1997). *De omgeving telt*. Amsterdam: Instituut voor Sociale Geografie.

DEN BROEDER, C. (1996). *Institutions At Work. Commitment and Flexibility on the German and Dutch Labour Markets*. The Hague: CPB Netherlands Bureau for Economic Policy Analyses.

DROOGLEEVER FORTUYN, J., and VAN KEMPEN, E. T. (1998). 'Oh, die asobuurt'. *Geografie*, 7(3): 32–4.

DRONKERS, J., ROELEVELD, J., LEDOUX, G., and ROBIJNS, M. (1999). 'Verandert het onderwijsachterstandsbeleid negatieve gevolgen van armoede?', in G. Engbersen, J. C. Vrooman, and E. Snel (eds.), *Effecten van armoede*, 173–90. Amsterdam: Amsterdam University Press.

DUNCAN, S. (1989). 'What is locality?', in R. Peet and N. Thrift (eds.), *New Models in Geography*. Vol. 2, 221–55. London: Unwin Hyman.

ENGBERSEN, G. (1990). *Publieke bijstandsgeheimen. Het ontstaan van een onderklasse in Nederland*. Leiden/Antwerpen: Stenfert Kroese.

——SNEL, E., and YPEIJ, A. (1998). 'De andere kant van het armoedebeleid. Beleid en realiteit in Amsterdam-Noord', in G. Engbersen, J. C. Vrooman, and E. Snel (eds.), *Effecten van armoede*, 143–74. Amsterdam: Amsterdam University Press.

ESPING-ANDERSEN, G. (1990). *The Three Worlds of Welfare Capitalism*. Cambridge: Polity Press.

FLEURKE, F., and DE VRIES, P. J. (1997). 'Armoedebestrijding met de bijzondere bijstand', in G. Engbersen, J. C. Vrooman, and E. Snel (eds.), *De kwetsbaren*, 179–292. Amsterdam: Amsterdam University Press.

GIDDENS, A. (1984). *The Constitution of Society. Outline of the Theory of Structuration*. Oxford: Polity Press.

GOETZE, R. (1979). *Understanding Neighborhood Change. The Role of Expectations in Urban Revitalization*. Cambridge, MA: Ballinger.

HENDERSON, J., and KARN, V. (1987). *Race, Class and State Housing: Inequality and the Allocation of Public Housing in Britain*. Aldershot: Gower.

HIRSH, F. (1977). *The Social Limits to Growth*. London: Routledge & Kegan Paul.

HOFF, S. (1998). 'Armoede en sociale relaties', in G. Engbersen, J. C. Vrooman, and E. Snel (eds.), *Effecten van armoede*, 115–28. Amsterdam: Amsterdam University Press.

JAHODA, M., LAZARSFELD, P. H., and ZEISL, H. (1933). *Die Arbeitslosen von Marienthal: Ein Soziographischer Versuch uber die Wirkungen Langdauernder Arbeitslosigkeit.* Leipzig: Verlag von S. Hirzel.

JOHNSTON, R. S. (1984). *Residential Segregation, the State and Constitutional Conflicts in American Urban Areas.* London: Academic Press.

JORDAN, B. (1996). *A Theory of Poverty and Social Exclusion.* Cambridge: Polity Press.

KASARDA, J. D. (1989). 'Urban Industrial transition and the Underclass'. *Annals of the American Academy of Political and Social Science*, 501: 26–47.

——(1990). Structural Factors Affecting the Location and Timing of Urban Underclass Growth. *Urban Geography*, 11(3): 234–64.

KEMPSON, E. (1996). *Life on a Low Income.* York, UK: Joseph Rowntree Foundation.

KROFT, H., ENGBERSEN, G., SCHUYT, K., and VAN WAARDEN, F. (1989). *Een tijd zonder werk; een onderzoek naar de levenswereld van langdurig werklozen.* Leiden/Antwerpen, Stenfert Kroese.

LEIBFRIED, S. *et al.* (1995). *Zeit der Armut. Lebensläufe im Sozialstaat.* Frankfurt am Main, Suhrkamp.

LEWIS, O. (1968). 'The culture of poverty', in D. P. Moynihan (ed.), *On Understanding Poverty; Perspectives from the Social Sciences*, 187–200. New York: Basic Books.

MADANIPOUR, A., CARS, G., and ALLEN, J. (eds.) (1998). *Social Exclusion in European Cities; Processes, Experiences and Responses.* London/Philadelphia: Jessica Kingsley.

MARSHALL, T. H. (1965). *Class, Citizenship and Social Development.* Garden City, NY: Anchor Books, Doubleday & Company.

MASSEY, D. (1994). *Space, Place and Gender.* Cambridge: Polity Press.

——and EGGERS, M. L. (1993). 'The spatial concentration of affluence and poverty during the 1970s'. *Urban Affairs Quarterly*, 29(2): 299–315.

MEERT, H., MISTIAEN, P., and KESTELOOT, C. (1997). 'The geography of survival: household strategies in urban settings'. *Tijdschrift voor sociale en economische geografie*, 88(2): 169–81.

MINGIONE, E. (1991). *Fragmented Societies; A Sociology of Economic Life beyond the Market Paradigm.* Oxford: Blackwell.

MORRIS, L. (1994). *Dangerous Classes. The Underclass and Social Citizenship.* London/New York: Routledge.

OECD (Organization for Economic Cooperation and Development) (1996). *The Employment Outlook 1996.* Paris: OECD.

OSA (1996). *Soepel geregeld. Instituties en efficiëntie van de arbeidsmarkt.* The Hague: OSA.

PAASI, A. (1991). 'Deconstructing regions: notes on the scales of spatial life'. *Environment and Planning: A*, 23: 239–56.

PAHL, R. E. (1985). 'The restructuring of capital, the local political economy and household working strategies', in D. Gregory and J. Urry (eds.), *Social Relations and Spatial Structures*, 242–64. London: Macmillan.

REES, A. M. (1996). 'T. H. Marshall and the progress of citizenship', in M. Bulmer and A. M. Rees (eds.), *Citizenship Today.* London: UCL Press.

RENOOY, P. H. (1990). *The Informal Economy. Meaning, Measurement and Social Significance.* Amsterdam: KNAG/Regioplan.

ROOM, G. (1995). 'Poverty and social exclusion: the new European agenda for policy and research', in G. Room (ed.), *Beyond the Threshold: The Measurement and Analysis of Social Exclusion*, 1–9. Bristol, UK: Polity Press.

ROMMELSPACHER, TH., and OELSCHLAGEL, D. (1989). 'Armut im Ruhrgebiet—Regionale Entwicklungstrends und kleinraumige Prozesse am Beispiel eines Duisburgers Elendsgebietes', in I. Breckner *et al.* (eds.), *Armut im Reichtum*, 275–92. Bochum, Germinal.

ROSCAM ABBING, R. (1999). 'Nieuwe kleur voor Millinxbuurt'. *NRC Handelsblad*, 20 October: 3.

SCHEP, G. G., and BOMMELJÉ, Y. (1994). *Een kwestie van geld. Over de financiële positie van cliënten van de sociale dienst*. Den Haag: Vuga.

SCP (Sociaal Cultureel Planbureau) (1996). *Sociaal cultureel rapport 1996*. Rijswijk: SCP.

——(1998). *Sociaal cultureel rapport 1998. 25 jaar sociale verandering*. Rijswijk: SCP.

SOJA, E. (1985). 'The spatiality of social life: towards a transformative retheorisation', in D. Gregory and J. Urry (eds.), *Social Relations and Spatial Structures*, 90–127. London: Macmillan.

STORPER, M. (1985). 'The spatial and temporal constitution of social action: a critical reading of Giddens'. *Environment and Planning: D*, 3: 407–24.

SULLIVAN, M. L. (1989). 'Absent Fathers in the Inner City'. *Annals of the American Academy of Political and Social Science*, 501: 48–59.

TESSER, P., and VEENMAN, J. (1997). *Rapportage minderheden 1997*. Rijswijk: Sociaal Cultureel Planbureau.

TESTA, M., ASTONE, N. M., KROGH, M., and NECKERMAN, K. M. (1989). 'Employment and Marriage among Inner-City Fathers'. *Annals of the American Academy of Political and Social Science*, 501: 79–91.

THRIFT, N. (1979). 'Unemployment in the inner-city: urban problem or structural imperative. A review of the British experience', in D. T. Herbert and R. J. Johnston (eds.), *Geography and the Urban Environment*. Vol. 2, 125–226. London: Wiley.

——(1983). 'On the determination of social action in space and time'. *Environment and Planning: D. Society and Space*, 1(1): 23–57.

TITMUSS, R. M. (1968). *Commitment to Welfare*. London: George Allen & Unwin.

TOWNSEND, P. (1987). 'Deprivation'. *Journal of Social Policy*, 17(2): 125–47.

VAN BERKEL, R., BRAND, A., and VROOMAN, J. C. (1997). 'Langblijvers in de bijstand', in G. Engbersen, J. C. Vrooman, and E. Snel (eds.), *De kwetsbaren*, 85–102. Amsterdam: Amsterdam University Press.

VAN DER PENNEN, T., and HOFF, S. (1999). 'De staat van het lokale armoede beleid', in G. Engbersen, J. C. Vrooman, and E. Snel (eds.), *Effecten van armoede*, 191–210. Amsterdam: Amsterdam University Press.

VAN KEMPEN, E. T. (1992). 'High-rise living: the social limits to design', in B. Danermark and I. Elander (eds.), *Social Rented Housing in Europe: Policy, Tenure and Design,* 159–80. Delft: Delft University Press.

——and TEIJMANT, I. (1990). *Onverwacht ontruimd?* Amsterdam: Instituut voor Sociale Geografie.

VEENMAN, J. (1996). *Heb je niets, dan ben je niets. Tweede generatie allochtone jongeren in Amsterdam*. Assen: Van Gorcum.

WACQUANT, L. J. D. (1993). 'Urban Outcasts: Stigma and Division in the Black American Ghetto and the French Urban Periphery'. *International Journal of Urban and Regional Research*, 17(3): 366–83.

WILSON, W. J. (1987). *The Truly Disadvantaged: The Inner City, the Underclass and Public Policy*. Chicago: University of Chicago Press.

——(1991). 'Studying inner-city dislocations: The challenge of public agenda research'. *American Sociological Review*, 56(1): 1–14.

13

States, Cities, and the Partitioning of Urban Space: Conclusions

Peter Marcuse and Ronald van Kempen

The focus in this book is, as we said in our Introduction, a central fear that states and cities are powerless to chart their own course, and to escape the inevitable spectre of globalization. Expressed more formally, we formulated the following questions:

1. How have cities been partitioned in past periods? What role has the state played in the historical processes of partitioning?
2. Do new forms of partitioning characterize changes in cities today? What role does the state play in the shaping of cities today, in a period in which globalization is generally seen as a dominating force, while at the same time the role of the state seems to be declining, or at least changing? Specifically, do changes in cities today come about because of the competitive market, in the face of an increasingly powerless state?

The individual contributions, in their description of changes in cities from seven countries around the globe, and our own brief historical overview, have provided evidence that partitioning has been an enduring aspect of city form over the long *durée*, but that there have been significant changes in the manner and driving forces behind those partitions over time. In this last chapter, we want to examine more generally the role that the state has played in bringing about and shaping those changes in partitioning that have in fact taken place in our time.

To summarize our conclusion:

The state has not been the driving force behind (or against) partitioning since the advent of modern capitalism, and often not before, but its actions have been critical in determining both the form and the extent of partitioning. The state today does not act autonomously; other forces, of which the distribution of wealth and power in the market, the drive for profit, national chauvinism, the pandering or independence of politicians and government officials, racism, religion, ideologies, international economic location, demographic changes, all combine to determine the state's actions and its effects. But the state's actions are crucial to implementing partitioning. By the same token, the state can be effective in countering the forces that lead to partitioning.   ·

The state can decisively influence whether and to what extent and in what form partitioning takes place.

The complex interplay between state power and other forces (private forces, as well as macro-structural developments) that lead to partitioning have not been extensively explored in the literature (Musterd and Ostendorf 1998). We have surveyed, in Chapter 3, the sociological and geographical explanations given in the established literature for the shape and divisions of cities, and found few in-depth explorations of the state's role. We find many explanations that explore the private forces that shape cities, but they generally implicitly assume that, to the extent state action is relevant, it is simply a reflection of those private forces. This is true of the Chicago School approaches, of factorial ecology, of social area analysis, of behavioural theories, and in ethnic-cultural discussions. We have also, less methodically, explored some of the literature specifically examining the state's role, as in our discussion of ghettoization in the United States in Chapter 6, and have found it often uni-dimensional in its explanation of changes, either treating the state as alone and autonomously decisive or as simply reacting to the forces of racism and the opposition to it. This is not to denigrate either body of literature, but simply to suggest that the precise focus of our concerns, the exploration of the relative powers and limits of state action on urban form under present-day circumstances, viewed in comparative and historical perspective, remains a field in which much work needs to be done.

Historically, certainly until the advent of capitalism, the power of the state in shaping urban form was indisputable, and almost universally it imposed partitions on cities, generally along lines designed to reinforce hierarchical divisions of power. Divisions reflecting cultural or functional economic relationships have also been widespread, but the evidence is much less clear as to the state's role here; in most cases those divisions seem to have come about autonomously, as a result of voluntary action within civil society not requiring state reinforcement. Thus, in medieval cities in Europe, for instance, the protected and dominant position of castle and cathedral were imposed from the top down, through the exercise of state power, but the separation of quarters for the respective guilds, or (more in non-European than in European countries) the clustering of residents by religion or national origin, proceeded independently of state action. The ghettoization of Jewish residents is a glaring exception to this generalization.

The advent of capitalism changed this picture dramatically, for with the commodification of land and housing (in separate steps) it purported to replace state decisions or voluntary agreements with market forces as the determinant of location, and thus of partitions. The ability to pay, and only the ability to pay, as influenced by the actions of those determining supply in the interests of profit, decided where people lived, or in what quarters. But that arrangement was not tenable in a complex urban society, and at least by the middle of the 19th century state action was increasingly called on to regulate urban development. The forces that produced Disraeli's 'two cities' were private; the measures to regulate building densities, provide infrastructure, lay out roads, clear slums, restrict conflicting uses, distribute public facilities, provide mass transportation, were all state measures.

Have these new functions of the state changed its role in reflecting and rein-forcing hierarchical relations of power in the form of the city? Here, the evidence suggests two different trends, two different possibilities. On the one hand, state power in the control of complex urban development can, under cover of efficiency, in fact exacerbate hierarchical divisions and inequalities and implement their reflection in urban space. On the other hand state action can recognize the likely impact of 'normal' efficiency-oriented actions on such divisions, and attempt to counter or ameliorate their impact. Experience in the United States suggests the first pattern—reinforcement of division; experience in the Netherlands the second—amelioration. In both cases, there are private forces pressing in both directions, but the balance represented and imple-mented by the state are quite different. The ambiguous experience of the former state socialist countries provides yet a third model.

Part of the pattern in the United States was described in Chapter 6. It shows the explicit implementation by government at all levels of the segregation of blacks in cities in the early years of the 20th century, building on the legal, that is to say state-established and enforced, enslavement of blacks for the hundreds of years preceding the Civil War. The state slowly retreated from such imple-mentation in the 1920s, shifting instead to the adoption of land use controls, such as large-lot zoning, having much the same partitioning effect. Not until after the Second World War was there any deliberate action by government in the opposite direction. In the following half-century, at the Federal level, anti-discrimination and fair housing laws were gradually adopted and strengthened, with varying levels of enforcement. At the same time, other policies, such as those encouraging suburbanization through the Interstate Highway system and Federal mortgage insurance policies, in effect reinforced segregation. A similar ambivalent pattern existed at the local level: anti-discrimination laws and human rights commissions aimed at reducing segrega-tion, while in other cases segregation was increased through policies of triage permitting abandonment of ghetto areas, through empowerment policies lim-ited to the partitioned space of those ghettos, and through implementation of gentrification in other areas. The net result, over time, implicates government in the enforcement, rather than in the dismantling of the historically inferior position of blacks through spatial partitioning. This result comes about, not because of the independent will of government, but rather as government responds to the pressure of racism and the private commodified market for land and housing provision. Thus we find private impetus and public implementation both in actions enforcing and in making milder partitioning based on 'race'.

The Netherlands have shown a very different picture. Immigration, segregation in cities, and the possible effects of spatial concentration and segregation of minority ethnic groups are relatively new topics. While immigration to the Netherlands has played a role for centuries, the possible problems have only arisen in the 1970s, as cities gradually became more multi-cultural with immigration from Mediterranean countries and from the former colony of Surinam.

The construction by the state of large numbers of affordable social rented dwellings of a rather good quality is one of the reasons spatial concentration of low-income groups in general and ethnic minority groups in particular has never been very high in Dutch cities. Because of their large numbers, social housing units could be found in many urban areas, which meant that low-income households could be found all over the city. Because of their good quality, social rented dwellings were not just occupied by low-income households. Although allocation rules prevented middle- and higher-income households from entering the social rented sector, after allocation it was impossible to force people to move out when their incomes rose; thus, over time, mixed income developments became common. Nevertheless, over the last decades there have been no explicit governmental plans to reduce ethnic or class segregation in Dutch cities. After 1997 that changed; under the policy of urban restructuring, local governments plan to build more expensive dwellings in low-rent areas and at the same time sell or demolish part of the social rented housing stock. Officially (without mentioning the ethnic component, however) this is done in order to diminish the homogeneity of the population of these areas. If this really leads to desegregation remains to be seen. It may very well lead to larger concentrations of the poor: as the number of affordable rented dwellings is diminished it becomes more and more difficult to find adequate housing elsewhere.

Local governments, national governments, and intermediate levels of government, do not always act in parallel. In the United States case, at least, the judicial branch of government frequently acted in contradiction to (or dictated) the partitioning or anti-partitioning actions of other branches of government. It is beyond the scope of the evidence adduced in this volume to generalize, but from our own experience the hypothesis might be formulated that, for the United States, the courts, within its constitutional system, and to a lesser extent the national government, have by and large acted to ameliorate the direct partitioning actions of many local governments in recent decades. This is because (again, to summarize a complex situation) local levels of government are generally more responsive to local real estate interests and landed property-owners than, on balance, is the Federal government.

The state socialist case is somewhat different. Here, market pressures were given, formally at least, much less scope to influence governmental action, and official governmental action was quite consistently anti-partitioning. Divisions were rather—and more strongly than in corresponding capitalist societies—oriented towards economic efficiency, and particularly rapid industrialization and the land use patterns that would best foster it. Thus, as appears implicitly in Chapters 8 and 9 of this volume, state socialist governmental policies, certainly in their early periods, rather reduced pre-existing partitioning than reinforced it, and produced a pattern in which neither income nor wealth nor 'race' determined residential location. Political power was indeed, if at the margin, reflected in housing provision, and economic policies to some extent had the effect of creating new forms of partition, but those policies of the state that were formally directed at spatial patterns acted, with the exceptions noted, effectively in the direction of reduced hierarchical divisions. The extent of the impact of those policies can in part be judged by the extent of the counter-movement, in the direction of increased partitioning, that has occurred dramatically since the end of the Soviet system.

Can we hazard a guess as to the future? Perhaps, but not by way of prediction, but by way of trends, alternatives, and possibilities. Economic developments internationally tend towards greater division among groups based on income, wealth, and occupation. Polarization is a partial description of the direction, increasing inequality is another. It involves not only greater distance between the top and the bottom in terms of income and power, but also greater differentiation in between. It also plays differentially to render divisions by 'race', ethnicity, and gender more extreme at levels of lesser power, perhaps moderated in between. More women and more blacks, in the United States, are below the poverty level, and fewer are among the ultra-rich; in between, progress toward equality is evident if spotty. Those trends are reflected in space, and 'partitioning' is an apt term for the result. We have described some details of the pattern elsewhere (Marcuse and Van Kempen 2000). At the same time, recognition of the ill effects of these trends is also growing, at least in some national and local contexts, and resistance to them and efforts to counter them are apparent.

Has the role of government been changed with respect to its possibilities of affecting these results? Some of the prevailing wisdom suggests it has been reduced: the power of the nation-state, in an era of increasing globalization, is declining, it is argued, and the pressures of international competition limits the options of local governments as well. There is truth to this observation, but it needs reformulation. For it is not the legal power of either the national state nor of the local state that is declining; on the contrary, the extensive action of each is increasingly required for the international economy to function smoothly. National laws must enforce international agreements, nation-states must come together to formulate binding trade policies, the security of global financial transactions and information exchange must be guaranteed at the level of each participating nation.

Likewise, actions of local governments are more and more required for the efficient conduct of business by global interests. Governmental planning and action is infinitely more important for the construction of a downtown skyscraper than for a log cabin. Infrastructure, utilities, transportation, control of discordant uses, are vital, and cannot be left to private initiative; only government can handle them effectively. True, economic competition, important for some (important) forces in a city, limits the likelihood that a local government will act in directions counter to their interests, but that is not for lack of legal ability of government to act otherwise, but because of the lack of powerful enough support for alternatives. In many cities around the world city leaders have sought policies that not only support economic competition by fostering increasing productivity and attracting businesses, but also have a positive social and environmental component (Andersen and Van Kempen 2001*a*; see also Friedrichs 2001). Alternative goals do not necessarily contradict each other. Attracting new businesses may increasingly depend on perceptions of social stability and social sustainability in the urban area, and a clean environment may be attractive for companies, as well as their employees.

So the formal power of government to affect the development of cities is, if anything, greater than it has been in the past, and the necessity on all sides for it to exercise that power is more urgent. To date, it has been more generally exercised to facilitate rather than counter the trends that lead to the partitioning of cities. Declining numbers of social rented dwellings in housing production, decreasing housing allowances for low-income households, the targeting of subsidies to specific neighbourhoods in urban areas (thereby excluding other areas) are indications not so much of a decreasing role of the state, but much more of deliberate policy choices for some and against other measures and favouring some and depriving other quarters and neighbourhoods within the metropolitan area. Of course, these policy changes are often formulated within a framework of decentralization, deconcentration, and privatization and have to do with a general attitude change towards government intervention. But the increasing reliance on market forces or the free market as the best allocator of resources and distributor of benefits (and ills?) has at least to be seen as a deliberate choice of government. It remains to be seen if this trend will in the end solve problems that have to do with spatial concentration and segregation within all kinds of different urban areas.

A simple indicator of the direction in which a government is moving is the extent of social housing provision; in almost all countries, the more social housing, the less segregation. Social housing can also be used to segregate, as, for instance, it often has been in the United States, but this is the exception rather than the rule. If social housing provision is the indicator, then, the direction internationally is for less, not more. Beginning with the Margaret Thatcher era in Great Britain and the Ronald Reagan era in the United States, the attack on social housing is almost a hallmark of our period. The pattern of increasing privatization of governmental facilities and services—privatization is, of course, an act of government, abdicating its powers, rather than a reflection of the absence of those powers—goes in the same direction.

Yet, there are alternative directions for governmental action. Governments have the power to counteract partitioning (by direct policies or as a consequence of indirect effects of policy) as well as to foster it. It is necessary here to return to the discussion in Chapter 2, and the distinction among partitions drawn along lines of culture, along lines of functional efficiency, and along lines of power. It is to the latter, to the partitions developed by and reinforcing hierarchical relations of economic, political, and social power, that our attention is directed, and to which the brief discussion of possible positive alternative measures with which we conclude this book is directed. What follows is really only a list of some possibilities, whose application will vary from city to city. It is intended more to demonstrate the falsity of the TINA ('There Is No Alternative') position than to be a menu of proven measures for adoption.

The following might be considered:

• Expanded provision of social housing in different urban areas (not only in areas that already have substantial social rented dwellings), planned as part of an overall programme for the mainstream of housing provision (Marcuse 1998). In areas that still have to be developed social housing should also be included. Inter-municipal agreements with respect to housing low-income households may be important here. Such agreements might especially be useful between cities and suburbs. Often, lower-income households are located in central cities, while suburban environments house the middle- and higher-income households. Building low-rent dwellings in suburbs, and giving high-income households the opportunity to move to central city areas by offering them good alternatives in these areas, may foster desegregation in the US context; in the others, reverse policies may have the same effect.

• Use of tax incentives to promote local economic development and job creation/expansion, within a broad integrative framework. This will give possibilities for unemployed people to get a job and a higher income and to move to better dwellings, permitting them to move from distressed areas, and permitting those remaining in such areas to change their economic status.

• Progressive real estate taxes, that would make local real property-based taxes progressive, redistributing some of the benefit of land appreciation to the entire community; Porto Alegre, in Brazil, has begun such a practice successfully.

• Capital gains and anti-speculation taxes, such as have been adopted in some places in the United States, which impose a high tax on profits resulting from purchase and sale of a property within a short time, at high levels if no significant improvements have been made justifying the profit; such taxes discourage speculation and displacement from rising prices in areas of gentrification.

• Inter-municipal agreements (or regulation at higher levels of government) can be used to prevent destructive competition among cities, such as often results in tax incentives or other financial incentives offered to businesses seeking new locations, generally resulting in a regressive redistribution of tax benefits and an increasing disparity among aided and unaided businesses and their employees.

• Provision of infrastructure and land use controls for local and equitable benefit, so that development desired for its contribution to equity and integration are favoured and support for citadel-like construction of insulated enclaves of the rich and powerful are discouraged. Provision of mass transportation with stations and stops in different kinds of areas may lead to the increase of economic activities in neighbourhoods that did not have good connections before.

• Regional planning and land use controls geared to equalizing benefits and burdens of development, so that suburbs are not permitted to escape the costs of urbanization while reaping all of their benefits. Proposals and policies discussed in Minnesota and by the Regional Plan Association in New York are examples.

• Community information as to public decisions, with broad decentralized control over neighbourhood developments, so that local communities can be enabled to resist segregating tendencies, whether gentrification or the dumping of undesired polluting or otherwise undesired facilities in already neglected ghetto or ghetto-like areas; New York City's Fair Share regulations are intended to be a step in this direction.

• Expansive provision of public space and opportunity for public communication, so that the movement in the direction of private control, with its market-based tendencies to segregate, can be counteracted, and the general sense of a diverse community be reinforced.

• Strong anti-discrimination action, as is particularly needed, and extensively if still inadequately used, in the United States.

• Anti-redlining and pro-greenlining legislation, often part of such efforts. Thus, the use of zoning and land use controls to steer new construction and commercial development in desired areas and limit it in undesired areas (see, e.g., Marcuse 1984–5);

• Legalization of squatting through national legislation affecting land titles and evictions and prohibition on confiscation or buying up of land by non-farmers, actions against landlessness, land reform, thus keeping down the push pressure of rural immigration to the cities. Measures such as these, often as part of comprehensive restructuring of property rights and property reform, have been extensively adopted or are under consideration in countries as diverse as Brazil and Turkey.

The range of policies that might reduce partitioning should in fact include the wide variety of measures that would reduce that inequality which is the underlying cause of partitioning. In the long run, for instance, measures such as steeply progressive income taxes, protection of the rights of women, limitations on the concentration of ownership and control of economic activity, environmental protection measures taking into account the just distribution of burdens and benefits, would all reduce undesired partitioning. To the extent that global/international pressures lead to or accentuate negative partitioning, international agreements establishing standards and limits on private actions from outside national borders should also be considered. But further consideration of such measures would bring us too far outside the scope of this volume, and are extensively dealt with in the growing literature of globalization and its consequences (see, e.g., Hirst and Thompson 1996).

The way policy is implemented may be as important as the content of the policy itself. 'Governance' is a general term that has come into vogue in many places for discussing measures for the control of urban development, including the handling of partitioning. The term suggests an involvement of all kinds of relevant partners. It implies inclusion of local public authorities (government) as well as actors representing private business and voluntary organizations:

The transformation of government to governance reflects the changing balance between government and capital. It includes not only a shift in overall ideology by the introduction of market principles in public services but also a shift in focus to consider local economic development issues. Furthermore, it includes a shift in discourse; i.e., from welfare maximization towards business efficiency and ultimately towards a reconstruction of the general perception of democracy and justice.   (Andersen and Van Kempen 2001a: 8)

Governance is neither inherently supportive of nor contradictory to any of the above measures, but approaches the issues from a different direction. Increasingly, it suggests, public goals are not reached by acts of governments alone, but by coalitions between governments and all kinds of other public and private partners, such as investors, voluntary organizations, the police, schools, and residents of neighbourhoods. Such partnerships and networks have become important, in some places, for increasing the quality of life in neighbourhoods and increasing the competitiveness of cities in the quality of life they afford.

The rationale for such policies lies in the apparently growing gap between available resources and the welfare demand facing many cities. Governments see themselves being forced to restructure their organization in order to increase their capacity. This can be achieved by forms of governance, by drawing other actors into the political process or by building networks of citizens, the private sector, and various organizations (both private and public). Some argue that no region or city can avoid the impending transformations accompanying globalization; to stay out is to drop out. Local governments are thus seen as being forced to reformulate their policies in order to mobilize local resources and make room for new and different forms of economic growth. To make this happen, a change from government to governance is seen as necessary (see Andersen and Van Kempen 2001b). Others argue that the forms of existing globalization themselves need to be changed, and that new and different forms of governmental action are required to protect the citizenry from the adverse effects of the present forms.

There are pros and cons to these concepts. Governance may increase governmental capacity, create a closer link with the community and the people for whose benefit policy is directed, and expand the possibility of building on existing resources. But the networks and partnerships of governance proposals also have clear disadvantages (see, e.g., Andranovich and Riposa 1998; Elander and Blanc 2001; Andersen and Van Kempen 2001*b*):

1. Governance bodies are not democratically elected.
2. The borders between public and private become cloudy.
3. Accountability is less clear.
4. Power lies in the hands of those who have the interest to participate.
5. Many governance structures are 'gated' or even closed.
6. Goals among partners conflict.
7. Governance arrangements are only suitable for specific topics, but do not help provide a holistic view or policy.
8. Administration in governance may be problematic.

The above discussion of approaches and listing of possible measures is not intended as a comprehensive guide to anti-partitioning actions, nor as a checklist of possibilities, nor even as a partial catalogue of desirable measures; some of the items may well be counter-productive under given circumstances, or wildly unfeasible, or less desirable than other measures not included. What is intended rather is a demonstration that, in our opinion, the argument that 'there is no alternative', the famous TINA position, is false. There are indeed alternatives, many of them. Whether they will be pursued or not depends, not on their inherent logic or justice, but on the forces in support of them and those arrayed against. A discussion of that question far exceeds the scope of what we hope to cover in this book. But it helps to put our discussion in a realistic perspective: whether the type of description and analysis we have tried to undertake in this volume will have any useful effect depends, ultimately, on the strengthening of the forces working towards the elimination of the destructive partitioning that is increasingly confronting our cities and cities all over the world.

References

ANDERSEN, H. T., and VAN KEMPEN, R. (2001*a*). 'Social fragmentation, social exclusion and urban governance: An introduction', in H. T. Andersen and R. van Kempen (eds.), *Governing European Cities. Social Fragmentation, Social Exclusion and Urban Governance*, 1–18. Aldershot: Ashgate.

————(eds.) (2001*b*). *Governing European Cities. Social Fragmentation, Social Exclusion and Urban Governance*. Aldershot: Ashgate.

ANDRANOVICH, G., and RIPOSA, G. (1998). 'Is governance the lost hard "G" in Los Angeles?' *Cities*, 15: 185–92.

ELANDER, I., and BLANC, M. (2001). 'Partnerships and democracy: A happy couple in urban governance?', in H. T. Andersen and R. van Kempen (eds.), *Governing European Cities; Social Fragmentation, Social Exclusion and Urban Governance*, 93–124. Aldershot: Ashgate.

FRIEDRICHS, J. (2001). 'Urban revitalization transforms urban governments: The cases of Dortmund and Duisburg, Germany', in H. T. Andersen and R. van Kempen (eds.), *Governing European Cities. Social Fragmentation, Social Exclusion and Urban Governance*, 191–212. Aldershot: Ashgate.

HIRST, P., and THOMPSON, G. (1996). *Globalization in Question: The International Economy and the Possibilities of Governance*. Cambridge: Polity Press.

MARCUSE, P. (1984–5). 'To control gentrification: Anti-displacement zoning and planning for stable residential districts'. *New York University Review of Law and Social Change*, XIII: 931–52.

—— (1998). 'Mainstreaming public housing: A proposal for a comprehensive approach to housing policy', in D. P. Varady, W. F. E. Preiser, and F. P. Russell (eds.), *New Directions in Urban Public Housing*, 23–46, New Brunswick, NJ: Center for Urban Policy Research.

—— and VAN KEMPEN, R. (eds.) (2000). *Globalizing Cities: A New Spatial Order?* Oxford: Blackwell.

MUSTERD, S., and OSTENDORF, W. (eds.) (1998). *Urban Segregation and the Welfare State: Inequality and Exclusion in Western Cities*. London/New York: Routledge.

Afterword

Peter Marcuse

It does not seem possible, sitting in New York City in December 2001, to let a book about cities and states go to press that ignores one of the most shattering events for at least that city in our age, perhaps as shattering a single event as anything since the great fire of 1774. 11 September 2001 has put in bold relief key trends in the relationship between states and cities that are the theme of this book. This Afterword tries to sketch out some of the specifics. What is possible thus far is more in the nature of speculations and conjectures than description of verifiable patterns or trends; the evidence is not yet in for a normal scholarly assessment. But even educated guesses may be provocative in a period of such rapid developments. What follows is strictly based on the situation in New York City and the United States since 11 September 2001.

The key trends, some apparently contradictory but, I believe, consistent in their underlying pattern, are as follows:

• Globally, there will be on the one hand a trend towards deglobalization because of the increasing prominence and willingness of the central governments of nation-states to control economic activities, and on the other hand an increasing global reach to the power of a single nation-state and its close subordinates and allies.

• The market will lead to urban decentralization in space, but not of control, and a psychologically accentuated spatial segregation and polarization.

• The state will play an expanded role in the physical patterns of cities, but in a skewed fashion, with considerations of physical security legitimating a diminution of urbanity and democracy and concealing a regressively distributed economic benefit of state action.
  • Privatization will be defrocked, its ideological hegemony limited and shifted in application.
  • Deplanning will be an appropriate name for the neglect of open and participatory democratic process in planning and the neglect of issues of social equity in that process.

• The impact of activities in the market and of state actions will be visible in many aspects of urban space, including

- decentralization within metropolitan areas of major service-sector business activities,
- accelerated residential suburbanization,
- increase in the concentration of immigrant enclaves and restrictions on immigrant freedom and opportunities,
- restrictions in the nature and use of public and semi-public space,
- citadelization of private space.

None of this is new; none is even a change of direction. But all of it is a significant acceleration of existing trends, and involves an ideological cover, under the name of 'security', that is indeed new in scope and intensity.

First, briefly, on the global context, then the market response at the city level, then the governmental response.

The Impact of Globalization/Deglobalization

'Globalization is going to be at a standstill for a while,' says Henry Kaufman, former vice-chair of Salomon Brothers and a guru for financial markets.[1] Niall Ferguson, Professor of Political and Financial History at Oxford, speaks of the 'nonglobal nature of globalization', and believes it is increasing; 'think of it as deglobalization', he writes.[2] That may be exaggerated; but the international aspects of globalization[3] will indeed be seriously affected. It is too early to tell whether the New York City pattern will be duplicated elsewhere, although there is anecdotal evidence of some parallel trends; for example, in Frankfurt there is talk of decentralization to avoid the threat of terrorism,[4] in skyscrapers there and in Kuala Lumpur fears of attack are reported, etc. But while the impact of the changes that will be manifest through the market, suggested below, are likely to have ramifications in many places, the point here is rather to put what is happening in New York City in context.

The mobility of capital will be somewhat more closely regulated; it is interesting to see how the arch-enemies of regulating capital, Dick Army in the United States House of Representatives and Phil Gramm in the United States Senate, who even opposed the mild transparency requirements the Clinton administration proposed, are now silent as the United States pushes other states to join it in tracing 'terrorist' funds and blocking accounts. The recently adopted USA Patriot legislation (discussed below) explicitly expands the Federal government's powers to monitor capital flows, and thus endangers some of the common practices in international trade that use offshore or multiple transactions to reduce and evade taxes, reducing the attractiveness of those global investments that depend on that advantage. The feasibility of national regulation and taxation of international transactions is correspondingly strengthened.

Globalization will be affected in a much more intangible way. There is sporadic anecdotal evidence that, at least for those in direct contact with the collapse of the World Trade Center (and that includes a large portion of those working in Lower Manhattan that day), the attraction of financial speculation has decreased; bond trading, stock brokerage, securities, become less valued as occupations, including their more global aspects. Likewise, the 'cocooning' that seems to be one result of the concern about terrorism may reduce the lure of high-pressure business and other riskier activities. The economic decline that preceded but was accentuated by the events of September 11 may accentuate both effects.

The mobility of labour across borders will clearly be impeded in the aftermath of September 11. Restrictions on immigration are being tightened, border checks made stronger, pursuit of those in violation of immigration rules more aggressive, civil rights of immigrants curtailed. Even 'normal' business travel is affected; delays at airports are substantially increased, and the hassle effect becomes worse. Movement of goods as well as of people across international borders will be more difficult. For those meeting particular profiles, or otherwise considered to be an endangering factor, the difficulties will be even more. 'RUSHDIE IS GROUNDED BY FAA', says a newspaper headline, because his presence on the plane increases the risk of an attack.[5]

Alan Greenspan told Congress of the danger that 'international travel will tank';[6] but while that is something of an exaggeration, perhaps targeted to supporting the airlines' request for their $15 billion dollar bailout, there is no question that there have been sharp reductions in air travel. Security proposals for airport access now speak of a special streamlined ID card for 'frequent travellers', that is, for business travellers; infrequent travellers, which includes most lower-income folk, will find themselves even more in second-class status.

The 'war on terrorism' has attracted the support of governments around the world because it is in each of their individual interests to increase their own powers within their own countries. Really existing globalization turns out not to see all forms of internationalization, all weakening of national boundaries, as desirable. The ideological contradictions in which conservatives, including the Bush administration, are caught by the need to respond to the attacks are thus major. Not only is there concern to limit and/or regulate free trade, otherwise anathema to the administration, not only are investments in high-tech weaponry like Star Wars conspicuously irrelevant yet part of their basic long-term programme, but perhaps most importantly the commitment to reduce the size of government is hardly viable today. The issue of Federal responsibility for airport security is perhaps symbolic; to the extent that security inspectors are 'federalized', it may be the first major deprivatization of a public service in several decades. What becomes clear is that the principled commitment is not in fact to reduce the size of government, but only to reduce certain of its functions, those having to do with welfare and social concerns. That can, in the long run, provoke widespread political discontent. These tensions remain to be resolved.

So does the tension around the role of the United States internationally. On the one hand, the United States has gone all out to use its power to achieve its purposes, both militarily (as in the assumption of its right to engage in 'nation-building', as in Afghanistan) and economically (in its unabashed use of international financial institutions to bribe cooperation, as in Pakistan). On the other hand, there is also a less visible desire to reassert national independence in some countries, and an unquietness about the intent and competence of United States leadership. Nor does the United States seem enthusiastic about the ratification of a number of international covenants and treaties. The result is still open.

Globalization is thus both advanced and retarded. Big and mainstream capital will continue to operate across borders without restriction, but where specific movements are not in a 'national interest', they will be stopped. Labour will continue to be permitted to cross borders where there is a particular economic interest in having it do so, but where there is no such interest its movement will be much more restricted. Trade will continue to grow, but in the long run militarization and the greater weight given to military production and investment in military development will be counterproductive for economic growth, certainly for equitable economic growth.

The net result is not so much a retreat of globalization as a sharpening of its skewed implementation.

The Market Response

Employment patterns have for some time been towards deconcentration of many types of jobs, with only a very narrow band of activities remaining regularly in the central business districts of major cities (primarily those of FIRE—fire, insurance, and real estate—and directly related services, government, advanced health care, entertainment, and media), and most other activities focusing on less central areas of the city, the suburbs, and edge cities, with a noticeable movement from primary cities to secondary and even tertiary (economically defined) cities. A number of factors come together to shape this trend: the availability of technology to make both transportation and communication easier across greater distances; the pressure on central real estate prices in a market dominated by private land ownership, the costs of congestion and environmental degradation; and, last but hardly least, the social tensions that result from increasing polarization of the population and the perception, outpacing the reality, of continuing racial and ethnic division. To these negative aspects of concentration there has been counterpoised the advantages of agglomeration: the efficiencies of shared services, the importance of face-to-face meetings, the reduced friction of transportation, the desirability of a creative, diverse, lively, urbane milieu, the urban 'quality of life'.

In this balance between ongoing pressures for deconcentration and concentration, the fear of terrorism now adds a significant weight on the side of deconcentration. Extreme agglomeration is equated with danger. In the centres of the more 'global' cities, this balance has hitherto been more on the side of concentration than it has in other cities; that balance will now noticeably change; they will no longer be exempt, even to the extent that they ever were. The pattern is already visible in New York City.

The hyper-concentrations of jobs in service-centre-oriented office buildings that is typical of the centres of the more globalized cities (and both the high- and the low-paying jobs associated with them) will shrink. The global status of the central business district(s) of New York City, but perhaps of other global cities as well, will change, as multinational businesses change their spatial strategies in the search for security in more outlying areas. The focus will initially be fairly close: for New York City, from the financial district to midtown and to Long Island City and central Brooklyn and Queens Plaza. It will overwhelmingly be within the same metropolitan region (e.g., American Express, Lehman Brothers, others, renting—on long-term leases—spaces in Jersey City, Stamford, etc.). Many major firms in New York City already had large satellite offices in fringe locations, to which they quickly moved after September 11; in some cases decisions to move more operations out of the city to those locations were simply accelerated by the attack.

The New York Stock Exchange is symbolically central for New York City. It won't build its long-planned new trading floor and 900-foot tower across the street from its current headquarters, but will likely expand in the city. It may build a secondary trading site outside Lower Manhattan. But some are raising questions about the very need for a large physical presence. More shares are traded on the NASDAQ stock market, which exists only on computer systems and the screens of its dealers, than on the big board. 'With faster computers and data transmission, traders no longer have to meet in person to buy and sell shares,' says the chief executive of the Cincinnati Stock Exchange.

Residential patterns, as well as business and commercial patterns, will change. In particular, the trend towards re-creating residential housing and residential environments in central business districts will suffer. In Washington DC, where the major business tenant is government, there will be a continuing trend to the decentralization of government offices, but the hopes for bringing multi-family residential development to the downtown are now given little chance.[7] The trend here is one of longer standing, as suburbs generate more and more of the accoutrements of urbanity that used to be confined to the centres of cities: the sidewalk cafés, the art galleries, the cultural centres, the symphony orchestras, the theatres. But the safety issue will accentuate the trend.

As a result, polarization and segregation will increase. Those with higher incomes will, if they choose to remain in the central city, have the resources to protect and insulate themselves from perceived threats to their security, and thus to separate themselves more and more from the day-to-day life of the city. Most will continue the trend to the suburbs, particularly if they are households with children. That means those with low incomes will be left behind in the 'unprotected' parts of the city, and the stratification along lines of income, colour, and ethnicity is likely to grow sharper.

As Paul Krugman, who holds himself out as a hard-headed economist and lives in the Jersey suburbs, wrote: '[I] felt perfectly safe on September 11; there are millions of people living and working nearby, but no obvious targets, because there's no there here.' The 'there' that isn't there is an urban centre, a city, and fewer will want that, given the trade-offs, than even before. The new 'there' may well be the edge cities (not just in Joel Garreau's narrow sense): Stamford, Jersey City, White Plains, and what are now being called 'boom-burgs': communities, on the outer parts of metropolitan regions, with 100,000 population or more and growing rapidly over an extended period of time.

The movement out of the centre will be not only to the immediately adjacent parts of the region. Over time the effects may lead to an even wider dispersal to other regions or urban enclaves. TIAA-CREF, the largest pension fund in the United States, now has 4,600 employees in New York City, 1,320 in Denver, and 597 in Charlotte, North Carolina. Their planned expansion will be over-whelmingly in Charlotte, hardly a global city. While larger cities will benefit, smaller cities will suffer: air connections, for instance, will be comparatively strengthened among larger centres, but curtailed among smaller. National Airport, Washington DC, for instance, will only initially connect to eight other centres, and will have special security arrangements on those flights; on the other hand, United Airlines is curtailing service to smaller cities like Little Rock, to the dismay of their Congressional representatives.

Citadelization, the aggressive fortification of business and residential space, will be further accentuated by the events of September 11, both within cities and in suburbs and edge cities. Again, citadels are nothing new; the mall at the basement of the World Trade Center towers may be taken as a partial example. But new ones will modify the form: walls and gates and guard posts, but more. They will be larger, more comprehensive, fortified centres, with high-tech metal detectors, fingerprint card entry, permanent visible security personnel, etc. The barriers (see below) to easy access will increase.

On the other hand, there will be fewer glamorous high-rise signature build-ings. The towers in Kuala Lumpur and Frankfurt were already evacuated the day after the World Trade Center collapse; workers in the Empire State Build-ing in New York and the Sears Tower in Chicago are already reported afraid to go up to their offices. Height will lose some of its attraction, and perhaps power will be less ostentatiously displayed.

Further, the location of future citadels will be in more dispersed locations than has been the practice. Already, many have been developed in smaller cities on the edge of the giant metropolitan agglomerations of the more global cities: Stamford, the northern cities of New Jersey, and the southern and eastern cities of Westchester County have such developments. This is where more of the future citadels will be built. The advantages of being right at the centre of a metropolitan region, already dwindling before September 11, will have an even greater counterweight when fears about terrorism are added to the disadvantages.

Polarization by income, by occupation, and by race will be spurred. The loss of jobs after September 11 disproportionately affected those at the extremes, the very high-paid and very low-paid workers. Professionals are relocated; the janitors and salad-bar preparers who served them are not. Those at the bottom of the economic ladder, those without accumulated resources, will be particularly hard-hit; some will end up in the soup kitchens.[8] Those at the top are producing a boom in the ex-urban real estate market in Connecticut, New Jersey, and upstate New York. Segregation will thus come about as a result of both residential developments and changes in employment patterns. Those able to move their home or where they work to out-of-town locations or to barricaded citadels will do so; those unable to do so will remain behind. The difference between the two groups will be, in the United States, both income- and race-related. The polarization will be both between city and suburb and within the city, with the focus of upper-income, disproportionately white, households concentrating in more tightly controlled citadels, and others more and more excluded and segregated, with sharper dividing lines between and among groups. So segregation and quartering will increase.

The Public Response

'The barricading of the city' is a good shorthand term to describe where public policy is heading. It will be readily visible in public spaces, within and near public buildings, in places of public assembly and use. 'Public space' will become less public; free access and free use will be limited. In public space that is public in ownership and control, e.g., streets, public plazas, public buildings, parks, the diversity of uses will be restricted and surveillance and control will be extended. In particular, aberrant uses will be restricted, and those of darker skin or conspicuously 'foreign' will feel themselves less welcome. The openness of public space will be reduced.

Some public spaces, like the park at the Federal Courthouse in Boston[9] or the plaza before City Hall in New York City and its adjacent recently renovated park, will simply be barred for open use. Mayor Giuliani had already prior to September 11 pioneered such a development with his restrictions on assemblies near City Hall and his attempts to limit the use of streets for parades, in the name of security, but the Democratic candidate in the municipal elections had, before September 11, pledged to reopen City Hall Plaza for public use; after September 11, he withdrew that pledge. Public buildings will be less freely accessible; metal detectors, demands for identification, will become normal, in a pattern reminiscent of eastern European and Soviet public buildings before 1989. Many places, from railroad stations to bus terminals to public streets and squares, will be subject to pervasive surveillance.

By the same token, controlled spaces, such as malls, will increase their attraction. Malls and private spaces apparently open to public access will multiply, both in the suburban and in central cities, but will at the same time become more patrolled by private security, more overseen by hi-tech security devices, with more limits on what may be done there without permission. Management practices, legitimated further by 'security' concerns, will reinforce barriers to free use.

Barricading is being reinforced by new legislation. The passage of what is called, officially, the USA Patriot Act of 2001[10] will extend the restrictions on customary civil liberties even further, with the Federal government centrally involved but local communities and their residents directly affected. Key provisions of the legislation allow investigators to use roving wiretaps, following a suspect rather than a particular phone. It also gives the government the power to detain immigrants for up to seven days if they're suspected of involvement with terrorists—up from two days. The bill calls for tripling the number of immigration and border patrol agents along the 3,000-mile border with Canada.[11]

Such measures will disproportionately affect immigrant communities in large cities. Immigrants, particularly those who are visibly identifiable as 'foreign', have already felt suspicion and hostility even in perfectly legal activities—passengers refusing to board a plane with turbaned fellow passengers—and their vulnerability to harassment, both social and legally, especially by the Immigration and Naturalization Service, is substantially increased. New York colleges, for instance, are now required to report those foreign students who are not attending class to the Immigration and Naturalization Service, and there are legislative efforts to 'track [non-citizens] more closely when they're here'.[12] As a result of all this, the tendency to group in enclaves will be increased, and the 'voluntariness' of such clustering together becomes blurred. Immigrant enclaves, and the sharply involuntary ghettos of many cities, will find themselves more neglected in terms of public investment infrastructure and services than before, as public investment goes to the protection of high-value business uses and private investment is increased by those who can afford to provide their own security and services.

Barricading will more broadly affect the active participation of all in democratic debate that has been a characteristic of life in cities. 'Stadt Luft macht freie', city air produces freedom, becomes less true. 'Security' becomes the justification for measures that threaten the core of urban social and political life, from the physical barricading of space to the social barricading of democratic activity. Stephen Graham goes further, and speaks of the 'accelerated militarisation of urban civil society' and the concomitant 'urbanisation of the military',[13] as serious military concerns (not of the Star Wars kind) focus on cities, how to defend them, and how to attack them.

Deplanning and the Role of the State

The events of September 11 have accentuated the skewed role of the state in urban development. On the one hand, the state is acting more directly and with greater weight on behalf of major real estate development and business inter- ests in the city. On the other hand, it is abdicating a more general role in urban planning and the overall direction of city development, and is reducing its involvement in social welfare and social-justice-oriented measures.

The overwhelming focus of governmental activities to deal with the conse- quences of September 11 in New York City has been in what is euphemistically called Lower Manhattan. What is meant is the financial district, and speci- fically the property owners and real estate concerns who have a major interest there. This is where Federal funds for 'rebuilding New York' will go, as well as where state and city aid will be targeted. The view is that this geographically defined area is the only area affected by the attack of September 11, and that within it the real estate industry is the key sector with which there needs to be planning concern. Steven Spinola, President of the Real Estate Board of New York, is quoted as saying: 'We believe we represent the people most affected, the owners and the tenants. When you add the Alliance for Downtown New York and labor, that's it.'[14] The Alliance for Downtown New York represents the business interests in that area, and by labour is meant primarily the con- struction trades, who are seen as having a common interest with property own- ers in building and reconstruction.

But New York City's political leaders, including the Chair of its Planning Commission, have taken the position that development in the area directly affected by the attack, which they uniformly consider to be the financial dis- trict, should proceed rapidly, with the normal procedures of the planning process set aside in favour of immediate response. Calls for a tsar to oversee rebuilding, a Reconstruction Commission of appointed officials, and various other proposals to 'streamline the planning and approval process' are frequent. The most prominent and probably most influential of the existing groups or new committees that have sprung up to influence what will be done in the built environment is the Rebuild New York City Task Force, renamed the Infrastructure Task Force ('nobody doesn't love infrastructure', says Herbert Muschamp, in explaining their public-relations-motivated decision[15]). It includes executives from leading real estate companies and corporate architec- ture firms; its early members were described as 'a *Who's Who* of major real estate developers and corporate architecture firms'.[16] Its early Statement of

Purpose recommends 'pragmatic implementation strategies that engage concerned parties before they coalesce into opposition'.[17] It sounds like the pragmatism of power, not of democracy.

The latest developments give further cause for concern. Mayor Giuliani and Governor Pataki have just created the Lower Manhattan Development Corporation, as a subsidiary of the Empire State Development Corporation. Its purpose is 'to rebuild lower Manhattan and distribute much of the federal aid for its reconstruction. . . . [It] will manage all aspects of revitalizing lower Manhattan south of Houston St. . . . it will generally oversee transportation and infrastructure improvements and attempt to stop the financial hemorrhaging of businesses affected by the terrorist attacks'.[18] So it will be planning and implementing the rebuilding of New York City. As head of the Corporation, the Governor has named John C. Whitehead, former co-chairman of the investment firm Goldman Sachs & Company and a major contributor to the Republican Party.

So positive governmental action is narrowly focused on the financial district of the city, and within it the support of real estate and business interests. What is not being done, however, is by contrast legion; the net result might better be called *deplanning* than planning.

The issues being swept aside in the current decision-making process include:

• regional review of the City's role in the tri-state area;

• economic planning about the role and future of the financial industry in New York City, the pros and cons of its intensive spatial concentration, and alternative directions of economic development;

• physical planning, looking at the best locations for new construction (including Manhattan outside the financial district and the other boroughs and beyond), and alternative uses for locations within the financial district;

• social planning, examining the distributional consequences of various alternatives;

• planning for housing, looking at the housing impacts outside the financial district on the majority of workers there (who did not live in Manhattan), in the context of dealing with the city's broader housing problems;

• historical and memorial concerns about the impact recent events and the longer-term history of the World Trade Center site have had on the lives of people;

• urban design, infrastructure, communications and transportation, environmental quality, and qualities of urban life (urbanity) outside the financial district;

• alternate investment strategies for the use of tax revenues and subsidies, including the costs of shifting from expenditures for social purposes such as education to support for financial district reconstruction.

The formal governmental decision-making process itself is geared to down-play or ignore these concerns, to limit the process to involve only the most nar-rowly defined 'stakeholders' in the financial district, and to ignore broad public participation. The furthest decisions have gone thus far is to involve the chair of Community Board #1 Manhattan on the Lower Manhattan Development Corporation, as one of nine members. But other communities in the city also have an interest in the outcome; labour, and particularly service workers, hotel and restaurant workers, janitors, health workers, etc., have a vital interest; and the broader issues outlined above need to be addressed. The city has a formal process for planning, including public hearings, environmental reviews, local Community Board hearings and votes, and votes by its Planning Commission and City Council, etc.; every indication is that these will be 'streamlined' as far as legally possible. The flavour of current thinking is given by a commentary by Gerry Khermouch, the Real Estate Board of New York's Vice-President, high-lighted in a special issue of *Business Week*:

lofty talk of a breakthrough regional approach . . . makes me nervous . . . The focus must be on the downtown business district. It's only when that area is restored to vibran-cy that other regional goals should be taken up . . . Forget about the big picture. New York needs to make rebuilding Lower Manhattan Job No. 1.[19]

Deplanning is certainly an appropriate term for this approach, since it implies ignoring the most basic principles of urban planning and bypassing existing legal planning procedures.

Conclusion

The September 11 attack on the World Trade Center will have major conse-quences at the urban level, not only for New York City but likely for major cities throughout the globe. What those consequences will be will depend both on how those in the private market react and on public policy decisions still being debated. Both in the market and in the political arena, the direction of change is likely to be a continuation of trends already well under way, rein-forced and aggravated by the reaction to the attack. The role of the state will be ever more central, but ever more skewed, in the process. In the name of security, government will play a more active role in fostering the prosperity of one part of the city. It will be supporting even further real estate and business activities, focusing on the higher end, particularly FIRE and its affiliated office uses. Concern with and expenditures for social welfare will be reduced. Per-ceiving a threat to their tax base and the political base of their established regimes, local governments, often with the support of central government, will set aside environmental and planning restrictions on tax-paying construction by businesses: deplanning the city. Those adversely affected by these develop-ments—labour, community groups, the unemployed and the ill-housed, immigrant and minority groups–have thus far barely been heard in the speech of security concerns and starkly visible immediate needs. Much depends on whether they will mount a vocal opposition and aggressively put forward alternative programmes in the immediate future—as well as on whether the recession deepens or evaporates.

The prognosis is not good for those interested in urban life, equity, and democracy. Each is threatened by market trends, and the official response is likely to aggravate the problem. The role of the state in city life has increased, but not necessarily for the better.[20]

Notes

My appreciation to my co-editor, Ronald van Kempen, for very helpful editorial assistance (but the opinions in this Afterword must remain my own responsibility), and to Anne Ashby, at Oxford University Press, who was open to entertaining an Afterword to a manuscript long after it would normally have been put to bed.

1. *New York Times* (14 Oct. 2001), sect. 3, p. 1.
2. Niall Ferguson, '2011', *New York Times* magazine (2 Dec. 2001), 78–9.
3. I take globalization in its really existing form to have three components: technological advance, concentration of economic power, and international exchange. See 'Introduction', in Peter Marcuse and Ronald van Kempen (eds.), *Globalizing Cities: Is there a New Spatial Order?* (London: Blackwell, 1999).
4. *Frankfurter Allgemeine Zeitung* (12 Oct. 2001), 20.
5. *New York Post* (21 Sept. 2001).
6. *Business Week* (22 Oct. 2001), 35.
7. According to a task force assembled by the mayor of the city, reported at GlobeSt.com (19 Oct. 2001).
8. ' "Our associates report a drastic increase in the number of those seeking help after Sept. 11," said Lucy Cabrera, executive director of Bronx-based Food for Survival, the country's largest food bank.' The example the story cites is of Dagoberto Hernández, who had worked at a $350-a-week job as a salad-maker at a ground floor restaurant at the World Trade Center, and had only once been at a soup kitchen before. Albor Ruiz, *Daily News* Staff Writer, 'Soup Kitchen Lines Longer since Tragedy', *New York Daily News* web site, *http://www.nydailynews.com/2001-10-30/News_and_Views/City_Beat/a-130299.asp* (30 Oct. 2001).
9. *New York Times* (2 Oct. 2001), A16.
10. HR 3162, 107th Congress. Its full title is Uniting and Strengthening America by Providing Appropriate Tools Required to Intercept and Obstruct Terrorism (United States Patriot Act) Act of 2001.
11. The summary is from the ABC News web site (26 Oct. 2001).
12. *Gotham Gazette*'s The Citizen web page (5 Dec. 2001), http://www.gothamgazette.com/citizen.
13. Stephen Graham, *In a Moment: On Glocal Mobilities and the Terrorised City*, *CITY* (forthcoming).
14. *New York Times* (29 Oct. 2001), B10.

15. Herbert Muschamp, 'Power, Imagination and New York's Future', *New York Times* (28 Oct. 2001).
16. Ibid.
17. Ibid.
18. As reported in the *New York Daily News* (6 Nov. 2001).
19. *Business Week* (22 Oct. 2001), 118.
20. There are no entries to the Afterword in the Index.

INDEX

(The afterword has not been indexed)